THE CAMBRIDGE COMPANION TO
AMERICAN GAY AND LESBIAN LITERATURE

This *Companion* examines the connections between LGBTQ populations and American literature from the late eighteenth to the twenty-first century. It surveys primary and secondary writings under the evolving category of gay and lesbian authorship and incorporates current thinking in U.S.-based LGBTQ studies as well as critical practices within the field of American literary studies. The *Companion* also addresses the ways in which queerness pervades persons, texts, bodies, and reading, while paying attention to the transnational component of such objects and practices. In so doing, it details the chief genres, conventional historical backgrounds, and influential interpretive practices that support the analysis of LGBTQ literatures in the United States.

Scott Herring is Associate Professor of English at Indiana University, Bloomington. His previous books include *The Hoarders: Material Deviance in Modern American Culture* (2014); *Another Country: Queer Anti-Urbanism* (2010); and *Queering the Underworld: Slumming, Literature, and the Undoing of Lesbian and Gay History* (2007). Herring's articles have also appeared in such journals as *American Quarterly, Modern Fiction Studies, GLQ,* and *PMLA.*

A complete list of books in the series is at the back of this book

THE CAMBRIDGE
COMPANION TO
AMERICAN GAY AND LESBIAN
LITERATURE

THE CAMBRIDGE
COMPANION TO

AMERICAN GAY
AND LESBIAN
LITERATURE

EDITED BY

SCOTT HERRING
Indiana University

CAMBRIDGE
UNIVERSITY PRESS

CAMBRIDGE
UNIVERSITY PRESS

32 Avenue of the Americas, New York NY 10013-2473, USA

Cambridge University Press is part of the University of Cambridge.

It furthers the University's mission by disseminating knowledge in the pursuit of
education, learning and research at the highest international levels of excellence.

www.cambridge.org
Information on this title: www.cambridge.org/9781107646186

© Cambridge University Press 2015

First published 2015

A catalogue record for this publication is available from the British Library

Library of Congress Cataloguing in Publication data
The Cambridge Companion to American Gay and Lesbian Literature / edited by
Scott Herring.
pages   cm. – (Cambridge Companions to Literature)
Includes bibliographical references.
ISBN 978-1-107-04649-8 (hardback) – ISBN 978-1-107-64618-6 (paperback)
1. Gays' writings, American–History and criticism.   2. Homosexuality and
literature.   3. Gay men in literature.   4. Lesbians in literature.
I. Herring, Scott, 1976–
PS153.G38C36   2015
810.9'920664–dc23   2014047270

ISBN 978-1-107-64618-6 Paperback

CONTENTS

CONTENTS

NOTES ON CONTRIBUTORS

MICHAEL P. BIBLER is Associate Professor of Southern Studies at Louisiana State University. He is the author of *Cotton's Queer Relations: Same-Sex Intimacy and the Literature of the Southern Plantation, 1936–1968* (University of Virginia Press, 2009). He is also the coeditor of the essay collection *Just below South: Intercultural Performance in the Caribbean and the U.S. South* (University of Virginia Press, 2007) and the reissue of Arna Bontemps's 1939 novel *Drums at Dusk* (Louisiana State University Press, 2009).

DANIELA CASELLI is Associate Professor at the University of Manchester. She is the author of *Improper Modernism: Djuna Barnes's Bewildering Corpus* (Ashgate, 2009) and *Beckett's Dantes: Intertextuality in the Fiction and Criticism* (Manchester University Press, 2005). Her work on gender, sexuality, and critical theory has appeared in *Textual Practice* (2006), *Feminist Theory* (2010), and *Parallax* (Forthcoming). She is currently working on a project on the figure of the child in modernism.

MICHAEL COBB is Professor of English at the University of Toronto. He is the author of three books: *Racial Blasphemies: Religious Irreverence and Race in American Literature* (Routledge, 2005); *God Hates Fags: The Rhetorics of Religious Violence* (New York University Press, 2006); and, most recently, *Single: Arguments for the Uncoupled* (New York University Press, 2012). Currently, he is working on two new projects: one on goodness, "The Good Book," and another on endurance, "Fagments, or Your Love Life in Ruins." He is also cowriting a small trade book with *The Atlantic Monthly*'s Kate Bolick on friendship and treacherous love addiction entitled *More*.

GUY DAVIDSON is Senior Lecturer in the English Literatures program at the University of Wollongong. He has published widely on sexuality and American literature. His book *Queer Commodities: Contemporary US Fiction, Consumer Capitalism, and Gay and Lesbian Subcultures* was published in 2012 by Palgrave Macmillan. He is also coeditor, with Nicola Evans, of *Literary Careers in the Modern Era* (Palgrave, 2015). His current research project examines literary celebrity, sexuality, and affect in the postwar United States.

TRAVIS FOSTER is Assistant Professor of English at Villanova University, where he is working on a book about popular genres, race, and social history in the wake of the U.S. Civil War. His work has also appeared in *American Literature*, *ESQ: A Journal of the American Renaissance*, and *American Literary History*.

MELISSA JANE HARDIE is Associate Dean (Undergraduate) in the Faculty of Arts and Social Sciences, University of Sydney, where she teaches literary and film studies. She is completing a book on the closet and queer theory, and she recently published a chapter on Djuna Barnes's *Nightwood* in the collection *Modernism and Masculinity*, as well as articles on the closet and Lindsay Lohan, true crime, and *Mad Men*.

SCOTT HERRING is Associate Professor of English at Indiana University, Bloomington. His books include *The Hoarders: Material Deviance in Modern American Culture* (University of Chicago Press, 2014); *Another Country: Queer Anti-Urbanism* (New York University Press, 2010); and *Queering the Underworld: Slumming, Literature, and the Undoing of Lesbian and Gay History* (University of Chicago Press, 2007).

LUCAS HILDERBRAND is Associate Professor of Film and Media Studies and Director of Visual Studies at the University of California, Irvine. He is the author of *Inherent Vice: Bootleg Histories of Videotape and Copyright* (Duke University Press, 2009) and *Paris Is Burning: A Queer Film Classic* (Arsenal Pulp Press, 2013).

ERIC KEENAGHAN is the author of *Queering Cold War Poetry* (Ohio State University Press, 2009) and a contributing author to *The Princeton Encyclopedia of Poetry and Poetics* (4th ed., 2012) and *The Cambridge History of Gay and Lesbian Literature* (2014). He has published widely on modernist poetry, sexuality, and politics, and he is currently writing a new book on philosophical anarchism and the politics of affect in mid-century American poetry. He teaches at the University at Albany, SUNY.

SEAN METZGER is Associate Professor in the UCLA School of Theater, Film, and Television. He is the author of *Chinese Looks: Fashion, Performance, Race* (Indiana University Press, 2014). His coedited volumes include *Embodying Asian/American Sexualities* (Lexington, 2009); *Futures of Chinese Cinema: Technologies and Temporalities in Chinese Screen Cultures* (Intellect, 2009); and special journal issues of *Cultural Dynamics* (2009) and *Third Text* (2014).

JULIE AVRIL MINICH is Assistant Professor of English, Mexican American and Latina/o Studies, and Women and Gender Studies at the University of Texas at Austin. She is the author of *Accessible Citizenships: Disability, Nation, and the Cultural Politics of Greater Mexico* (Temple University Press, 2014). Additionally, her articles have appeared in journals such as *Comparative Literature, Modern Fiction Studies,* and the *Journal of Literary and Cultural Disability Studies.*

MARTIN JOSEPH PONCE is Associate Professor of English at The Ohio State University. His teaching and research interests focus on U.S. ethnic literatures, histories of U.S. empire, and queer of color and queer diasporic critique. He is the author of *Beyond the Nation: Diasporic Filipino Literature and Queer Reading* (New York University Press, 2012).

JUDITH ROOF is William Shakespeare Chair in English at Rice University. She is the author of *A Lure of Knowledge: Lesbian Sexuality and Theory* (Columbia University Press, 1991); *Come as You Are: Sexuality and Narrative* (Columbia University Press, 1996); *All about Thelma and Eve: Sidekicks and Third Wheels* (University of Illinois Press, 2002); and the forthcoming *Remaking Gender* (University of Minnesota Press), among other monographs.

L. H. STALLINGS is Associate Professor of Gender Studies at Indiana University. She is the author of *Mutha' Is Half a Word: Intersections of Folklore, Vernacular, Myth, and Queerness in Black Female Culture* (Ohio State University Press, 2007) and coeditor and contributing author to *Word Hustle: Critical Essays and Reflections on the Works of Donald Goines* (Black Classic Press, 2011). Her second book, *Funk the Erotic: Transaesthetics and Black Sexual Cultures,* is forthcoming from the University of Illinois Press.

KYLA WAZANA TOMPKINS is Associate Professor of Gender Studies and English at Pomona College. She is the author of *Racial Indigestion: Eating Bodies in the Nineteenth Century* (New York University Press, 2012), which won the Lora Romero Prize for best first book from the American Studies Association.

CHRONOLOGY

1799–1865

1799	Charles Brockden Brown, *Ormond; or, The Secret Witness*
1808	Leonora Sansay, *Secret History; or, The Horrors of St. Domingo*
1810	Anonymous, *Rosa; or, American Genius and Education*
1823–1841	James Fenimore Cooper, "Leatherstocking Tales"
1830	Emily Dickinson born; letters to sister-in-law Susan Huntington Gilbert taken as evidence of lesbian desire by feminist critics in later twentieth century
1835	Augustus Baldwin Longstreet, "A Sage Conversation"
1839	Edgar Allan Poe, "William Wilson"
1841	Walt Whitman, "Bervance: or, Father and Son" and "The Child's Champion"
1846	Herman Melville, *Typee: A Peep at Polynesian Life*
Late 1840s	Julia Ward Howe, *The Hermaphrodite* (unpublished until 2004)
1851	Nathaniel Hawthorne, *The House of the Seven Gables*
1851	Herman Melville, *Moby-Dick; or, The Whale*
1852	Nathaniel Hawthorne, *The Blithedale Romance*
1854	Bayard Taylor, *A Journey to Central Africa; or, Life and Landscapes from Egypt to the Negro Kingdoms of the White Nile*

1855	Walt Whitman, *Leaves of Grass* (first edition)
1857	Anonymous, "The Man Who Thought Himself a Woman"
1858	Rose Terry Cooke, "My Visitation"
1863	Harriet Elizabeth Prescott Spofford, "The Amber Gods"

1866–1889

1866	Augusta Jane Evans, *St. Elmo*
1869	Bret Harte, "Tennessee's Partner"
1870	Bayard Taylor, *Joseph and His Friend: A Story of Pennsylvania*
1871	Frederic W. Loring, *Two College Friends*
1875	Henry James, *Roderick Hudson*
1876	Constance Fenimore Woolson, "Felipa"
1880	Alice French, "My Lorelei"
1882	Oscar Wilde tours United States
1884	Sarah Orne Jewett, *A Country Doctor*
1885	Oliver Wendell Holmes, *A Mortal Antipathy*
1885	Charles Warren Stoddard, *The Lepers of Molokai*
1886	Henry James, *The Bostonians*
1886	Richard von Krafft-Ebing, *Psychopathia Sexualis, with Especial Reference to Contrary Sexual Instinct: A Medico-Legal Study* (English translation published in the United States in 1892)
1887	Mary Eleanor Wilkins Freeman, "Two Friends"
1888	James Lane Allen, "Two Gentlemen of Kentucky"
1889	Alfred J. Cohen (Alan Dale), *A Marriage Below Zero: A Novel*

1890–1899

| 1890 | Harriet Riddle Davis, *Gilbert Elgar's Son* |
| 1896 | S. Weir Mitchell, *Hugh Wynne: Free Quaker* |

1897	Alice Brown, "There and Here"
1897	Sarah Orne Jewett, "Martha's Lady"

1900–1909

1900	Pauline Hopkins, *Contending Forces: A Romance Illustrative of Negro Life North and South*
1902	Pauline Hopkins, *Winona: A Tale of Negro Life in the South and Southwest*
1902	Henry James, *The Wings of the Dove*
ca. 1902	Mark Twain, "How Nancy Jackson Married Kate Wilson"
1903	Henry James, "The Beast in the Jungle"
1903	Gertrude Stein, *Q. E. D.*
1903	Charles Warren Stoddard, *For the Pleasure of His Company*
1905	Willa Cather, "Paul's Case: A Study in Temperament"
1909	Gertrude Stein, *Three Lives*

1910–1919

1910	Jane Addams, *Twenty Years at Hull-House*
1910	Sigmund Freud, *Three Essays on the Theory of Sexuality* (English translation)
1912	Edith Maude Eaton (Sui Sin Far), *Mrs. Spring Fragrance*
1912	James Weldon Johnson, *The Autobiography of an Ex-Colored Man*
1914	Gertrude Stein, *Tender Buttons*
1915	Djuna Barnes, *The Book of Repulsive Women*
1915	Willa Cather, *The Song of the Lark*
1916	Angelina Weld Grimké, *Rachel*
1917	Edna St. Vincent Millay, *Renascence and Other Poems*

1918	Willa Cather, *My Ántonia*
1918/1919	Ralph Werther (other aliases include Earl Lind and Jennie June), *Autobiography of an Androgyne*

1920–1929

1921	Zitkala-Ša, *American Indian Stories*
1924	Marianne Moore, *Observations*
1925	Willa Cather, *The Professor's House*
1925	Countee Cullen dedicates "Heritage" to Harold Jackman
1925	Robert McAlmon, *Distinguished Air (Grim Fairy Tales)*
ca. 1926–1935	Harlem (New Negro) Renaissance supports queer artists, such as Langston Hughes, Countee Cullen, Claude McKay, Nella Larsen, Carl Van Vechten, Wallace Thurman, and Richard Bruce Nugent
1926	Richard Bruce Nugent, "Smoke, Lilies and Jade," published in avant-garde journal *FIRE!!: A Quarterly Devoted to Younger Negro Artists*, edited by Wallace Thurman et al.
1927	Mae West, *The Drag*
1928	Djuna Barnes, *Ladies Almanack*
1928	Claude McKay, *Home to Harlem*
1928–1929	Obscenity trial for Radclyffe Hall's 1928 *The Well of Loneliness* in America
1929	Nella Larsen, *Passing*

1930–1939

1930	Hart Crane, *The Bridge*
1930	Carl Van Vechten, *Parties: Scenes from Contemporary New York Life*
1931	Blair Niles, *Strange Brother*
1932	Wallace Thurman, *Infants of the Spring*

1933	Charles Henri Ford and Parker Tyler, *The Young and Evil*
1933	Gertrude Stein, *The Autobiography of Alice B. Toklas*
1933	José Garcia Villa, *Footnote to Youth: Tales of the Philippines and Others*
1934	Lillian Hellman, *The Children's Hour*
1935	H. T. Tsiang, *The Hanging on Union Square*
1937	Djuna Barnes, *Nightwood* (American publication)
1938	Gertrude Stein, *Doctor Faustus Lights the Lights*

1940–1949

1944	Charles Jackson, *The Lost Weekend*
1946	Carson McCullers, *The Member of the Wedding*
1947	Kenneth Anger, *Fireworks* (film)
1947	Edith Eyde (Lisa Ben) edits and publishes *Vice Versa*
1948	Truman Capote, *Other Voices, Other Rooms*
1948	Alfred Hitchcock, *Rope* (film)
1948	Alfred C. Kinsey, Wardell B. Pomeroy, and Clyde E. Martin, *Sexual Behavior in the Human Male*
1948	Gore Vidal, *The City and the Pillar*
1949	Thomas Hal Phillips, *The Bitterweed Path*

1950–1959

1950s	Height of what historian David K. Johnson refers to as the "Lavender Scare," or the extreme scrutiny and oppression of U.S. government–affiliated lesbians and gays
1950	Mattachine Society founded
1951	Langston Hughes, "Café: 3 a.m."
1951	Edward Sagarin (Donald Webster Cory), *The Homosexual in America: A Subjective Approach*

1952	Patricia Highsmith (Claire Morgan), *The Price of Salt*
1952	ONE, Inc., founded in Los Angeles
1952	*Diagnostic and Statistical Manual of Mental Disorders* lists homosexuality as "Sexual Deviation" alongside "transvestitism, pedophilia, fetishism and sexual sadism"
1953	William S. Burroughs (William Lee), *Junkie: Confessions of an Unredeemed Drug Addict* (subsequently released as *Junky*)
1953	Alfred C. Kinsey, Wardell B. Pomeroy, Clyde E. Martin, and Paul H. Gebhard, *Sexual Behavior in the Human Female*
1954	Tennessee Williams, *Hard Candy: A Book of Stories*
1955	Elizabeth Bishop, *Poems: North & South/A Cold Spring*
1955	Tennessee Williams, *Cat on a Hot Tin Roof*
1955	Daughters of Bilitis formed
1956	James Baldwin, *Giovanni's Room*
1956	Jeannette Howard Foster, *Sex Variant Women in Literature: A Historical and Quantitative Survey*
1956	Allen Ginsberg, *Howl and Other Poems*
1957	Jack Spicer, *After Lorca*
1957	Ann Weldy (Ann Bannon), *Odd Girl Out* (published under pen name A. Bannon); Weldy launches first in series "The Beebo Brinker Chronicles" (1957–1962)
1958	Tennessee Williams, *Suddenly, Last Summer*
1959	Lorraine Hansberry, *A Raisin in the Sun*

1960–1969

1962	Edward Albee, *Who's Afraid of Virginia Woolf?*
1962	James Baldwin, *Another Country*
1962	William S. Burroughs, *Naked Lunch* (American publication; originally published in Britain in 1959)
1963	John Rechy, *City of Night*

1963	Jack Smith, *Flaming Creatures* (film)
1963	Guy Strait publishes *The Lavender Baedeker*
1963	John Kennedy Toole, *A Confederacy of Dunces* (published in 1980)
1964	Christopher Isherwood, *A Single Man*
1964	Frank O'Hara, *Lunch Poems*
1964	Susan Sontag, "Notes on 'Camp' "
1964	Andy Warhol, *Blow Job* (film)
1965	Elizabeth Bishop, *Questions of Travel*
1966	Samuel M. Steward (Phil Andros), *$tud*
1966	Queer protest riots at San Francisco's Compton's Cafeteria
1967	Oscar Wilde Memorial Bookshop opens in New York City's Greenwich Village
1968	Gore Vidal, *Myra Breckinridge*
1969	Queer protest riots at New York City's Stonewall Inn

1970–1979

1970s	Rise of lesbian and gay independent presses
1970	William Friedkin, *The Boys in the Band* (film)
1970	Radicalesbians, "The Woman-Identified Woman"
1971–1972	The Furies Collective, a Washington, DC–based lesbian separatist organization; Rita Mae Brown a notable member
1972	Sidney Abbott and Barbara Love, *Sappho Was a Right-On Woman: A Liberated View of Lesbianism*
1973	Rita Mae Brown, *Rubyfruit Jungle*
1973	Toni Morrison, *Sula*
1974	Ann Allen Shockley, *Loving Her*
1974	Gay Caucus for the Modern Languages founded within the Modern Language Association

1975	John Ashbery, *Self-Portrait in a Convex Mirror*
1975	Joanna Russ, *The Female Man*
1976	Lisa Alther, *Kinflicks*
1976	Bertha Harris, *Lover*
1977	María Irene Fornés, *Fefu and Her Friends*
1977	Barbara Smith, "Toward a Black Feminist Criticism"
1977	Anita Bryant launches Save Our Children campaign, which advances rise of New Christian Right
1978	Andrew Holleran, *Dancer from the Dance*
1978	Harvey Milk assassinated
1979	*Conditions: Five*, special issue titled "The Black Women's Issue"; includes essay on Angelina Weld Grimké's queerness
1979	Moral Majority, an antigay Christian organization, founded by Jerry Falwell

1980–1989

1980	Howard Cruse releases first issue of *Gay Comix*
1980	William Friedkin, *Cruising* (film)
1980	Adrienne Rich, "Compulsory Heterosexuality and Lesbian Existence"
1980	Edmund White, *States of Desire: Travels in Gay America*
1980	Split Britches Company founded
1980	WOW (Women on Women) Café founded
1980	Human Rights Campaign Fund founded
1981	Audre Lorde, *Uses of the Erotic: The Erotic as Power*
1981	Cherríe Moraga and Gloria Anzaldúa coedit *This Bridge Called My Back: Writings by Radical Women of Color*
1981	*The New York Times* publishes article "Rare Cancer Seen in 41 Homosexuals," the newspaper's first notification of what would later become standardized as HIV/AIDS

1982	Audre Lorde, *Zami: A New Spelling of My Name: A Biomythography*
1983	Alison Bechdel, *Dykes to Watch Out For*
1984	David Leavitt, *Family Dancing*
1984	Charles Ludlam, *The Mystery of Irma Vep*
1985	Beth Brant, *Mohawk Trail*
1985	Larry Kramer, *The Normal Heart*
1986	Joseph Beam edits *In the Life: A Black Gay Anthology*
1986	*Bowers v. Hardwick* affirms U.S. sodomy laws
1987	Gloria Anzaldúa, *Borderlands/La Frontera: The New Mestiza*
1987	Michelle Cliff, *No Telephone to Heaven*
1987	Randy Shilts, *And the Band Played On*
1987	ACT UP (AIDS Coalition to Unleash Power) founded in New York City
1988	Samuel R. Delany, *The Motion of Light in Water: Sex and Science Fiction Writing in the East Village, 1960–1965*
1988	David Henry Hwang, *M. Butterfly*
1989	First annual Lambda Literary Awards

1990–1999

1990	Judith Butler, *Gender Trouble: Feminism and the Subversion of Identity*
1990	Jessica Hagedorn, *Dogeaters*
1990	Jennie Livingston, *Paris Is Burning* (film)
1990	Eve Kosofsky Sedgwick, *Epistemology of the Closet*
1990	Pomo Afro Homos performance group organized
1990	Queer Nation, an AIDS activist organization, founded in New York City

1990	Phrase "queer theory" coined by academic scholar Teresa de Lauretis
1990	National Endowment for the Arts revokes funding for "NEA Four" (Karen Finley, John Fleck, Holly Hughes, and Tim Miller)
1991	Dennis Cooper, *Discontents: New Queer Writers*
1991	Melvin Dixon, *Vanishing Rooms*
1991	Jewelle Gomez, *The Gilda Stories: A Novel*
1991	E. Lynn Harris, *Invisible Life*
1991	Essex Hemphill edits *Brother to Brother: New Writings by Black Gay Men*
1991	Eileen Myles, *Not Me*
1991	Carla Trujillo, *Chicana Lesbians: The Girls Our Mothers Warned Us About*
1991	David Wojnarowicz, *Close to the Knives: A Memoir of Disintegration*
1992	Dorothy Allison, *Bastard Out of Carolina*
1992	Essex Hemphill, *Ceremonies: Prose and Poetry*
1992	Paul Monette, *Becoming a Man: Half a Life Story*
1992	Cherríe Moraga, *Heroes and Saints*
1992	Sandy Stone, "The *Empire* Strikes Back: A Posttransexual Manifesto," published in academic journal *Camera Obscura*
1992	Phrase "New Queer Cinema" coined by critic B. Ruby Rich; associated directors include Todd Haynes, Cheryl Dunye, Kimberly Pierce, and Rose Troche
1993	Henry Abelove, Michèle Aina Barale, and David M. Halperin coedit *The Lesbian and Gay Studies Reader*
1993	Leslie Feinberg, *Stone Butch Blues*
1993	David M. Halperin and Carolyn Dinshaw coedit first volume of *GLQ: A Journal of Lesbian and Gay Studies*

1993	Part One of Tony Kushner, *Angels in America: A Gay Fantasia on National Themes, Millennium Approaches*, wins Pulitzer Prize
1993	March on Washington for Gay, Lesbian, and Bi Equal Rights and Liberation
1993	Intersex Society of North America (ISNA) launched by Cheryl Chase (Bo Laurent)
1994	Don't Ask, Don't Tell (DADT), a U.S. government policy punitive toward out lesbians and gays in the military, initiated
1995	R. Zamora Linmark, *Rolling the R's*
1995	Andrew Sullivan, *Virtually Normal: An Argument about Homosexuality*
1996	Holly Hughes, *Clit Notes: A Sapphic Sampler*
1996	Cherríe Moraga, *Watsonville: Some Place Not Here*
1996	Defense of Marriage Act (DOMA) defines marriage as "only a legal union between one man and one woman as husband and wife"
1997	Rafael Campo, *The Poetry of Healing: A Doctor's Education in Empathy, Identity, and Desire*
1997	Sex Panic! activism begins in New York City
1998	Lawrence Chua, *Gold by the Inch*
1998	Michael Cunningham, *The Hours*
1998	Stephen Trask and John Cameron Mitchell, *Hedwig and the Angry Inch*
1999	José Esteban Muñoz, *Disidentifications: Queers of Color and the Performance of Politics*

2000–

2001	Naomi Iizuka, *36 Views*
2001	Craig Womack, *Drowning in Fire*
2002	Jeffrey Eugenides, *Middlesex*

2002   Richard Greenberg, *Take Me Out*

2003   Monique Truong, *The Book of Salt*

2003   *Lawrence v. Texas* strikes down *Bowers v. Hardwick*; includes amicus brief coauthored by LGBTQ historians and social critics, such as George Chauncey, Estelle B. Freedman, Mark D. Jordan, John Howard, and Elizabeth Lapovsky Kennedy

2005   Ang Lee, *Brokeback Mountain* (film); screenplay adapted from E. Annie Proulx's 1997 short story

2006   Alison Bechdel, *Fun Home: A Family Tragicomic*

2009   Terry Galloway, *Mean Little Deaf Queer: A Memoir*

2010   Justin Spring, *Secret Historian: The Life and Times of Samuel Steward, Professor, Tattoo Artist, and Sexual Renegade*

2011   Don't Ask, Don't Tell (DADT) repealed

2012   Kate Bornstein, *A Queer and Pleasant Danger: A Memoir*

2012   Samuel R. Delany, *Through the Valley of the Nest of Spiders*

2013   *United States v. Windsor* overturns Defense of Marriage Act (DOMA)

2013   Gender Identity Disorder relisted as Gender Dysphoria in fifth edition of *Diagnostic and Statistical Manual of Mental Disorders (DSM-5)*

SCOTT HERRING

Introduction: What Do We Mean by the Phrase "American Gay and Lesbian Literature"?

How do we compile an institutional history of the phrase "American Gay and Lesbian Literature" as it developed in the U.S. academy? Although we should be cautious of any conclusive moment of origin, one place to start would be a December 27, 1974, forum at the annual Modern Language Association (MLA) Convention in New York City. Titled "Homosexuality and Literature" and moderated by Catharine Stimpson, the panel's presenters included Louis Crompton, Bertha Harris, and Christopher Isherwood.[1] Each proved to be elemental to gay and lesbian literary studies as it cohered in the late twentieth-century United States. A professor of English at the University of Nebraska-Lincoln, Crompton stoked controversy with a course on the topic of homosexuality. Known for novels such as *A Single Man* (1964) and *Goodbye to Berlin* (1939), Isherwood was an "uncle" of Gay Liberation Front (GLF) activists.[2] Harris published her lesbian-themed novel *Lover* in 1976, and Stimpson established the feminist studies journal *Signs* in 1974. Together these four writers and intellectuals courageously broached subjects such as "The Suppression of Homosexual Literature" and "The Lesbian as Literature" – topics removed from other panels on authors like Boccaccio and John Updike.[3]

This panel and other gay-themed events at the 1974 MLA Convention helped to foster, if not to launch, the study of gay and lesbian literature across the United States. Along with Kent State University professor Dolores Noll, Crompton also organized a session complementary to the "Homosexuality and Literature" forum that resulted in the institutionalization of the Gay Caucus for the Modern Languages. The MLA Executive Council formalized this organization in 1975 and recorded in its Professional Notes and Comments that "Discussion Groups on Children's Literature and on Gay Studies in Language and Literature shall be established."[4] Still operative, this group has hosted hundreds of panels on an assortment of topics. Take but three examples: "Homosexuality in Film: *The Celluloid Closet*" in 1982; "The Queer Child" in 1997 with a talk on "Psychoanalysis and Race in Asian American Childhood"; and a special session in 2002 on "Queer Atlantics" with presentations on "Black and Queer Geographies" and "The Material and Literary Production of 'Coming Out' Narratives in the Americas."[5] As these eclectic panel titles suggest, the caucus supports cross-disciplinary research under the auspices of "Gay Studies in Language and Literature" by expanding this domain beyond both U.S. borders and the aesthetic medium of literature. This *Companion* does so as well.

That this group emerged in the mid-1970s is also telling: it testifies to a growing excitement inside and outside U.S. academies around the broad topic of "homosexuality and literature." Archives housed at the University of Nebraska record that Crompton taught one of the nation's first seminars on "Homophile Studies" at his home institution in the autumn of 1970. This course integrated a section on literature with a bibliography of novels and plays by African American, Chicano, and Anglo American gay male novelists and playwrights, such as James Baldwin, Mart Crowley, and John Rechy.[6] Provisional discussion topics for this class included "The Lesbian Novel," "Incidental Treatment of Homosexuality in Hemingway, Fitzgerald, and Faulkner," and "Modern American Poetry: Crane, Ginsberg, and Auden."[7] Confirming the richness of gay and lesbian literatures in the midst of national homophobia, Crompton's course also began to construct and categorize this field according to genre, periodization, gender, literary movement, and, implicitly, nation-state. Although he was not alone in this disciplinary formation, his class stands as a noteworthy moment in the field's institutional inception.

The 1970s were pivotal, but we should also keep in mind the labors of the years prior. A seminar topic like "The Lesbian Novel" would have been inconceivable without contributions such as Jeannette Howard Foster's *Sex Variant Women in Literature*, which was self-published in 1956. As Stimpson notes in her influential 1981 essay "Zero Degree Deviancy: The Lesbian Novel in English," Foster's work remains a "pioneering survey of the figure of the lesbian in Western literature."[8] As a University of Chicago–trained librarian, Foster researched this text, her biographer tells us, "for at least two decades."[9] On modern lesbian American literature, Foster was prescient, and she singled out Amy Lowell, Edna St. Vincent Millay, Gertrude Stein, and Djuna Barnes. *Sex Variant Women* thus stands as but one fight against the suppression of homosexuality in literature, and it memorializes the risky work of librarians in what is known as the pre-Stonewall era. Honoring these professionals, Foster's acknowledgements in *Sex Variant Women* state that "an even heavier debt is due all the librarians who made available rare or restricted material, negotiated interlibrary loans, or merely rendered much ordinary service."[10]

We should also not forget the marginalized presence of gay men of color and, especially, lesbians of color from many of these developments. Perhaps another place to mark the embryonic idea of American gay and lesbian literature, then, would be at the MLA Convention two years *after* the "Homosexuality and Literature" forum. As the African American lesbian feminist Barbara Smith recollects in her classic 1977 essay, "Toward a Black Feminist Criticism," "at the 'Lesbians and Literature' discussion at the 1976 Modern Language Association Bertha Harris suggested that if in a woman writer's work a sentence refuses to do what it is supposed to do, if there are strong images of women and if there is a refusal to be linear, the result is innately lesbian literature."[11] Another of Harris's theories stirred Smith – if women "are the central figures, are positively portrayed and have pivotal relationships with one another," then the said work of literature should be stamped lesbian – and she reformatted this claim in "Toward a Black Feminist Criticism."[12] Using Harris's comments to address matters of race in homoerotic women's literature, Smith published her article in *Conditions*, a feminist journal devoted to lesbian topics. Here she argues that "all segments of the literary world – whether establishment, progressive, Black, female, or lesbian – do not know, or at least act as if they do not know, that Black women writers and Black lesbian writers exist."[13] She then follows this shattering claim with a close reading of Toni Morrison's 1973 novel *Sula*.

The same decade that Crompton, Noll, Stimpson, and other white scholars institutionalized gay and lesbian literary studies, African American lesbians such as Smith thus legitimized the homoerotic work of persons of color. As a follow-up to her "Black Feminist" essay, Smith coedited an issue of *Conditions* with Lorraine Bethel entitled *The Black Women's Issue* in 1979. This volume extended Smith's earlier claims. Their introduction "disproves the 'non-existence' of Black feminist and Black lesbian writers" and notes that the "restrictive effect of racial/sexual politics on Black women's writing is made clear for us by the fact that at least one lesbian writer felt the need to publish in this issue using a pseudonym."[14] They find that the issue of same-sex sexuality is "appropriate for courses in women's literature, Black women writers, lesbian literature, Black women's studies, lesbian studies, the contemporary women's movement, feminist theory, etc."[15]

Essays featured in this fifth issue of *Conditions* were just as innovative as Smith's introduction. In her piece entitled "'Under the Days': The Buried Life and Poetry of Angelina Weld Grimké," Gloria T. (Akasha) Hull analyzed the eroticism in Grimké's poetry. A writer unfairly passed over by literary critics at the time, Grimké appears in Hull's account as one of the Harlem (New Negro) Renaissance's outstanding lesbian poets.[16] In another essay, Ann Allen Shockley made mention of her own 1974 novel *Loving Her* as well as *Ruby*, a 1976 novel "authored by the West Indian writer, Rosa Guy."[17] Although she did not frame her findings in this interpretive light, her essay widened the scope of African American lesbian literature beyond conventional U.S. borders to include a Trinidadian-born writer. In so doing, Shockley situated lesbian literatures by women of color within "diasporic literature," or what the 2002 MLA panel referenced at the outset of this introduction called "Queer Atlantics."

These accomplishments took place several years before the rise of queer theory and the 1993 publication of the edited collection, *The Lesbian and Gay Studies Reader*. To their credit, the *Reader*'s editors mark this timeline in their introduction: "[W]hat now looks like work in lesbian/gay studies has been going on for well over two decades."[18] They correctly claim, however, that "until now there has been no single, inclusive, cross-disciplinary anthology of scholarly and critical essays in lesbian/gay studies."[19] The *Reader* reprinted the work of Smith and Stimpson and also cited the work of Foster and Crompton in its "Suggestions for Further Reading". Interdisciplinary in scope, it testified to the primacy of American gay and lesbian literature. Entitled "Between the Pages," the *Reader*'s final section offered analyses of Harlem Renaissance writer Nella Larsen and pulp novelist Ann Bannon, as well as Cherríe Moraga and Gertrude Stein. In an example of historical continuities between lesbian, gay, and queer literary studies that I have briefly sketched above, Stimpson penned this last piece on Stein.

The Lesbian and Gay Studies Reader is remarkable for the bridge that it established between the lesbian and gay studies of the 1990s and those of earlier decades. At the same time, it documents how American gay and lesbian literary studies absorbed the intellectual apparatus of what is now known as "queer theory" or "queer studies." The editors, in fact, included some of the most prominent queer theorists – Eve Kosofsky Sedgwick, Lee Edelman, and Teresa de Lauretis, to name but three – and many of these thinkers made their institutional homes in departments of English. Coterminous with the HIV/AIDS crisis (which is conventionally, if problematically, historicized from the early 1980s until the introduction of antiretroviral medications in the later 1990s), queer theory's initial methodology embraced clashing aims. First, it sought greater presence in sexuality studies for sexually nonnormative individuals, such as transgender persons, bisexuals, or heterosexuals who did not identify as lesbian or gay. Second, queer theory treated sexual categorization as a mode of identity management. American literature was often used to play out these competing objectives. To cite one example: Sedgwick's 1990 *Epistemology of the Closet* – an indispensable text for U.S. queer theory that is partly excerpted in the *Reader* – offers post-structuralist readings of American-born authors, such as Henry James.

During and after the 1990s, fault lines within queer theory enriched American literary studies as the field further intersected with issues of race, ethnicity, class, region, religion, disability, and nation-state. The *Reader* was percipient on many of these fronts. It notes that "we have reluctantly chosen not to speak here and in our title of 'queer studies,' despite our own attachment to the term."[20] In one of their introduction's penultimate lines, the editors state that "our choice of 'lesbian/gay' indicates no wish on our part to make lesbian/gay studies look less assertive, less unsettling, and less queer than it already does."[21] At the same time, with its reprint of the Caribbean American author Audre Lorde's "The Uses of the Erotic: The Erotic as Power," the *Reader* hinted at the soon-to-be-flourishing field of "queer of color theory," a field that would continue the work of scholars such as Hull and Smith.

This last reference to Lorde's nonfiction piece alerts us to the dynamic status of the adjective "American" in U.S. lesbian, gay, and queer literary study. Throughout her writings, Lorde critiqued the idea of America, and her 1982 memoir *Zami: A New Spelling of My Name: A Biomythography* references the nation as a lowercase "america."[22] Some post–World War II writers adopted this stylization to mark their fury with the U.S. nation-state and its oftentimes draconian policies toward minority populations, or what *Zami* refers to as the "hostile surroundings" and "this plastic, anti-human society in which we live."[23] Lorde consequently points us to the unstable status of "America" as it impacts homoerotic writing and critique.

Writers such as Lorde – as well as many others mentioned in forthcoming chapters – direct us, finally, to the significant roles that internationalism and transnationalism play within the evolving concept of American gay and lesbian literature. So too does this *Companion*, which is composed of authors from three continents and four nations who survey primary and secondary writings under the admittedly inadequate category of "gay and lesbian authorship" in the United States. Their cosmopolitanism extends the intellectual traditions just outlined, and they prove "American Gay and Lesbian Literature" to be an ongoing and malleable concept.

This *Companion* distributes itself across three parts that lay out formal, contextual, and critical parameters of interpretation: (1) genres; (2) historical contexts; and (3) critical approaches. Part I outlines four major genres that cut across periodization – novel, drama and performance, poetry, and life writing – and ends with a consideration of American cinema as it does and does not overlap with American literature.

In his chapter on the LGBTQ novel, Michael Cobb's "Queer Novelties" (Chapter 1) explores the pleasures and discomforts that this narrative form affords readers. Examining fiction by James Baldwin, Djuna Barnes, and Michael Cunningham, Cobb argues that the novel supplies queer individuals with a mode of voicing same-sex desire at the same time that it records the frustrations, disappointments, and yearnings of same-sex eroticism and camaraderie. Merging his close readings with insights from some of queer theory's crucial thinkers, Cobb demonstrates that the LGBTQ novel's pleasures lay in and beyond the genre's historical moments: "For the queer novel permits us to be quite novel – novel as in new, as in giving us news about our often confusing, often inchoate understandings of sexuality, which will disturb, no doubt, our senses of time."

In Chapter 2, Sean Metzger focuses on the genre of queer theater and performance and widens this category beyond the stage and into the embodied aesthetics of solo performance and radical queer productions. After offering an overview of avant-garde performance, he then provides a detailed close reading of Richard Greenberg's 2002 Broadway play, *Take Me Out*. By examining how this homoerotic production enables scholars to interrogate intersecting claims about race, ethnicity, nation-state, and sexuality via "queer Asian/American critique," Metzger presents a useful model of how to analyze a queer performance, its reviews, and its larger cultural meanings.

Turning his attention to three centuries of queer poetics, Eric Keenaghan tracks how verse has been essential to recording queer desire across gender, race, and ethnicity. In Chapter 3, which considers a range of works, from Walt Whitman's *Leaves of Grass* to transgender poet kari edwards's *obedience* (2005), Keenaghan makes a strong case that the genre of poetry enables queers to mark their historical realities-at-hand and to imagine other spaces of same-sex desire. "Poetry," he remarks, "imaginatively supplements those bleak realities, thus making readers conscious of them and ready to transform them." To support this claim, he offers readers a panoply of poetics that highlights works by the Harlem Renaissance poet Langston Hughes, the San Francisco Renaissance poet Jack Spicer, and the Washington, DC–based lesbian-feminist collective The Furies. Although he remains attuned to the historical specifics of these publications, Keenaghan, like Cobb, nonetheless offers a complementary argument that connects these disparate texts: "The actual character of LGBT poetry, like most other poetries, is that it is future-oriented, invested in imagining and articulating life and its possibilities differently from what is currently known."

Julie Avril Minich's chapter on "Writing Queer Lives: Autobiography and Memoir" (Chapter 4) turns to queer life writing and its commentary on events such as the AIDS epidemic and the corporeal disability that alienates one from normative worlds. This focus enables her "to think about why queer lives matter, about what we might learn from their unusual embodiments and their nonnormative unfoldings in time and space." One example of this dynamic appears in her reading of Gloria Anzaldúa's 1987 *Borderlands/ La Frontera: The New Mestiza*. Exploring the appeal for "a new race, / half and half – both woman and man, neither – / a new gender" in *Borderlands*, Minich also teases out how queer disability informs this poetic text.[24] The critical yield of her interpretations becomes obvious: queer writers across gender, class, race, and literary period, she suggests, have reformatted "traditional life events associated with heteronormative constructions of time" into a genre that announces new forms of connection, healing, and embodiment.

Capping this part on genre, Lucas Hilderbrand's contribution, "Queer Cinema, Queer Writing, Queer Criticism" (Chapter 5), addresses how important cinema has become for LGBTQ populations as the visual medium distinguishes itself from its textual compeer. Focusing on a handful of post-Stonewall film adaptations of literary texts – including director Ang Lee's 2005 *Brokeback Mountain*, with a screenplay based on a 1997 short story by E. Annie Proulx; William Friedkin's 1970 *The Boys in the Band*, adapted from the 1968 stage play of the same title; and Isaac Julien's 1989 *Looking for Langston*, based partially on Richard Bruce Nugent's 1926 short story "Smoke, Lilies and Jade," to name three examples amidst other films that he discusses – Hilderbrand looks at how the genre of film has been useful for visualizing literary representation while also modeling how to analyze queer film "on its own terms." His chapter usefully supplements the literary analyses that precede it.

The second part of this *Companion*, "Historical Contexts," elucidates how lesbian and gay writing responded to historical transitions across decades of aesthetic innovation that the first part gauged. Part II moves chronologically and follows standard historical outlines of sexuality's emergence in the later nineteenth century United States; its growing crystallization in the first half of the twentieth century; and the intensification of political activism in the mid-twentieth century and thereafter. At times, its contributors look beyond this periodization to stress how queerness – as discrete from lesbian and gay social identity – appears outside sexuality's emergence in modern American cultural media.

In his chapter on "Nineteenth-Century Queer Literature" (Chapter 6), for example, Travis Foster suggests that queerness enveloped literary productions for decades before a hetero-/homosexual binary took hold in

American reading publics. Although Foster does not ignore the impact of this historical construction, he attends to both canonical works, such as Herman Melville's 1851 *Moby-Dick*, and lesser known texts, such as Rose Terry Cooke's 1858 short tale "My Visitation" composed prior to the rise of the field of sexology (the scientific study of sex). In so doing, he explores how literatures in an era of "presexology" recorded same-sex erotics that encompassed desires across the threshold of the living and, in the case of Cooke's tale, the dead.

Turning to the literary and sexual advances produced in the interwar years, Daniela Caselli's chapter (Chapter 7) highlights links between formalist experimentalism; the calcification of hetero- and homosexual identity; and the emergence of lesbian and gay sexual subcultures in globalizing spaces such as twentieth-century New York City. To do so, she provides readers with historicized readings of three major texts of queer American modernism: Richard Bruce Nugent's 1926 short story "Smoke, Lilies and Jade," Charles Henri Ford and Parker Tyler's 1933 novel *The Young and Evil*, and Djuna Barnes's 1936 *Nightwood* (published in the United States in 1937). Situating these avant-garde texts within cultural milieus such as the Harlem Renaissance, queer scenes of Manhattan, and Parisian lesbian subcultures, Caselli shows that these works grappled with developing norms of sexual and racial identity via innovative aesthetic techniques. As they did so, each of these writers provided audiences of their moment – as well as those to come – with insight into questions of queer childhood, interracial desire, and temporality.

Furthering the historical trajectory begun by Foster and Caselli, Michael P. Bibler's chapter on Cold War–era LGBTQ literatures (Chapter 8) charts how lesbians and gays responded to a conventionally unsympathetic moment in twentieth-century America: the decades immediately before the advent of gay liberation. Intriguingly, Bibler contends that this era was extraordinarily fruitful for LGBTQ literatures, because it saw the reformatting of the closet that Caselli also discusses – the idea that the sexual orientation of queer individuals remains hidden in a predominantly heterosexual society. Surveying literatures by Tennessee Williams, Patricia Highsmith, Ann Bannon, and others, Bibler counterintuitively describes how the social and sexual stranglehold of this cultural era allowed these writers to queer genres such as pulp fiction, the southern gothic novel, postmodernist poetry, and the melodramatic Broadway production.

Guy Davidson's chapter on "The Time of AIDS and the Rise of 'Post-Gay' " (Chapter 9) concludes the "Historical Contexts" part. Focusing on writings from the 1980s to the twenty-first century, Davidson takes up the bearing of the HIV/AIDS crisis on LGBTQ literatures as well as the subsequent mainstreaming of LGBTQ communities. With regards to the AIDS crisis, Davidson interprets a wide range of texts, such as Rafael Campo's *The Poetry of Healing* and Jewelle Gomez's *The Gilda Stories*, that each developed unique strategies for navigating fictional and nonfictional accounts of HIV/AIDS. He then turns to several readings of mainstream white gay male authors, such as David Leavitt and Michael Cunningham. Treating a few of their works as exemplary of a growing conservatism among LGBTQ reading publics, Davidson concludes that contemporary queer literatures such as the novels of Samuel R. Delany will nonetheless carry forth "vigorous and diverse" sexual and aesthetic innovation.

Part III, "Critical Approaches," orients readers to five strains of criticism useful for understanding the genres and historical backgrounds of the American gay and lesbian literatures that are outlined in Parts I and II. They encompass: (1) feminist/gender theory; (2) intersectional/queer of color critique; (3) psychoanalytic theory; (4) post-structuralist theory and affect theory; and (5) transnational criticism.

L. H. Stallings's chapter, "Gender and Sexuality" (Chapter 10), explains how LGBTQ criticism emerged as an offshoot of feminist scholarship. After overviewing writings that recuperated forgotten female authors, Stallings then turns to scholarship on race and ethnicity by theorists such as Gloria Anzaldúa, Trinh T. Minh-ha, and others that augments these innovations in feminist criticism. These contributions, she suggests, set the stage for later post-structuralist examinations of gender and sexuality as performance (as seen in the writings of Judith Butler); the application of masculinity to female-identified bodies (as seen in the work of Judith [Jack] Halberstam); and the development of queer women of color critique (as seen in the theories of Barbara Smith and Deborah McDowell).

In her chapter on "Intersections of Race, Gender, and Sexuality: Queer of Color Critique" (Chapter 11), Kyla Wazana Tompkins complements Stallings to further the intellectual gains of LGBTQ theories across race and ethnicity. Taking a long historical view of how racialization impacts cultural matters of sexual nonnormativity, Tompkins illuminates that "to be black then was to be always already sexualized as against white citizens and therefore to be always and already deviant." She then details how "queer of color critique articulates queer theory from the heart of these and other histories, although at times it also intervenes in and complicates mainstream and Euro-American queer theory." To do so, she rehearses the findings of theorists such as Sara Ahmed, Gloria Anzaldúa, David L. Eng, José Esteban Muñoz, and Jasbir Puar, who crafted critical tools for understanding the social damages launched against racialized queers as well as the means for surpassing such hostilities.

Judith Roof vigilantly walks readers through the uses of psychoanalysis in her chapter, "Psychoanalytic Literary Criticism of Gay and Lesbian American Literature" (Chapter 12). Beginning with Sigmund Freud's and Carl Jung's famous 1909 visit to Massachusetts-based Clark University, Roof details how beneficial psychoanalytic thinking has been for LGBTQ scholars and authors. Roof touches on how French feminists incorporated the theories of Jacques Lacan, which were then embraced by American academics; how gay male theory by thinkers such as Leo Bersani and Tim Dean established a generation of new thinking about pleasure and sexual relations; and how works by Judith Butler, Teresa de Lauretis, and Lee Edelman have helped us understand identity as a performance and the psycho-social demands placed on queer individuals in a world that often urges biological reproduction.

As a match to Roof's chapter, Melissa Jane Hardie's contribution, "Post-Structuralism: Originators and Heirs" (Chapter 13) offers a sharp discussion of how "the perverse orientation of" post-structuralist thinkers such as Michel Foucault, Eve Kosofsky Sedgwick, Judith Butler, Samuel R. Delany, and others influenced the analysis of American literature. Considering deconstruction's far-reaching impact on the field of queer theory, Hardie grants insight into foundational texts such as the first volume of Foucault's *The History of Sexuality*, Butler's *Bodies That Matter*, and Sedgwick's *Epistemology of the Closet*. She then traces how these texts assisted a critical swerve as queer literary and cultural studies began to explore issues of affect related to LGBTQ works and personages.

Concluding this *Companion*, Martin Joseph Ponce's "Transnational Queer Imaginaries, Intimacies, Insurgencies" (Chapter 14) addresses critical accounts of American literatures inside and outside U.S. borders. As Ponce writes at the start of his chapter, "to bring to bear a transnational analytic to the study of queer U.S. literature is to interrogate the national frame of 'America' as the organizing principle of literary and sexual history and to open up the field to hemispheric, oceanic, postcolonial, and diasporic approaches." Making good on this claim, Ponce embraces queer literatures from the 1930s to the late twentieth century that theorize the methodology that he identifies as a central aspect of any study of American literature. Importantly, these literary theorizations – enhanced with scholarship by Gloria Anzaldúa, Inderpal Grewal, and Debra A. Castillo, among others – also include discussions of queer Native literatures keen on "dismantling settler colonialism and asserting Native sovereignty." Fittingly, then, Ponce's chapter autocritiques the nationalism of U.S. LGBTQ writing that has both informed and, in some instances, thwarted the literary efforts of writers across the genres and the historical periods that the earlier chapters detail. It is a necessary end to this *Companion*, which begins with my recapitulation of a 1974 MLA Convention panel in New York City on "Homosexuality and Literature" but concludes with a more sprawling notion of this idea across time and, especially, the globe.

NOTES

1 "Forum: Homosexuality and Literature," *PMLA* 89, no. 6 (1974): 1180.
2 Quoted in Jaime Harker, *Middlebrow Queer: Christopher Isherwood in America* (Minneapolis: University of Minnesota Press, 2013), 165.
3 "Forum: Homosexuality and Literature," *PMLA* 89, no. 6 (1974): 1180.
4 "Professional Notes and Comments," *PMLA* 90, no. 4 (1975): 744.
5 "Homosexuality in Film: *The Celluloid Closet*," *PMLA* 97, no. 6 (1982): 1092; "The Queer Child," *PMLA* 112, no. 6 (1997): 1302; "Queer Atlantics," *PMLA* 117, no. 6 (2002): 1491.
6 Louis Crompton, "Homophile Course, Designated Texts, Bibliography," fall 1970, box 12, folder 7, Louis Crompton Papers, Archives and Special Collections, University of Nebraska-Lincoln.
7 Louis Crompton, "Homophile Course, Topics List," fall 1970, box 12, folder 8, Louis Crompton Papers, Archives and Special Collections, University of Nebraska-Lincoln.
8 Catharine R. Stimpson, "Zero Degree Deviancy: The Lesbian Novel in English," *Critical Inquiry* 8, no. 2 (1981): 363.
9 Joanne Passet, *Sex Variant Woman: The Life of Jeannette Howard Foster* (Cambridge, MA: Da Capo Press, 2008), 181.
10 Jeannette Howard Foster, "Acknowledgments," in *Sex Variant Women in Literature: A Historical and Quantitative Survey* (1956; London: Frederick Muller, 1958), 7.
11 Barbara Smith, "Toward a Black Feminist Criticism," *Conditions: Two* 1, no. 2 (1977): 33.
12 Ibid.
13 Smith, "Toward a Black Feminist Criticism," 25.
14 Lorraine Bethel and Barbara Smith, introduction to "The Black Women's Issue," ed. Lorraine Bethel and Barbara Smith, special issue, *Conditions: Five* 2, no. 2 (1979): 11–12.
15 Ibid., 14.
16 Gloria T. Hull, "'Under the Days': The Buried Life and Poetry of Angelina Weld Grimké," in "The Black Women's Issue," ed. Lorraine Bethel and Barbara Smith, special issue, *Conditions: Five* 2, no. 2 (1979): 17–25.
17 Ann Allen Shockley, "The Black Lesbian in American Literature: An Overview," in "The Black Women's Issue," ed. Lorraine Bethel and Barbara Smith, special issue, *Conditions: Five* 2, no. 2 (1979): 137.
18 Henry Abelove, Michèle Aina Barale, and David M. Halperin, introduction to *The Lesbian and Gay Studies Reader*, ed. Henry Abelove, Michèle Aina Barale, and David M. Halperin (New York: Routledge, 1993), xv.
19 Ibid., xvi.
20 Ibid., xvii.

21 Ibid. Another fine analysis of this overlap is Linda Garber, *Identity Poetics: Race, Class, and the Lesbian-Feminist Roots of Queer Theory* (New York: Columbia University Press, 2001).

22 Audre Lorde, *Zami: A New Spelling of My Name: A Biomythography* (Berkeley: Crossing Press, 1982), 187.

23 Ibid., 149, 181.

24 Gloria Anzaldúa, *Borderlands/La Frontera: The New Mestiza* (San Francisco: Aunt Lute Books, 1987), 216.

PART I

Genres

I

MICHAEL COBB

Queer Novelties

Writing anything definitive about queer American novels will always be unsatisfying, if not impossible. Unsatisfying, because the romances they contain are uncertain and, quite often, doomed: heartbreak, violence, and persecution pepper nearly every page. Impossible, because the genre's terrain is as vast and uncertain as America itself: the spaces, characters, plots, ideas, and dynamics are too varied. The minute you say one thing, you could say another. And perhaps that might be the point. As one character from Djuna Barnes's lesbian novel *Nightwood* puts it, "[w]ith an American anything can be done."[1] We could say the same about the queer American novel.

If there is anything consistently connecting this genre, it is that it features, however obliquely, the effects that characters (usually American, but not always) have as they seek reasons for why they have sexual feelings for those that are not obvious or traditional object choices. Frequently, these effects instruct characters in their pursuit of self-knowledge and self-understanding, especially if others have pathologized their desires (and America has and does pathologize its queers). In her autobiographical graphic memoir *Fun Home*, Alison Bechdel tells a story about a variety of discoveries that books, be they explicitly queer or not, can inspire. During the same afternoon when she acknowledges that she is a "lesbian," she also finds herself asking a professor to let her take his course on James Joyce's *Ulysses* – her father's favorite book. As we move from the captions to the meticulous, stylized drawings, canonical books acquire an increasingly important role: books become guides to how Bechdel will produce "a convergence" with her "abstracted father."[2] That is, reading the "classics" enables Bechdel to relate to her distant and closeted father. She can explore his passions for high art and aesthetics, which *Fun Home* understands as part of a larger expression for his queer passions.

One book leads to many, and as she reveals to her dad that she is taking a course on *Ulysses*, he advises her on what she "needs" to know, thickening her reading of Joyce with other books. Not accidentally, he gives her a copy of Colette's autobiography, *Earthly Paradise*. Like clockwork, Colette stirs Bechdel's lesbian self-awakening, leading to more books that she reads alongside (and often instead of) Joyce – a series of readings she says she could have called an independent study on Contemporary and Historical Perspectives on Homosexuality: Virginia Woolf's *Orlando*, Radclyffe Hall's *The Well of Loneliness*, and Rita Mae Brown's *Rubyfruit Jungle*, among others (205). Bechdel styles the world of queer literature as an Odysseus-like journey of self-understanding, as these scenes of reading and queer discovery highlight the capacious quality of the queer novel, especially in the American context, for many novels, well beyond those with explicit lesbian, gay, bisexual, trans, or queer subject matter, can be brought into anyone's queer critical imagination. Almost any piece of writing can find a rather fun home in queerness if the reader is up for it.

Eve Kosofsky Sedgwick pictures the scene of queer reading when she introduces her influential collection on queer fiction, *Novel Gazing*:

> Yet what seems least settled [about the essays in the volume] is any predetermined idea about what makes the queerness of a queer reading. Often these readings begin from a move toward sites of same-sex, interpersonal eroticism – but not necessarily so. It seems to me that an often quiet, but very palpable image here – a kind of *genius loci* for queer reading – is the interpretive absorption of the child or adolescent whose sense of personal queerness may or may not (*yet?*) have resolved into a sexual specificity of proscribed object choice, aim, site, or identification. Such a child – if she reads at all – is reading for important news about herself, without knowing what form that news will take; with only the patchiest familiarity with its codes; without even, more than hungrily hypothesizing to what questions this news may offer an answer. The model of such reading is … [a] speculative, superstitious, and methodologically adventurous state where recognitions, pleasures, and discoveries seep in only from the most stretched and ragged edges of one's competence.[3]

So when readers hunt for queer "news," all sorts of novels, bits of language, or, really, any expressive object can be part of that speculative, superstitious, and adventurous project. Any novel is a queer frontier in the imagination of one of America's most brilliant queer theorists, as it might be in your own. We could say that Sedgwick thinks of queer reading as a form of amateurism, resisting cultivated competencies or knowing what "news" one can learn about oneself before the act of interpretation. The amateur has a child-like openness, which means that all sorts of imagination will accompany the meanings about sexuality he or she generates. Such a figure of the queer reader is apt, given that any attempt to say anything definitive or expert about the queer novel is slightly silly. How, for instance, do we even know what constitutes lesbian, gay, bisexual, or trans (not to mention all the other initials we could legitimately add to the ever-growing list)? Certainly, such confusion about sexual identity only points to the vagueness of sexuality in general: Is sexuality about the rubbing and touching of erogenous zones of the body? Or is it about something more? Do nations have sexualities? Does sexuality have something to do with desire? Love? Would desire or love for a commodity count as sexuality? If not, what about commodities related to sex or love? Are there specific words, plots, temporalities, anxieties, pleasures, or losses that would count as sex? If so, what makes any of this queer? The childlike amateur image – the one that feels like anything but an expert – is especially appropriate then, because love and sexuality make amateurs of us all. Queer reading is an apprenticeship in paying attention to your sexual amateurism.

So how best to proceed? Sedgwick herself uses two great American fictions, Herman Melville's *Billy Budd, Sailor* and Henry James's "The Beast in the Jungle," in her influential readings of queer texts, so we can see queerness where some might only be hinted at, felt, or understood when close attention is paid to the text.[4] Readers have been curious about why so many are so attracted to Billy Budd, "The Handsome Sailor." An officer, soon after discovering that Billy was a foundling, cruises and flirts: "'*Found*, say you? Well,' throwing back his head and looking up and down the new recruit; 'well it turns out to have been a pretty good find.'"[5] Might this be queer? Or what is the deep secret that John Marcher and May Bartram share in James's novella? Was the "beast" in the "jungle" really the "beast" in the "closet," as Sedgwick argues?[6] If you are game for this type of close reading, then you might also approve of why literary critic Deborah McDowell, quite some time ago, convincingly argued that Nella Larsen's Harlem Renaissance novel *Passing* – a novel about the pleasures and perils of light-skinned African American women in the 1920s passing for white – is also about female-female desire.[7] There is nothing explicitly sexual between the two main characters, Clare Kendry and Irene Redfield, but Clare exudes a seductive quality that attracts Irene, eventually violently. Irene, for instance, receives a letter from Clare at the beginning of the novel, and even the description of the white envelope suggests the seduction: "[T]he long envelope of thin Italian paper with its almost illegible scrawl [...] And there was, too, something mysterious and slightly furtive about it. A thin sly thing which bore no return address [...] Furtive, yet some peculiar, determined way a little flaunting?"[8] Or later, a phone call: "She'd done it again. Allowed Clare Kendry to persuade her into promising to do something [...] What was it about Clare's voice that was so appealing, so very seductive?" (52). The novel is riddled with these oblique, curious, titillating moments, and one can (and many have) read all sorts of queer desires into such sentences.

So how could you teach people to be comfortable being the queer amateurs, the queer children they already are (or once were), so that they can
pick up on these readings? What might a canonical survey of queer American
literature include? Certainly, there is a list of books that scholars might tell
you should be included. Perhaps: Ralph Werther's *Autobiography of an
Androgyne*; Truman Capote's *Other Voices, Other Rooms*; Gore Vidal's *The
City and the Pillar*; John Rechy's *City of Night*; Christopher Isherwood's
A Single Man; Andrew Holleran's *Dancer from the Dance*; Audre Lorde's
Zami: A New Spelling of My Name: A Biomythography; Edmund White's
A Boy's Own Story; Alice Walker's *The Color Purple*; Leslie Feinberg's
Stone Butch Blues; Dorothy Allison's *Bastard out of Carolina*; and Jeffrey
Eugenides' *Middlesex*, among many others. Any list is always unsatisfying,
however, because it is idiosyncratic; people cherish and respect novels that
mean a lot to them, to their sense of what sexuality, if not queer sexuality,
means. But a canon of queer books is starting to take shape now that lesbian and gay studies has lingered around the professional literary academy
for more than a quarter of a century. One could even cement that list by
historicizing these titles' meanings by referring to the major epochs that
have affected queer life in the United States: the legacies of degeneracy and
psychological pathologization in the late nineteenth-century era of indus-
trialization and urbanization; the demimonde of expatriated Americans in
Paris in the 1920s; the closeted but provocative time of the Mattachine
Society in the 1950s; the emergence of gay and lesbian pride (alongside the
rise of second-wave feminism and racial civil rights movements) marked
most symbolically by the Stonewall riots of 1969; the hedonism and
disco-drug cultures of gay-liberating San Francisco and New York City in
the 1970s; the impacts of the HIV/AIDS epidemic on expressions of a subculture marked for annihilation in the 1980s and early 1990s; and the early
twenty-first-century push for mainstream acceptance and normalcy as new
mediated social networks and mainstream legal gains make queer people,
entertainment, politics, and cultures visible, standardized, and ubiquitous.

This codification of a distinct and distinctive subculture and genre of literature makes sense and produces superb work.[9] Some lesbian and gay studies
scholars even have strong investments in making sure that something coherent and knowable will be transmitted by the interpretations we develop as
we make our queer readings mean something, that we can study these novels
within rigorous historical considerations of the past, that we can "practice
a queer historicism dedicated to showing how categories, however mythic,
phantasmatic, and incoherent, came to be."[10] There is something about the
precision of rigorous historical contextualization and interpretation that

makes us more certain of the claims we're trying to make when we offer up a meaning for consideration.

Kathryn Bond Stockton, however, offers an alternative to such a commonplace methodology. She believes we're still being adventurous, speculative, and superstitious even when we think we're putting things into a canonical, historical sequence:

> History, however much it changes, is itself a synchrony, in the largest sense. It is All the Views of Historical Sequence that Exist to be Read at This Time. Hence I cannot "go back" to texts, historical or fictional, so as to think their meanings in their own time. No one can. They can exist for me only now as the reader I am, a reader who is using (at this current moment) a raft of ideas from decades of reading so as to read texts that themselves are extremely complex amalgams of various times.[11]

Any kind of historical rigor, or even understanding of what a text might reveal to you about, say, something like sexuality, is only a synchronic understanding of what you have been able to discern for yourself as a reader. The only real history you might get is a history of you, for this moment and perhaps only for a moment.

Bechdel agrees with Stockton. Her graphic memoir constantly loops backward, rehearsing moments and shifting time, so it cannot make easy sense of discrete epochs. All gathers into the present moment of reading. On one page of drawings, we see Bechdel having oral sex with another woman in a room with historical remnants of feminist and lesbian feminist activism (including an old shirt, hung on the wall, with a sickle and the words "Lesbian Terrorist" and a protest placard that reads "Keep Your God Off My Body"). But the panel's captions reference Homer's *Odyssey*, where her reading of Joyce has taken her, and we learn: "Like Odysseus on the island of the Cyclops, I found myself facing a 'being of colossal strength and ferocity, to whom the law of man and god meant nothing.'" The terrifying being: her new lover's vulva. Then, "[i]n true heroic fashion, I moved toward the thing I feared." And in the third panel, "[y]et while Odysseus schemed desperately to escape Polyphemus's cave, I found that I was quite content to stay here forever" (214). The joke about the prolonging of enjoyment – of lingering over the act of cunnilingus (cunnilingering?) with a one-eyed monster – aside, we have the historical context of the college-room lesbian sex (T-shirt, protest sign) drenched in epic reference. No easy history can organize and contain the textual expression of sexual expression, so Bechdel enables a synchrony of antiquity, recent past, and contemporary memoir to be the way she represents her first taste of lesbian sexuality.

Moreover, the wish to stay anywhere "forever" is the wish to refuse conventional time and timing (or at least the hope that such conventions can be suspended), which is one of the features of the queer novel we should consider *before* we begin disciplining the genre into meaning something that can be read as belonging to a kind of time or to a literary tradition of the time's greatest literary hits. The queer novel permits us to be quite novel – novel as in new, as in giving us news about our often confusing, often inchoate understandings of sexuality, which will disturb, no doubt, our senses of time. The diary entry of Virginia Woolf that Michael Cunningham uses as an epigraph to his queer novel *The Hours* (which swirls in time around the story of Virginia Woolf and her novel *Mrs. Dalloway*) quite suggestively states, "I have no time to describe my plans. I should say a good deal about The Hours, & my discovery; how I dig out beautiful caves behind my characters; I think that gives exactly what I want; humanity, humour, depth. The idea is that the caves shall connect, & each comes to daylight at the present moment."[12] The novel gives us a startling sense of presence, if only for the present. Cunningham wants us to focus on how the zone of "no time" can enable depth, or "beautiful caves," to be carved out of the queer characters tangled in the understandings, in various ways, of *Mrs. Dalloway*.

Being tangled in novel time gives us our dark holes, inspiring our cave explorations into what happens to characters as they experience the mysteries of having atypical desires. Geoff Ryman, in his novel about HIV/AIDS (among many other things), also fixates on another novel from the past. Not *Ulysses*, not *Mrs. Dalloway*, but L. Frank Baum's *The Wonderful Wizard of Oz*, featuring one of the most iconic characters from gay life in the late twentieth century – Judy Garland/Dorothy from the film *The Wizard of Oz* – which inspired the phrase "Friends of Dorothy," a euphemism for gays and lesbians in America. In Ryman's book, we have Dorothy Gael (the novel's fictional presentation of a real Dorothy), who is an orphan physically abused by Auntie Em and sexually abused by Uncle Henry. Dorothy swells with indignity, tragedy, and poverty as she becomes a nightmare adolescent. Baum is cast as a substitute teacher who encounters a teenaged Dorothy, "a great lump of a girl."[13] He soon develops a connection with her, one that is nearly flirtatious, only to traumatize her by trying to get her to open up to him. The way the Substitute looked at her ("not unlike the look Uncle Henry gave her") made her "wan[t] to shrug away her love of him," for "[t]he love hurt" (172), but she cannot help but want to comply with his wish for her to write something for him. The assignment exposes too much of her hurt, sorrow, and indignation, and she implodes. The Substitute's (L. Frank Baum's) response to the meltdown: he is inspired to write the story of the life she should have had, which becomes, in Ryman's imagination, *The Wonderful Wizard of Oz*.

Throughout, the novel blends biographical details of Dorothy's story with those of Judy Garland as she grows up into the woman who plays the young role of Dorothy in the iconic movie. Ryman also weaves into his novel details about those involved in the production of the iconic Oz movie; and he complements this Dorothy matrix by mixing in a storyline about Jonathan, a gay actor dying of AIDS-related causes in the late 1980s, who grew up obsessed with *Oz* and who, as a form of coping with and therapy for his terminal illness, desires to go to Kansas to find out what happened to this "real" Dorothy – the "great lump of a girl" who has been obscured by the cyclone of images generated by the Substitute's fantastical telling of her story. As he searches for Dorothy, "[t]ime seemed to be leapfrogging over itself. Parts of it were missing" (319). His search takes him to a cemetery where he looks for Dorothy's family name, and as he stares at the old tombstones, he inexplicably starts to sing a version of the Civil War patriotic fight song "The Battle Hymn of the Republic." Jonathan marches out of the cemetery toward the prairie, but he gets tangled in a barbed-wire fence. Here, he assumes a scarecrow-like posture, which recalls his love of playing the scarecrow when he performed the *Oz* role when he was younger, and then he returns to cemetery, back "among the dead" (340), where he miraculously finds the graves of Uncle Henry and Auntie Em. In this scene, we watch Jonathan get snarled in the historical details he is seeking. Soon, both he and his travel companion, Bill (his psychiatrist), are able to find Dorothy's farm and perhaps her school, or at least the place where it might have been. His response to his success it that he quite alarmingly flees and then vanishes: "'Where are you?' Bill started to run across the fields, toward Dorothy's farm and then stopped. This is crazy, he thought. There's nowhere to hide. If Jonathan was ahead of him, he would see him, running. If he had fallen over, he would still see him, there was no cover, Bill could see every clump of dirt" (347–348). The mystery of the time travel that leads to the inexplicable loss of a gay man dying of AIDS-related causes is never illuminated by an adequate answer to the question, "Where are you?" He is here one moment and gone the next.

So Jonathan's denouement frustrates because we do not learn what happens to him. We're not permitted to know. Ryman explains, in an unconventional coda to the novel, that he is "a fantasy writer who fell in love with realism," and he lists some of the details of the novel that are true and some that are made up. He does the historicist's work, and just when you think he reveals his mysteries, he leaves us befuddled, caught up in the barbed wire of fact and fiction. He insists that he had to tell the story of Jonathan and all the other friends of Dorothy as a constant battle between history and fantasy:

> I fell in love with realism because it deflates myths, the unexamined ideas of fantasy. It confronts them with forgotten facts. It uses truth – history.
>
> I love fantasy because it reminds us how far short our lives fall from their full potential. Fantasy reminds us how wonderful the world is. In fantasy, we can imagine a better life, a better future. In fantasy, we can free ourselves from history and outworn realism.
>
> Oz is, after all, only a place with flowers and birds and rivers and hills. Everything is alive there, as it is here if we can see it. Tomorrow, we could decide to live in a place not much different from Oz. We don't. We continue to make the world an ugly, even murderous place, for reasons we do not understand.
>
> Those reasons lie in both fantasy and history. Where we are gripped by history – our own personal history, our country's history. Where we are deluded by fantasy – our own fantasy, our country's fantasy. It is necessary to distinguish between history and fantasy wherever possible.
>
> And then use them against each other.
>
> (368–369)

Ryman makes explicit what happens throughout a variety of queer novels and for quite some time: the queer novel instructs one in a queer methodology; even as we sort out fantasy from history, we still cannot help but leap-frog from time to time and only end in a confrontation without anything specific or settled. The costs of being too gripped by personal or national histories or fantasies are great indeed; being too gripped does not allow us to make our own lives like the one Dorothy dreams she finds over the rainbow, where "everything is alive." Ryman's methodology is not unlike Sedgwick's speculative, adventurous, even superstitious queer readings, and it does have many resonances with queer theory's deep connection with notions of performativity (gender/sex and sexuality as accumulated performances of understood markers and citations of identity) that both Sedgwick and Judith Butler, and really most others, now understand as axiomatic.[14] Butler articulated this issue rather well:

> So I am skeptical about how the "I" is determined as it operates under the title of the lesbian sign, and I am no more comfortable with its homophobic determination than with those normative definitions offered by other members of the "gay or lesbian community." I'm permanently troubled by identity categories, consider them to be invariable stumbling-blocks, and understand them, even promote them, as sites of necessary trouble. In fact, if the category were to offer no trouble, it would cease to be interesting to me: it is precisely the *pleasure* produced by the instability of those categories which sustains the various erotic practices that make me a candidate for the category to begin with.

> To install myself within the terms of an identity category would be to turn against the sexuality that the category purports to describe; and this might be true of any identity category which seeks to control the very eroticism that it claims to describe and authorize, much less "liberate."[15]

Something about energy, intensity, life, and unpredictability produce the pleasures of eroticism, which resists any easy categorization. History, fantasy, lesbian – really any "identity category" or term that must rest on its laurels, as it were – cannot be erotic, cannot count as belonging to sexuality's force. We have to be "permanently troubled," "forever" stuck staring at the face of sexuality's mysteries, and something about the novel's ability to stop our conventional notions of time strands us in frustratingly atypical desire. No category will do. We'll never be satisfied if what we're looking for is coherence and strong expression. Instead, we should be lost in Woolf's caves, plumbing the depths of what makes the character much more than a type. What an amateur craves, then, is something other than a strong category (lesbian, gay, straight, bisexual, trans, and so forth). Hortense J. Spillers puts it this way: "As I see it the goal [of sexuality work] is not an articulating of sexuality so much as it is a global restoration and dispersal of power. In such an act of restoration, sexuality becomes one of several active predicates. So much depends on it."[16]

"Global" is obviously an enormous scale, but that is why the drama of sexuality, which can so often feel like a small, personal anxiety deep inside one's fretting mind, is really of the largest scale. This is why the work of understanding the sweep and scope of the queer novel goes beyond the interpersonal and solitary trouble and torment of specific characters. The trick of queer reading is that one needs to suggest the large scale of the crisis of relation without falling prey to the lures of normative categories, discrete and sequential time periods, specific canons, and sentimental slogans. Such lures obstruct the potentially expansive network of any character's dark caves from connecting, except for in the eye of an expert, which otherwise codifies and makes coherent – in other words, makes smaller – the eroticisms that fuel characters' lives. Something about the predicate of sexuality troubles not just sexuality, and not just us. So much depends on sexuality.

No wonder, then, that race, gender, class, and all sorts of other identity categories vex our experiences of eroticism. Sexuality has the habit of touching every category, if not everyone and everything. James Baldwin's second novel (and his second queer novel), *Giovanni's Room*, features David, whose literal and figurative reach is figured as global: he travels to Europe to leave the hurt and anxiety of being a gay man in mid-twentieth-century America only to fall in love with an Italian expatriate, Giovanni. The whole novel casts itself as a big journey to understanding the small, lurking, sexual things David knew and worried about as a child:

> Perhaps, as we say in America, I wanted to find myself. This is an interesting phrase, not current as far as I know in the language of any other people, which certainly does not mean what it says but betrays a nagging suspicion that something has been misplaced. I think now if I had any intimation that the self I was going to find would turn out to be only the same self from which I spent so much time in flight, I would have stayed at home. But, again, I think I knew exactly what I was doing when I took the boat for France.[17]

Quite literally, he is a child of the world, and his status as an amateur, a fool, enables him to explore, deeply, why he cannot seem to proficiently learn how to "say Yes to life" (10).

This is a lesson our queer amateur David, we are told quite early in the novel, will not learn because he gives up on his desire and love for Giovanni; he refuses to become an expert in his relationship. Giovanni tragically ends up being put to death (after a series of mistakes that Giovanni makes in his life after David leaves). Instead of a coherent sense of self or relationship, what remains in David is a constant return, a haunting, an unsatisfied imagination that forever animates his refusal to just say yes and to be:

> I think we [David and Giovanni] connected the instant that we met. And remain connected still, in spite of our later *separation de corps*, despite the fact that Giovanni will be rotting soon in unhallowed ground near Paris. Until I die there will be those moments, moments seeming to rise up out of the ground like Macbeth's witches, when his face will come before me, that face in all its changes, when the exact timbre of his voice and tricks of speech will nearly burst my ears, when his smell will overpower my nostrils ... I will see Giovanni again, as he was that night [we first met], so vivid, so winning, all of the light of that gloomy tunnel trapped around his head.
>
> (59)

The tunnel (cave) behind this character's head is where David will inevitably always wind up, bringing him back, over and over again, to his attachment to a love that cannot die even when its object of affection does. The experience pushes David almost to his limits; it overwhelms him (especially his ears and his nose), and even though we know that any experience of gay sex refers back to his initial worries when he first had sex with a boy, Joey, back in America (before David fled), the male body in David's head is now forever Giovanni's. The male body will always be "the black opening of a cavern in which I would be tortured till madness came, in which I would lose my manhood" (15). Even at the novel's end, we're still in a world of dark, gloomy "long corridors" where death moves toward Giovanni (as David imagines his final moments). And David imagines as much as he stares at the mirror and then at his own body, which is also "under sentence of death" (223). He can only come up with shadowy insights: "It [David's body] is lean, hard, and cold, the incarnation of a mystery. And I do not know what moves in this body, what this body is searching. It is trapped in my mirror as it is trapped in time and it hurries toward revelation" (223). How does one grow up and say yes to life? He cannot. Not life as any of us know it. He cannot stop glaring at "his troubling sex," wondering "how it can be redeemed," how he "can save it from the knife" (223). Any categorical understanding of his sex cannot redeem David. The desire to know will only live on as frustrated, troubled desire. And as we know, desire survives only if it is never satiated.

The final sentences of the novel have David tearing up the letter announcing Giovanni's execution, throwing these pieces up into the air, "watching them dance, watching the wind carry them away" (224). In the last line, we have a crucial ambiguity: "Yet, as I turn and begin walking toward the waiting people, the wind blows some of them back on me" (224). Are the pieces of writing about Giovanni blowing back on to him? Or are some of the waiting people blowing back on to him? We're not allowed to know, and we can be disturbed because, in a gust of wind, the story of Giovanni is also the story of the unnamed, waiting people that will, in concert, touch David and move him as he tries to understand what his failed romance means. Those people could be anyone or everyone: different races, genders, sexualities, classes, and nationalities. The possibilities are as wide as the black opening of the cavern that consumes David all of the time.

Djuna Barnes's *Nightwood* also scatters and blends people who are in states of confusion that are hardly sanguine or hopeful. At the ripped-apart heart of the novel is the relationship between two women, Robin Vote and Nora Flood, which is doomed because Robin is a sleepwalker, an object of puzzling allure that will never stay still, always wandering and never dwelling with any one admirer for too long. "Robin told only a little of her life, but she kept repeating in one way or another her wish for a home, as if she were afraid she would be lost again, as if she were aware, without conscious knowledge, that she belonged to Nora, and that if Nora did not make it permanent by her own strength, she would forget" (55). What Nora will not forget, however, is Robin, because the feeling she has for her is love, and this queer feeling has the power even to stop time:

> Love becomes the despot of the heart, analogous in all degrees to the "findings" in a tomb. As in one will be charted the taken place of the body, the raiment, the utensils necessary to its other life, so in the heart of the lover will be traced, as an indelible shadow, that which he loves. In Nora's heart lay the fossil of Robin, intaglio of her identity, and about it for its maintenance ran

Nora's blood. Thus the body of Robin could never be unloved, corrupt, or put away. Robin was now beyond timely changes, except in the blood that animated her.

(56)

Nora, like David, is stuck in no ordinary time. Her heart is turned into stone, which is also a fossil, and she cannot help but crave the one who is always fleeing, even after she decides she cannot continue the relationship. The sequencing of their relationship, then, makes no easy sense, and long passages of the novel seek out inadequate and sometimes contradictory explanations for why Robin cheats on Nora. As Nora processes the relationship (and as she thinks of the dolls that Robin gives her as tokens of their infantilizing love), she seeks out an acquaintance, Doctor O'Connor, who tells her something we all kind of know but do not want to admit: the desire for love, well

> that's what makes most people so passionate and bright, because they want to love and be loved, when there is only a bit of lying in the ear to make the ear forget what time is compiling. So I ... say, creep by softly, softly, and don't learn anything because it's always learned of another person's body; take action in your heart and be careful whom you love – for a lover who dies, no matter how forgotten, will take somewhat of you to the grave.

(147)

Love, especially queer love, which has been constantly rendered dangerous throughout the twentieth century, is a precarious pedagogy that will take away something of you, something that will be hidden forever in the caves in the ground – graves where all the time we have shared in the world is literally piled up. We pretend these piles are not waiting for all of our deepest desires and passions – our bodies. The animation, the childlike brightness of wanting to be loved, will not last forever, for time will stop, and even if your lover does not die (Robin does not in the novel), the love will, which will make the lover in someone (Robin) dead to you (Nora). In every case, though, we're all going to die.

Do not despair. There is something novel here, at least for now. In what might be the best queer novel (composed, ironically, of poetic verse), Canadian-born Anne Carson's *Autobiography of Red*, a lonely, "broken-heart" of a boy, Geryon, reflects on love's harsh lessons for years after he has lost his first boyfriend, Herakles: "'What is time made of?' ... *Time is an abstraction – just a meaning / that we impose upon motion.*"[18] This is more or less the question we ask when we read novels about queer desire, for desire is made of motion; desire makes us move (why reach and try to touch that particular body or not)? We're trying to amass an understanding of queerness that unfolds as people move in the world, turned by their attractions, turned into selves that seem strange and upsetting but are inevitable, even if they are marked as precarious and deadly. As we move across the words on the page, we can try to impose a chronology, a sequence, a set of ideas that unfold in time that will make coherent all the hours we spend loving and losing the people who are teaching us about the depths of ourselves in love. But any specific news – any specific identity, history, category, or paraphrase – is just an abstraction, an imposition, because at heart we are more like long-lost fossils (permanently troubled and lost in darkness) than members of a group that can come into the light and be known. Carson ends the romance with the ex-lovers staring at all the bright lights, amazed: "And now time is rushing toward them / where they stand side by side with arms touching immortality on their faces / night at their back" (146). Everything connects in this moment, and in true Woolfian fashion, all the darkness gathers behind the characters, who will not be explained by time, which they must watch assault them. It is a perfect ending, for at the end of any day (darkness), the queer novel astonishes rather than explains.

NOTES

1 Djuna Barnes, *Nightwood* (New York: New Directions, 1937), 39; hereafter cited in text.
2 Alison Bechdel, *Fun Home: A Family Tragicomic* (Boston: Houghton Mifflin, 2006), 203; hereafter cited in text.
3 Eve Kosofsky Sedgwick, "Paranoid Reading and Reparative Reading; or, You're So Paranoid, You Probably Think This Introduction Is about You," in *Novel Gazing: Queer Readings in Fiction*, ed. Eve Kosofsky Sedgwick (Durham: Duke University Press, 1997), 2–3.
4 See Eve Kosofsky Sedgwick, *Epistemology of the Closet* (Berkeley: University of California Press, 1990).
5 Herman Melville, *Billy Budd, Sailor*, in *Great Short Works of Herman Melville*, ed. Warner Berthoff (New York: Perennial Classics, 2004), 437.
6 Sedgwick, *Epistemology of the Closet*, 195–212.
7 Deborah McDowell, "'It's Not Safe. Not Safe at All': Sexuality in Nella Larsen's *Passing*," in *The Lesbian and Gay Studies Reader*, ed. Henry Abelove, Michèle Aina Barale, and David M. Halperin (New York: Routledge, 1993), 616-625.
8 Nella Larsen, *Passing* (New York: Knopf, 1929), 3; hereafter cited in text.
9 The list of studies here could be endless.
10 Valerie Traub, "The New Unhistoricism in Queer Studies," *PMLA* 128, no. 1 (2013): 35.
11 Kathryn Bond Stockton, *The Queer Child, or Growing Sideways in the Twentieth Century* (Durham: Duke University Press, 2009), 9.
12 Virginia Woolf, diary, August 30, 1923, second epigraph from Michael Cunningham, *The Hours* (New York: Picador USA/Farrar, Straus and Giroux, 1998), n.p.

13 Geoff Ryman, *Was* (New York: Penguin, 1992), 178; hereafter cited in text.

14 See the great classics of queer theory: Judith Butler, *Gender Trouble: Feminism and the Subversion of Identity* (New York: Routledge, 1990); Judith Butler, *Bodies That Matter: On the Discursive Limits of "Sex"* (New York: Routledge, 1993); and Sedgwick, *Epistemology of the Closet*.

15 Judith Butler, "Imitation and Gender Insubordination," in *The Lesbian and Gay Studies Reader*, ed. Henry Abelove, Michèle Aina Barale, and David M. Halperin (New York: Routledge, 1993), 308.

16 Hortense J. Spillers, *Black, White, and in Color: Essays on American Literature and Culture* (Chicago: University of Chicago Press, 2003), 175.

17 James Baldwin, *Giovanni's Room* (New York: Dell, 1956), 31; hereafter cited in text.

18 Anne Carson, *Autobiography of Red* (New York: Vintage, 1998), 70, 93 (emphasis in the original); hereafter cited in text.

2

SEAN METZGER

Queer Theater and Performance

To invoke queer theater and performance is to expand and perhaps confound the rubric of gay and lesbian American literature. For example, any survey of theatrical production in the United States and Canada would quickly reveal that William Shakespeare has been and continues to be one of the most produced playwrights in North America.[1] The Bard's scripts have influenced a veritable Shakespeare industry, producing well-known queer variations, from Anne-Marie MacDonald's play *Goodnight Desdemona (Good Morning Juliet)* (1998) to any number of twenty-first-century youthful gay love stories on screen, including Tom Gustafson's *Were the World Mine* (2008) and Alan Brown's *Private Romeo* (2011). Often trading on the bawdy and the burlesque (with all of the latter word's connotations), such adaptations situate Shakespearean performance within competing discourses of sexuality, even as they demonstrate how Shakespeare's language produces some of those discourses. However, even though homoeroticism suffuses such displays, these productions maintain relatively traditional narrative structures. What does it mean, then, to invoke "queer" in relation to a form (narrative theater, broadly construed) that is so frequently seen, at least in content, *as* queer?

Gregory W. Bredbeck's work, which was written primarily to elucidate narrative and narrativity, provides a lead that assists us in particularizing the potential of queer theater and performance. Bredbeck argues that queer narrative manifests a specific "attitude toward power and toward strategies of social change."[2] Gay narratives (which perhaps too easily also seem to encompass lesbian, if not transgender, writing) "expose the dominant modes of production which result in the hegemony of a particular social formation, and ... intervene in these modes and/or offer alternatives to them"; in contrast, queer narrative, which he aligns with pure critique, "seeks to expose a system in its entirety *as a system*."[3] Bredbeck elaborates this last point, arguing that "new queer narrative effectively blocks the ability to produce new sites of subjective cohesion and immanence, and at the same time it exposes all aspects of narrative itself as illusory constructs devoid of immanence and productive only of false cohesion."[4] Bredbeck, of course, recognizes that the kind of critique embedded in queer narrative cannot be completed. Nevertheless, he finds this schematic useful (as do I) for thinking through the politicization of lesbian, gay, bisexual, and transgender (LGBT) liberation discourse in the 1990s and the legacies of those struggles.

To follow what we might call "American queer theater and performance" is thus to reflect on the regulatory norms that produce and discipline subjects. Rather than locating actual or proto–lesbian and gay people in the theater, therefore, I am more interested in outlining critical framings that can assist in thinking through problems of LGBT historiography and its American contexts. My use of the term "queer" refers not so much to a social formation as it does to a critical project that interrogates romantic and erotic acts in relation to theatrical aesthetics. This investigation of stage, narrative, and critique draws on Bredbeck's earlier formulations. But, as José Esteban Muñoz has illustrated, such considerations also have a genealogy in American theater history in what he calls the "weird and resplendent book" of Brecht (not, however, *Bertolt* Brecht).[5] Stefan Brecht's *Queer Theater* (1978) identifies several performances in New York during the 1960s and 1970s that engaged in "Dadaist travesty," which required "the sort of scattered, multiple concentration needed to play several opponents in chess simultaneously."[6] He traces specific currents of the avant-garde, even as he provides often lengthy asides that offer thick descriptions of performances, explicitly editorialized. These create less a coherent picture and more a kind of textual reproduction of a queer encounter. The reader must relish in contradictions, such as Brecht's origin story of the New York–based, avant-garde group called Theatre of the Ridiculous (which centered around the camp of figures, including John Vaccaro and Charles Ludlam, beginning in the mid-1960s): "All of this history I have also myself gotten from the principals, but I never trusted any information of theirs qua history."[7] Queer emerges for Brecht through an avant-garde populated by artists who practiced, staged, and, indeed, flaunted same-sex desire as constitutive of their aesthetic experimentation.

The provocations of Brecht's weird and resplendent book together with Bredbeck's significant if rather more dour theorization of queer narrative and critique lead to a different articulation of queer theater and performance than one that might be produced by moving through a more conventional frame (e.g., a chronological history from, for instance, Lillian Hellman to Edward Albee). Here, queer disrupts linearity. It seizes on aesthetic departures from what is generally considered normative. In twentieth-century U.S. theater, that norm is often realism and its attendant style of stage performance: method acting. A queer intervention into theater and performance forges new pathways that generate new contexts for considering genealogies of LGBT theater and its theorizations.

Queer Letters/Queer Times

Letters and punctuation constitute the building blocks of the playwright; consolidated in epistles and verse, they also constitute a tradition of romantic friendship upon which much LGBT historiography relies. We witness an early American illustration of this relationship in the amorous affection of Sor Juana Inés de la Cruz for the Marquise de Mancera and the Marquise de la Laguna. The seventeenth-century nun's love poems often address the two female political figures; their textual affiliations create an archive that enables Jesusa Rodriguez's performances centuries later. The textual performativity facilitates a time warp in which the mores of seventeenth-century Mexico rub against those of our contemporary moment. In a somewhat related vein, Yone Noguchi's passionate letters to Charles Warren Stoddard perform and testify to intimacies between Japan and the United States at the turn of the nineteenth century. Such documents assist today's audiences in reimagining the implications of bohemian communities in that period and also in considering the implications of those theatrical spaces that evoke *la vie bohème*.[8] That both Sor Juana and Noguchi also crafted plays might be coincidental, but the assemblage of parts into a kind of whole anticipates, at the scales of the forms in which they worked and of their biographies, the more complex assemblages of the U.S. playwright Gertrude Stein, who spent a good portion of her writer's life in Paris.

Despite the fact that Stein located herself in various ways in the City of Light, she has been called "the foremost dramatist of the early American avant-garde."[9] She is also a writer of consummate queerness. Her works potentially render private intimacies public on the page, particularly for those who would follow the intricacies of her prose to extradiegetic referents. In the tradition of romantic friendship and erotic epistles, Stein often collapses the distance between lover and beloved. *The Autobiography of Alice B. Toklas* (1933) evinces such a collapsing of distinctions even as it performs a kind of ruse that could be traced back to Noguchi's *The American Diary of a Japanese Girl* (1901). However, unlike Noguchi's novel, *The Autobiography of Alice B. Toklas* manifests through performativity an actual person, one whose material assistance facilitated Stein's career. In this manner, Stein holds more in common with her elected compatriots in France, Claude Cahun (née Lucie Schwob) and Marcel Moore (née Suzanne Malherbe). The kind of dual subjectivity that pertains to these pairs

Stein/Toklas and Cahun/Moore also corresponds with, for example, the "I" whose name is "Marguerite Ida and Helena Annabel" in Stein's play *Doctor Faustus Lights the Lights* (1938). Rather than being coterminous with ideas of individual, rights-bearing Enlightenment subjects, these characters and the subjects they seek to index emerge through a play of textual performance, identification, fragmentation, relationality, and desire. Their refusal of the presumed grounds of representation offers a queer critique and a set of queer performance practices the legacies of which emerge in several disparate examples.

To an extent, my effort to name specific examples attempts to create a genealogy of queer theater and performance that works against the foreclosure of women from a more traditional gay canon structured around male playwrights (e.g., from Tennessee Williams to Tony Kushner). On both coasts of the continental United States, various female performance collectives have emerged. These include the founding of the Sacred Naked Nature Girls (SNNG) in the early 1990s, and its later dispersion, as well as the much longer-lived Split Britches, which emerged through New York's WOW (Women on Women) Café in the late 1970s and early 1980s.[10] Such groups encourage a reconsideration of the constitutive exclusions in Brecht's comments on the New York avant-garde. Where were the women? Given women's limited access to modes of production until relatively recent decades, the frame for such an inquiry might be located outside of the commercial theatrical house in other kinds of performance venues. Such a shift in location also helps bring into relief the literal and metaphorical spaces between full disclosure and the unspeakable, between public and private in solo or small ensemble performances that foreground gender and sexuality. From figures like Gladys Bentley and Josephine Baker to lesbian feminist performance art, this genealogy includes Kate Bornstein, Patrisse Cullors, Carmelita Tropicana, Holly Hughes, and Denise Uyehara, among others.

What many, if not all, of these performances share are different investments in time that radically diverge from the causal linearity of theatrical realism. From Baker's invocation of primitivism to Uyehara's homage to domestic incarceration in Japanese internment camps, these performances promise to collapse the distance between the private/personal and the public/spectacular. In other words, they proffer an intimate encounter to audiences but one generally premised on access to some sort of "real" experience to which the performer enjoys a privileged proximity. To return to Stein once more as a kind of provacatrice: one potential effect of such performance is to queer time through a rather sudden intimate encounter, to see performers (she says "actors") who are present to the audience "right away," without the spectators having had much time to familiarize themselves with the characters. Stein suggests that the temporal disjunctions between our lives outside the performance space and the events that happen within it elicit certain forms of excitement. Ultimately, she refers to her own theatrical works as landscapes to suggest the kinds of relations that interest her. Stein's notions of disjunctive time, intimacy, and relationality anticipate the ongoing discussions of queer time that have linked eroticism with temporality in productive, if often divergent, ways.[11]

The Gay White Way: Queer Failure

To an unfortunately large degree, the apotheosis of theater for many audiences in the United States remains Broadway. The requisites of wide commercial appeal limit, with few exceptions, the potential kind of experimentation and lack of narrative cohesion that are associated with queer in this chapter. The analytical stakes of Broadway lie in thinking differently about how the most commodified of theatrical spectacles might nevertheless produce meanings outside of logics of narrative development and profit-making. To queer the Great White Way, I investigate a single play and think through the contradictions of Broadway theater (here understood expansively as big budget, high production value, narrative-driven stage performances in both New York stage and touring incarnations).

Regardless of how Broadway does or does not facilitate queer critique, certainly the history of the Great White Way not only tracks but also shapes the shifting contexts that render sexual norms at any given moment. As one illustration, the very different reactions to the Broadway productions of Sholem Asch's play *God of Vengeance* in 1923 and Duncan Sheik and Steven Sater's musical *Spring Awakening* in 2006 attest to the sea change in normative perspectives regarding teen sexuality. The initial stage premieres of Asch's work (1907) and the eponymous source material for *Spring Awakening* (1906) generated controversy, but the Broadway performance of *God of Vengeance* in 1923 elicited charges of obscenity for which cast members were arrested. The musical, on the other hand, created a "frisson of surprise and excitement" through its "adaptation of the once-scandalous 1891 play by Frank Wedekind" (fifteen years elapsed between the writing of the drama and its first staging in Europe); the review in *The New York Times* of the adapted musical specifically celebrated its depiction of "the confusion and desperation that ensue when the onrushing tide of hormones meets the ignorance of children raised by parents too embarrassed or prudish to discuss what those new urges signify."[12] These productions illustrate the ways in which Broadway registers and helps produce American sexual norms – in these cases by appropriating narratives initially written in response to other cultural frameworks – but they do little, in my view, to challenge the norms of narrative form itself.

However, for some fans, the musical as a genre always calls attention to its narrative structure. For the scholar D. A. Miller, the musical's "frankly interruptive mode-shifting" produces "the same miraculous effect on him as on every character, no matter how frustrated in ambition and devastated by a broken heart, who felt a song coming on: that of sending the whole world packing."[13] In other words, the musical enables possibilities for imagination and identification that might circumvent given norms or even enable spectators to iterate differently the normative conditions that structure our lives.[14] Notwithstanding such interpretive practices, I understand Broadway as a mode of production that seeks to engage the mainstream in an attempt to generate massive profits. This assertion and Miller's are not mutually exclusive, but it is perhaps only the uncommon Broadway spectacle that might generate a critique of the mode of production and the ways in which it is tied to normative discourses of race and sexuality. One example is Richard Greenberg's 2002 Tony-award winning play *Take Me Out*.

"What a fuck of a season, huh?" The biracial star of *Take Me Out* thus describes the tribulations of a fictional baseball team called The Empires.[15] Greenberg's character voices an inadequate summation of a period in which the tenuous boundary between claims of truth and fiction dissolved specifically within the celebrations and lamentations attending national sports culture and the articulations of race, class, gender, and ability that structure such spectacular formations more generally. "Fuck of a season" as an intentionally vague yet volatile phrase indicates, even as it substitutes for, a failure of narrative coherence and encapsulation.

In the play, of course, "fuck of a season" gestures toward the events that constitute the dramatic action, most of which centers around the star player Darren Lemming. These events include his public coming out, the hiring and firing of the homophobic and racist relief pitcher Shane Mungitt, the emergence of an intimate – albeit not sexual – relationship between Lemming and his financial manager Mars Marzac, the dissolution of the friendship between Lemming and the shortstop Kippy Sunderstrom, the death of friend and rival Davey Battle, and The Empires' final victory in the World Series. The play ultimately resists threading all of its narrative elements into a definitive statement of meaning. "Fuck of a season," then, marks within the theatrical world of *Take Me Out* the apparently inexplicable illogic of a chronology structured by chance. However, this line, uttered by two of the principal characters in the very last moments of the play, forestalls an analysis of precisely the thing that "fuck of a season" replaces: failure.

Lemming's self-outing precipitates the team's collapse as a cohesive unit. Insofar as they fail as a team, the narrator Sunderstrom offers a detailed description of the ailing pitching staff. At the center of these men stands the "ace" Takeshi Kawabata, who "came with a dazzling arsenal of pitches, a breathtaking contract, and a truly stupendous lack of English-language skills, which at times seemed willful."[16] Kawabata rarely speaks during the play. Near the top of Act Two, however, the pitcher delivers a monologue in Japanese. For spectators who are not proficient in this language, his words become intelligible through Sunderstrom's translation. In the Broadway production, the shortstop occupied center stage, and Kawabata delivered his monologue from stage right. The translation describes Kawabata's background, including his grandmother who was interned in the United States, his relatives who were killed in Hiroshima and Nagasaki, and his more recent transition to the U.S. Major League, a journey that brought on unexplained familial scorn and subsequent isolation. On the one hand, baseball becomes Kawabata's salvation in a celebration of the opportunities afforded by liberal multiculturalism. On the other hand, by tracing Kawabata's life through some of the destructive events of World War II and positing baseball as a kind of therapeutic response to these historical traumas, Sunderstrom constructs Kawabata as a case study of male subjectivity in crisis.[17] Kawabata can attempt to rewrite the "dominant fiction" (theorist Kaja Silverman's term) of U.S. history that has erased Japanese/American suffering and celebrated the emergence of the United States as a superpower from the 1940s onward.[18] In this vein, Kawabata's monologue critiques the United States from the empire's/Empires' own bullpen, both figuratively and literally.

But two factors mitigate such critique. First, when Kawabata begins to lose, the hope of The Empires falls to the relief pitcher, Shane Mungitt. In spite of the fact that Kawabata can claim a win even after he breaks down (significantly, he always pitches through the sixth inning, which means a win is counted as his), his success depends on a racist white man. Second, the staging choices link Kawabata to other marginal figures on stage. For example, the Latino duo Rodriguez and Martinez share a penchant for not speaking in English, and Sunderstrom also translates their exchanges. The trio of Kawabata, Rodriguez, and Martinez become a group of subjects that The Empires have absorbed and to whom they have given means of expression both through the opportunity to play as well as through a white male translator. Of course, Sunderstrom also attempts to translate the inchoate sentiments of Mungitt, whose own impoverished background has rendered him, in the dramaturgical logic, uncommunicative. Mungitt's difference becomes legible through Sunderstrom as a kind of universal cipher whose translations restore the marginalized to the team. On multiple levels, then, Sunderstrom stands at the center of the play.

The shortstop tells the audience, "You need to know some stuff before I can get to Shane. You need a little *back* story" (6). The emphasis on back story anticipates expository information on the featured teammates at the same time as it intimates the revelation of repressed narratives. Such stories have already emerged, obliquely, as in Sunderstrom's initial description of Lemming:

> A five-tool player of such incredible grace, he made you suspect there was a sixth tool. Something only he had. Something you couldn't name. In addition to all the other stuff: the one-man-emblem-of-racial-harmony stuff. His white father. His black mother. Their triumphant yet cozy middle-class marriage.
>
> (5)

The shortstop alters the focus of his monologue from reciting biographies to exploring other potential beginnings of the theatrical narrative. For example, Sunderstrom mentions "a diamond made out of four bases set ninety feet apart" and transitions to "a really beautiful *park*" occupied by "a man, a woman, a serpent, and this *tree*" (6; emphasis in original). Sunderstrom's wide vision maps the metaphysical space of the biblical garden on to the geographic space of the baseball field. He moves the tale of the nation's pastime literally past time, that is, beyond the physical or temporal boundaries of an individual game or season into the realm of Western metaphysics. Situating The Empires within the sphere of the ontological from almost the moment after the play opens encourages the consideration of a subject's intelligibility within a Western spiritual body.

That Western spiritual body, what Ernest Renan might have called a nation, exists both in tandem with and in contradiction to the carnal forms that occupy the stage.[19] The actor's bodies – whether engaging in the "baseball-ography" of the show's sports sequences or, more often, glistening naked under the water of the onstage showerheads – insist on the material presence of flesh (I overheard a fellow spectator say after the show, "I have never seen so many penises in all my life"). But, as Benedict Anderson has demonstrated, the nation depends on the imagining of individuals whom each community member will never actually meet. Although the audience can observe the physiological reactions of the performers to onstage stimuli, including the spray of the showers, and although this play was popularly received in terms of its explicit depiction of masculine physiques (*The New Yorker*, for example, described it as a "kind of well hung homoerotic heaven"), the show produces onstage carnality as meaningful only in the sense that even if these men come equipped in different proportions, they come with the same instruments.[20] The parade of nudity asserts corporeality but evacuates that physicality of any significance, so that nakedness serves to mark sameness instead of difference. Furthermore, even when clothed, the men appear more often than not in nearly identical uniforms. The site of the body thus serves to link the men together in the larger unit of the team.

Nudity here has largely lost any radical potential it might have had on stage.[21] In contrast to much feminist performance art, like that of Carolee Schneeman's Eye Body series, where naked bodies often exposed the unequal power dynamics structuring women's oppression (that is, they exposed precisely the ways in which patriarchal discourse reduces women to objects), bare flesh has become a mostly banal part of the spectacle in gay theater. One director even locates this sort of shift in the wake of what he calls the "'Take Me Out' Revolution."[22] Indeed, the sorts of relatively youthful, athletic bodies on display align as closely with a conformist fascist aesthetic as they do with a disruptive one.

Despite this alignment, the play nevertheless articulates a kind of queer critique through a discourse of failure. Consider Mason Marzac, Lemming's at first subdued and finally flamboyant financial advisor. Marzac is The Empires' unlikely convert. After meeting Lemming for the first time and congratulating him for doing a "wonderful thing for the community," Marzac describes his own affiliation with LGBT social circles: "Of course, I don't really have a community. Or, more precisely, the community won't really have me. And I don't like communities in general. I avoid them. I'm outside them. (Beat). Possibly beneath them" (31–32). Marzac is the play's abject figure, and he finally connects to baseball and democracy because they both involve failure. Marzac becomes enamored of baseball, concluding that the sport is a metaphor for hope in a democracy:

> What could be more generous than to give everyone all these opportunities and the time to seize them in as well? ... And then, to ensure that everything remains fair, justices are ranged around the park to witness and assess the play. And if the justice errs, an appeal can be made. It's invariably turned down, but that's part of what makes the metaphor so right ... And baseball is better than democracy ... because, unlike democracy, baseball acknowledges loss. While conservatives tell you, "Leave things alone and no one will lose," and liberals tell you, "Interfere a lot and no one will lose," baseball says, "Someone will lose." Not only *says* it – insists upon it! So that baseball achieves the tragic vision democracy evades. Evades *and* embodies. Democracy is lovely, but baseball's more mature.

> (36–37)

This embrace of failure usefully correlates with the play's construction of the inscrutable Japanese/American pitcher.

Kawabata's physical ability renders him meaningful in this dual articulation of democracy and baseball. His collapse on the mound motivates the recruitment of the relief pitcher and thus sets in motion the bulk of the dramatic action. The play is, to some degree, specifically structured around Asian/American failure. However, the victories and defeats are understood by Kawabata in ways that are incommensurate with the playful logic of win or lose that Marzac's monologue establishes, for Kawabata's personal narrative links him to historical ruptures that challenge U.S. national fictions of fair play and equal opportunity – that is, the logics of liberal multiculturalism. Although the pitcher does not choose to express this history to his teammates, he is nevertheless interpolated by the translator Sunderstrom into the narrative of fall and redemption that Sunderstrom has verbally constructed as context. In other words, the shortstop makes the pitcher legible to the audience as a liberal subject.

In his last monologue at the opening of Act Three, Kawabata explains his potential opposition to being marked as a subject and his certain resistance to his sociability within what Marzac has framed as the sports equivalent of democracy:

> In the clubhouse, there is a steady noise, a constant low hum of conversation. But I am very fortunate; My first act in the Major League was to dismiss my translator. It served me well. I know all the English necessary to me: *Sutoraiku wan. Sutoraiku tsuu. Sanshin.* Shall I be saying to myself, "If only that pitch had been less fat, if only I had gotten that third out"? No. Why must things have meanings? *This* is how I try to be an American: I make my mind a prairie. I think nothing. I think of great flat stretches of nothing.
>
> (83–84)

Far from being an ideal democratic subject, Kawabata participates in The Empires' shared project with reluctance. He refuses, for the most part, linguistic engagement with his peers and evacuates the mythological coupling of open space, open opportunity. The failure that Kawabata embodies, then, does not simply emerge from the decline of his throwing prowess in the seventh inning. He also represents a failure of interpolation. He renders suspicious the liberal subject and the claims articulated for that subject in terms of predetermined legibility, equality, and justice. Even though the play ultimately reintegrates Kawabata through his body's presence on stage and his understood role in the triumphant narrative of a "win" at the World Series (where the United States has always already won), the character momentarily disrupts the discourse of democracy and its assumed subjects that the play finally seems to promote. This sort of disruption, I aver, functions productively in the confusion of multiple identitarian claims about recognition and legal injury articulated under the aegis of liberal multiculturalism. In this reading, Kawabata figures a queer Asian/American critique. His desires remain illegible in the dramatic world and for the extradiegetic audience. His presence evokes the fissures of American democracy by indexing its most spectacular failures, from the bombings of Hiroshima and Nagasaki to the domestic World War II internment camps. Unlike either the biracial, gay baseball star or the abject financial advisor, Kawabata can never quite be integrated into the play's logics of multicultural belonging.

Kawabata as a figure of queer Asian/American critique thus works in the context of "intersectionality."[23] Black feminist legal studies scholar Kimberlé Crenshaw defined this term in her 1989 article "Demarginalizing the Intersection of Race and Sex"; for Crenshaw, intersectionality names the concurrent experience and compounding effects of numerous forms of oppression and claims of identity. She specifically identifies and examines the effects of Title VII, which facilitated discrimination suits on the basis of either racial or gender discrimination.[24] Such legal constructions of bias, as Crenshaw points out, erased women of color's claims to damages resulting from simultaneous, multiple, and layered discriminatory acts. Crenshaw's provocation is to think through the conditions of possibility that are established through the juridical to mark oppression. Her critical project flags failures of the law. Kawabata shifts the perspective of an intersectional analysis in order to consider the ways in which the United States has scripted transnational discourses of belonging. These include elective affiliations, such as those with American sports teams and corporate sponsors. But it also includes forced political and affective relationships, such as those that are created when the United States occupies foreign territory.

Merging Crenshaw's critiques with later scholarship, I here pick up on Kandice Chuh's notion of Asian Americanist critique as a "subjectless discourse."[25] For Chuh, "subjectlessness ... create[s] the conceptual space to prioritize difference by foregrounding the discursive constructedness of subjectivity ... a 'subject' only becomes recognizable and can act as such by conforming to certain regulatory matrices."[26] A queer Asian/Americanist critique invests in what Chuh calls "collaborative antagonisms," an epistemological project of doing and undoing.[27] I inflect Chuh's provocations in a specific direction. If Asian/American critique registers the problems attendant to the formations of legible subjects, it also marks the *failures* of idealization in the processes of subject formation.

Liberal multiculturalism celebrates categories of difference and models of uplift. Witness The Empires as a fictional case in point. Intersectionality shifts the discourse to acknowledge *axes* of difference that merge to create particularized subjects under the law. Intersectionality renders legible the ostensible hero of *Take Me Out*: Darren Lemming as the racialized, gay baseball player seeking respect on those terms. In contrast, a queer Asian/ American critique reveals the limits of knowing. Enter Kawabata. Rather than producing an inviolable subject, Kawabata presents a fractured history communicated through two languages. His presence encourages a rethinking of what becoming a subject through The Empires might mean. As a figure, Kawabata generates continuous internal dissent. Instead of attempting to produce a facile notion of resistance to hegemony, Kawabata fractures the Empires' (American) narrative from the inside; he never resolves the contradictions of which he speaks and that he represents. His status as a desiring sexual subject remains out of view, explicitly cut off from the frames through which the play allows us to know its characters.

Like many Broadway plays, women simply do not feature at all in *Take Me Out*. By juxtaposing one tradition of queer performance that is particularly aligned with women and a theatrical production that explicitly excludes them, I hope to have demonstrated the need to consider a wide range of theater and performance practices under the rubric of queer.[28] I further hope to have illustrated and challenged the easy alignment of queer with gay male visibility. Queer fails in part when it prioritizes hegemonic masculine gender constructions over other possibilities. Such failure is both productive and problematic. In the latter sense, queer might work to destabilize certain narratives even as it maintains the norms that structure Broadway as a mode of production. This critique has been directly, if somewhat flatly, leveled in relation to the 2014 Tony Awards, where various parties objected to the lack of women writing for Broadway.[29] Nevertheless, such calls to action attest to the continued need for alternative venues, like New York's Women's Project Theatre and the WOW Café, to produce differently in order to generate a more extensive queer critique.

If we are to take "queer theater and performance" as a category in this collection, then the term "queer" should also destabilize any easy assertion of American literature. I have included Canadian, Mexican, American expatriate, and Japanese figures and literary works here to interrogate the idea of a national literary tradition. My use of queer time aims to encourage more thinking about how notions of Americanness consolidate and support specific understandings of sexuality, and vice versa. As Bredbeck suggests, ultimately queer critique cannot be completed – that is, it must fail in order for us to reconsider the elusive traces of desire.

NOTES

1 The body of critical literature on Shakespeare and sexual desire is massive, but two useful studies that contextualize sexual desire in relation to the

specific moment and location of Shakespeare's writing and production are
Bruce R. Smith, *Homosexual Desire in Shakespeare's England: A Cultural
Poetics* (Chicago: University of Chicago Press, 1995); and Valerie Traub, *The
Renaissance of Lesbianism in Early Modern England* (Cambridge: Cambridge
University Press, 2002).

2 Gregory W. Bredbeck, "The New Queer Narrative: Intervention and Critique,"
Textual Practice 9, no. 3 (1995): 478–479.

3 Ibid., 479–480; emphasis in original.

4 Ibid., 489.

5 José Esteban Muñoz, *Disidentifications: Queers of Color and the Performance
of Politics* (Minneapolis: University of Minnesota Press, 1999), ix.

6 Stefan Brecht, *Queer Theatre* (Frankfurt am Main: Suhrkamp, 1978), 34, 43.

7 Ibid., 29.

8 See Amy Sueyoshi, *Queer Compulsions: Race, Nation, and Sexuality in the
Affairs of Yone Noguchi* (Honolulu: University of Hawai'i Press, 2012).

9 Sarah Bay-Cheng, "Atom and Eve: A Consideration of Gertrude Stein's *Doctor
Faustus Lights the Lights*," in *Theater of the Avant-Garde, 1890–1950*, ed. Bert
Cardullo and Robert Knopf (New Haven: Yale University Press, 2001), 422. On
Stein and queer performance, see Nick Salvato, *Uncloseting Drama: American
Modernism and Queer Performance* (New Haven: Yale University Press, 2010).

10 See Sue-Ellen Case, *Split Britches: Lesbian Practice/Feminist Performance*
(New York: Routledge, 1996). On SNNG, see Meiling Cheng, *In Other Los
Angeleses: Multicentric Performance Art* (Berkeley: University of California
Press, 2002).

11 See, for example, Elizabeth Freeman, "Introduction," *GLQ: A Journal of
Lesbian and Gay Studies* 13, no. 2–3 (2007): 159–176.

12 Charles Isherwood, "In 'Spring Awakening,' a Rock 'n' Roll Heartbeat for
19th-Century German Schoolboys," *The New York Times*, June 16, 2006,
http://www.nytimes.com/2006/06/16/theater/reviews/16awak.html?page
wanted=all&_r=0.

13 D. A. Miller, *Place for Us: Essay on the Broadway Musical* (Cambridge,
MA: Harvard University Press, 2000), 3.

14 See also John Clum, *Something for the Boys: Musical Theater and Gay
Culture* (New York: St. Martin's Press, 2001); and Stacy Wolf, *A Problem Like
Maria: Gender and Sexuality in the American Musical* (Ann Arbor: University
of Michigan Press, 2002).

15 After premiering in London, *Take Me Out* opened at the Joseph Papp Public
Theater in New York in the fall of 2002 and transferred to Broadway in
February of 2003, where the show ran for 355 performances.

16 Richard Greenberg, *Take Me Out* (New York: Faber and Faber, 2003), 33–34;
hereafter cited in text.

17 Here it might be useful to think of Kaja Silverman's elaboration of "historical
trauma" and "dominant fiction" in relation to World War II. See Kaja Silverman,
Male Subjectivity at the Margins (New York: Routledge, 1992). Certainly
Silverman offers a means to think through Kawabata's masculinity in relation
to Japanese/American history. However, I use the representation of Japanese/
American masculinity as a touchstone for another kind of project, so I inflect my
discussion in a different direction.

18 I follow David Palumbo-Liu's articulation of the slash to demonstrate that "the proximity of Asian Americans [to the ideal of American] … should be read as a history of persistent reconfigurations and transgressions of the Asian/American 'split,' designated here by a solidus that signals those instances in which a liaison between 'Asian' and 'American,' a *sliding over* between two seemingly separate terms, is constituted. As in the construction 'and/or,' where the solidus at once instantiates a choice between two terms, their simultaneous and equal status, and an element of indecidability, that is, as it at once implies both exclusion and inclusion, 'Asian/American' marks *both* the distinction installed between 'Asian' and 'American' *and* a dynamic, unsettled, and inclusive movement." David Palumbo-Liu, *Asian/American: Historical Crossings of a Racial Frontier* (Stanford: Stanford University Press, 1999), 1.

19 See Ernest Renan, "What Is a Nation?," in *Nation and Narration*, ed. Homi Bhabha (New York: Routledge, 1990), 8–22. In Renan's translated words, "A nation is a soul, spiritual principle" (19).

20 John Lahr, "Play at the Plate: Losing It in the Locker Room," *The New Yorker* 78, no. 20 (July 22, 2002): 80–81.

21 For an extended treatment of this topic, see Sue-Ellen Case, "The Emperor's New Clothes: The Naked Body and Theories of Performance," *SubStance* 31, no. 2–3 (2002): 186–200.

22 Winter Miller, "Beyond Cute Boys in Their Underpants," *The New York Times*, August 7, 2005, http://www.nytimes.com/2005/08/07/theater/newsandfeatures/07mill.html?ex=1124856000&en=5f468f62d17bc1d7&ei=5070&emc=eta1&_r=0.

23 I use "intersectionality" here following Crenshaw's elaboration of the term, although another productive and overlapping, if longer, genealogy might trace the term through queer of color art and critique (in which intersectionality is both invoked and critiqued). This list would include authors and theorists such as Gloria Anzaldúa, David L. Eng, Roderick A. Ferguson, Sharon P. Holland, E. Patrick Johnson, Audre Lorde, Jasbir Puar, Kitty Tsui, and many others. Perhaps one of the most explicit and sustained engagements with the term appears in Robyn Wiegman, *Object Lessons* (Durham: Duke University Press, 2012), 239–300.

24 See Kimberlé Crenshaw, "Demarginalizing the Intersection of Race and Sex: A Black Feminist Critique of Antidiscrimination Doctrine, Feminist Theory, and Anti-Racist Politics," *The University of Chicago Legal Forum* 139 (1989): 139–167.

25 Kandice Chuh, *Imagine Otherwise: On Asian Americanist Critique* (Durham: Duke University Press, 2003).

26 Ibid., 9.

27 I have elaborated this conjunction of theater and Asian/American critique in relation to Naomi Iizuka's plays, albeit without much explicit explication of her oeuvre's queerness. Nevertheless, I refer the interested reader to my discussion of Iizuka's *36 Views* as one entry point into this discussion in Sean Metzger, "At the Vanishing Point: Theater and Asian/American Critique," *American Quarterly* 63, no. 2 (2011): 277–300. I would also highlight David Henry Hwang's much-discussed *M. Butterfly* as another theatrical investigation of queer Asian/

American critique and, as a more recently developed stage production, Qui Nguyen's *Soul Samurai*.

28 The alignments and misalignments among queer theory and feminist theory have been taken up in several publications, but two useful compilations of such work are Naomi Schor and Elizabeth Weed's collection *Feminism Meets Queer Theory* (Bloomington: Indiana University Press, 1997); and a compilation of essays on the theme of the reparative turn in the journal *Feminist Theory* 15, no. 1 (2014): 3–49.

29 See, for example, Michele Willens, "The Sexist Reality That the Tony Nominations Just Highlighted," *The Atlantic*, April 29, 2014, http://www.theatlantic.com/entertainment/archive/2014/04/broadways-shockingly-resilient-glass-curtain/361340/.

3

ERIC KEENAGHAN

Queer Poetry, Between "As Is" and "As If"

As an African American, gay, and HIV-positive man with an urban, working-class background, the late poet Reginald Shepherd felt that identity categories did him and his work an injustice. "Identity poetics is *boring*, giving back the already known in an endless and endlessly self-righteous confirmation of things as they are," he wrote in 2003. "It is also constraining, limiting the imaginative options of the very people it seeks to liberate or speak for."[1] Composing work through the lens of any identity would render him "entirely too visible, the object of scrutiny, labeling, and categorization."[2] Instead, he preferred poetry that offered "a venture into the unknown" or "an image of who or what I could be, of what the world itself could be, an image of the 'as if' rather than of the 'as is.' "[3] Poetry, for Shepherd and other queer writers, is a subjunctive art of possibility. Instead of merely representing life and humanity as they are known, it imagines them otherwise. Thus, poets labeling their work with any socially determined identity category would detract from their art's possibilities.

If we date openly queer American poetry back to Walt Whitman's life-work *Leaves of Grass* (1855–1892, seven editions), we might recognize that Shepherd's preference for imaginatively pursuing the "as if," rather than expositing the "as is," is not unique, or even new, among lesbian, gay, bisexual, or transgender (LGBT) poets. Certainly, much of that book-length poem does celebrate same-sex eroticism and intimacies, and Whitman's homoerotic construction of himself as "the new husband" and "the comrade" for a primarily male audience, as he imagined it, has influenced many LGBT writers.[4] However, as the Good Gray Bard famously proclaims in "Song of Myself": "I am large, I contain multitudes." Instead of being a vehicle for expressing his sexual difference, his poetry is a medium through which otherwise silenced voices speak ("Through me many long dumb voices") and by which he sympathetically identifies with those persons ("In all people I see myself, none more and not one a barleycorn less"). Thus, even as Whitman acknowledges his strong sense of self ("I know perfectly well my own egotism"), he ultimately rejects an autonomous or even a self-cohesive identity.[5] After World War II, the bisexual modernist Muriel Rukeyser noted her affinity for Whitman's poetics not because he was a gay predecessor who had resolved his identity crises, but instead because he was "able to identify at last with both the people in their contradictions and himself in his."[6] Thus, for her, Whitman was "the poet of possibility" who strategically imagined identities as provisional and changing, not static and fixed.[7] Striving after a "poetry of the future" that would unite a country recently ravaged by the American Civil War, Whitman hoped to restore community by working "to arouse and initiate, more than to define or finish."[8] He even desired "races of orbic bards" to proselytize democratic ideals globally.[9] Consequently, his *Leaves of Grass* implicitly undermines the idea of separating any individual or minority group from the rest of human commonality.

Rukeyser's contemporary Robert Duncan read Whitman similarly – as "moved by generative urgencies toward the fulfillment of a multitude of latent possibilities."[10] Duncan acknowledged the homoerotic significance of Whitman's poetics, yet he also characterized his predecessor's "seminal" work as *reproductive*: the poems bear the "seeds of sons Whitman never fathered" and, through imagined intercourse with companionate readers and later poets, the poems rear a metaphorical progeny.[11] When Duncan delivered this appraisal one year after the 1969 Stonewall riots, his queerly reproductive reading – not heteronormative, yet not exactly gay – shocked many LGBT readers, who expected a prominent homosexual poet's state- ment about an important precursor to validate their own nonreproductive desires. However, his reading should not have come as a surprise. Since the 1940s, Duncan had openly proclaimed his homosexuality's personal sig- nificance and disavowed gay coteries, sensibilities, or argot because these characteristics foreclosed his poetry's universal appeal. His 1944 essay "The Homosexual in Society" notes that every poet must "disown *all* the spe- cial groups (nations, churches, sexes, races) that would claim allegiance" in order to demonstrate "a devotion to human freedom, toward the liberation of human love, human conflicts, human aspirations."[12] Three decades later, Duncan complained in a 1976 interview that "even now the word 'homo- sexual' has not transcended prejudice where you can write about your gay life because it *is* a human life and not a bizarre anomaly; we still invite hatred and bigotry."[13] He even claimed, "I don't see myself as gay at all," for that identification would tie him and his work to an increasingly codified social minority and market niche.[14] His fellow poet and gay liberation activ- ist John Wieners remarked that such outspokenness led to Duncan unfairly being "put out to sea" and ignored by activists.[15] They could not abide his warning that the closed minority identification denoted by the label "gay" might impede the "true liberation" of founding a changing, all-inclusive human commonality.[16]

Such continually repeated warnings deserve notice at the outset of a chapter about LGBT American poetry. As a *category*, queer poetry is a fiction. Yet, invoking an idea Duncan held dear, we might say that the idea of LGBT poetry is what he called a *fictive certainty*, an imagined possibility treated by art as a foregone truth "to come to the idea of what the world of worlds or the order of orders might be."[17] Such a critical approach understands the art as providing something more than a window on, or a confession of, present or past queer experience. Rather, queer poetry offers a humanizing, inclusive vision of the world that does not discount queer desire. Much (although not all) queer poetry does not set out only to represent sexual or gender difference; it just happens to do so. The actual character of LGBT poetry, like most other poetries, is that it is future-oriented, invested in imagining and articulating life and its possibilities differently from what is currently known. For those who give themselves over to poetry in their reading and study, it is a resource for liberating their selves and their love, allowing same-sex desire and relationships to be included in, even imagined as a starting place for, new social commonalities. LGBT poets have geared their writing toward such liberating, future-oriented ends while also testifying to, and representing, the fictive certainty of queer experience's fundamental humanness. That double objective is not without its attendant conflicts. Despite the undesirability of reducing any poetic project to an LGBT moniker, queer poetry's universal political and ethical viability ultimately depends on the poet's or the readers' minority identification; that is, achieving universality paradoxically depends on some form of identity poetics. To realize a transcendent ethic, a poem must deploy representative identity logics to elicit readers' sympathy, if not empathy. My brief account of a few scenes from queer American poetry's past is not exhaustive, but the discussed poets exemplify, in different ways, the productive tensions that have arisen between their representations of LGBT identity and their desire to transcend minoritizing categories.

The Dilemma of LGBT Representation during the Harlem Renaissance

About twenty years ago, Gregory Woods announced it was "high time" that poets from the Harlem Renaissance (ca. 1918–1935) "be reappraised by and for gay readers."[18] He identifies several luminaries – including Countee Cullen, Langston Hughes, and Claude McKay – as "gay" and even claims they belonged to "a cohesive gay community."[19] Like many later critics, Woods unearths same-sex erotic subtexts and explores explicit homoerotic themes as evidence of gay self-expression. However, we must be careful of such modes of recovering "gay" poetry by uncovering hidden same-sex themes. Such reading strategies risk impoverishing the poetry as well as our understanding of the authors' lives. As Cullen's biographer, Charles Molesworth, writes, "centering" an analysis of a poem "in a diffuse but uncontainable homoerotic desire [...] obscures, or at least subordinates, some of the other forms of desire which Cullen [or any queer Harlem Renaissance writer] was seeking to represent."[20] Those "other forms of desire," Molesworth specifies, might include eroticism associated with familial, social, even spiritual relationships. As is evident in Hughes's antiracist translations, eroticism and related power dynamics pervade individuals' relationships even with language.[21] Desire is a complex and multifaceted phenomenon, wherein various currents intersect and interfere with one another. We ignore that fact if we focus on same-sex desire without acknowledging any other sort, or if we assume that a representation of queer desire presupposes the author's affiliation with an existing or emergent minority. This is not to say that queer analyses of Harlem Renaissance poetry are impossible, but we should not approach the poems solely through the lens of LGBT-defined identity, community, or desire.

Certainly, several writers associated with the Harlem Renaissance did experience same-sex sexual contacts or transgressive gender identifications. The cultural climate of this predominantly black upper Manhattan neighborhood – with its cabaret and jazz scenes, drag balls, gay and lesbian subcultures, sex workers, and interracial sexual tourism – also supported spaces for LGBT experience. However, much occurred in those settings that conflicted with what many community leaders and artists saw as the Renaissance's primary aim of generating positive representations of *race*, not sexuality or gender. Identity-based readings of queer Harlem Renaissance poets "by and for gay readers" can lead to what Eve Kosofsky Sedgwick calls "a paranoid project of exposure," which valorously seeks to affirm minority identity as it is known now by searching out and redeeming past experiences of injury, ranging from the silencing of LGBT subjects to homophobic violence.[22] Such a critical orientation does have value. For instance, it has spurred the recovery of Angelina Weld Grimké's mostly unpublished verse by scholars such as Gloria T. (Akasha) Hull. Yet, on close examination, one finds that Grimké's work often exposits not just lesbian desire but also, contrary to Woods's claims about LGBT Renaissance writers' sense of community, feelings of alienation. Perhaps Grimké felt estranged because she contributed to Harlem Renaissance magazines from a distance, not in the city itself. However, she often describes her estrangement in Romantic or existential terms, not social ones. For instance, in "Where Phillis Sleeps," death has divided the narrator, "a soul alone," from her lover, over whose grave she pines.[23] If we were to recover Grimké's poetry as "lesbian" verse, her often-depressed lyrics would suggest that, historically, black women's experiences of lesbian desire were doomed to misery and loneliness. Such paranoid conclusions are teleological, for they assume that LGBT readers today are impossibly invulnerable to loneliness, even violence and oppression. Such assumptions also foreclose discoveries of unexpected connections with the past that might provoke readers' imaginations.

In another poem by Grimké entitled "Life," desire-related alienation produces an aristocratic attitude. Her narrator stands apart from "the people crawling by" because she "may feel the fierceness of great love / With all its agony and rare delights." Unlike the masses, she has "lived."[24] Some might judge the poem elitist, willfully disconnected from community. But what if we read Grimké as suggesting empowerment by embracing, not being incapacitated by, the crises attending lesbian desire? She could be read here as challenging our expectations by paradoxically expressing not just an awareness of marginalization but also the subjective *pleasures* of homosexual lovers' recognition of their difference. The alternative to paranoid reading strategies, Sedgwick theorizes, is a "reparative" mode permitting "hope."[25] She argues that "because the reader has room to realize that the future may be different from the present, it is also possible for her to entertain such profoundly painful, profoundly relieving, ethically crucial possibilities as that the past, in turn, could have happened differently from the way it actually did."[26]

Sedgwick does not prescribe what constitutes a reparative project, but Harlem Renaissance poetry offers opportunities for exploring some possibilities. Much like Sedgwick's paranoid queer reader, the Renaissance's leadership was invested in countering maligning and socially and politically injurious representations of their racial minority group. Cultural principles such as W. E. B. Du Bois, the leader of the National Association for the Advancement of Colored People (NAACP) and the editor of *The Crisis*, believed that representations of African Americans needed to remediate prevalent racist stereotypes. Among the most problematic misperceptions of black men and women was the erroneous belief that African Americans were hypersexualized, less-than-"civilized" primitives. Aesthetic renderings of black homosexuality – indeed, sexuality in any form – was feared to interfere with positive representations of African American persons and cultures. Yet, patronage systems were suffused with homoeroticism. Gay black cultural leaders, such as the philosopher Alain Locke, and white homosexual literati such as Carl Van Vechten, used "flirtation," as the critic Marlon Ross describes it, to develop "homoerotic coterie[s] in private."[27] A'Lelia Walker, a lesbian who hosted an important literary salon, also hosted orgies. She demanded that her guests in both settings tolerate sexual and gender variance.[28] The disconnection between the queer historical actuality of the Renaissance and its leadership's desire to desexualize images of African Americans placed "a burden of representation" on black artists.[29] Even when LGBT writers published poetry attesting to their queer experience, the ideological imperative that the Renaissance represent racial, not sexual, inequities led to misprision. Richard Bruce Nugent recalls how his 1925 poem "Shadow" – whose narrator is represented as "A dark shadow in the light" and "Lacking color / Or vivid brightness" – "created a kind of sensation" when it appeared in the magazine *Opportunity* because readers believed it was "a race poem."[30] However, decades later, he claimed that he had used tropes of light and dark in the poem to depict his intersectional experience of marginalization as a gay black man.

Around the time that Nugent's poem was published, public debate erupted about representative propriety. Several writers took issue with the idea that art should function as cultural propaganda that abides by norms for positive representations of *any* subjects and communities. Langston Hughes was a prominent voice in that controversy. He argued that Du Bois and other leaders exhibited an "urge within the race toward whiteness, the desire to pour racial individuality into the mold of American standardization, and to be as little Negro and as much American as possible."[31] Tellingly, he describes assimilation as an "urge" and "desire." Preserving the artists' individuality and freedom depends on acknowledging other forms of desire in black populations. Hughes gravitated toward jazz, "the eternal tom-tom beating in the Negro soul," to express his own desire to "revolt against" standardization and assimilation.[32] Much of what is queer about his work from the period is not homosexual per se but instead is related to his poetic pursuit of freedom and a truer representation of his individual experience; that was a different kind of "desire" and "urge" than what the NAACP mandated, and thus it was read as contesting standards of an emergent black heteronormativity. As he wrote in an unpublished essay inscribed to his (gay) patron Carl Van Vechten, "My poems are indelicate. But so is life."[33]

The "indelicate" nature of Hughes's poetry from the 1920s, especially of early poems such as "Cabaret" and "Harlem Night Club," might be attributed to his frank treatment of eroticism. However, these poems are not necessarily homosexual. Lines such as "They say a jazz-band's gay" or "White girls' eyes / Call gay black boys" do play on the double signification of the word "gay," but those moments only weakly encode same-sex desire.[34] More importantly, these poems explicitly represent a licentiousness and eroticism associated with cabaret culture, where illicit sexuality of all types – heterosexual, interracial, homosexual – flourished, even though the venues were banned by New York City's anti-vice Comstock Laws and Prohibition's Volstead Act. As a result, the performance studies scholar Shane Vogel argues, even Hughes's seemingly straight cabaret poems evoke a historically actual temporal and spatial zone of queer experience. Hughes figuratively seeks to keep these spaces open by composing his jazz poems in an improvisational style, rather than with the closed forms characteristic of his queer colleagues Cullen or McKay.[35]

Vogel's reading is reparative, but he still historically inscribes Hughes's work as representative of Harlem LGBT life in the 1920s. He even reads "Café: 3 a.m.," from Hughes's Cold War–era sequence *Montage of a Dream Deferred*, as a "poem out of time," which he wishes had been written three decades earlier because of its subject matter.[36] I prefer to push Vogel's reading of Hughes's "anticlosural impulses" and imagine the poet returning to his Renaissance poetry's cabaret themes to reopen those queer spaces and give them new lives, *as if* they still existed.[37] "Café: 3 a.m." represents "fairies" trailed by vice cops outside a 1950s iteration of the old Harlem cabaret. Amid McCarthyism's Red- and queer-baiting, Hughes's narrator intercedes, perhaps empowered by remembering past queer freedoms associated with similar sites, and argues against homosexuality's perceived degeneracy: "But God, Nature, / or somebody / made them that way."[38] Although he does not goes so far as to grant LGBT subjects agency in determining their own identities, he does take a step in that direction by urging readers to acknowledge sexuality's constructed nature, whether by a higher power or "somebody," a human agent. Such constructivism certainly benefits LGBT citizens, but, in the larger context of *Montage*, everyone stands to benefit from this stance. In the volume's headnote, Hughes refers to the book-length sequence as a jazz-inspired "jam session" celebrating "a community in transition."[39] African American gays, lesbians, and transgender persons are only a part of that community and its song. Just as "Café: 3 a.m." suggests that LGBT persons' identities are socially constructed, the rest of Hughes's sequence implicitly posits that the identities of the community's other members are similarly subject to open processes of reimagining. Increased inclusivity and a community's transformation begin by recognizing that fact, and everyone living during the Cold War's containment culture desperately needed the poetic lessons that Hughes had learned from past experience at queer sites like this poem's titular café.

Poetry and Early LGBT Activism

After the Second World War, LGBT communities emerged in the United States as identifiable and politicized minorities, rather than collectivities of similarly "deviant" individuals acting on outlawed desires. During the homo-phile movement – the first wave of queer American politics in the 1950s and 1960s – poetry was regularly included in nationally circulated activ-ist publications. Such poems were more than representative texts affirming individuals' identity and desire. They actually helped raise other LGBT indi-viduals' consciousness that a queer community could exist because others had similar experiences. Self-expression had to be coupled with an impulse to construct, to reimagine one's social and political world, because minority life, as it was known in later decades, simply did not exist.

The inaugural issue of *The Mattachine Review*, the first U.S. homo-phile magazine, appeared in 1955. Among stories about antigay legisla-tion and psychiatry's pathologization of sexual inversion is a poem titled "The Cigarette."⁴⁰ The author, Donal Norton, contributed journalistic articles to later issues, but his first verse publication relays a personal narrative, even if the byline is probably an assumed name. (Many in the homophile movement assumed pseudonyms to avoid possible repercus-sions.) Norton's narrator imagines himself in a "single bed" with another man, sharing a postcoital smoke. The smoldering fag silently says all that must be said, "as our communings are felt, / Without word, without mea-sure." The lovers, bereft of community, have only private "communings." Still, their shared cigarette begins a new "universe" – both "compact" and "inclusive," "more real" than the one their lovemaking "so recently tore a-sunder." "The Cigarette" imagines how same-sex encounters might not only create a new life for two intimates but also, more romantically, destroy universes. Although aesthetically unremarkable, this self-affirming gay poem also significantly marks a political desire to move away from inherited notions of community. Norton hopes to make history and the world queerly anew by beginning over in the present with himself and his partner.

Like Norton, the San Francisco Renaissance poet Jack Spicer was a mem-ber of the Mattachine Society. He became disillusioned with its politics, though, when the organization abandoned the radical vision of its foun-der, Harry Hay, and instead adopted an assimilationist politics. A decade after leaving the movement, Spicer published his 1962 prose poem "Three Marxist Essays." As with Norton's poem, the first part, "Homosexuality and Marxism," romantically associates same-sex love with ruin; but in Spicer's poem, the capitalist state, specifically, is destroyed:

> Homosexuality is essentially being alone. Which is a fight against the capi-talist bosses who do not want us to be alone. Alone we are dangerous.
>
> Our dissatisfaction could ruin America. Our love could ruin the universe if we let it.

> If we let our love flower into the true revolution we will be swamped with offers for beds.[41]

Despite his narrator's lonesomeness, Spicer, who cultivated local poetic coteries, was aware that poets are not truly "alone." Indeed, they are "dangerous" because poetry necessitates others. Both interlocutors and readers are intimates who help realize a poem's "flower[ing]," its development from a composition written in relative isolation into a shared text serving as the basis for a "true revolution." The dawning of Spicer's new historic epoch, his queer revolution, paradoxically produces a community of loners whose history begins – much like in "The Cigarette" – with the prospect of shared beds and poems. Emphasizing individual autonomy or, at best, lovers' oxymoronic private society, Spicer, like many of his LGBT contemporaries, encounters his own rhetorical limit. Collective politics takes a backseat to the bedroom. Even when the author himself tried to avoid self-expression (Spicer believed that his poems broadcast language like a radio, and he was just the receiver), any potential transformation effected by poetry remains largely personal, limited to the persons of the poet and the reader who intimately engages his work like a lover.

In this New Left era, though, politics were imagined as beginning with the personal, with raising individuals' consciousnesses about oppression. From that knowledge emerged resultant affinities with others who were similarly disenfranchised. Those connections presaged collective empowerment and action. Hence, second-wave feminists' famous slogan: *The personal is political.* Spicer did not live to see gay liberation or lesbian feminism emerge after the 1969 Stonewall riots, but he was aware of the New Left political ethos that informed those later movements. Neither activists nor poets associated with the gay liberation and lesbian feminist movements represented a minority as it is, though. Rather, both sought to define and construct minority identity out of their individual experiences so as to refigure the nation. Literature was crucial to that effort, for it helped consolidate an ethnic group identity that could evolve further. Past poetries offered a sense of shared history and cultural tradition, and contemporary poetry helped articulate changing paradigms of sexual subjectivity. In the early and mid-1970s, gay and lesbian presses published important anthologies – *The Male Muse* (1973), *Angels of the Lyre* (1975), and *Amazon Poetry* (1975) – that included work by activist-poets and sympathetic experimental poets. In *Angels of the Lyre*, the editor, Winston Leyland, also reprinted poets who were personally remiss to identify with the movement, like Robert Duncan. He also included recently deceased gay and bisexual poets, such as Stephen Jonas, Frank O'Hara, and Paul Goodman. The activist-poet William Barber contributed a raw, prosaic narrative about a pick-up in which "our backs and asses twisted all night / long."[42] In striking contrast is surrealist Charles Henri Ford's baroque elegy mourning the recent passing of Candy Darling, the transgender superstar of Andy Warhol's Factory:

> I saw the fiendish treatment you gave to a young pearl
> To identify the opposites of an artificial order a dwarf was sewn to your
>   abdomen with secret threads
> Bereft of origin and change wrapped in wire cloth white hard but malleable
>   they buried you in the skin of a black deer[43]

We should read such anthologies as polyvocal, even discordant, collections that provide insight into how poetry offered readers a spectrum of queer possibilities. LGBT life, as read through its poets, encompassed mourning others, expressing one's fears or desires, celebrating episodes of one's own sexual liberation, and offering political origin narratives. An anthology's multiplicity of styles and registers signals poetry's inability to definitively represent homosexual identity as a single entity; rather, it embodies a universe of options from which readers might choose their preferred means of imagining themselves and constructing their minority.

Gay liberation and lesbian feminist periodical publications also illustrate how poetry was one discourse among several that facilitated a dialogue about what queer identity and community could be, rather than what it supposedly was. The Furies Collective, a Washington, DC–based lesbian separatist group, printed in their newsletter, alongside consciousness-raising articles and announcements of political events, poems that affirmed same-sex desire, protested homophobia and heterosexism, and praised nascent communities. Selections from Judy Grahn's *Edward the Dyke and Other Poems* were used in such a fashion in the inaugural issue from 1972. Her poem "A History of Lesbianism" narrates how "The subject of lesbianism / is very ordinary" because it consists of caretaking communities of "women-loving-women."[44] This poetic definition immediately precedes Charlotte Bunch's manifesto "Lesbians in Revolt," with its proclamation that "LESBIANISM IS A POLITICAL CHOICE" and "LESBIANISM IS THE BASIC THREAT TO MALE SUPREMACY."[45] Grahn's characterization of lesbianism as ordinariness and Bunch's theorization of it as choice seem diametrically opposed. Yet the poem and manifesto do not dismiss one another. Published together, these two discursive forms implicitly participate in a dialogue. Each piece does not just represent lesbian identity as the respective author believes it supposedly to be, but instead they actually work cooperatively to form that identity (or plural, identities) and the social spaces that lesbian communities might inhabit.[46] Identity is provisional and contingent, not essentialist and fixed. When writing of Grahn's poetry, Adrienne Rich reminds us that power inheres in "the language we are using and that is using us."[47] "Poetry is, among other things, a criticism of language" that springs from a poem's "magic," or how "it lets us hear and see our words [and the power relations running through them] in a new dimension."[48]

The epitome of such "magic" is Black Mountain- and Beat-affiliated poet John Wieners's 1975 *Behind the State Capitol: Or Cincinnati Pike*, a curious book published by a press affiliated with the Boston Gay Liberation Front. Consisting of a heady mixture of prose vignettes, experimental lyric, and collages of photocopied ephemera, including photos of starlets and Jacqueline Kennedy Onassis, newspaper clippings, and gay pornography, Wieners's book defies easy description. One poem provides a glimpse of the author's ambitions for this textual mélange, though. The narrator longs for a one-hour liaison with an unnamed lover instead of cruising, or perhaps just fantasizing about cruising, "in the downstairs Washington Street subway stop in my / mind." His writing of this poem enables that possibility, even if only imaginatively. For him, poetry's purpose is to liberate reality's potential: "I write poems for little children / and imagine a world, fulfilled in reality."[49] Wieners wrote for the "little children" of the emergent LGBT community, whose erotic and sexual fantasies, like his own, connected them to another world, which they labored to actualize in their art, lives, and politics. *Behind the State Capitol* enables that subjunctive imagination to be shared with readers so that they, too, might discover their pleasures and search out new possibilities. LGBT poetry does not extend that other world without also realistically exposing queer persons' pains and vulnerabilities, including their subjection to language and heteronormative and homophobic institutions. Yet poetry imaginatively supplements those bleak realities, thus making readers conscious of them and ready to transform them. The art's magic resides in its ability to spur readers to take action, to move toward the possible.

Contemporary Queer Poetics

Gay liberation initiated an identity politics whose legacy is seen in many recent civic and political advances: the Supreme Court ruling that anti-sodomy statutes are unconstitutional with *Lawrence v. Texas* in 2003; the legalization of same-sex marriage in certain states from 2004 onward; the 2010 congressional repeal of "Don't Ask, Don't Tell"; and the Supreme Court overturning of the Defense of Marriage Act in 2013. Perhaps such progressive reforms made it easier for LGBT poets like Reginald Shepherd, with whom we began this chapter, to claim that identity poetics is "boring." However, it would better serve us to read twenty-first-century queer

American poetry as continuing to exhibit tensions between minority representation and subjunctive transformation that are similar to, although differently articulated from, what I've explored in relation to LGBT Harlem Renaissance and gay liberation poetries. Contemporary queer poets are not necessarily "post-identity" writers who reject identity categories. Rather, despite any rhetoric they might use to disavow minority representation, they tend to use LGBT identities as springboards for poetically addressing issues that affect all populations. Indeed, to refer to a form of poetry as "queer," rather than as "LGBT," is to acknowledge how its authors challenge rigid and potentially divisive identity logics so as to forge new connections and alliances between communities and groups.[50]

A new paradigm of queer poetry emerged out of the HIV/AIDS epidemic. In the 1980s and 1990s, the crisis revived the failed politically coalitional spirit of the Gay Liberation Front. Alliance was a political and social necessity because people living with AIDS (PLWA) – including the seropositive, loved ones, and caregivers – cut across social, economic, and even geopolitical demographics. Poetry of the epidemic by Eileen Myles, Mark Doty, Essex Hemphill, Aaron Shurin, Thom Gunn, James White, Leland Hickman, and Tim Dlugos signaled rage and upset while also registering the apocalyptic experience of living in a climate where the failure of representation – one's inability to represent oneself or loved ones, or the representative government's unwillingness to enact life-saving policies – produced a murderous silence. Minority representation alone was not possible and could not suffice, and, given the climate, perhaps it was not a reliable vehicle for change. Still, these writers struggled to represent their experiences as PLWAs, while also hopefully reaching out to all, firing readers' imaginations and sympathies and laying the personal groundwork for collective action. Take, for instance, Dlugos's last poem "D.O.A." Reflecting on living with AIDS close to the end of his life, he does not regret his affliction. He has come to see his seroconversion not as the consequence of "Lust, addiction" but instead as proof of "a kind of love," an "Absolute fidelity / to the truth of what I felt."[51] While cooking dinner for his lover, a quotidian domestic task and another kind of loving act, Dlugos remarks that despite his catalogue of physical symptoms, this is "A day / like any, like no other. Not so bad / for the dead."[52] His articulated hope to live and love in the unrepeatable present compels us, later generations of audiences, to follow his lead, no matter our orientations or HIV statuses. To dedicate oneself to one's principles and feelings – whether they are collectively political or personally sexual – is to live as if those principles and feelings could be the tenets of a personal faith, as if they were not deemed marginal, deviant, or illegal.

No matter the recent gains in public visibility, civil rights, and legal protections, other political objectives remain to be met – including nationwide transgender health care and workplace protections, LGBT naturalization rights, among others. Poetry will continue to be a resource for reimagining the world, one that might originate in LGBT subjects' specific experiences of oppression and marginalization but that ultimately works toward inspiring new coalitions and universal inclusivity. Queer poetry's continuing subjunctive, visionary ethos is best summed up in the late transgender poet kari edwards' *obedience*. Her 2005 book-length poem accounts for "this language plague," linguistic structures that reinforce everyone's social, economic, and cultural disenfranchisement; she attempts to redress that situation and "to cure" our shared affliction by writing as "a body" that struggles to unfix itself from that linguistic disorder.[53] Despite the injury she has experienced as a transgender woman, and despite the linguistic traumas to which she subjects her readers in turn via a heavily fragmented and painfully difficult text simulating her own experience, *obedience* concludes in the hopeful, future-oriented Whitmanic spirit noted at the outset of this chapter. Moving through this painful process together, edwards invites us to join her as she renews the struggle, pushing through the pain so as to discover new queer horizons: "let's begin again."[54]

NOTES

1 Reginald Shepherd, "The Other's Other: Against Identity Poetry, for Possibility," in *Orpheus in the Bronx: Essays on Identity, Politics, and the Freedom of Poetry* (2003; Ann Arbor: University of Michigan Press, 2007), 42.
2 Ibid., 43.
3 Ibid., 42, 43.
4 Walt Whitman, "Whoever You Are Holding Me Now in Hand," in *Leaves of Grass and Other Writings*, ed. Michael Moon (1860; New York: W. W. Norton, 2002), 100.
5 Walt Whitman, "Song of Myself," in *Leaves of Grass and Other Writings*, ed. Michael Moon (1855; New York: W. W. Norton, 2002), 77, 46, 42, 67.
6 Muriel Rukeyser, *The Life of Poetry* (1949; Ashfield, MA: Paris Press, 1996), 77.
7 Ibid., 83.
8 Walt Whitman, "Poetry To-Day in America," in *Specimen Days and Collect* (1880; New York: Dover, 1995), 294.
9 Walt Whitman, "Democratic Vistas," in *Specimen Days and Collect* (1870; New York: Dover, 1995), 241.
10 Robert Duncan, "Changing Perspectives in Reading Whitman," in *A Selected Prose*, ed. Robert J. Bertholf (1970; New York: New Directions, 1995), 64.
11 Ibid., 84.
12 Robert Duncan, "The Homosexual in Society," in *A Selected Prose*, ed. Robert J. Bertholf (1944; New York: New Directions, 1995), 47, emphasis in original.

13 Robert Duncan, "A Conversation with Robert Duncan, Part I," interview by Robert Peters and Paul Trachtenberg, in *A Poet's Mind: Collected Interviews with Robert Duncan, 1960–1985*, ed. Christopher Wagstaff (Berkeley: North Atlantic Books, 2012), 190, emphasis in original.

14 Robert Duncan, "A Conversation with Robert Duncan, Part II," interview by Robert Peters and Paul Trachtenberg, *Chicago Review* 44, no. 1 (1998): 95.

15 John Wieners, "Charley Shively Interviews John Wieners," in *Selected Poems 1958–1984*, ed. Raymond Foye (Santa Barbara: Black Sparrow, 1986), 298.

16 Robert Duncan, private correspondence, quoted in *Selected Poems 1958–1984*, ed. Raymond Foye (Santa Barbara: Black Sparrow, 1986), 298.

17 Robert Duncan, "Man's Fulfillment in Order and Strife," in *Fictive Certainties: Essays* (1968; New York: New Directions, 1985), 111–112.

18 Gregory Woods, "Gay Re-Readings of the Harlem Renaissance Poets," *Journal of Homosexuality* 26, no. 2–3 (1994): 128.

19 Ibid.

20 Charles Molesworth, "Countee Cullen's Reputation: The Forms of Desire," *Transition* 107 (2012): 75.

21 Eric Keenaghan, "Intimacy and Injury: The Queer Transfiguration of Racialized Exclusion in Langston Hughes's Translations of Nicolás Guillén," *Translation Studies* 2, no. 2 (2009): 163–177.

22 Eve Kosofksy Sedgwick, *Touching Feeling: Affect, Pedagogy, Performativity* (Durham: Duke University Press, 2003), 139.

23 Angelina Weld Grimké, "Where Phillis Sleeps," in *Selected Works*, ed. Carolivia Herron (New York: Oxford University Press, 1991), 29.

24 Angelina Weld Grimké, "Life," in *Selected Works*, ed. Carolivia Herron (New York: Oxford University Press, 1991), 48–49.

25 Sedgwick, *Touching Feeling*, 146.

26 Ibid., 146.

27 Marlon Ross, *Manning the Race: Reforming Black Men in the Jim Crow Era* (New York: New York University Press, 2004), 289.

28 Lillian Faderman, *Odd Girls and Twilight Lovers: A History of Lesbian Life in Twentieth-Century America* (New York: Penguin, 1992), 76.

29 See A. B. Christa Schwartz, *Gay Voices of the Harlem Renaissance* (Bloomington: Indiana University Press, 2003), especially 25–47.

30 Richard Bruce Nugent, "Shadow," in *Gay Rebel of the Harlem Renaissance: Selections from the Work of Richard Bruce Nugent*, ed. Thomas H. Wirth (1935; Durham: Duke University Press, 2002), 269; Richard Bruce Nugent, "You See, I Am a Homosexual," in *Gay Rebel of the Harlem Renaissance: Selections from the Work of Richard Bruce Nugent*, ed. Thomas H. Wirth (1983; Durham: Duke University Press, 2002), 268.

31 Langston Hughes, "The Negro Artist and the Racial Mountain," in *The Collected Works of Langston Hughes*, ed. Christopher C. De Santis (1926; Columbia: University of Missouri Press, 2002), 9:32.

32 Ibid., 35.

33 Langston Hughes, "These Bad New Negroes: A Critique on Critics," in *The Collected Works of Langston Hughes*, ed. Christopher C. De Santis (1927; Columbia: University of Missouri Press, 2002), 39.

34 Langston Hughes, "Cabaret," in *Collected Poems*, ed. Arnold Rampersad (1923; New York: Vintage, 1994), 35; Langston Hughes, "Harlem Night Club," in *Collected Poems*, ed. Arnold Rampersad (1926; New York: Vintage, 1994), 90.
35 Shane Vogel, *The Scene of Harlem Cabaret: Race, Sexuality, Performance* (Chicago: University of Chicago Press, 2009), 104–131.
36 Ibid., 119.
37 Ibid., 129.
38 Langston Hughes, "Café: 3 a.m.," in *Collected Poems*, ed. Arnold Rampersad (1951; New York: Vintage, 1994), 406.
39 Langston Hughes, headnote to *Montage of a Dream Deferred*, in *Collected Poems*, ed. Arnold Rampersad (New York: Vintage, 1994), 387.
40 Donal Norton, "The Cigarette," *Mattachine Review* 1 (1955): 28.
41 Jack Spicer, "Three Marxist Essays," in *My Vocabulary Did This to Me: The Collected Poetry of Jack Spicer*, ed. Peter Gizzi and Kevin Killian (1962; Middletown, CT: Wesleyan University Press, 2008), 328.
42 William Barber, "A Fuck Poem in the Tradition of Reality," in *Angels of the Lyre: A Gay Poetry Anthology*, ed. Winston Leyland (San Francisco: Panjandrum/Gay Sunshine, 1975), 16.
43 Charles Henri Ford, "Candy Darling," in *Angels of the Lyre: A Gay Poetry Anthology*, ed. Winston Leyland (San Francisco: Panjandrum/Gay Sunshine, 1975), 82.
44 Judy Grahn, "A History of Lesbianism," *The Furies Lesbian/Feminist Monthly* 1 (1972): 7.
45 Charlotte Bunch, "Lesbians in Revolt," *The Furies Lesbian/Feminist Monthly* 1 (1972): 8–9.
46 On women's liberation, poetry, and the imagining of new communal spaces, see Stephen Voyce, *Poetic Community: Avant-Garde Activism and Cold War Culture* (Toronto: University of Toronto Press, 2013), 162–201.
47 Adrienne Rich, "Power and Danger: Works of a Common Woman," in *On Lies, Secrets, and Silence: Selected Prose 1966–1978* (1977; New York: Norton, 1979), 247.
48 Ibid., 248.
49 John Wieners, "Physical Wanting," *Behind the State Capitol: Or Cincinnati Pike* (Boston: Good Gay Poets, 1975), 57.
50 See Eric Keenaghan, "Queer Poetry," in *The Princeton Encyclopedia of Poetry and Poetics*, ed. Roland Greene, Stephen Cushman, Clare Cavanagh, Jahan Ramazani, and Paul Rouzer, 4th ed. (Princeton: Princeton University Press, 2012), 1139–1141.
51 Tim Dlugos, "D.O.A.," in *A Fast Life: The Collected Poems of Tim Dlugos*, ed. David Trinidad (1990; Callicoon, NY: Nightboat, 2011), 535.
52 Ibid., 536.
53 kari edwards, *obedience* (n.p.: Factory School, 2005), 38.
54 Ibid., 82.

4

JULIE AVRIL MINICH

Writing Queer Lives: Autobiography and Memoir

But every memoir now is a kind of manifesto, as we piece together the tale of the tribe. Our stories have died with us long enough. We mean to leave behind some map, some key, for the gay and lesbian people who follow – that they may not drown in the lies, in the hate that pools and foams like pus on the carcass of America.

– Paul Monette, *Becoming a Man*

I now find myself enamored of the memoir. The good ones thrill me every bit as much as the great novels, but it's the crappy ones I've lost my heart to. [...] I feel intensely proud of the whole lot of lousy writing that has found its way to print because I smell in those stinkers a fecund democracy. Every sort of half-coherent loser getting their say. Maybe even mean little deaf queers like me.

– Terry Galloway, *Mean Little Deaf Queer*

The epigraphs to this chapter offer very different visions of queer life writing. For Paul Monette, queer memoir and autobiography are an antidote to the hate-filled "lies" of a homophobic America, a "key" that will unlock gay and lesbian stories hidden in the country's closet and a "map" to a better place.[1] For Terry Galloway, the point is not to create a map but to disrupt our faith in clear paths; she privileges not a singular truth but the "fecund democracy" of every "half-coherent loser getting their say."[2] These divergent perceptions of queer life writing provide a starting point for looking more closely at the genre.

We might observe, at the outset, that Monette and Galloway differ not only in their understandings of *queer life writing* but also in their understandings of *queer life*. Is a queer life solely one in which a person's primary emotional and sexual bonds are to others with the same gender identification, or is it also a life lived queerly – that is, against the grain of social norms? In *Becoming a Man* (1992), Monette describes queerness as a historically consistent identity that has "always existed, 'different' from the

mainstream but crucial to the health of the race" (11), although he acknowledges that "the modern queer, his brothers and sisters no longer hidden,
engages a larger identity than his mute ancestors ever could" (12). In *Mean
Little Deaf Queer* (2009), Galloway shows that a normative life script cannot tell her story, carrying us from the hearing loss of her ninth year, when
"the voices of everyone I loved had all but disappeared" (ix) through her
"first summer as a crippled child" (43) and finally through her transformation "from tomboy to child freak to adolescent geek" (125) to performance
artist. Although her title designates her as queer, she is provocatively unclear
about why she is queer: Is it because of her relationships with women, her
deafness, or her dedication to art? The queerness of Galloway's life story
resides not only in her sexuality but also in her rejection of multiple social
scripts that diminish her experience.

Beyond asking what constitutes a queer life, we might ask what constitutes *queer writing*. If we imagine queerness as more than just sexual object
choice, we might wonder if there is a formal or thematic distinction to queer
writing. The feminist autobiography scholars Bella Brodski and Celeste
Schenck critique the notion that "autobiography is a transparency through
which we perceive the life, unmediated and undistorted," an illusion rooted
in "the Western ideal of an essential and inviolable self" from which women
are left out; they conclude that life writing by those who are excluded from
"the masculine representative self" exposes *in its very form* the mediated,
subjective nature of life writing and foregrounds "the problematic status
of the self."[3] These insights dovetail with the work of queer theorists like
Heather Love who interrogate a "linear, triumphalist view of history" that
posits oppression and loss as remnants of a queer past that has now been
"overcome" by the LGBT rights movement.[4] Read together, the work of
Brodski, Schenck, and Love caution us against the temptation to mine queer
life writing for representative lives or achievements. They suggest that we
look instead for formal elements and thematic concerns that disrupt notions
of an essential queer self or a forward-moving queer history.

This chapter privileges contemporary examples of queer life writing that
resist both the impulse to universalize individual lives and the conventions
of teleological narrative. This is not to neglect earlier instances of the genre,
like Gertrude Stein's 1933 *The Autobiography of Alice B. Toklas* or Langston
Hughes's 1940 *The Big Sea*, but rather to ask what post-Stonewall texts
reveal about the stakes of refusing a narrative of progress. This periodization also locates my analysis within a cultural moment marked by what
G. Thomas Couser calls "the memoir boom"; Couser shows that contemporary life writing is "often about what it's like to have or to *be*, to live in or
as, a particular body – indeed, a body that is usually odd or anomalous" and

that, therefore, "the much ballyhooed 'memoir boom' has also been a boom in disability life writing, although publishers and reviewers rarely, if ever, acknowledge it as such."⁵ It is significant that so many of the texts considered here – which are more often read and taught as queer life writing than as disability life writing – also grapple prominently with bodily and mental vulnerability. Indeed, both queer theorists and disability theorists reject narratives of heroic overcoming in favor of stories about (as Love puts it) "what it is like to bear a 'disqualified' identity, which at times can simply mean living with injury – not fixing it" (4). I suggest that the telling of such stories helps us understand sexuality in its full complexity not because these texts claim to represent a universal queer experience but because of their emphasis on what Brodski and Schenck call "a model of nonrepresentative, dispersed, displaced selfhood" (6). Furthermore, following Couser's claim that disability memoir shows us that "people with odd or problematic bodies are in a position to remind us all of our embodiment, a fundamental dimension of the human condition" (11), I suggest that queer life writing is similarly crucial to knowledge about human sexuality in its many and diverse manifestations.

Given these arguments, my opening epigraph from Monette describing queer memoir as a "map" (implying a path forward) may seem counterintuitive. In many ways, of all the texts considered in this chapter, Monette's comes closest to offering a story of progress, evincing a desire for narrative resolution in the face of the HIV/AIDS crisis. However, this resolution evades even Monette. He writes:

> I can't believe it myself sometimes, how fresh the wounds of the deep past sting, how sharp the dry-eyed tears are even at this distance. The very act of remembering begins to resemble a phobic state – feeding on every missed chance, stuck forever in the place without doors. What's crazy about it is, I forget that I ever got out. For an hour or a day the pain wins.
>
> (172)

Although Monette longs to assign his pain to the "deep past," its continued "sting" reveals the elusiveness of that infallible map forward.

We see a similar dynamic in his description of the search for a life partner, whom he calls his "laughing man": "I had no choice but to keep on looking in the wrong places for the thing I'd never even seen: two men in love and laughing" (178). At the end, when he meets his beloved Roger, the reader knows that the search has ended because "the laugh that erupted between us was unlike anything I'd ever felt" (277). Finding his laughing man in Roger, Monette appears to end on a victorious note, but even here his triumph is haunted by ghosts of the pandemic, although "at least they're the ghosts of full-grown men, proof that all of us got that far, free of the traps and the lies" (278).

Galloway's memoir is organized episodically, composed of chapters that collectively create a larger narrative but also stand on their own; this makes it less directed toward a resolution than Monette's is. Instead of being organized around the search *for* love, her memoir focuses on the flight *from* a presence she calls "them":

> "Lucky to have made it no thanks to them" is a popular mantra among my disabled friends, the *them* shifting with the circumstance, the story. They can be upper-class parents who stick you in an institution when you're a toddler because your spine twists where it shouldn't; or scientists who conduct thirty-six exploratory operations so they can test their theories on your eleven-year-old body; or just superstitious passersby who gawk at the newborn you like you're some kind of nasty insect and they wish they had a swatter. [...] They can even be you, hating your own screwed-up body, wanting it dead.
>
> (9–10)

Them for Galloway are not specific people but rather cultural norms defining how bodies should function. Unlike Monette, who finds his laughing man at the end, Galloway never claims to escape them: "I will always be caught up in a web of resentment at the accident that befell me before I was even born" (227). Even her resolution is not a resolution: she states her decision to get cochlear implants that will restore her hearing but adds that she will wait until the technology improves. Therefore, even an event that might seem to represent a definitive "cure" is presented as another development in the struggle with them: "So much of my identity hangs on being little-*d* deaf. It is how I have defined and measured myself all my life. Without my deafness, who will I be?" (226).[6] By ending with this question instead of its answer, Galloway refuses to offer a triumphant story of progress or to depict her life as representative of a larger experience.

As this opening discussion reveals, an examination of queer autobiography and memoir has much to offer broader conversations about the significance of queer lives and queer history. To borrow Judith (Jack) Halberstam's phrasing, a consideration of the genre helps us understand queer lives as characterized by "strange temporalities, imaginative life schedules, and eccentric economic practices" and helps us think about "those forms of representation dedicated to capturing these willfully eccentric modes of being."[7] In other words, the texts discussed in this chapter invite us to think about why queer lives matter, about what we might learn from their unusual embodiments and their nonnormative unfoldings in time and space, and about the literary modes, genres, and formal strategies that represent them.

Queer Lives, Queer Knowledge: Audre Lorde and Samuel R. Delany

Although they were published in the 1980s, Audre Lorde's *Zami: A New Spelling of My Name: A Biomythography* (1982) and Samuel R. Delany's *The Motion of Light in Water: Sex and Science Fiction Writing in the East Village: 1960–1965* (1989) focus on life before Stonewall. Lorde explores her childhood in New York City as the legally blind daughter of Caribbean immigrants, the suicide of her high school friend Gennie, her time as a factory worker in Connecticut and as a student in Mexico, and her immersion in the Greenwich Village gay scene of the 1950s. Delany describes the beginning of his writing career, his sexual coming-of-age, and his marriage to poet Marilyn Hacker. Whereas Love argues that queer pain and loss are not confined to the past, Delany and Lorde show that pre-Stonewall queer life was not devoid of pleasure, joy, or intellectual richness. Engaging the intersection of sexuality and race, Lorde and Delany challenge dominant narratives about the history of both queer lives and queer theory. In doing so, they coincide with the work of critics like Ernesto Javier Martínez who reject a version of queer intellectual history that depicts queer theory emerging in the late 1970s and gaining academic prominence only in the early 1990s and who charge that this narrative ignores the intellectual contributions of queers of color.[8] This section builds on my introductory discussion of queerness's potential to "open up new life narratives" by examining the knowledges that these new narratives produce (Halberstam 2).

Lorde's exploration of experience-based knowledge coalesces in a chapter describing queer life in Greenwich Village. The chapter begins: "I remember how being young and Black and gay and lonely felt."[9] It describes how Lorde's social circle was, in the 1950s, already characterized by the kind of cross-racial alliances that would later contribute to the intellectual development of queer feminisms:

> We not only believed in the reality of sisterhood, that word which was to be so abused two decades later, but we also tried to put it into practice, with varying results. [...] Lesbians were probably the only Black and white women in New York City in the fifties who were making any real attempt to communicate with each other; we learned lessons from each other, the values of which were not lessened by what we did not learn.
>
> (179)

Here Lorde frames the Greenwich Village "gay-girl scene" as a site of rigorous inquiry, suggesting that the lives of racially diverse lesbians in 1950s New York constitute a source of theoretical knowledge about sexuality, feminist community, and the mutual constitution of race, gender, and sexuality.

Given that Lorde writes from the vantage point of the 1970s and 1980s – at a moment when conflicts about sexuality and race were a deep concern for many feminists – it is important to underscore here both the sense of community and the sense of struggle that Lorde identifies in both historical moments.[10] The knowledge she derives from these lessons, in other words, is not about building a singular, utopic, conflict-free women's community but rather about negotiating the discord that inevitably emerges within interracial feminist communities.

Lorde provides examples of the kinds of experiences from which she and her friends gained (and did not gain) theoretical knowledge about coalitions and conflicts, such as her struggle to tell friends why she avoids "gay-girl" bars:

> [T]he bouncer was always asking me for my ID to prove I was twenty-one, even though I was older than the other women with me. [...] And we would all rather die than discuss the fact that it was because I was Black, since, of course, gay people weren't racists. After all, didn't they know what it was like to be oppressed?
>
> (180)

It is worth noting here that the dismissal of Lorde's experience by her friends parallels at the level of embodied practice what Martínez understands to be a similar dismissal at the level of theory: "a long-standing pattern of rendering questions of race, intersectionality, and queer people of color marginal within contemporary theory" (16). Yet she goes on to elaborate how this experience prompted her, decades later, to arrive at a nuanced understanding of the significance of her identity: "In a paradoxical sense, once I accepted my position as different from the larger society as well as from any single sub-society – Black or gay – I felt I didn't have to try so hard" (181). In this way, she links experience to the creation of knowledge.

The Motion of Light in Water similarly depicts moments in Delany's life that – like Lorde's experience at the bar – do not become available to him as knowledge until later. Early in the memoir, Delany states: "My father's death, my subsequent dropping out of school, and my hasty marriage speak of a young man interested in writing and music, but under fair emotional strain. With the facts that I was black and Marilyn was white, that I was gay and both of us knew it, the implication of strain – for both of us – only strengthens."[11] Yet he also reveals that these facts are not "the story *I* remember from that time," because despite recalling "vivid moments, rich details, complexes of sensation, deep feelings, the texture of sensation," he retains "no sense that one came along to interrupt the other" (13, emphasis in original). With this opening, Delany concedes that the "careful and accurate biographer can, here and there, know more about the biographical subject than the subject him- or herself" (14). He also insists, however, that the knowledge of the memoirist, although less factually accurate, is more complete. Like Lorde, he privileges the depth of understanding that experience provides.

In subsequent chapters, Delany narrates how the "emotional strain" of his early adulthood and marriage brings him to seek psychiatric treatment. These chapters explore his struggle to claim an identity as a black, gay writer during a time when there were "only Negroes and homosexuals, both of whom – along with artists – were hugely devalued in the social hierarchy" (364). Three questions, separated by line breaks and punctuated by ellipses, represent this struggle: "A black man ... ? / A gay man ... ? / A writer ... ?" (327). Here he also offers a discussion of dyslexia that might seem – at first – to be a digression, invoking a series of stressful encounters in school that left him and his teachers struggling to understand "the obvious gap between my intelligence and my appalling spelling" (331). After being diagnosed, he concludes: "So much of what I had learned, what I had done, what I had searched out could be seen as silent, brutal compensation for this heretofore unnamed condition. What would have been the differences in me, I wondered, if I had grown up thinking of myself as having a learning disability from the beginning?" (332). Reflecting on his dyslexia allows Delany to contemplate the difference it makes to name and claim an identity: "What might the word have given me? / What might it have taken away?" (332). This, in turn, allows him to conclude these chapters by replacing his questions with three declarations: "A black man. / A gay man. / A writer" (364). Yet to read these declarative statements as a resolution would, I argue, be a mistake. (For one thing, this episode takes place in the middle of the text, and Delany goes on to narrate other struggles.) Rather, these declarative statements make a similar gesture as Galloway's conclusion does, revealing Delany's investment in living with (rather than fixing) what Love calls "disqualified identities," a rejection of the social imperative to triumph over adversity.

My opening discussion about Monette and Galloway explores different possibilities for understanding the significance of queer life writing. A consideration of Lorde and Delany extends this analysis by demonstrating how racialized queer lives – those occupying what Delany describes as "hugely devalued" social positions – might expand our understanding of queer history and queer knowledge. The following section further broadens this discussion by considering two texts that represent not only devalued identities but also devalued bodies.

Life in Queer Time: Gloria Anzaldúa and David Wojnarowicz

In terms of form, the Chicana feminist Gloria Anzaldúa's *Borderlands/La Frontera: The New Mestiza* (1987) and David Wojnarowicz's *Close to the Knives: A Memoir of Disintegration* (1991) veer further from conventional narrative structure than the texts discussed in the previous sections do. Both lack concrete plots that can be neatly summarized. *Borderlands/La Frontera*, which explores Anzaldúa's queer mestiza consciousness and its connection to the U.S.-Mexico borderlands where she grew up, consists of seven essays followed by a selection of poems. The text is more commonly cited and taught as feminist theory than as memoir; Anzaldúa describes it as "autohistoria-teoria," meaning "personal essay that theorizes."[12] *Close to the Knives*, which is designated in its subtitle as a memoir, is structured as a series of eight essays on such topics as homelessness among queer youth, the HIV/AIDS pandemic, and aesthetic representations of sexuality; some of these are best described as political or social commentary, others as autobiographical narrative. As with Galloway's memoir, Wojnarowicz's essays can be read in any order; unlike Galloway's vignettes, Wojnarowicz's essays do not constitute a linear chronology of the facts of his life. In addition to these formal considerations, both texts document brief but influential lives: Wojnarowicz was a painter, photographer, filmmaker, and performance artist who died of AIDS-related causes in 1992 at age thirty-seven; Anzaldúa was a scholar, poet, essayist, and children's author who experienced lifelong health complications and died of diabetes in 2004 at age sixty-one.[13] Although Anzaldúa lived longer than Wojnarowicz did, her illnesses (and inconsistent access to health care) significantly affected her ability to write, and her relatively sparse publications register the challenging bodily conditions under which she labored. As testaments to the vulnerability of bodies marked as queer, both texts inscribe what Halberstam calls *queer time*: "alternative temporalities" producing "futures that can be imagined according to logics that lie outside of those paradigmatic markers of life experience – namely, birth, marriage, reproduction, and death" (2).

Although Anzaldúa never identified as disabled, her work is now often claimed by disability scholars. Robert McRuer, for instance, describes her as a "crip theorist,"[14] employing the word "crip" as a "reclaimed" slur that functions similarly to the word "queer." References to bodily anomaly pervade *Borderlands/La Frontera*; for instance, Anzaldúa famously likens the border to a wound: "The U.S.-Mexican border *es una herida abierta* where the Third World grates against the first and bleeds. And before a scab forms it hemorrhages again, the lifeblood of two worlds merging to form a third country – a border culture."[15] It is noteworthy that Anzaldúa uses an image of comingling blood to represent border culture but disarticulates this comingling from heterosexual reproduction; instead, it is the wound that is imbued with generative possibility. In this way, Anzaldúa rejects what Halberstam calls the "logic of reproductive temporality" (4). In addition to describing the borderlands in terms of corporeal difference, Anzaldúa also identifies its inhabitants in terms of their nonnormative physicality: "The prohibited and the forbidden are its inhabitants. *Los atravesados* live here: the squint-eyed, the perverse, the queer, the troublesome, the mongrel, the mulato, the half-breed, the half dead; in short, those who cross over, pass over, or go through the confines of the 'normal'" (25). Here her attention to "the half dead" further overlaps with Halberstam's discussion of nonnormative life trajectories as well as with age studies scholar Margaret Morganroth Gullette's critique of an "age ideology" that privileges a "sense of rising through an institutionalized and secure and progressive age hierarchy."[16] Gullette, like Anzaldúa, asks us to reconsider the value of people whose lives do not "support progress and progress narratives" (19) contained in dominant understandings of "the life course" (15). By resisting the dominant life course paradigm, Anzaldúa privileges the forms of knowledge, spiritual practices, and cultural interventions of the wounded, the nonreproductive, the ill, the physically vulnerable, and those marked for death.

As an illustrative example, the poem "To live in the Borderlands means you" inscribes the physical challenges with which inhabitants of the borderlands live, "carrying all five races on your back / not knowing which side to turn to, run from" (216). Here the poem's speaker and interlocutor both represent Anzaldúa's mestiza consciousness. As a result, the poetic form itself illustrates Anzaldúa's border identity, depicting a subject who inhabits both "sides" of the poem – its speaking voice and the object of its address. As in the beginning of the book, where Anzaldúa describes the border's inhabitants as "perverse," the border is depicted as a site of racial and gender ambiguity: the subject of the poem is the "forerunner of a new race, / half and half – both woman and man, neither – / a new gender" (216). Although this notion of a "new" race and gender implies optimism – the potential to enact race and gender in innovative, potentially unoppressive ways – the poem is also explicit about the violence enacted on bodies whose gender or race is illegible: "[Y]ou are the battleground / where enemies are kin to each other [...] you are wounded, lost in action / dead, fighting back" (216). The fact that the subject of the poem is both "dead" and "fighting back" speaks to the radical temporality that Anzaldúa presents throughout, acknowledging both the profound challenges that border identities pose to normative social life and the material fact that lives lived outside the parameters of social acceptability are often brutally cut short. In this way, the text refuses to (as Halberstam puts it) "pathologize modes of living that show little or no concern for longevity" (4), even as it also condemns the social forces that lengthen some lives at the expense of others.

Wojnarowicz even more directly rejects the concern for longevity, even as he (like Anzaldúa) seeks to hold accountable the social forces that have shortened his life, as well as the lives of his friends, lovers, and fellow artists. Wojnarowicz writes: "Some of us are born with the cross hairs of a rifle scope printed on our backs or skulls. [...] I don't receive the kind of paycheck to take out a seventy-year lease on my life."[17] Depicting futurity as a luxury good – belonging only to those with the right kind of "paycheck" – Wojnarowicz presents no incentive to live according to what Gullette describes as the dominant life course, slowly accumulating wealth and prestige.

Although Wojnarowicz created art in different media – including traditionally lucrative media like painting and sculpture – the sections of his memoir that discuss photography are particularly helpful for considering how he frames the brevity of his life. He writes, for instance, of the democratic potential of the photograph: "In the art world, photography is one of the most misunderstood mediums because the camera is accessible to almost everybody. A good portion of the population in america owns cameras" (140). He links the aesthetic value of photography to its lack of economic value: "You can always get *something* on film and if it is blurry and out of focus or 'badly' lit you only have to claim INTENT and the art world will consider it. [...] This is why the art world will not throw billions of dollars at photography the way it has at painting; and that is what makes it an interesting medium" (141). Rejecting the social imperative to pursue longevity for its own sake, however, Wojnarowicz also expresses a desire for the images that he produces to endure:

> I try to think of what it meant to be engaged in the act of picture-taking. I thought at the time that it would be making pictures of the world I lived in. One that was never seen on the television sets [...] Or it was possibly an act of validation of our lives, something of value being implied in the preservation of our bodies.

(142)

The form of the photograph as described by Wojnarowicz, then, bears a structural similarity to the form of his life: economically nonlucrative, anticapitalist, and lacking in cultural prestige. The difference is that the photograph endures where the physical body of the artist and his loved ones do not; in this way, Wojnarowicz privileges the longevity of the aesthetic rendering of the body over that of the physical body. Indeed, this represents a point of connection between his text and Monette's, even though the form of Monette's is much less experimental: writing from within "the cauldron of plague" (2), Monette too imagines the survival of his text beyond that of his body, envisioning how the former will serve "the women and men of my tribe" (1).

Although both Anzaldúa and Wojnarowicz worked in a variety of aesthetic forms, it is telling that their memoirs, which are so concerned with the discursive and physical violence directed at queer bodies, should employ and theorize aesthetic forms linked to brevity. Instead of the book-length memoir form adopted by Monette, Galloway, Lorde, and Delany, they privilege the essay, the poem, and the photograph. They are concerned with lives that do not proceed through the traditional life events associated with heteronormative constructions of time and produce texts that are similarly punctuated and interrupted in unexpected ways. To build on this discussion of vulnerable queer embodiment and to conclude my overall discussion of queer life writing, I now turn to a text that centers on the representation of a queer death.

Mourning Queer Lives: Alison Bechdel

Alison Bechdel's graphic memoir *Fun Home: A Family Tragicomic* (2006) tells a story about growing up lesbian in rural Pennsylvania with a father who, although married to Bechdel's mother, had sexualized encounters with adolescent boys (including the family babysitter). Bechdel characterizes her father's death (which occurred shortly after her own coming-out) as a suicide but acknowledges its ambiguous circumstances; he was hit by a truck while clearing brush from a yard. Ann Cvetkovich argues that in *Fun Home*, the death of "someone who might be categorized (however problematically) as a pedophile, suicide, or closet homosexual, raises the possibility that there are some lives that are not 'grievable,' certainly not in a public context," and she explores how the text claims "historical significance and public space not only for a lesbian coming-out story but also for one that is tied to what some might see as shameful sexual histories."[18] The memoir thus coalesces many concerns of this chapter by exploring the inadequacy of queer progress narratives, the knowledges that emerge from marginalized life stories, and the alternative life trajectories that result from the vulnerability of bodies marked as queer.

Permeating her text with allusions to such canonical queer autobiographical writings as Marcel Proust's *In Search of Lost Time* (1913–1922), the novels of Colette, and Kate Millett's *Flying* (1974), Bechdel simultaneously acknowledges the seductiveness of teleological life narratives and rejects the logic of causality that undergirds them. She writes: "The idea that I caused his death by telling my parents I was a lesbian is perhaps illogical. Causality implies connection, contact of some kind, and however convincing they might be, you can't lay hands on a fictional character."[19] She speculates that her father timed his death so that it would take place at the same age as that of F. Scott Fitzgerald but then dismisses this speculation: "But that would only confirm that his death was not my fault. That, in fact, it had nothing to do with me at all. And I'm reluctant to let go of that last, tenuous bond" (86). In her struggle to insist that her father's death has something to do with her, to cling to that "tenuous bond," Bechdel complicates Monette's notion of a historically consistent gay and lesbian "tribe," but this does not mean that she jettisons the idea of queer identity and community: "Perhaps my eagerness to claim him as 'gay' in the same way I am 'gay,' as opposed to bisexual or some other category, is just a way of keeping him to myself – a sort of inverted Oedipal complex" (230). Her desire to "keep" her father even as she acknowledges the complexity of imposing on him her own gay identity dovetails with Love's claim for the continued cultural significance of marginalized queer lives. Love writes: "I insist on the importance of cling-ing to ruined identities and to histories of injury. Resisting the call of gay normalization means refusing to write off the most vulnerable, the least pre-sentable, and all the dead" (30). For Bechdel, "clinging to ruined identities" is not a matter of rejecting out of hand all discourses of queer pride and affirmation but rather a matter of acknowledging and honoring those whose lives and histories cannot fit within those discourses. By aligning, moreover, with Couser's point about how the stories of lives lived in anomalous bod-ies help us all understand our embodiment, Bechdel insists that her father's fraught queerness can inform her own, more legibly gay, sexual identity.

Because of the way *Fun Home* touches on multiple theoretical insights that have informed this chapter, this discussion provides an apposite ending point. *Fun Home* is not unique among the texts discussed here in its call-ing attention to the mediated, subjective, and inherently unreliable nature of autobiography. As noted earlier in the chapter, Delany even explicitly states that a biographer would provide more factually accurate information about his life than he does. Nor is Bechdel's the only text to question how adequately one queer life can represent others or to pose difficult questions about how belonging and affirmation are conferred in queer communities. By memorializing her father within her own story of coming-out, however, Bechdel provides a powerful account of how and why life stories that do not make representative claims to the universal are nonetheless important. Indeed, Galloway's half-coherent losers, Delany's devalued, Anzaldúa's per-verse/queer/troublesome, Love's most vulnerable or least presentable, and others like them have much to teach us about how communities are formed, who represents them, and which lives and life stories are valued within them.

NOTES

1 Paul Monette, *Becoming a Man: Half a Life Story* (New York: Perennial Classics, 1992), 2; hereafter cited in text.
2 Terry Galloway, *Mean Little Deaf Queer: A Memoir* (Boston: Beacon Press, 2009), x–xi; hereafter cited in text.
3 Bella Brodski and Celeste Schenck, introduction to *Life/Lines: Theorizing Women's Autobiography*, ed. Bella Brodski and Celeste Schenck (Ithaca: Cornell University Press, 1988), 1, 5, 2, 2; hereafter cited in text.
4 Heather Love, *Feeling Backward: Loss and the Politics of Queer History* (Cambridge, MA: Harvard University Press, 2007), 3; hereafter cited in text.
5 G. Thomas Couser, *Signifying Bodies: Disability in Contemporary Life Writing* (Ann Arbor: University of Michigan Press, 2009), 2; hereafter cited in text.
6 Galloway uses the term "little-*d* deaf" to distinguish herself – as one who grew up with a hearing impairment in a hearing family and culture – from those born to Deaf parents who grow up immersed in Deaf culture and fluent in American Sign Language.
7 Judith Halberstam, *In a Queer Time and Place: Transgender Bodies, Subcultural Lives* (New York: New York University Press, 2005), 1; hereafter cited in text.
8 Ernesto Javier Martínez, *On Making Sense: Queer Race Narratives of Intelligibility* (Stanford: Stanford University Press, 2012); hereafter cited in text. Martínez challenges a history that ties queer theory's emergence in the United States to the publication and translation of the first volume of Michel Foucault's *The History of Sexuality,* vol. 1, *An Introduction,* trans. Robert Hurley (New York: Pantheon Books, 1978) and its acceptance into the U.S. academy to the publication of Judith Butler's *Gender Trouble* (New York: Routledge, 1990) and Eve Kosofsky Sedgwick's *Epistemology of the Closet* (Berkeley: University of California Press, 1990).
9 Audre Lorde, *Zami: A New Spelling of My Name: A Biomythography* (Berkeley: Crossing Press, 1982), 176; hereafter cited in text.
10 Here I refer to the conflicts that have come to be known as the Feminist Sex Wars – a series of acrimonious debates between groups of feminists that have in turn come to be characterized (somewhat reductively) as anti-porn feminists and sex-positive feminists – whose most famous clash took place at the 1982 Barnard Conference on Sexuality.
11 Samuel R. Delany, *The Motion of Light in Water: Sex and Science Fiction Writing in the East Village: 1960–1965* (New York: Masquerade Books, 1988), 12–13; hereafter cited in text.
12 Gloria E. Anzaldúa, "now let us shift ... the path of conocimiento ... inner work, public acts," in *this bridge we call home: radical visions for transformation*, ed. Gloria E. Anzaldúa and AnaLouise Keating (New York: Routledge, 2002), 578.
13 Readers interested in Wojnarowicz's life will also wish to consult Cynthia Carr, *Fire in the Belly: The Life and Times of David Wojnarowicz* (New York: Bloomsbury, 2012).

14 Robert McRuer, *Crip Theory: Cultural Signs of Queerness and Disability* (New York: New York University Press, 2006), 39.

15 Gloria Anzaldúa, *Borderlands/La Frontera: The New Mestiza*, 4th ed. (1987; San Francisco, Aunt Lute Books, 2012), 25; hereafter cited in text.

16 Margaret Morganroth Gullette, *Aged by Culture* (Chicago: University of Chicago Press, 2004), 18; hereafter cited in text.

17 David Wojnarowicz, *Close to the Knives: A Memoir of Disintegration* (New York: Vintage, 1991), 58; hereafter cited in text.

18 Ann Cvetkovich, "Drawing the Archive in Alison Bechdel's *Fun Home*," *Women's Studies Quarterly* 36, no. 1–2 (2008): 111, 112. Cvetkovich builds on the idea of a "grievable life" that Judith Butler proposes in *Precarious Life: The Power of Mourning and Violence* (New York: Verso, 2004), 20.

19 Alison Bechdel, *Fun Home: A Family Tragicomic* (New York: Mariner Books, 2006), 84; hereafter cited in text.

5

LUCAS HILDERBRAND

Queer Cinema, Queer Writing, Queer Criticism

Both homosexuality and cinema were invented in the late nineteenth century, yet gay cinema can only be understood to begin in tandem with the gay liberation era, which dates to the 1960s. In part, the turn toward gay community and acts of self-acceptance at that time was signaled through new strategies of imaging and imagining sexuality in the media. In his 1973 *Screening the Sexes*, the film critic and experimental modernist writer Parker Tyler offered one of the first published explorations of homosexuality on screen. Perhaps overzealously, he proclaimed the cinema's centrality in shifting sexual politics:

> What today we rather facilely call the Sexual Revolution can be located centrally *in the movies.* ... If we read aright the signs of sexual style in the movies – read them with intelligence and an open, enlightened spirit – we can descry the true, the actual, the varied features of the whole repertory of human sexuality.[1]

Less than a decade later, Vito Russo authored an acclaimed survey of filmic representations of homosexuality, but his *The Celluloid Closet* was far less celebratory. As Russo commented in his introduction, few friends or other interlocutors could even imagine the serious value of his undertaking as he researched and wrote his book:

> They reflected the closeted mentalities of gay people themselves. Almost all the people I spoke with reacted as though they had never considered a discussion of homosexuality as anything but potential gossip; the idea of examining some images of gay people onscreen was a barely legitimate concept to most.[2]

These two film critics, respectively, suggest the stakes and range of perspectives on the history of gay, lesbian, bisexual, and transgender representations (although most attention has been paid to gay male ones) that bookended the foundational era of gay liberation. Much of what we might call gay cinema and queer film studies has been about the search for representations of queer characters in otherwise straight narratives or films that have been appropriated by queer audiences as part of their own subcultural canon.

Since the publication of Russo's book, gay cinema has been understood as a struggle over representations, with a general historical arc from homophobic to affirming to queer to assimilationist. Although studies of representations have largely fallen out of favor in film studies as a dated analytical framework, cinema continues to be a major popular medium that reflects and informs broader cultural ideologies – and also provides validation or shame for audiences who may feel starved for reflections of their own experiences on screen. The well-rehearsed history of cinematic representations of gay and lesbian life before the liberation era shows that such characters were typically sinister and often killed by the end of the movie. For instance, Russo's book concludes with a "necrology": a listing of queer characters who die by their respective films' final reels. Strikingly, the most acclaimed queer-themed films of the fin de siècle – *Gods and Monsters* (Bill Condon, 1998), *Boys Don't Cry* (Kimberly Pierce, 1999), *The Hours* (Stephen Daldry, 2002), *Brokeback Mountain* (Ang Lee, 2005), and *Milk* (Gus Van Sant, 2008) – appeared decades after the rise of the gay rights movement and efforts to reshape media images of queerness, but each features the death of its lead character – with the major connotative difference being that these denouements are tragic rather than deserved.

This chapter gives particular attention to two of the most commented-on gay films that span the gay cinema era: *The Boys in the Band* (William Friedkin, 1970) and *Brokeback Mountain*. On first look, these films could not be more different: one is a chamber piece confined to a one-bedroom Manhattan apartment on a single night, whereas the other boasts mountain vistas and spans decades. Yet I turn to these films to suggest that they open up larger questions of gay cinema, from the issue of affirmative images to the composition of their imagined audiences. As the most mainstream gay films of their respective moments, they not surprisingly focus primarily on white males (although there is a black gay character among the ensemble in *Boys*). Despite the acclaim for *Brokeback*, it may actually be a less progressive film about gay life than the historically maligned *Boys* is. But both have also suffered the burden of representing the totality of gay life in a single text as the Zeitgeist films of their respective moments. Playing off these two mainstream films, I also turn to two films – *Looking for Langston* (Isaac Julien, 1989) and *Go Fish* (Rose Troche, 1994) – by a gay and lesbian filmmaker, respectively, that bookended the late 1980s–early 1990s moment of New Queer Cinema and signaled transitions in the strategies and sensibilities of more explicitly queer cinema.

There have been historical parallels between queer literature and queer cinema, as well as crossovers between their audiences, from early expressions being constrained by censorship to later pornographic, activist, and ultimately middlebrow narratives; this chapter, however, focuses specifically on film on its own terms because the medium has its own distinct histories of commercial production and visual forms. A number of the films surveyed here are adaptations of different genres: *The Boys in the Band* was adapted by a playwright from his own stage play; *Brokeback Mountain* is based on a short story; and *Looking for Langston* draws from numerous authors to pay tribute to a poet.[3] Yet, despite the literary origins of these films, I suggest that each of them, as well as *Go Fish*, develops a distinctively cinematic form for representing queer experiences and narratives. Although one might deploy narratological analysis from literary studies for these productions, one of the fundamental tenets of film studies is that to understand a text, one must not only examine the plot and dialogue but also recognize the expressive grammar of film form (shot composition, editing, sound); in addition, film studies has explored how films address their audiences, construct imagined subject positions, and reinforce dominant ideologies through the power of the gaze.[4]

The contrast between the major gay films of 1970 and 2005 suggests a stunning counter-narrative to the accepted one of historical progress toward liberation. Rather, *The Boys in the Band* and *Brokeback Mountain* suggest turns from community to the closet, from speech to silence, from life to death, and from gay audiences to straight ones. This historical comparison may be reductive and schematic, but nonetheless it allows for a provocative rethinking of the historiography of gay cinema as simply teleological toward affirmation – precisely the kind of questioning and ruptures that are offered in the films of the New Queer Cinema.

In the Band and in the Sand

The Boys in the Band was made for an assumed emergent gay audience, one that had already been demonstrated by niche-reading publics. Although it is often called a "Hollywood" film, it was produced and released outside the major studio system in order for playwright and screenwriter Mart Crowley to maintain creative control. The film has had a longer influence than have the contemporaneous gay-themed films that the bigger studios did make, such as the adaptations of *Staircase* (Stanley Donen, 1969) or *Myra Breckinridge* (Michael Sarne, 1970). *The Boys in the Band* is widely mythologized as the first major Hollywood film to portray gay male protagonists – not unlike the way in which the 1969 Stonewall riots are understood to be the symbolic start of the gay liberation era – and its representations and reception reflected shifting publicity and politics for gay culture across media.

Boys had been the most prominent play to represent gay life to date, and it offered a range of characters who struggled with their own self-acceptance yet who had found a community. The stage play, written by openly gay Crowley, debuted in New York in 1968 and was met with acclaim for its radical candor and empathy toward a circle of gay male friends who gather for a birthday party. The dialogue offers both a compendium of gay witticisms and, in a milieu in which the dramas of Tennessee Williams and Edward Albee had stood as the model, requisite dramatic monologues and histrionics. The cast of characters range from the unabashed sissy Emory (Cliff Gorman) to the newly divorced bisexual Hank (Laurence Luckenbill) to the caustically campy but self-accepting Harold (Leonard Frey) to Michael (Kenneth Nelson), the party's host, who indulges his queeny tastes for the finer things but is ultimately haunted by Catholic guilt. The characters, aging and middle-class, do not speak of gay liberation.

After 1,001 off-Broadway performances, the play was adapted into a film with the same cast (most of whom were at least semi-closeted) but a new straight director (Friedkin). The character Michael's self-loathing and the torturous taunts between friends already seemed retrograde to some of its politicized gay audiences by 1970. As is remarked in almost all of the commentary on the film, the play and film adaptation neatly appeared pre- and post-Stonewall, respectively. Although it was radical for a major film to represent gay life with any kind of depth or nuance, the film was not affirmative enough for many viewers – instead, it reveled in internalized homophobia rather than advocating activism. Despite complaints that the film supposedly reflects pre-Stonewall ideologies, the characters still remain perhaps the most fully developed ensemble of gay men assembled on film. As I suggested, the play and film operate in the mode of Albee's 1962 *Who's Afraid of Virginia Woolf?*, where alcohol lubricates character self-revelations. Early in the film, Michael reveals that he has been sober for five weeks, but subtly we see him switch from drinking club soda to pouring himself cocktails over the course of the birthday party, and he consequently becomes more vicious. In many ways, the characters' dilemmas – including parental issues, monogamous or open relationship rules, body issues, and debt – remain relevant for gay men in the twenty-first century. When viewed in retrospect, what remains striking about the film is its wit and dialogue, written and performed with rapid-fire gay camp. Although many viewers might see the film as an anachronism of homophobia, I see it as a time capsule of gay argot and probing psychological realism.

The ambivalence of responses to the film was legible from the start. Russo cautiously recognized the film's power:

In spite of itself, Crowley's passion play was part catharsis and part catalyst. ... The internalized guilt and self-hatred of eight gay men at a Manhattan birth-day party formed the best and most potent argument for gay liberation ever offered in a popular art form. It supplied concrete and personalized examples of the negative effects of what homosexuals learn about themselves from the distortions of the media. ... It was a gay movie for gay people, and it imme-diately became both a period piece and a reconfirmation of the stereotypes.[5]

The film's (and play's) most pronounced gay liberation declaration actually comes from Michael, the protagonist who appears to be the most tortured, when he declares, "If we ... if we could just ... not hate ourselves so much. That's it, you know, if we could just *learn* not to hate ourselves quite so very much." A moment later, Michael flippantly queries, "Who was it that used to always say, 'You show me a happy homosexual, and I'll show you a gay corpse'?"

The film's emotional arc is signaled in its visual strategies as well as in its dialogue and performances. The look and feel of the film shifts from bright and airy afternoon scenes to dark and closed-in late night ones, and from brisk and lively camera movement to static, claustrophobic fram-ings. Friedkin displays a range of camera techniques to vary the experience of a film that might otherwise feel stagy, as it is primarily confined to a single, small apartment; moments of frenetic handheld camera movement alternately signal the spirited cutting-loose of the festivities, the chaos and distress of a homophobic fight scene, and ultimately the loss of control as Michael drunkenly stumbles (in one of the few moments clearly presented as a point-of-view shot). In more contemplative or morose moments, the camera is static, and the high-contrast lighting creates visual tension.

Pointing to medium-specific shifts between the effects of the play and those of the film, Tyler writes, "On the stage ... there was a special dramatic focus in the ensemble acting that is lost amid the closeups and attention to detail in the movie," which are the product of separate camera set-ups and editing.[6] A later scholarly analysis of the film likewise turned attention to the politics of the film's shot structure: "The screen often only shows one man, suggesting that he is not part of a community, but alone, separate, emo-tionally isolated."[7] Although isolating close-ups do increase in frequency as the film progressively becomes more tense, these scholars downplay the frequent camaraderie embodied by group shots, particularly with a shifting configuration of characters in dialogue.

At the film's end, Harold's searing monologue indicting Michael's self-destructive ambitions ("You're a sad and pathetic man. You're a

homosexual, and you don't want to be") is shot, first, through a pan following Harold as he saunters across the room in his queenly fashion. The
film cuts to an extreme close-up of Michael's face in profile with Harold
facing the camera head-on behind him. This framing suggests that they are
split elements of the same personality or that Harold sees directly through
Michael as he declares that Michael will be a homosexual "always. Until the
day you die." It is perhaps the most cinematic moment in the film, one that
could not have been constructed on stage.

An essential part of *Boys*'s legacy in gay culture and in cinema is its pornographic cousin. Playing off of the title of *The Boys in the Band*, Wakefield
Poole's *Boys in the Sand* (1972) is widely considered the first gay male porn
feature film. The film was advertised in *The New York Times* and reviewed
in the leading entertainment industry trade journal *Variety*, in addition to
being publicized in the gay press. In other words, the film was visible even
to mainstream culture and, significantly, established pornography as the
most prominent genre of gay cinema made by openly gay filmmakers and
as reflective of gay liberationist values. Despite the longstanding claims of a
paucity of representations of gays and lesbians in cinema, in the 1970s there
were dozens of films made for these audiences, and they were increasingly
made by self-identified gay and lesbian filmmakers; the distinction is that
most were not Hollywood-style productions but instead were pornographic,
documentary, experimental, or independent films.

New Queer Cinema in Black and White

At the turn of the 1990s, an interlude of radically queer cinema exploded on
film festival, art house, and public television screens and became hailed as
the New Queer Cinema. Informed by AIDS activist strategies, this moment
came out of an urgent move to reclaim and reinvent queer imaging practices, and many of its key artists had shaped their politics and aesthetics
as members of ACT UP (AIDS Coalition to Unleash Power). This cycle of
films also coincided with the explosive first moments of queer theory in the
academy, which sought to question the fundamental categories of identity,
gender, and sexuality – including homosexuality. The films of this informal
movement, including most famously *Tongues Untied* (Marlon Riggs, 1989),
Poison (Todd Haynes, 1991), *Paris Is Burning* (Jennie Livingston, 1991),
Swoon (Tom Kalin, 1992), and Sadie Benning's video shorts, achieved
unprecedented awards, critical acclaim, and mainstream visibility for queer
cinema.[8]

In the 1970s and 1980s, a number of documentaries, such as *Word Is
Out* (The Mariposa Group, 1977) and *Before Stonewall* (Greta Schiller and

Robert Rosenberg, 1984), had begun the project of earnestly reconstructing an affirmative gay and lesbian history by and for gay and lesbian audiences through testimonies and archival documents. *Looking for Langston* signaled a more experimental rethinking of the queer past – or rather, a queering of the past. In part, the film's project was to shift discourses on the black American poet Langston Hughes toward a more intersectional understanding that foregrounded the homoeroticism in his life and work in addition to his blackness. Because it is more lyrical than either a documentary or a narrative, the forty-minute essay film transcends standard feature film structures yet has found a significant and enduring influence and audience. By fusing quotation and gorgeous recreations, *Looking for Langston* offers a meditation on Langston Hughes and the queerness of the Harlem Renaissance.

Looking constructs a highly stylized, romanticized, and eroticized vision that evokes both past and present, playing with anachronism by interjecting jeans, leather jackets, and public sex practices of the 1980s into scenes set in Jazz Age Harlem. The film weaves a genealogy of influences, including not only Hughes but also various blues singers, Richard Bruce Nugent, George Platt Lynes, Jean Cocteau, James Baldwin, Robert Mapplethorpe, Essex Hemphill, and Voguing and House music. (Some of this material was likewise explored in *Tongues Untied*.) The film's layering of documents, quotations, and dramatizations – like its languorous camera movements that play with still and moving images – reflects the inextricable blurring between the actual past and mediated memory. This film opened the door for the vaunted postmodern citationality and (at times campy) play with history that marked other New Queer Cinema works, including *Urinal* (John Greyson, 1989), *Poison, Hours and Times* (Christopher Munch, 1991), *Edward II* (Derek Jarman, 1991), *Swoon, Orlando* (Sally Potter, 1992), and later *The Watermelon Woman* (Cheryl Dunye, 1996) and *Velvet Goldmine* (Todd Haynes, 1998).[9] Indeed, this film plays with history as much as it does with race, sexuality, genre, and form.

As its title suggests, *Looking* stages a search and recovery mission for the underrepresented history of black gay life, or perhaps, as Kobena Mercer has suggested, for a contemporary black gay subjecthood. Mercer writes, "the film looks for Langston, but what we find is Isaac [Julien]."[10] As he suggests, this structure of *looking* also foregrounds the lustful glances between characters and the reenvisioning of the past as specifically cinematic.[11] *Looking* is also transnational, a British production that examines a specifically American cultural legacy. Julien features the British cultural studies scholar Stuart Hall's commentary in voice-over and makes visible London landmarks, such as King's Cross and the Thames riverfront – thereby problematizing not only temporality but also nationality in this meditation on Hughes's significance.

Go Fish initiated a different transition, from the experimental aesthetic of the New Queer Cinema to the more conventional indie romantic comedies that would dominate gay and lesbian cinema for the remainder of the 1990s, such as *Jeffrey* (Christopher Ashley, 1995), *The Incredibly True Adventures of Two Girls in Love* (Maria Maggenti, 1995), *Billy's Hollywood Screen Kiss* (Tommy O'Haver, 1998), and *But I'm a Cheerleader* (Jamie Babbit, 1999). In part, *Go Fish* was celebrated for changing the genre of lesbian romance from drama (and its implicit sense of anxiety or tragedy) to comedy – although, as Maria Pramaggiore suggests, it managed to do so without conforming to rigid heterosexual narrative conventions for crossover address.[12]

Despite its black-and-white film stock and impressionistic montage interludes, *Go Fish* presents a remarkably simple and straightforward story about the formation of a lesbian couple, Max (Guinevere Turner, also cowriter of the film) and Ely (V. S. Brodie). In fact, there are few narrative obstacles to the central romance beyond questionable attraction, and the film's quirky aesthetic is determined by economic restraint as much as it is by intention. Yet even here the style is meaningful: the film grain is almost exaggerated as a mark of youthful independence rather than being lit for elegance as in *Looking for Langston*. This difference in sensibility is reflected in their films' respective visual intertexts: the photographs of George Platt Lynes and Robert Mapplethorpe for Julien versus the experimental videos of Sadie Benning and Cheryl Dunye for Troche.[13]

Even with a slight central story, the film articulates its burden of representation by opening with a women's studies seminar in which the students speculate about historical lesbians. Kia (T. Wendy McMillan), the professor, tells her class in the first scene that "throughout lesbian history there has been a serious lack of evidence that'll tell us what these women's lives were truly about. I mean lesbian lives and lesbian relationships – they barely exist on paper, and it is with that in mind and understanding the power of history that we begin to want to change history." These statements regarding print culture and historical erasure are intercut with the opening credits, suggesting the status as a thesis statement for the film.

Later in the film, upon returning home from their first date, Max and Ely also debate the politics of representations as well as audience desires for validation:

MAX: That movie sucked. Why do queers always have to be so pathetic? I mean, I'm queer, and I'm finding it relatively easy not to hate myself.

I mean, the man is a gay filmmaker. I feel like he has a certain responsibility to represent us in a positive way.

ELY: I don't know. I really liked the film. There were so many beautiful things about it. We expect queer filmmakers to take the responsibility to represent the entire community, and I think that's really a lot to ask anyone.

MAX: I know, but I just don't feel like we can withstand such negative representation from within our own ranks. Do you know what I mean?

ELY: Well, if he hates himself for being gay – I mean a lot of people do. I think we want him to represent everyone, and he's just representing what he sees in the community.

Despite its at times didactic dialogue, the film clearly has a sense of humor about the need for visible and affirming lesbian representations. Lisa Henderson praised the film for capturing "the felt survival value of whimsy, self-irony, and representations of group culture" in its recognizable take on urban lesbian culture during the early 1990s.[14]

Go Fish plays with lesbian stereotype in-jokes for its core audience yet maintains a commitment to inclusive politics: for instance, the film sends up the range of herbal teas at Ely's house, while at the same time conscientiously featuring an interracial cast (although the central couple is white). Importantly, part of the film's pleasure is its winking sex-positivity, including: discussions of pet euphemisms for female genitals (e.g., "honey pot," "love mound") during one of its Greek chorus-style interludes; a running joke about Daria's (Anastasia Sharp) rotating cast of girlfriends; a dinner party at which the host has slept with almost every woman in the room; and the use of nail clipping as foreplay for a tryst between Max and Ely. Even lesbian object-choice is satirized in a fantastical sequence in which Daria is interrogated about her lesbian allegiances after sleeping with a man.

In contrast to the historical fascinations and anachronisms of so much New Queer Cinema, however, this film encapsulates the early to mid-1990s not only because of its baggy fashions and Dr. Martens boots but also because of how its characters express anxiety about perpetuating a 1970s version of stereotypical women's culture or butch/femme role playing. In building an affable movie for a recognizable and increasingly mainstream lesbian culture, this film also inadvertently helped open the door for numerous increasingly bland comedies and coming-of-age films to come.

Millennial Mourning

After these cycles of gay liberationist and queer cinemas produced for the gay and lesbian niche markets, a handful of films have crossed over to mainstream success and acclaim (including numerous Academy Award nominations and wins) at the turn of the 2000s, including the afore-mentioned *Gods and Monsters*, *Boys Don't Cry*, *The Hours*, *Brokeback Mountain*, and *Milk*. Marketed as "prestige" independent films, driven by strong dramatic performances, and mostly written and directed by gay or lesbian filmmakers (*Brokeback* is the notable exception), these films signaled a couple of departures. First, although they were advertised prominently in the gay press, distributors for these films strategically avoided allowing the films to become "ghettoized" as "gay films" by refusing to book them in gay film festivals or by using other traditional strategies for building a specifically niche gay audience. Secondly, and perhaps more importantly, the films themselves reflected a return to narratives in which the central queer character dies by each film's end; yet, reflecting a liberal turn in representations, such characters' deaths were treated as tragedies rather than punishments.[15]

Despite three decades of building gay audiences and, arguably, acceptance, it was widely reported that *Brokeback Mountain*'s distributor, Focus Features, presumed that the movie could not be commercially viable if it only appealed to gay audiences. Rather, the straight female audience was courted as central to its crossover success. Accordingly, the film adaptation of E. Annie Proulx's 1997 short story is remarkably faithful in most respects but develops the female characters and tones down some of the original text's homoeroticism. Made by (the director, screenwriters Larry McMurtry and Diana Ossana, and cast are all straight-identified) and largely for straights, *Brokeback Mountain* was characterized by Robin Wood as "precisely the film about gay men that the general public is ready for and can accept."[16] In a more prickly (but on-point) take on the film, the queer literary and film theorist D. A. Miller remarked, "erotic disappointment may well be the only genuine homosexual response to *Brokeback Mountain* – and hence the only genuine basis for a political critique of the film."[17]

Although *The Boys in the Band* had been considered dated by some audiences by the time of its release, it was ultimately a contemporary film. *Brokeback Mountain*, in contrast, is a period piece (although its pastoral setting suggests an ahistorical feel), beginning in 1963 and extending beyond the gay liberation era into the early 1980s. In other words, it presents another portrait of *The Boys in the Band*'s period, but that portrait is untouched by any awareness of the gay rights movement or gay community beyond the dark alleys of Juarez, Mexico. *Brokeback Mountain* portrays the decades-long love affair between two men who forge a connection while spending a summer working as shepherds deep in the mountains. Ennis (Heath Ledger) is the stoic type, a man who rarely speaks and only mumbles when he does talk. Jack (Jake Gyllenhaal) is the more impulsive of the two. The film's first act offers a pastoral narrative of romance that flowers away from civilization. The second act brings the men back to their "real world" relationships and commitments, including wives and children, prior to the men's reunion. The third act establishes Ennis's refusal to make a life with Jack following his own divorce and the emotional toll of his withdrawal from intimacy. After the long and lush opening, with mountainous skylines, grassy hills, and charming flocks of sheep providing the setting for the men's infatuation, the film has a pervasive tone of sadness – not just Ennis's or Jack's but also their wives' – because none of the characters live the lives they want. Although the film suggests the impossibility of living a gay life in the 1960s and 1970s American West, it is as sympathetic to the women whom they have married out of social convention as it is to the men. (As a crossover film, it is also significant that there is as much female nudity as male nudity and as many heterosexual sex scenes as gay ones.) This is an empathetic and touching film by straight people that suggests that the lives of men who have sex with men are sad.

Formally, *Brokeback Mountain* constructs desire and disclosure through the characters' looks: Jack's desire – and later longing – for Ennis is presented by him gazing at Ennis in the rearview mirror of his truck. Peering through binoculars (represented through an insert point-of-shot), their boss detects their affair from a distance, inferring from their shirtless wrestling that something more unseemly is happening. Ennis's wife, Alma (Michelle Williams), witnesses her husband passionately kiss Jack upon their first reunion, despite Ennis's attempt to hide his actions from view. The film even visualizes Ennis remembering a formative moment from his childhood when his father took him to witness the castration and murder of a local gay man – which was intended as a warning to the young boy; later, Ennis envisions Jack being killed in a hate crime, countering the story of an accident that his wife (Anne Hathaway) offers as an explanation for his death. The only instance among these in which a character actually explains what we see is the flashback to Ennis's traumatic childhood. Everything else in the film is communicated through looks, expressions, gestures, or dialogue that refuses to speak the truth.

Ennis and Jack's reunion, in particular, suggests the spare and efficient ways that narrative information is conveyed without didactic dialogue – and thus the inverse of the verbosity of *The Boys in the Band*. One day, when Ennis arrives home, Alma tells him he's received a postcard from Jack via "general delivery." Ennis looks at the card and sees a brief message, written in a manly cursive scrawl, that Jack is going to be passing through the area. To convey Ennis's excitement, the film quickly cuts to an exterior shot of the local post office and then to Ennis writing a terse message – "You bet!" – on a postcard that he immediately drops into the outgoing mail slot. The film cuts to Ennis looking out his living room window, nervously fidgeting and smoking in excitement. Alma, on the couch, has clearly prettied herself up with a fitted and cheerful dress and even lipstick. It is a subtle touch, one that goes unremarked, but it clearly communicates that this is a special day, that she supports her husband, and that she has no idea that she is about to be eclipsed from Ennis's life.

When Jack's truck pulls up, seen in a point-of-view shot through a window from Ennis's perspective, Ennis rushes down the stairs to greet him. In a quick handheld medium close-up, Ennis not only embraces Jack but rushes him under the stairs to kiss him. Compared to the almost entirely static camera compositions throughout the rest of the film, this one gesture is shot to exude a rush of feeling. Although this moment establishes that Ennis makes the first move, it is shot and edited so that it crosses the 180-degree line, creating a flush of disorientation as the men twist and kiss passionately in tight framing. An insert shot of Alma standing at the front door, closed behind the glass, reveals her sudden discovery and the ways in which she is cut off from Ennis's passion; a point-of-view shot from her perspective, looking down at the men, confirms what she sees and allows us to feel not only the joy of the men's reunion but also her own sudden sense of alienation. This sequence is, narratively and emotionally, at the center of the film, and almost none of its important information is communicated through language but instead through framing and editing.[18]

By the film's final act, Ennis has chosen a self-imposed life of solitude, refusing Jack's dreams of living together but occasionally engaging in weekend trysts with him. Jack has taken to crossing the border to Mexico in search of sexual pick-ups and has begun an affair with a local friend to tide himself over between visits to Ennis.[19] They remain emotionally committed to each other, even though both have made decisions that keep them apart. After Jack's death, Ennis visits Jack's parents' house and discovers the shirts from their first farewell nestled together and hanging in Jack's closet. The film ends with a shot of the two shirts hanging inside Ennis's closet, the door of which is apparently only opened when Ennis is alone. The *closet* here is obviously a metaphor, but it is an effective one.

Revisiting the history of gay cinema and some of its post-liberation literary adaptations both challenges simplistic narratives of progress and reopens the question of who the audiences for these movies should be. Should films reflect the particularities of gay life with queer aesthetics for community-based audiences? Or should the goal be mainstream acceptance and assimilation via crossover appeal? Answers vary depending on the period, the context, and who asks these questions. In the wake of *The Boys in the Band*, gay and lesbian filmmakers produced a number of pornographic, documentary, and experimental films to represent the advances of gay liberation. In the New Queer Cinema of the 1990s and the crossover character studies of the 2000s, gay- and lesbian-identified filmmakers (as well as Lee) have created films that embody a sense of oppositional politics or loss that are suggestive of queer negativity rather than gay affirmation.

NOTES

1 Parker Tyler, *Screening the Sexes: Homosexuality in the Movies* (1973; New York: Da Capo, 1993), xxiii.
2 Vito Russo, *The Celluloid Closet: Homosexuality in the Movies* (1987 revised edition; New York: Quality Paperback Book Club, 1995), xi–xii.
3 Many of the major works of lesbian and gay literature have never been adapted into films, including Radclyffe Hall's *The Well of Loneliness*, Gore Vidal's *The City and the Pillar*, James Baldwin's *Giovanni's Room*, John Rechy's *City of Night*, Rita Mae Brown's *Rubyfruit Jungle*, Andrew Holleran's *Dancer from the Dance*, and Leslie Feinberg's *Stone Butch Blues*.
4 Although this essay focuses on film, it would be misrepresentative to overlook the fact that by the 1990s, television would also become an important venue for adaptations and documentaries, including *The Lost Language of Cranes* (Nigel Finch, 1991), *Tales of the City* (Alastair Reid, 1993), *And the Band Played On* (Roger Spottiswoode, 1993), *Coming Out under Fire* (Arthur Dong, 1994), and *The Celluloid Closet* (Rob Epstein and Jeffrey Friedman, 1995). By the turn of the 2000s, many of the most popular gay representations and narratives – particularly those narrowcasting to queer audiences – were made for television, including *Queer as Folk* (BBC, 1999–2000, Showtime, 2000–2005), *The L Word* (Showtime, 2004–2009), *RuPaul's Drag Race* (LOGO, 2009–present), and *Orange Is the New Black* (Netflix, 2013–present).
5 Russo, *The Celluloid Closet*, 175, 177.
6 Tyler, *Screening the Sexes*, 47.
7 Joe Carrithers, "The Audiences of *The Boys in the Band*," *Journal of Popular Film and Television* 23, no. 2 (1995): 65.
8 On the New Queer Cinema, see Michele Aaron, ed., *New Queer Cinema: A Critical Reader* (New Brunswick: Rutgers University Press, 2004); and B. Ruby Rich, *New Queer Cinema: The Director's Cut* (Durham: Duke University Press, 2013).
9 Such interest in anachronism would later figure in queer theory's interrogations of temporality.
10 Kobena Mercer, "Dark and Lovely, Too: Black Gay Men in Independent Cinema," in *Queer Looks*, ed. Martha Gever, Pratibha Parmar, and John Greyson (New York: Routledge, 1993), 250.
11 Ibid., 251. For a more recent alternative reading of *Looking for Langston*, see David Marriott, *Haunted Life: Visual Culture and Black Modernity* (New Brunswick: Rutgers University Press, 2007), 106-22.
12 Maria Pramaggiore, "Fishing for Girls: Romancing Lesbians in New Queer Cinema," *College Literature* 24, no. 1 (1997): 59–75.

13   Rich, *New Queer Cinema*, 62.

14   Lisa Henderson, "Simple Pleasures: Lesbian Community and *Go Fish*," *Signs* 25, no. 1 (1999): 37.

15   *Gods and Monsters* was adapted from Christopher Bram's 1995 novel *Father of Frankenstein*, and *The Hours* was adapted from Michael Cunningham's 1998 novel. *Boys Don't Cry* and *Milk* were biopics based, respectively, on historical figures: Brandon Teena (1972–1993) and Harvey Milk (1930–1978).

16   Robin Wood, "On and around *Brokeback Mountain*," *Film Quarterly* 60, no. 3 (2007): 28.

17   D. A. Miller, "On the Universality of *Brokeback Mountain*," *Film Quarterly*, 60, no. 3 (2007): 50.

18   Miller likewise pays close attention to the structures of looking and conditions of being under surveillance in the film, and he connects these gazes to the author Proulx's own origin story. See Miller, "On the Universality," 52.

19   For the original audiences of *Boys Don't Cry* and *Brokeback Mountain*, which both take place in the Western United States, the widely reported crucifixion of gay college student Matthew Shepard in Wyoming in the fall of 1998 would have presented a resonant intertext. For geographic readings of *Brokeback*, see Martin F. Manalansan IV, "Colonizing Time and Space: Race and Romance in Brokeback Mountain," *GLQ: A Journal of Lesbian and Gay Studies* 13, no. 1 (2006): 99; and John Howard, "Of Closets and Other Rural Voids," *GLQ: A Journal of Lesbian and Gay Studies* 13, no. 1 (2006): 101.

PART II

Historical Contexts

6

TRAVIS FOSTER

Nineteenth-Century Queer Literature

Because, really, what isn't queer about nineteenth-century American literature?

Take, for example, "The Man Who Thought Himself a Woman" (1857), an anonymously published short story whose protagonist spends seven years secretly "making ... a perfect suit of garments appropriate for [her] sex" and then hangs herself, leaving behind a suicide note regretting that she has "passed so long, falsely, for a man."[1] Or Anna Seward's "Elegy" (1796), which dwells sensually on the beauty of her beloved Honora Sneyd. Or Julia Ward Howe's *The Hermaphrodite* (ca. 1846), whose ambiguously gendered protagonist challenges the very foundations of patriarchal sexual norms, attracting the desires of women and men alike. Or perhaps the stories of Sui Sin Far, such as "The Smuggling of Tie Co" (1900) and "A Chinese Boy-Girl" (1904), which frequently use cross-dressing as a trope to destabilize any seemingly self-evident terms purporting to categorize gender, desire, race, and citizenship. And that does not even include the canon, where we find Charles Brockden Brown locking *Ormond's* (1799) narrator, Sophia Westwyn, in a struggle with Ormond for the affections of Constantia Dudley; Emily Dickinson refiguring female eroticism through the behavior of flowers, birds, and bees; Herman Melville marrying off *Moby-Dick's* (1851) narrator, Ishmael, to the heroic Queequeg; Walt Whitman celebrating the virtues of urban cruising; Louisa May Alcott crafting her beloved Jo as a male-identifying woman whose "heterosexual" desires arise out of shared masculinity; and Sarah Orne Jewett highlighting the remarkable lives of spinsters who fashion lives outside the confines of marriage or, indeed, coupledom of any sort.[2] None of this even gets us to Henry James, the novelist with by far the highest number of hits (fifty-seven and counting) when you perform a keyword search for "queer" in the Modern Language Association's International Bibliography of secondary criticism.

In short, where nineteenth-century American literature is concerned, there is plenty of queerness to go around. This remains true if we take the term "queer" at its most narrow to denote same-sex desire and deviance from those gender roles prescribed by compulsory heterosexuality; and it becomes even more so if we instead follow broader scholarly (and nineteenth-century) uses of the term to indicate that which undermines taken-for-granted social structures and misalignment with the normal (as in Nathaniel Hawthorne's description of *The House of the Seven Gable's* [1851] Holgrave as "queer and questionable").[3] The challenge, then, lies not in locating queer texts written during the nineteenth century but instead in knowing how to interpret or understand those texts. As Jordan Alexander Stein describes the problem: "It's becoming easier (in part because so many more people are looking) to find apparent evidence for queer sex and homoerotic relationships in pre-twentieth-century texts. But it is no easier to determine what exactly this evidence is evidence *of*."[4]

Consider a famous case of delightfully suggestive queer intermingling: the ninety-fourth chapter of *Moby-Dick*, "A Squeeze of the Hand," which describes a group of sailors re-liquefying cooled spermaceti:

> Squeeze! squeeze! squeeze! all the morning long; I squeezed that sperm till I myself almost melted into it; I squeezed that sperm till a strange sort of insanity came over me; and I found myself unwittingly squeezing my co-laborers' hands in it, mistaking their hands for the gentle globules. Such an abounding, affectionate, friendly, loving feeling did this avocation beget; that at last I was continually squeezing their hands, and looking up into their eyes sentimentally; as much as to say, – Oh! my dear fellow beings, why should we longer cherish any social acerbities, or know the slightest ill-humor or envy! Come; let us squeeze hands all round; nay, let us all squeeze ourselves into each other; let us squeeze ourselves universally into the very milk and sperm of kindness.[5]

The critic and novelist Caleb Crain describes first encountering this passage at age twenty and experiencing a pronounced identification with its author. Seeing the chapter as a thinly veiled expression of Melville's homosexual desire, Crain summarizes his initial impression thus: "To me, in my youthful misery, these sentences seemed to convey a secret meaning. They said that people like Melville and me had to accept that we were not going to be happy; we were going to have to settle. The closest we were ever going to come to what we really wanted was a metaphor."[6] Crain's Melville is, if not gay himself, then at least closeted, and the scene's erotic pleasures cover thwarted realities and offer, at best, a literary inheritance that retroactively fashions the paradox of shared isolation. Other critics interpret the scene in ways that leave virtually no breathing room for such a cross-century identification or, indeed, for one another. In their hands, the scene represents not tragedy but "a comically anarchic sensuality"; not gay yearning but "a vision of sexual pleasure ... without sex," which "cannot be said, strictly speaking, to be homosexual or modern in any way"; and not sexual but instead merely social, "a moment of fraternal community."[7] These competing interpretations, selected from dozens, underscore the trickiness that contemporary readers face when attempting to apprehend queer representations from more than a hundred years ago. Yet they simultaneously underscore precisely what is queer about *Moby-Dick*, pointing us toward queerness as an object of study and analysis that resists being pinned down or wedged into any one framework or conclusion.

All of this foregrounds what this chapter will not do, what it cannot do: adjudicate between interpretations, stifle the present's myriad and ever-shifting investments in the past, or distill the vast corpus of pre-1900 queer American literature into a neatly chronological survey. Instead, I provide some tools for the reader's own interpretive work by suggesting two historical axes – sexology and race – along which queer representations might be positioned. I begin with sexological knowledge, which, for the most part, succeeded in coalescing the dispersed erotic life of the nineteenth century into the identities, such as gay and straight, that many now take for granted. I then shift to the related axis of race, examining how literary representations of queerness take shape, implicitly and explicitly, in tandem with the histories of racialization, racism, imperialism, settler colonialism, and white supremacy.

Sexological Knowledge

It has become a familiar story: as the nineteenth century unfolded, the very nature of sex shifted. Sex was enthusiastically taken up as an object of study and entered the realm of science, where psychologists, psychiatrists, and doctors promised to decode entire populations according to whom or what they desired. Michel Foucault's now famous term, *scientia sexualis*, emerged, tasking itself with the bold discovery of new perversions and the rigorous categorization of new sexual types, in the process launching what we now know as sexual modernity and what we now recognize as specific sexual subjects.[8] No longer a set of desires and acts – some sanctioned, many labeled sinful – sex became a key marker of being and a core component of self-definition.

We cannot pinpoint exactly when or how this transition began or even if it ever entirely ended (certainly, previous models have yet to be completely supplanted), but we can identify certain moments during the late nineteenth century when its pace quickened.[9] One such moment occurred with the popularity of Richard von Krafft-Ebing's *Psychopathia Sexualis, with Especial Reference to Contrary Sexual Instinct: A Medico-Legal Study*, first published in German in 1886 and then translated into English in 1892. In his study, which was quickly followed by others in a similar vein, Krafft-Ebing coupled sexual acts with deeply ingrained identity categories – for instance, linking sex between men to sexual inversion, which he defined as an all-encompassing mismatch between the sex of one's body and the sex of one's very soul. Another moment occurred in 1892, after a middle-class white woman slashed the throat of her female lover in downtown Memphis, Tennessee, staging an exceptional public event that became the international focus of not merely journalists but also medical and scientific professionals. And another occurred just three years later with the transatlantic sensation of the Oscar Wilde trials, which presented Wilde less as a transgressing individual than as a very specific type of person, complete with a deeply seated thing that we now call sexuality explaining nearly all of his behavior.[10] Taken together, these events and others propelled a medical-psychological model of homosexuality into transatlantic consciousness, providing queer writers with ample material to work with – and, of course, against.

By the end of the nineteenth century, therefore, it is difficult to imagine many writers who did not have some consciousness of emergent sexual types. Sarah Orne Jewett, for instance, seems to resist the rise of this new configuration of sex when she presents the heroine of her 1884 Bildungsroman, *A Country Doctor*, against sexological notions of the self. As the novel's narrator puts it, Nan Prince belongs to a "class of women who are a result of natural progression and variation," formed as much by exposure to her surroundings as she is by intrinsic (or, to use a term favored by Krafft-Ebing, "congenital") forces.[11] Hence, once Nan has grown to adulthood, she finds herself "more than ever before surprised to see the connection of one thing with another, and how some slight acts had been the planting of seeds which had grown and flourished long afterward" – suggesting a multitude of possible outcomes arising from an impossible-to-predict complexity of "slight acts" (232). In this sense, the narrator's "class of women" does not correspond to a static, transhistorical identity type but instead emerges within an evolutionary logic in which difference produces variation rather than reproducing itself.

Alternately, in his *Autobiography of an Androgyne*, which was begun during the late nineteenth century but not published until 1919, Ralph Werther wholeheartedly embraces sexological vocabulary and invokes a sexological explanation for his homosexuality, even to the point where he presents his own story as a case study in which one specific individual becomes the basis for an entire group's characteristics. He writes, for instance, "I have been doomed to be a girl who must pass her earthly existence in a male body," thereby embracing the notion of homosexuality as gender inversion, and he provides section titles, such as "Typical Temptation of Inverts," that seem to have been pulled from a scientific text rather than an autobiography.[12] Whereas Jewett places her heroine in a model of subject formation that refuses to collapse differences into identities, Werther values a model that articulates affinities and deep identifications between himself and his fellow inverts.

Literary representations under the sway of sexology or even modern lesbian and gay identity categories sometimes seem to contract knowingly on the specificity of their characters, labeling them as just this or that sort of person, but presexological representations frequently dilate under even the slightest critical pressure, expanding to create room for an ever-increasing range of possibilities and lending themselves to what we might call a refreshing unknowingness.[13] This is what Peter Coviello stresses when he reminds us "that the appearance of what we might want to call queer identity, or modern homosexual identity, was not a fate fixed in the stars, and was not the target toward which all emergences were speeding, arrow-like, across the century" – and that, in fact, "presexology writers ... might in fact know things we do not, or that we have over the course of time lost the ability to see clearly."[14] Thus, although presexological representations can suggest appealing and valuable back stories for modern-day queerness, they also invite us to dispense as best we can with our assumptions about what any given representation might mean or imply – to entertain alternate ways of being sexual and alternate ways of organizing sexual difference.

To explore these interpretive problems, I consider, at some length, the competing ways in which we might position a single text vis-à-vis the emergence of modern sexual categories: Rose Terry Cooke's remarkable and surprisingly underread ghost story, "My Visitation," published in *Harper's New Monthly Magazine* in July 1858. The story follows an unnamed first-person narrator who is orphaned at age fifteen and sent to live with her guardian. After a year, Eleanor Wyse, the guardian's beautifully statuesque cousin, comes to live in the home, and within a month of Eleanor's arrival, the narrator has fallen "passionately in love." "I speak advisedly in the use of that term," she hastens. "[N]o other phrase expresses the blind, irrational, all-enduring devotion I gave to her; no less vivid word belongs to that madness."[15] A relationship between the two girls soon transpires, although it is always on Eleanor's terms and is thus fraught with unequal distributions of emotion and expression. At the very least, we learn, Eleanor finds in the narrator's blind adoration and "constant yearnings" a "receptivity that suited her" (30, 28). This state of affairs continues, with brief interruptions because of distance, for roughly eight years before coming to no fewer than three separate ends: first, when Eleanor confesses to an unnamed yet apparently cruel deception (more on this narrative gap in the next section); second, when Eleanor marries and moves west; and third, when she dies. In the months after her death, "*It*" – that is, Eleanor's ghost – begins visiting the narrator: "*It* was there beside me! – unseen, unheard, but felt in the secretest recesses of life and consciousness" (37). This haunting, which most frequently occurs at night and accompanies a series of distinctly erotic touches, continues until Christmas morning, when the ghost identifies herself and asks forgiveness. Ultimately, these visits enable the narrator to reconcile her love for her new male suitor and fiancé, Herman, and her still intense feelings for her deceased lover: "Herman and Eleanor both loved me – I had forgiven; I was forgiven" (42).

We have ample evidence to read this story as a lesbian narrative, one that anticipates the twentieth century's translation of sexology, with its clinical approach, into the pathological representation of lesbianism as either an immature girl's rehearsal for heterosexual adulthood or an abject lover's tragic desire, doomed to unrequited heartbreak. Hence, Kristin Comment argues that the story fictionalizes warnings against female masturbation and the female attachments found in mid-century guidebooks, ultimately "foreshadowing ... the clinical pathologization of lesbianism."[16] In this sense, the ghost stands in for a durable social order that perseveres stubbornly into the present. Take the narrator's description of one visitation, the closest the story comes to describing an erotic encounter between the two girls or, at least, between the narrator and Eleanor's ghost:

> At first I felt only a sense of alien life in a room otherwise solitary; then a breath of air, air from some other sphere than this, penetrative, dark, chilling; then a sound, not of voice, or pulse, but of motion in some inanimate thing, the motion of contact; then came a touch, the gentlest, faintest approach of lips and fingers, I knew not which, to my brow; and last, a growing, gathering, flickering into sight.

(38)

The narrator's hesitation here, in which the faint "sense of alien life" builds gradually into the indeterminate "approach of lips and fingers," bespeaks a desire that fears itself; she is timid or even terrified to embrace the "penetrative, dark, chilling" force for which she so desperately longs. In this sense, the description suggests a scene of masturbation in which a fantasy of sex with Eleanor gathers and flickers just at the edge of consciousness as a doomed possibility the narrator can only barely allow herself to entertain. Such a reading invites us to group the two girls in "My Visitation" within what Heather Love terms the "wicked sisterhood" of "perverse schoolgirls, vampires, and poetesses" that looms in the "genealogy of the modern lesbian," who typically meet with tragic ends and whose presence, like that of a ghost, continues to make itself felt in contemporary representations of lesbian desire, such as David Lynch's *Mulholland Drive* (2001).[17]

Alternately, in a related reading, we might focus on the genre of the ghost story as a remarkably prescient choice on Cooke's part, the perfect vehicle for identifying a pattern in which, to cite Judith Roof's influential paradigm, lesbianism appears time and again as a "representational impossibility" – which is to say that even after lesbianism was created as a meaningful sexual category, it nevertheless lacked the terms through which to appear in ways that do not flicker in and out of sight.[18] "Why is it so difficult to see the lesbian – even when she is there, quite plainly in front of us?," Terry Castle asks before then answering, "In part because she has been 'ghosted' – or made to seem invisible – by culture itself."[19] Perhaps, we can reasonably speculate, Cooke is making a similar point. In this case, the ghostliness of pleasure-inducing lips and fingers stems not from failed masturbatory fantasy but from thwarted potential, or interruption by a social order that at best defers the narrator's desire until another time and place. Hence, Ralph Poole's argument that the ghost here prophesizes "future fulfillment."[20] Both of these readings depend on a method that begins with the present and works backward to the terms of Cooke's story – one that, put differently, reads sexual modernity into its just barely pre-modern past. The value of the readings, to return to Heather Love's term, lies in the construction of a genealogy that can make visible the ways in which past remnants continue to impact how we conceive of homosexuality and how we represent contemporary lesbian and gay experience.

However, we might instead take as our starting point not the modern lesbian but the precise terms Cooke uses when representing her heroine's experience, thereby following the inductive method "for interpreting sexuality before 'homosexuality'" suggested by Jordan Alexander Stein in which we begin with the evidence on the page and then move outward to our categories of analysis.[21] In this vein, I return to the passage cited earlier in this section and its scene of ghostly visitation. At its most literal, Cooke uses this passage to describe the sensory (and sensual) aspects of her narrator's encounter with an otherworldly and ephemeral presence, "a sense of alien life in a room otherwise solitary." Yet in so doing, she also seems to be working against a model of sexuality based solely on the object of one's core desires. The narrator finds herself immersed in an eroticism that externalizes desire, in which stimulation arises from the frictions and vibrations caused by contact between herself, an ephemeral "breath of air" from another realm, and the seemingly paradoxical liveliness of the material world ("motion in some inanimate thing"). Take, as one small example of the scene's charge, the striking repetition of "air," separated by only a comma ("air, air"), as though, given the right conditions, even air has the ability to rub against itself, initiating vibrations that impact the narrator's pleasure and fright. At its broadest, then, the scene imagines a sexuality that is more likely to define settings than people, particularly settings that enable the rubbing together of things and realms – human and inhuman, animate and inanimate, material and immaterial, secular and spiritual. It is true that we later learn "*It*" is also Eleanor, so the scene's eroticism includes something like homosexuality, the desire of one female for another; yet homosexuality alone cannot begin to account for the full range of the scene's desires and experiences.

Indeed, one of the striking things about these pre-sexological representations is how inadequate something like *sexuality* becomes in any reckoning with the vocabularies and grammars that are used when describing erotic experience. In Cooke's case, for instance, we may require a religious account as well – specifically one that turns to Spiritualism, a movement involving communication and contact with spirits of the dead that was popular in the United States from the 1840s to the 1920s. Such an association becomes particularly apt if we note that the story itself seems to invoke Spiritualist channeling when it directs its final two sentences not to the reader but to "thee, Eleanor" (42). Whereas our modern, post-sexological categories of sexual definition tend to privatize eroticism and desire as a kind of property belonging to individual subjects, Spiritualism had a very different impulse. As Molly McGarry argues, "crossing the boundary of life itself worked to unsettle a whole series of earthly boundaries," particularly those between "religion, politics, sexuality, gender, and less easily named modes of existence."[22] In this sense, we might see "My Visitation" less as a lesbian narrative anticipating medicalized demarcations of sexual desire than as a narrative striving to align spiritual embodiment with sexual experience in a way that renders both roomier and better primed to accommodate multiple forms of deviance.

Sex and Race

If sexology constitutes an obvious axis along and against which to place nineteenth-century queer texts, a second axis, racialization, remains still too frequently ignored – an omission that becomes particularly vexing when we consider the degree to which the epistemologies of race and sex interacted in nineteenth-century America. Racialization, which refers to the historical production of racial identities and to the ways that certain characteristics become attached to racially marked bodies, presaged the categorization of sexual behaviors, even as queerness became a potent stigma for reifying racial hierarchies. Yet these interconnections do not mean we can rest on any easy analogies between racial and sexual histories; nor, as we shall see, do they mean that white queerness always misaligns with white supremacy. Here then, I trace a series of uneven, sometimes contradictory, processes through which race and sex interacted in queer texts.

In *Queering the Color Line*, Siobhan Somerville tracks a history in which mid-nineteenth-century scientific racism, with its insistence on document-ing and specifying racially distinct kinds of people, helped clear a path for *scientia sexualis*, with its insistence on documenting and specifying sexually distinct kinds of people. Moreover, scientific racism's obsession with the mixed-race figure and the "unnaturalness" of interracial sex became a useful analogy for the later interest in the invert and the pathology of homosexual sex.[23] As Somerville argues, this conflation between the mulatto, to use the era's common terminology, and the invert emerges perhaps most clearly in the fiction of Pauline Hopkins, particularly in *Contending Forces* (1900) and *Winona* (1902–1903).[24] For instance, when the mulatta heroine, Winona, cross-dresses as Allen Pinks and becomes "the prettiest specimen of boy-hood," Hopkins registers the conflation of anxieties surrounding both male and female homosexuality as well as mixed-race identity.[25] Indeed, we might return to "My Visitation," where one possibility for the content of Eleanor's discovered deception is that she initially hid her own mixed-race identity. Although the evidence for this is inconclusive, it is also far from absent. The text describes Eleanor with tropes that are conventionally used for the tragic mulatta, noting her "long, melancholy eye, with curved, inky lashes," the contrast between her "scarlet lips" and "tiny pearl-grains of teeth," and her "soft, oval cheeks, colorless but not pale, opaque and smooth, betraying Southern blood" (26). We also know that racial passing constituted a keen interest for Rose Terry Cooke, who explores it more explicitly in her short story "A Hard Lesson." When read as a story about homosexual and interra-cial desire, "My Visitation" reveals the mixed or ambiguously raced person as not only an object of cultural anxiety but also an object of intense erotic interest and fascination.

For at least some queer white men, indigenous peoples, both inside and outside the U.S. territorial border, constituted just such an ambig-uously racialized source of erotic fascination that was at once a lur-ing source of homosexual possibility and a threat to be contained. James Fenimore Cooper's *Leatherstocking Tales* (1823–1841), for instance, fre-quently register Natty Bumppo's attraction toward the body and manners of Chingachgook, whom the texts represent as being at once immensely appealing and barbaric. In a somewhat different vein, Melville's South Sea novels *Typee* (1846) and *Omoo* (1847) both, as Caleb Crain argues, figure cannibalism as a stand-in for same-sex desire, which perhaps explains why they seem likely to have been read in late-century homosexual underworlds and found readership among British sexologists, including Havelock Ellis, whom historians credit with the first use of the word "homosexual" in English.[26] Likewise, Gregory Tomso argues that Charles Warren Stoddard's Pacific travel narrative *The Lepers of Molokai* (1885) turns to indigeneity as a site of homosexual potential by figuring native Hawaiians, with their perceived racial difference, as uniquely susceptible to homosexuality and leprosy. In the narrative, Tomso writes, Stoddard "presents leprosy as a spectacle of the flesh that is at once horrifying and erotic, at once forbidding in its evocation of fears of national and racial pollution and alluring in its suggestion of intimate contact with supposedly hypervirile Hawaiian natives."[27] The narrative, that is, renders disease and homosexuality as twinned contagions that, regardless of their Orientalist appeals for Stoddard, threatened the sanctity of national whiteness.[28]

As the century unfolded, this whiteness – or, more precisely, the family-making white couple through which whiteness reproduced itself – increasingly came to occupy an unquestioned norm against which racial and sexual others were measured. Hence, for instance, the turn to heterosexuality in the wake of the Civil War, when writers sought to reconcile the white North with the white South through romance reunion narratives and the marriages and intersectional progeny they featured.[29] Such a tightening around both race and sex of just what counts as normal corresponded to an expansion of what counts as deviant, and this requires us to consider the possibility that we might find queerness in the places we are least likely to go looking, including ostensibly heterosexual relationships that somehow stand apart from privatized, nuclear arrangements. As Cathy J. Cohen writes, "a simple dichotomy between those deemed queer and those deemed heterosexual" lacks the critical subtlety to analyze nonnormative experience.[30] Breaking from this "simple dichotomy" allows us to begin seeing the ambivalence toward queerness that marks so many nineteenth-century queer texts, which vacillate between imagining alternatives to hetero-familial paths, on the one hand, and at least partially embracing those paths, on the other hand. For Mark Rifkin, the essays and short stories of the Dakota writer Zitkala-Ša manifest exactly this tension. Zitkala-Ša's writings clearly resist governmental efforts to use Indian education to position "real and stable love, home, and family" at the center of Indian life, "instead connecting romance to the maintenance of indigenous collective identity and forms of self-determination"; yet they simultaneously disavow "social identities and practices that might be taken by white readers as sexually *non*normative."[31] For Rifkin, this knotty complexity suggests that we need to consider the "layered quality" of nonnormative representations, perhaps particularly those by writers of color, as well as the different ways in which writers, readers, and characters experience their distance from the family-making white couple.[32]

Such a "layered quality" emerges as well in texts where homosexuality allies itself with white supremacy. A rather blunt example occurs in Leonora Sansay's 1808 epistolary novel *Secret History; Or, The Horrors of St. Domingo*, which takes the form of letters primarily written by Mary, a white American woman who witnesses firsthand what would come to be known as the Haitian Revolution. At one point, Mary wishes that "the negroes" could again be "reduced to order," so that she might "be fanned to sleep by the silent slaves, or have [her] feet tickled into extacy [sic] by the soft hand of a female attendant."[33] Sansay represents what Aliyyah Abdur-Rahman terms "the linkage of sexual abuse, homoeroticism, and racial dominance" under slavery, a linkage that Harriet Jacobs also explores in *Incidents in the Life of a Slave Girl* (1861), which represents the continued sexual exploitation of a slave, Luke, by his master.[34] Frederic Loring's Civil War novel *Two College Friends* (1871) represents a related connection between homoeroticism and racial dominance by aligning white homosexual romance with racially exclusive nationalism. Although the romantic ties between Ned and the breathtakingly beautiful Tom are cut short with Ned's honorable death, the novel circulates its accumulated passions of homosexuality as a way of compensating for the potential flatness of more large-scale affective attachments, such as those between citizens. The novel's penultimate sentence underscores the point, beginning with "These friends, these brothers," a phrase in which the second half corrects the first by redirecting the intimacy of "friends" toward the fraternity of "brothers."[35] In this way, the novel participated in a larger culture of nationalist sentiment, including the romance reunion narratives that were popular through the end of Reconstruction and the rise of Jim Crow segregation.[36] In his analysis of white supremacist literature, Mason Stokes provides one plausible explanation for why white supremacy, even as it idealized and incorporated the heterosexual couple, may have needed a homosocial, even homoerotic collaborator; he argues that heterosexuality in a racially diverse society always comes with the threat of miscegenation. In a system where the biological reproduction of whiteness "risk[s] contamination," homosexuality might comprise "the only structure of desire that can keep whiteness white."[37]

Taken together, these patterns of race and sex underscore the difficulty of disentangling racialization from the history of sexuality or of predetermining the nature of their relationship. Moreover, similar arguments could be made that this conclusion characterizes not only sex and race but also sex

and religion, sex and region, sex and nation, sex and freedom, sex and terror, sex and sovereignty, sex and democracy, and sex and reform – a list that
only barely gets us started. Knowing this, our readings into the queer past
become an open engagement with a broad, unexpected world, leaving us, to
return to Sarah Orne Jewett's apt phrase, "more than ever before surprised."

NOTES

1 "The Man Who Thought Himself a Woman," *The Knickerbocker* (Dec. 1857): 609.
2 For good places to begin research on these canonical depictions of queerness, see, respectively, H. Jordan Landry, "Animal/Insectual/Lesbian Sex: Dickinson's Queer Version of the Birds and the Bees," *The Emily Dickinson Journal* 9, no. 2 (2000): 42–54; Leo Bersani, "Incomparable America," in *The Culture of Redemption* (Cambridge, MA: Harvard University Press, 1990), 136–154; Kathryn R. Kent, *Making Girls into Women: American Women's Writing and the Rise of Lesbian Identity* (Durham: Duke University Press, 2003), 43–104; and Heather Love, "Gyn/Apology: Sarah Orne Jewett's Spinster Aesthetics" *ESQ: A Journal of the American Renaissance* 55, no. 3-4 (2009): 305–334.
3 Nathaniel Hawthorne, *The House of the Seven Gables* (New York: Penguin, 1986), 154. When citing these two versions of queerness, scholars frequently claim that the latter, more general definition at least includes the former, which pertains more specifically to homosexuality. One thing the nineteenth century has to teach us, however, is that it is also possible to identify moments of clear separation when homosexuality aligns itself comfortably with everyday normalcy.
4 Jordan Alexander Stein, "*The Blithedale Romance*'s Queer Style," *ESQ: A Journal of the American Renaissance* 55, no. 3–4 (2009): 214.
5 Herman Melville, *Moby-Dick; Or, The Whale*, in *The Writings of Herman Melville*, ed. Harrison Hayford, Hershel Parker, and G. Thomas Tanselle (Chicago: Northwestern University Press, 1988), 6:416.
6 Caleb Crain, "Melville's Secrets," *Leviathan* 14, no. 3 (2012): 6.
7 Leo Bersani, *The Culture of Redemption* (Cambridge, MA: Harvard University Press, 1990), 145; Cesare Casarino, *Modernity at Sea: Melville, Marx, Conrad in Crisis* (Minneapolis: University of Minnesota Press, 2002), 175; Elizabeth Barnes, *Love's Whipping Boy: Violence and Sentimentality in the American Imagination* (Chapel Hill: University of North Carolina Press, 2011), 78.
8 Michel Foucault, *The History of Sexuality*, vol. 1, *An Introduction*, trans. Robert Hurley (New York: Vintage, 1990), 53–73.
9 Here I refer to events that popularized and propagated sexual categorization schemes. Historians of sexuality also point to previous significant events in the history of sexology, including Heinrich Kaan's publication of an earlier *Psychopathia Sexualis* in 1844; Karl Heinrich Ulrichs's use of *Urning*, a term roughly synonymous with "invert," in 1862; and Karl Maria Kertbeny's use of the term "homosexual" in 1868.
10 Useful places to begin research on key sexological texts, the Wilde trials, and the "girl lovers" murder trial include, respectively, Lucy Bland and Laura Doan, eds., *Sexology in Culture: Labeling Bodies and Desires* (Chicago: University of

Chicago Press, 1999); Ed Cohen, *Talk on the Wilde Side* (New York: Routledge, 1992); and Lisa Duggan, *Sapphic Slashers: Sex, Violence, and American Modernity* (Durham: Duke University Press, 2000).

11 Sarah Orne Jewett, *A Country Doctor* (New York: Penguin, 2005), 223. See also Josephine Donovan, "Nan Prince and the Golden Apples," *Colby Library Quarterly* 22, no. 1 (1986): 17–27.

12 Ralph Werther, *Autobiography of an Androgyne* (New York: Rutgers University Press, 2008), 45, 55. For sexology's influence on Werther, see Scott Herring's introduction, especially xviii–xxiv.

13 I have in mind here Scott Herring's useful phrase "sexual unknowing" in *Queering the Underworld: Slumming, Literature, and the Undoing of Lesbian and Gay History* (Chicago: University of Chicago Press, 2007), 60.

14 Peter Coviello, *Tomorrow's Parties: Sex and the Untimely in Nineteenth-Century America* (New York: New York University Press, 2013), 16, 42.

15 Rose Terry Cooke, "My Visitation," in *Two Friends and other Nineteenth-Century Lesbian Stories by American Women Writers*, ed. Susan Koppelman (New York: Meredian, 1994), 26; hereafter cited in text.

16 Kristin M. Comment, "'When It Ceases to Be Silly It Becomes Actually Wrong': The Cultural Contexts of Female Homoerotic Desire in Rose Terry Cooke's 'My Visitation,'" *Legacy* 26, no. 1 (2009): 26–47. In a similar vein, Elizabeth Ammons reads the story as a journey wherein the narrator's fulfilled same-sex desire is repressed, forcing her to become monstrous to herself and ultimately leading her into madness. Elizabeth Ammons, introduction to *"How Celie Changed Her Mind" and Selected Stories*, by Rose Terry Cooke (New Brunswick: Rutgers University Press, 1986), ix–xxxviii.

17 Heather Love, "Spectacular Failure: The Figure of the Lesbian in *Mulholland Drive*," *New Literary History* 35, no. 1 (2004): 121.

18 Judith Roof, "The Match in the Crocus: Representations of Lesbian Sexuality," in *Discontented Discourses: Feminism, Textual Intervention, and Psychoanalysis*, ed. Marleen S. Barr and Richard Feldstein (Urbana: University of Illinois Press, 1989), 103.

19 Terry Castle, *The Apparitional Lesbian: Female Homosexuality and Modern Culture* (New York: Columbia University Press, 1993), 4.

20 Ralph J. Poole, "Body Rituals: The (Homo)Erotics of Death in Elizabeth Stuart Phelps, Rose Terry Cooke, and Edgar Allan Poe," in *Soft Canons: American Women Writers and Masculine Tradition*, ed. Karen L. Kilcup (Iowa City: University of Iowa Press, 1999), 257.

21 Stein, "*The Blithedale Romance*'s Queer Style," 214. In a related argument, Dana Luciano suggests that historians of sexuality ought to "understand the category of 'sex' as speculative rather than given." Dana Luciano, *Arranging Grief: Sacred Time and the Body in Nineteenth-Century America* (New York: New York University Press, 2007), 11.

22 Molly McGarry, *Ghosts of Futures Past: Spiritualism and the Cultural Politics of Nineteenth-Century America* (Berkeley: University of California Press, 2008), 159–160.

23 Siobhan B. Somerville, *Queering the Color Line: Race and the Invention of Homosexuality in American Culture* (Durham: Duke University Press, 2000), 15–38.

24 Ibid., 77–110.
25 Pauline Hopkins, *Winona: A Tale of Negro Life in the South and Southwest*, in *The Magazine Novels of Pauline Hopkins* (New York: Oxford University Press, 1988), 388.
26 See Caleb Crain, "Lovers of Human Flesh: Homosexuality and Cannibalism in Melville's Novels," *American Literature* 66, no. 1 (1994): 25–53; George Chauncey, *Gay New York: Gender, Urban Culture, and the Making of the Gay Male World, 1890–1940* (New York: Basic Books, 1994), 284; and Jordan Alexander Stein, "American Literary History and Queer Temporalities," *American Literary History* 25, no. 5 (2013): 862–863.
27 Gregory Tomso, "The Queer History of Leprosy and Same-Sex Love," *American Literary History* 14, no. 4 (2002): 747.
28 For a related account of the interaction between heterosexuality and colonialism, see Ann Laura Stoler, *Race and the Education of Desire: Foucault's History of Sexuality and the Colonial Order of Things* (Durham: Duke University Press, 1995).
29 See Nina Silber, *The Romance of Reunion: Northerners and the South, 1865–1900* (Chapel Hill: University of North Carolina Press, 1997).
30 Cathy J. Cohen, "Punks, Bulldaggers, and Welfare Queens: The Radical Potential of Queer Politics," *GLQ: A Journal of Lesbian and Gay Studies* 3, no. 4 (1997): 440.
31 Mark Rifkin, "Romancing Kinship: A Queer Reading of Indian Education and Zitkala-Ša's *American Indian Stories*," *GLQ: A Journal of Lesbian and Gay Studies* 12, no. 1 (2006): 29–30.
32 Ibid., 48.
33 Leonora Sansay, *Secret History; Or, The Horrors of St. Domingo and Laura* (New York: Broadview Press, 2007), 73.
34 Aliyyah I. Abdur-Rahman, "'The Strangest Freaks of Despotism': Queer Sexuality in Antebellum African American Slave Narratives," *African American Review* 40, no. 2 (2006): 231.
35 Frederick Loring, *Two College Friends* (Boston: Loring, 1871), 161.
36 See Travis M. Foster, "Campus Novels and the Nation of Peers," *American Literary History* 26, no. 3 (2014): 462–483.
37 Mason Stokes, *The Color of Sex: Whiteness, Heterosexuality, and the Fictions of White Supremacy* (Durham: Duke University Press, 2001), 18.

7

DANIELA CASELLI

Literary and Sexual Experimentalism in the Interwar Years

In her classic *Epistemology of the Closet*, Eve Kosofsky Sedgwick asks, tongue firmly in cheek:

> Has there ever been a gay Socrates?
> Has there ever been a gay Shakespeare?
> Has there ever been a gay Proust?
> [...] A short answer, and a very incomplete one, might be that not only have there been a gay Socrates, Shakespeare and Proust but that their names are Socrates, Shakespeare and Proust.[1]

A very incomplete list of experimental American authors in the decades between the two World Wars (1918–1939) who have been discussed in relation to LGBT identities might include: Djuna Barnes, Natalie Clifford Barney, Willa Cather, Countee Cullen, Floyd Dell, H.D., Janet Flanner, Charles Henri Ford, Langston Hughes, Robert McAlmon, Claude McKay, Richard Bruce Nugent, Gertrude Stein, Edna St. Vincent Millay, Wallace Thurman, Parker Tyler, and Carl Van Vechten.

We know by heart the resentful objections to compiling such lists. In the case of American literature produced in the period under consideration, the argument has often been: either "same-sex genital relations may have been perfectly common during the period under discussion" – hence, "they must have been completely meaningless"; or, if we follow a less historically informed but even more popular line, "attitudes towards homosexuality were intolerant back then, unlike now – so people probably didn't do anything."[2] There are often variations on these protestations, such as questions about the roles played by T. S. Eliot and Ezra Pound, who by virtue of their absence relegate our list back to its marginal position and whose heterosexuality has only occasionally received discussion.[3] However, the most insidious argument that seems to be raising its head again in the post-gay twenty-first century is the one that states, again in Sedgwick's formulation, that "the author or the author's important attachments may very well have been homosexual – but it would be provincial to let so insignificant a fact make any difference at all to our understanding of any serious project of life, writing, or thought."[4] After all, *A New Literary History of America*, for all its protestations of liberal inclusion of contrasting and yet dialoguing voice, produces only a resounding LGBT silence. Rather than "made in America," in this new literary history, LGBT firmly belongs to "another country."[5]

But even though it is hard to find "a framework in which to ask about the origins or development of individual gay identity that is not already structured by an implicit, trans-individual Western project or fantasy of eradicating that identity," this chapter, in looking at the relationship between experimentalism and same-sex desire, does not redress the censoring of certain authors' sexual identity by expanding a list.[6] It looks instead at a few select texts that reflect to the reader her own desire for queer history as a problem of legibility. This is, of course, also a problem of historical contextualization, because a number of the authors in the list at the beginning of the chapter vehemently refused such identifications. More importantly, during the past two decades, cultural historians have compellingly argued that in the period under consideration, the disjunction between same-sex desire and identity (and, as Terry Castle reminds us, these two terms are far from self-evident) is to be thought of not principally in terms of repression or self-censoring but rather as one of the very markers of modernity's understanding of sexuality.[7]

One way to keep alive an LGBT American canon (an institution that is perhaps still more precarious than we may be prepared to admit) is to question its foundational ideologies through texts that were never comfortably assimilated by either the straight or the LGBT tradition. The works of Nugent, Ford and Tyler, and Barnes were written between 1926 and 1936; although Barnes was regarded as a major modernist author until World War II and then forgotten until the 1990s, the other authors gained some queer literary visibility only in the 1990s (even though Tyler and Ford had already made careers for themselves in film and art criticism, respectively).[8] Michael Cobb has pointed out that Nugent's "Smoke, Lilies and Jade" (1926) was mysteriously left out from the reprinting of *Fire!! A Quarterly Devoted to Younger Negro Artists* in the *Norton Anthology of African American Literature*.[9] Ford and Tyler's *The Young and Evil*, a novel that merrily transgresses the line that precariously divides literary eroticism from obscenity, was tellingly published in Paris in 1933 by Obelisk Press and remained out of print for three decades, even though it enjoyed the unfailing support of Stein and Barnes. And although Barnes would almost certainly have hated the idea of being discussed in a *Companion to American Gay and Lesbian Literature*, her *Nightwood* (1936) is not even mentioned in *A New Literary*

History of America, which unwittingly reinforces her position as "the most famous unknown of the century."[10]

These texts entertain a complex relationship with legibility that confines them to the margins of mainstream literary history. Unsurprisingly, they are exhilaratingly contrary and politically unviable; after Barnes, we can say that their work "did not fall into oblivion, it was predestined to it from the outset."[11] What they and other texts show us, however, is the peculiar, even curious, problem of sexual legibility and linguistic experimentalism in America between the wars.

"Ain't Nobody's Business What I Do"

In a 1983 interview, Richard Bruce Nugent looked back to his Harlem of the mid-twenties and claimed:

> I have never been in what they call "the closet." It has *never* occurred to me that it was anything to be ashamed of, and it never occurred to me that it was anybody's business but mine. You know that good old Negro song: "Ain't Nobody's Business What I Do"? And the times were very different then. Everybody did whatever they wanted to do. And who cared? There was a great admixture – the mixture of blacks and whites during that particular two or three years. Whites making p-i-l-g-r-i-m-a-g-e-s to black Harlem, *doing* the cabarets or Clinton Moore's private parties, whites being able to mingle freely in every way, including sexual, with blacks. Blacks suddenly having the freedom to have white sex partners ... Blacks very sought-after for everything, from cabarets to *everything*. And my particular shtick was that I liked men.[12]

Best known for his prose fragment "Smoke, Lilies and Jade," which appeared in the first and only issue of *Fire!!*, Nugent was at the center of the ironically self-defined group of "Niggeratti" that in 1926 gave voice to one of the most explosive and controversial expressions of dissatisfaction with the progressive politics of Harlem intellectuals such as Alain Locke and W. E. B. Du Bois. Throughout his life, Nugent wrote, painted, illustrated, acted on Broadway, taught ballet, and was involved in gay rights activism; in the seventies and eighties he became a key source for cultural historians of Harlem (he died in 1987) and was invested by literary scholars with the title of the first openly gay writer of the Harlem Renaissance.[13]

In a 1933 letter to Ezra Pound, Tyler wrote that *The Young and Evil* would not "contribut[e] anything to textbook knowledge of homosexuality." For Tyler, "homo information is not homo rendition; there is plenty of homo information unaided by poetic insight but psychologically psychology never had any interest for me nor would mere transcribed orgy. [...] The main point [of the novel] is NOT whether there are any new 'scientific' conclusions but whether there are any new phenomena."[14] Tyler makes clear the anti-mimetic allegiance of his and Ford's 1933 novel, invoking but resisting (through a slapdash redundant formulation) the psychological notion of depth and favoring instead a phenomenological take that is able to move from "homo information" to "homo rendition," thus bringing to the fore its interpretive and temporary quality. Staying true to the anti-mimetic project of their early novel, Ford, the longtime partner of the Russian artist Pavel Tchelitchew, went on to become one of the most important curators of surrealist art in America, whereas Tyler became a pioneer film critic who argued in favor of a psychoanalytic approach to cinema. He wrote on gay icons such as Mae West and Greta Garbo and authored one of the first monographs on homosexuality in film.

Having survived her mythical 1920s and 1930s persona, Barnes wrote to Michael Perkins on July 19, 1971: "My dear Mr Perkins: Thank you for your generous article; I could wish it had not got itself to *Gay*. I quarrel with it in one or two places, but that's to be expected. Do send along the SELECTED WORKS, I will send it back inscribed."[15] More vehemently, however, she wrote next to her own copy of Perkins's article: "[In spite of some idiocy] Nice article – disgusting paper."[16] Voicing that most common of homophobic sentiments, disgust, this attack against *Gay* comes from the legendary author of *Nightwood*, a love story between two women that was published by Faber in London in 1936 (and in New York in 1937 with a preface by Eliot). That Barnes's first collection of poetry in 1915 was called *The Book of Repulsive Women* only adds to the stark opposition between the revulsion against *Gay* that she voiced in the early 1970s and the attention given in her literary corpus to the spectacularization of desire. Partner of the artist Thelma Wood for eight years in the 1920s, Barnes allegedly stated in 1935, when asked by her friend Emily Coleman if she considered herself "really Lesbian": "I might be anything. If a horse loved me, I might be that."[17]

The experimental works by Nugent, Ford and Tyler, and Barnes produce same-sex desire narratives while also relentlessly questioning the nature of what we see on the page. If *case study* might appear to be a notion too closely imbricated in the oppressive history of LGBT pathologization, it is also the phrase used by Raymond in Thurman's *Infants of the Spring* (1932) to describe the "stimulating personalities," for the most part "more than a trifle insane," with whom he needs to surround himself "in order not to curdle and sour."[18] In typical post-Romantic fashion, Thurman's character collapses genius and madness, whereas these case studies – "Smoke, Lilies and Jade," *The Young and Evil*, and *Nightwood* – stage their anachronistic backward glance toward the literary movement of decadence. Written after

World War I and throughout the Great Depression, these works inscribe their own lateness and demonstrate a keen awareness of the American and Parisian economy around bohemia and the avant-garde. Having abandoned the possibility of presenting themselves as children of the new era, these texts riff on the trope of the child in order to put pressure on key literary notions such as productivity, generation, legacy, and futurity. They belong to oeuvres that range across a much longer period of time, spanning from 1913 to 1982 in the case of Barnes, from 1925 to 1987 for Nugent, and from the early 1930s to the 1950s and 1970s for Ford and Tyler, respectively.

All three texts stage their backward gaze to the Naughty Nineties as if openly disregarding Mr. Nixon's warning in Pound's *Hugh Selwyn Mauberley (Contacts and Life)*: "Don't kick against the pricks, / Accept opinion. The 'Nineties' tried your game / And died, there's nothing in it."[19] Although the shadows of the Oscar Wilde and *The Well of Loneliness* trials are perceptible (the former is openly cited in *Infants*), we are most definitely not dealing with the output of the beautiful bohemian dead, but of the stubbornly death-driven ones, who survived long enough to witness the 1960s enchantment with the 1920s but died before the term "queer" became a politicized notion during the AIDS crisis. By squeezing the potential of European decadence over American Whitmanian legacies or "a healthy paganism based on African traditions" (*Infants* 235), these texts resist a modernism that by the mid-1920s was already a crystallized institution.

Although these authors reacted very differently to the nascent notion of homosexual identity that, through writers such as James Baldwin, Audre Lorde, and Truman Capote, led to the literary ferment of post-Stonewall America, they all refused to treat the issue of same-sex desire in literature as a theme and turned it instead into a formal problem. They were all writing before the "essential American drama" became, as in Baldwin's *Another Country*, one in which "characters desperately seek to escape from the parody of themselves which has been constructed for them."[20] Putting their own literariness in question, they established a clear link between a language that refuses to behave nicely and a sexuality that can only be improper. In this sense, all three are post-sexological and post-Freudian narratives, in which sexuality and textuality are forms of experimentation to be kept alive in the wake of Joyce, Stein, Eliot, and Pound.

Another common feature affecting the legibility of these works is their refusal to transparently present same-sex desire. They do so to avoid transforming that desire into a commodified spectacle of marginality. Nevertheless, by playing with genres that nod toward the sensationalist, they display a keen awareness of the impossibility of an aesthetic project outside of a capitalist economy. They unbearably insist on asking what counts as sexuality and on testing the hypothesis that language might be conceived as being outside the realm of the sexual. Against the backdrops of Harlem, Greenwich Village, and Paris (with forays into Berlin, London, and elsewhere), in Nugent, Tyler and Ford, and Barnes's works, even the negative comfort provided by the possibility of an antagonistic normative heterosexual perspective unravels, and it is not replaced by an uplifting subversive alternative: language and sex are confounding, "bouleversing," and "moving"; they refuse to stay in their proper place.[21]

Homosexuality, from this perspective, does not become an already-known critical object to be observed in its past incarnations. It is a problem, but it is not a moral one, as is made clear in Thurman's *Infants of the Spring*. When Samuel interrogates Paul Arbian (the alter-ego of Nugent), Samuel is the one to be shamed: "'[D]id you ever ... ' he lowered his voice, 'indulge in homosexuality?' 'Certainly.' Samuel turned red. The others in the room tried no longer to restrain their laughter" (47). "Smoke, Lilies and Jade" teases us by questioning our own investment in seeing something right in front of our eyes, thereby echoing the problem, although not the agony, of racial and sexual visibility in Nella Larsen's *Passing* (1929) and Ralph Ellison's *Invisible Man* (1952).[22] In *The Young and Evil*, "the lines between the strange and the common," between minority and majority, are being redrawn, and the question, "But you are aren't you? [...] But you are aren't you? but you are aren't you?," is parodically voided.[23]

Infants of the Spring

> No, Steve, there is not yet a return to normalcy, and certainly not for the Negro who has never known such a state (*Infants* 222).

Having been described as "a child's adolescent revolt against his parents," the single issue of *Fire!!* sensationally paraded its rebellious agenda.[24] According to Nugent's playful reminiscing, the contributors' courting of notoriety was dictated by a wish to provoke the banning of the Afro-modernist magazine in Boston, which would secure its economic survival. Both wishes failed. The artists who wrote in *Fire!!* described themselves as *enfants terribles* who were desperate to make a splash by going against their paternal figure, Alain Locke. Even though Locke, in turn, did not cast himself quite in the position of the progenitor, he famously resorted to a procreative simile when he depicted himself as a "philosophical midwife to a generation of younger Negro Poets," and his preposterous fictional rendition as Dr. Parkes in Thurman's *Infants of the Spring* persistently plays "mother hen to a brood of chicks" (180).[25]

The Harlem Renaissance has often been periodized as a familial narrative that, as Henry Louis Gates, Jr. reminds us, involves the necessary and paradoxical reconstruction of yet another New Negro generation.[26] The texts produced by the provocatively self-defined "Niggeratti" rejected the values of previous generations, thus conforming to a familiar schema.[27] However, although they kept this model alive, they also archly embraced a pre–World War I wish for the "suicide" and "sterility" of the entire "human race," questioning through their contrary temporality the ideology of family, lineage, and productivity that had been central to the reconstruction of black history and legitimacy in the previous two decades (255–256).

Nugent's "Salt Lake Saga" section in his 1930s *roman à clef Gentleman Jigger* gives us a fictional account of Thurman's background. An irreverent send-up of religious traditions and moral values, "Salt Lake Saga" spares nothing and nobody: Jewish, Mormon, and Christian traditions; regional social climbing; blacks who think themselves too black or not black enough; children whose main achievement is dying at a young age; nymphomaniac mothers; rapist sons; and queers. These genealogical components contribute to the ambivalent advent of Raymond "Rusty" Pellman, "one of the most promising Negro upstarts. And a full-fledged Negro, too. So Black! So handsome! So small and so brilliant! He had come at last to Harlem."[28] In a similarly impudent but more palatable vein, Thurman's *Infants of the Spring* exploits the pious image of the Christian child to evoke a 1920s Harlem "altogether different than The New Negro's sanitized and mythopoeticized 'promised land' ":[29]

> Beloved, we join hands here to pray for gin. An aridity defiles us. Our innards thirst for the juice of juniper. Something must be done. The drought threatens to destroy us. Surely, God who let manna fall from the heavens so that the holy children of Israel might eat, will not let the equally holy children of Niggeratti Manor die from the want of a little gin. Children, let us pray.
>
> (102)

Severing the link between cultural and spiritual production that had been established by Locke, the blasphemous prayer for gin shows us how the progressive, high-achieving youth at the center of the New Negro program and celebrated in *The Crisis* had no place in *Fire!!*, whose contributors' main point of commonality nevertheless remained belonging to a younger generation.[30] This playful kidding about Niggeratti Manor takes apart the figure of the child as an unquestioned symbol of futurity, generational renewal, and fruitful legacy.[31] In *Infants*, Dr. Parkes, addressing the participants in his short-lived salon, claims: "I am somewhat fearful of the decadent strain which seems to have filtered into most of your work. Oh, yes, I know you are children of the age and all that, but you must not, like your paleface contemporaries, wallow in the mire of post-Victorian license" (234).

Such wallowing characterizes the queer child of *Fire!!*, Nugent's "Smoke, Lilies and Jade." Nugent's piece performs the synesthetic indolence of a penniless black genius kid smoking from an ivory cigarette holder inlaid with jade and green. The text overtly displays its fin de siècle allegiances to John Ruskin, Joris-Karl Huysmans, and Oscar Wilde, which were immediately picked up by Locke, who, from his first reaction to the publication, wished for a more American literary genealogy. The shameless quality of this allegiance is connected to an unapologetically anachronistic aesthetics that queers notions of authorship and originality, as echoed in a passage in *Spring* in which Paul Arbian replies to Stephen's interest in his artwork by saying:

> "I'm a genius. I've never had a drawing lesson in my life, and I never intend to take one. I think that Oscar Wilde is the greatest man that ever lived. Huysmans' Des Esseintes is the greatest character in literature, and Baudelaire is the greatest poet. I also like Blake, Dowson, Verlaine, Rimbaud, Poe and Whitman. And of course Whistler, Gaugin, Picasso and Zuloaga."
> "But that's not telling me anything about your drawings."
> "Unless you're dumber than I think, I've told you all you need to know."
>
> (24)

Just like Barnes between the 1910s and 1930s, Nugent was still playing around with decadent aesthetics, not out of nostalgic wallowing but rather to figure the anachronistic, contrary, and openly unoriginal aesthetics that queers his authorial self-descriptions. Huysmans's excess of immobilized capital (such as jewel-encrusted turtles, perfumes, silks, and damasks) is mechanically reproduced and thus mobilized in "Smoke," turning on its head an eminently antimodern agenda while also rejecting an aesthetics based on productivity.

Alex, just like Stuartt in *Gentleman Jigger*, luxuriates "in the fact that he had no money, no job, and no responsibilities" and stubbornly refuses to present his musings on the page as a valuable and original aesthetic object (191). The single object invested with the evocative power of art for art's sake is the cigarette holder; its solitary stillness in the squalor casts everything else as transitory, fast-moving, and certainly not very distant from the muck in which Langston Hughes's gutter boy plays in the lines quoted in the text (79–80). Des Esseintes's rare scents turn into the acrid smell of horse manure, stale fried fish and dirty milk bottles in "the odorous tenement" – which Alex finds, counterintuitively, pleasant.[32]

In traditional modernist fashion, this story estranges, but Alex's own strangeness and the strangeness of his experiences are firmly grounded in everyday ordinariness: he is "hungry and comfortable" (76). The peculiarity of his father's death is that paradoxically "it hadn't seemed so strange" (75). Even Alex's own artistic sensibility ineluctably carries a whiff of cliché: Alex archly declares "beautiful sunsets" or "music" to be "the things that hurt, the things to sympathize with" (75). "Smoke, Lilies and Jade" is bereft of tragedy, denies pathos, and vindicates instead an attachment to the transitory encounter.

Synesthesia fails to dematerialize modernity into a sophisticated effort at stillness in this tale. Stillness and movement are both natural to Alex, who is never bored enough to be sophisticated: just as he "smokes thoughts," so too he "walks music" (78). "Smoke, Lilies and Jade" thus defamiliarizes the energy of the city by turning it into a transitory fairy tale landscape, which nevertheless does not allow us to forget that money is central to the narrative movement: its absence, its circulation, and Alex's memories of his mother reproaching him for his inability to earn enough of it figure prominently in this only apparently self-indulgently abstracted piece.

The family is very much a part of this modern economy. Alex disappoints his mother's wishes by refusing to become "a little man" and contribute to the family economy after his father's death (75). It may be tempting to argue that the "Niggeratti" listed in the text by their recognizable first names are "a substitutive kinship structure," an artistic community able to produce a nourishing environment.[33] But "all people he had loved ... loved one by one and together ... and all had died ... he had never loved a person long before they died ... in truth he was tragic ... that was a lovely appellation ... The Tragic Genius ... think ... to go through life known as The Tragic Genius ... romantic ... but it was more or less true ..." (78). The loved ones (in that ambivalent formulation "one by one and together") are firmly placed in the realm of the dead and are opportunistically used to produce a painfully self-conscious romantic image of the self. Forno, the fleeting stage where "everyone came," is a place of encounters and networks, not of community (85).[34] The text also rejects any psychological characterization that would create a causal link between individual personalities and choices of love, or even affiliation. Names do not even congeal into characters, just as the literary names dropped throughout the text – notably, Wilde, Sigmund Freud, Giovanni Boccaccio, and Arthur Schnitzler – do not provide Alex with a heritage to perpetuate. Beauty does not emerge from a genealogy but rather appears, anonymously, in a street, and an equally anonymous room is the stage of his encounter with Alex. Beauty is encountered. And its effect has more to do with timing than it does with essence.

We can read in the same light the text's knowing nod to the literary association between sexual desire and making a pact with the devil: Beauty, a Latino, stops Alex and asks for a match. He addresses Alex formally ("usted") in Spanish and uses the word "fósforo" for "match" (81): although simply referring to the match's tip, phosphorous is very obviously "the devil's element."[35] But this guilt and shame-free sexual encounter is not the same as "going down the vortex of time," which requires the pretextual confessing of Barnes's *Ryder*.[36] It creates instead a counterpoint to the moment of shame Alex feels when looking at his mother during his father's funeral.

Echoing what will remain a fixture of Nugent's writing, from the discussion about "being queer" in *Gentleman Jigger* to *Geisha Man* to his 1980s interviews, the text invites speculations on sexual identity but refuses to work as its revelation, defending surface over depth, natural artificiality over essence. Alex's "short disconnected thoughts" are produced through free indirect discourse and ellipses, which do not, however, create an effect of depth but instead suggest fleetingness, to the point that the writing on the page presents itself not as writing but as thinking and smoking (75). To "write or draw … or something" are Alex's unformed wishes and not, apparently, what is already under our eyes (75). Drawing attention to its linguistic materiality through the ellipses, "Smoke" presents itself as ephemera, something hardly there at all, both superficial and transient – but not meaningless. Although they are suggested by the very dreaminess of this smoky text, no deep truths are concealed or revealed, even though something is definitely taking place. This evanescent text vindicates its power of being unfinished and disappointing, just like Alex is for his mother. Whereas Radclyffe Hall's trademark "that night they were not divided" is eloquent in its restraint, the climax of Alex's night encounter with Beauty does not renounce its undecidability by presenting itself as obvious: "no need for words … they had always known each other … undressing beautiful body … they talked and … slept …" (82). There is absolutely no doubt about the sexual and pleasurable nature of the relationship between Alex and Beauty, just as there is no doubt about his relationship with Melva. As critics unfailingly notice, the narrator repeats that "one *can* love two at the same time" (87); however, only Alex's relationship with Beauty creates a "confusion" that "does something" that is never experienced with Melva: the "not knowing" (and not the loving) leads to "doing something" outside of a reproductive paradigm. That "something" refuses to call itself "writing," "drawing," "something about the things he felt and thought," or even "sex," but it can only happen with Beauty, thanks to Beauty's body (72). Hidden in plain sight, such a protean artistic credo is imbued with the queer aesthetics of an everyday encounter in Harlem.

An Adult Fairy Tale

"Well said the wolf to Little Red Riding Hood no sooner was Karel seated in the Round Table than the impossible happened. There before him stood a fairy prince and one of those mythological creatures known as Lesbians. Won't you join our table? They said in sweet chorus" (4). This opening of Ford and Tyler's *The Young and Evil* presents us with the problem of its illegible sensationalism. Holding George Chauncey's *Gay New York* as our Baedeker, we can decode, as Joseph Allen Boone and Sam See have done, this space of drag queens, wolves, fairies, and, after the 1928 Hall trial, those most definitely mythical lesbians. Recognizing that "the famous Greenwich Village club owner Eve Addams is evoked in the novel's first – and self-consciously mythic – working title, *Eve's Adam*" and that the Round Table was a popular Greenwich Village restaurant add to our illusion of being in the know.[37]

And yet, this is not a book that encourages a tour of the Village and a discovery of its sites; rather, it is one that creates a queer underworld as a mythological place. Tyler, who became a major film critic after the war, writes in his influential *Magic and Myth of the Movies* (1947) that "*desires* may have the same power over the mind and behavior, indeed a much greater power, than *facts*."[38] Openly citing James Frazer but adopting Freudian rather than Eliotian language, Parker's later text echoes *The Young and Evil*'s take on modernism's mythical method, which articulated queerness "not as tangentially 'alternative' but as central to literary modernist experience," asking, in one of the protagonists' voices, "Where is the line between the strange and the common?" (109).[39]

The text sabotages the possibility of drawing that line, deviously quipping and contrarily equivocating, so as to present itself, in paradoxically literal fashion, as a fairies' tale uninnocently punning on its orality while also making us wonder whether "all things of course are going backwards past" our ears, as Julian admiringly says of Barnes (18). Obscenely light-hearted and technically superficial, *The Young and Evil* is not, pace Gertrude Stein's witty remark on the novel's dust jacket, a book that "creates this generation as *This Side of Paradise* by Fitzgerald created his generation. It is a good thing, whatever this generation is, to be the first to create it in a book." Van Vechten's *Nigger Heaven* (1926), Claude McKay's *Home to Harlem* (1928), Barnes's *Ladies Almanack* (1928), and Thurman's *Spring* had all fused the genre of the modernist *roman à clef* with the older slumming narratives to knowingly produce the literary 1920s; Stein's *The Autobiography of Alice B. Toklas* (1933) and Barnes's *Nightwood* can be read as belonging to the same tradition, too.[40]

Unmistakably looking back (and forward) to these texts, *The Young and Evil* is not, however, a celebration of a new queer generation. It mobilizes instead the radically individualist figure of the American adolescent (as opposed to old Europe) to sabotage its central role as a guarantor of futurity; if there are brilliance, vigor, and youthfulness in this book, they are presented as neither productive nor generative. Resisting, in more sensationalist ways than Nugent did, the analogy between creating art and perpetuating the logic of the family, this book is not about a generation but rather about a network refusing to accept its modernist lateness. Parents unsuccessfully try to kill off modernism, but they cannot be trusted: disbelief meets Frederick's mother's announcement that "James Joyce was dead. Dead! said Julian" (125). On the other hand, the task of keeping modernism alive is not one predicated on reproduction: when Julian soppily muses about writing "more beautiful than ever poetry," Gabriel thinks "was it so nice being wasn't it barren" (83). In chapter 11, "Love and Jump Back," even the unknown (but self-described "old son-of-a-bitch") character loitering outside Karel and Louis's room (who is invited in exclusively because he is holding a gallon of wine) preposterously claims to be taking the wine to "his childless mother," and it is only when Frederick is told by the magistrate "you don't live with your parents" that we are reminded, in one of the book's rare moments that tentatively points in the direction of realism, that these characters are supposed to be just kids (68–69, 118).

Even though trench-mouth is one of the "tangible spectres" of the past that makes New York what it is (127), Ford and Tyler's novel does not mourn the stolen children of the previous generation. Instead it places a queer childish pleasure at the center of its aesthetics by assembling surrealist images and techniques, squeezing to its last drop the titillating potential of half-a-century-old slumming literary conventions and heavy-handedly citing as its presiding authorities Barnes, Stein, and E. E. Cummings. The *éminence grise* of this text is, however, Wilde, on whose *Dorian Gray* Tyler later wrote wonderful pages in his *Magic and Myth of the Movies*:

> The whole thesis of Wilde's art was the reality of make-believe not merely in childhood but in youth and manhood too. [...] Wilde was too impatient to bother with much erudition, too realistic to confine himself to historico-literary symbols. He determined to be an up-to-date anachronism, and that is precisely what his Dorian Gray was.[41]

"Up-to-date anachronism" is an apt definition for this book, which rejects political duty and community and disputes the literary logic of legacy, reproduction, and futurity while also subverting the trope of arrested development to reflect on the legibility of its verbal pyrotechnics. Building off nineteenth-century tropes of arrested development and "the imitation of art by life," *The Young and Evil* attempts to produce, in parallel with Hollywood cinema more so than with high modernist Europe, the "fundamental eye trickery that is a genius of the camera – you see the object, yet it isn't there."[42] The "surrealist eye" at work in this text – fragmenting, decomposing, dissecting – produces a trickery that is also magic – "magic lantern metamorphoses" – rather than a method.[43]

It is difficult to attribute a coherent aesthetics to a text whose "scattering into oblivion rather than congealing into community" is not simply a theme but a dazzling clash of temporary, contradictory, and non-coinciding points of view.[44] Yet there is no doubt that the decadent child presides over the impossible verbal and sexual innocence of this text. And this insufferably precocious child is a form of resistance to what Tyler identifies after the Second World War as "one of the diseases of American culture: that salesmanship can be an esthetic value."[45] Julian says to himself that "Louis and Gabriel are very like children; if I had sons I would train them up like them: debonair, destitute, devouring" (122). Hypothetical progeny is trained up for a decadent act that, rather than being opposite to the preestablished innocence of the child, is what comes closest to being genuine. In her exploration of queer in relation to childhood, Kathryn Bond Stockton argues that:

> The child is precisely who we are not and, in fact, never were. It is the act of adults looking back. It is a ghostly, unreachable fancy, making us wonder: Given that we cannot know the contours of children, who they are to themselves, should we stop talking of children altogether? Should all talk of the child subside, beyond our critique of the bad effects of looking nostalgically in fantasy?[46]

Stockton's complex defense of fantasy shows us how much cultural work the child can silently do. Brilliantly queer, the child is for Stockton not a being but a troubling act of looking at the self: this is why the child vindicates the strangeness of any form of sexuality. Indeed, these hypothetical models for future "trained up," "debonair, destitute," and "devouring" children that we see incarnated in Louis and Gabriel are not so much proto-gay children or a backward fantasy of a queer future as they are part of a world that is in any case declared to be "ninety-five percent [...] just naturally queer" (88).[47] Against the "strangely mature [...] continent," this American text is painfully aware that it is "talking like a kid" in its search for a "natural behavior," and as soon as it is wished for, it is turned into something far from "agreeable" and most definitely not the site of moral goodness (90). But this text is childish also because of the chiseled quality of many of its statements, ranging from the Dadaesque "I am waiting for the day Louis said when I can destroy all definitions" (67) to the decadently witty "I must do something septic to boredom" (77).

Paradoxically adopting a Wildean tradition that "cuts its own roots from beneath itself," the queering and turning taking place in this brilliant text are not thematic concerns but formal preoccupations.[48] The novel's in-your-face illegibility is determined by male same-sex desire, which is here the perspectival problem of the surrealist's eye, by the paradoxical claim to orality as a form of pleasurable disorientation, and by a diction that, in both homage and echo, reproduces Stein's childish prose: "But Karel was thinking of Louis turning queer so beautifully gradually and beautifully like a chameleon beautifully and gradually turning. [...] A man cannot want a woman and a woman cannot want a man he thought not really. He thought so looking at Gabriel" (75).

A "Meet of Child and Desperado"

In the May section of Barnes's 1928 *Ladies Almanack*, Evangeline – the sapphic amazon named after the heroine of Henry Wadsworth Longfellow's *Evangeline: A Tale of Arcadie* – fabricates with distinctive missionary zeal her own mythical past, an imaginary "early eighties."[49] In the satirical vein that characterizes the almanac, in Dame Musset's day, she was "a Pioneer and a Menace, it was not then as it is now, *chic* and pointless to a degree, but as daring as a Crusade, for where now it leaves a woman talkative, so that we have not a Secret among us, then it left her in Tears and Trepidation."[50] The almanac constructs the 1920s not as the pinnacle of sexual and textual daring experimentalism but as the moment of lateness, when sapphism had already lost its edge. Lateness and anachronism characterize the entire Barnes oeuvre, from the early journalism (1913-1921) mocking the tourists hungry for a Bohemia that is elusive if not quite certifiably dead to *The Book of Repulsive Women* (1915), which contradictorily capitalizes on that same bohemia. *Ladies Almanack*, written and published in Paris in 1928, sports a mish-mash of sixteenth-century vocabulary and generic conventions, eighteenth-century comedy of manners, and parodies of *The Well of Loneliness*. It makes its own lateness visible through both its linguistic antiquarianism and satirical targets: the sapphic coterie's main problem lies in its being not a subversive artistic and sexual group but rather a toxic composite of well-bred inward-lookingness, purple prose, religious conservatism, and gossipy objectification of the female body.

The problem of lateness in *Nightwood* is figured through a language that refuses to belong to its time but instead is in perpetual "locomotion," just like Robin, the unendingly elusive object of Nora's desire, the unreadable "girl with the body of a boy" (72). Language refuses to stay in place, moving toward John Donne and the metaphysical poets, resurrecting and subverting fin de siècle sexological projects of classification and decadent bohemia, and sporting a Benjaminian fascination with the baroque. Predictably, Barnes's peculiarly American novel about moving around the underground of European capitals was considered too queerly decadent. "She belongs temperamentally to the elder generation of living writers who present life in its essential nakedness and seeming hopelessness," claims *The Spectator*. "Only by a miracle, it would seem, can *Nightwood* escape the affectionate, destroying hands of some twittering literary cult," adds *The New Yorker*, and Mark Van Doren claims in *The Nation* that "Miss Barnes has strained rather than enriched our sensibilities. *Nightwood* is more fascinating than interesting," quipping that the novel is mouse meat to be nibbled at "page after page with a special kind of joy. But great fiction is more ordinary than this, and ultimately more nourishing. Beefsteak and apple pie."[51] Alain Locke had wished away Nugent's suspiciously French associations; ten years later, Mark Van Doren advocated an equally healthy (although clearly from WASP New England and not pagan Africa) alternative diet.

The anxiety linking the obscure with the sexual is palpable in these reviews, and yet *Nightwood*'s darkness is openly visible, calling for a theory of reading that vindicates surface over depth, simile over metaphor, the horizontal over the vertical. When answering some of her translator's queries, Barnes unflinchingly explains: "And 'and the lining of my belly, flocked with *the* (which you left out) locks cut off love in odd places that I've come on' ... what it says, implying that among other things will be found xxx in [sic] his stomach body hair, implication obvious considering that he is homosexual."[52] Of Tiny O'Tool, she writes: "Of course here, in the scene in the church, the doctors sex-organ. It is an Irish play on words. O'Tool being an Irish name but also tool is a slang word for penis."[53] These explanations show how meaning in *Nightwood* is oblique and camp, but it is not a secret to be disclosed; the lack of transparency is there for all to see. *Nightwood* ultimately invests all language with the power of equivocation rather than resorting to a historically specific subcultural argot, as Tyler and Ford do. As Barnes writes in a vitriolic letter to Coleman: "[A]nd if you think for that matter that the people here [in *Nightwood*] are not normal, hadn't you better read the history of mankind (slightly at least) and then see how you would come up yo[ur] statement."[54]

Echoing such a rejection of a predetermined notion of normality, the doctor in *Nightwood* uses Robin as the subject of his serious parody of the sexological theories of inversion that theorized same-sex desire as an inborn reversal of gender traits:

Very well – what is this love we have for the invert, boy or girl? It was they who were spoken of in every romance that we ever read. The girl lost, what is she but the Prince found? The Prince on the white horse that we have always been seeking. [...] We were impaled in our childhood upon them as they rode through our primers, the sweetest lie of all, now come to be in boy or girl, for in the girl it is the prince, and in the boy it is the girl that makes a prince a prince – and not a man. [...] They are our answer to what our grandmothers were told love was, and what it never came to be; they, the living lie of our centuries.

(194–195)

Authentic love is fashioned as the outcome of stories, so that gender is no longer a point of origin and authenticity. Opposites construct each other, and gender becomes exclusively relational. The invert is here the figure of fascination because it spells out the mutual implication of girl lost and prince found: the girl both *is* the prince and *makes* the prince a prince, and the present is fashioned as the original past created by our desire. Because the most authentic love is the living lie of the century, the possibility of expressing a true self is undone. Nobody can play innocent in the unlicensed practitioner's "feminine finery" that has suffered "venery," watching the girl with the body of a boy, dreaming of Nora's grandmother's camp appearance, and fantasizing about Nikka's tattooed black body, whose member at a stretch spelled Desdemona but is rumored to be as ineffectual as that of the aging Count Onatorio Altamonte. *Nightwood*'s language "give[s] even the most innocent a sensation of having been accomplice" (116).

Anachronistically mobilizing decadence to figure their lateness, "Smoke, Lilies and Jade," *The Young and Evil*, and *Nightwood* refuse to place the category of the homosexual as an object of direct knowledge and discovery as they collectively turn same-sex desire into a problem of legibility. The legibility of same-sex desire, just like the legibility of modernist experimentalism, is figured in the period between the late 1920s and the mid-1930s as a modern problem of the circulation of capital, as the repartee between Julian and Karel pithily illustrates: "[I] wanted to know how he felt about homosexuality and he told me. You must have paid for the information" (107). These texts do not claim to be able to escape this logic, and yet they resist it by rejecting the notion that their oeuvres are forms of cultural capital, legitimate inheritors of the high modernist legacy, and progenitors of experiments to come. They are not so much precocious as up-to-date anachronistic, disrupting the linearity of literary history but not leading to a revolutionary change, and figuring instead the very crisis in critical mastery that has often obscured their exhilarating, ephemeral, and irreducible power to make strange.

NOTES

1 Eve Kosofsky Sedgwick, *Epistemology of the Closet* (Berkeley: University of California Press, 1990), 52–53.

2 Ibid., 53.

3 See, for example, Wayne Koestenbaum, *Double Talk: The Erotics of Male Collaboration* (New York: Routledge, 1989); and Cassandra Laity and Nancy K. Gish, eds., *Gender, Desire, and Sexuality in T. S. Eliot* (Cambridge: Cambridge University Press, 2004).

4 Sedgwick, *Epistemology of the Closet*, 53.

5 Greil Marcus and Werner Sollors, eds., *A New Literary History of America* (Cambridge, MA: The Belknap Press of Harvard University Press, 2009), xxiii.

6 Sedgwick, *Epistemology of the Closet*, 41.

7 On gay, lesbian, and queer historiography, see Terry Castle, *The Apparitional Lesbian: Female Homosexuality and Modern Culture* (New York: Columbia University Press, 1993); George Chauncey, *Gay New York: Gender, Urban Culture, and the Making of the Gay Male World, 1890–1940* (New York: Basic Books, 1994); Laura Doan, *Disturbing Practices: History, Sexuality, and Women's Experience of Modern War* (Chicago: University of Chicago Press, 2013); Laura Doan, *Fashioning Sapphism: The Origins of a Modern English Lesbian Culture* (New York: Columbia University Press, 2001); Laura Doan and Jane Garrity, eds., *Sapphic Modernities* (New York: Palgrave Macmillan, 2006); Martin Duberman, Martha Vicinus, and George Chauncey, Jr., eds., *Hidden from History: Reclaiming the Gay and Lesbian Past* (New York: Meridian, 1990); Lee Edelman, *Homographesis: Essays in Gay Literary and Cultural Theory* (New York: Routledge, 1994); David M. Halperin, *How To Do the History of Homosexuality* (Chicago: University of Chicago Press, 2002); Scott Herring, "Catherian Friendship; Or, How Not To Do the History of Homosexuality," *Modern Fiction Studies* 52, no. 1 (2006): 66–91; Jonathan Ned Katz, *The Invention of Heterosexuality* (New York: Penguin, 1996); Heather Love, *Feeling Backward: Loss and the Politics of Queer History* (Cambridge, MA: Harvard University Press, 2007); Valerie Traub, *The Renaissance of Lesbianism in Early Modern England* (Cambridge: Cambridge University Press, 2002); and Joanne Winning, "Lesbian Modernism: Writing in and beyond the Closet," in *The Cambridge Companion to Gay and Lesbian Writing*, ed. Hugh Stevens (Cambridge: Cambridge University Press, 2011), 50–64.

8 Joseph Allen Boone, *Libidinal Currents: Sexuality and the Shaping of Modernism* (Chicago: University of Chicago Press, 1998). For a discussion of the history of Barnes's reception, see Daniela Caselli, *Improper Modernism: Djuna Barnes's Bewildering Corpus* (Burlington: Ashgate, 2009).

9 Michael L. Cobb, "Insolent Racing, Rough Narrative: The Harlem Renaissance's Impolite Queers," *Callaloo* 23, no. 1 (2000): 329.

10 Djuna Barnes, letter to Natalie Clifford Barney, May 31, 1963, series II, box 1, folder 45, Djuna Barnes Papers, Special Collections, University of Maryland Libraries, College Park. Further references are to this same collection are with kind permission of the Author's League Fund.

11 Djuna Barnes, letter to Cristina Campo, 1969, series II, box 2, folder 43, Djuna Barnes Papers.

12 Richard Bruce Nugent, "You See, I Am a Homosexual," in *Gay Rebel of the Harlem Renaissance*, ed. Thomas H. Wirth (Durham: Duke University Press, 2002), 268–269; hereafter cited in text.

13 I gather this biography from Wirth, *Gay Rebel*, 1–64; Scott Herring, *Queering the Underworld: Slumming, Literature, and the Undoing of Lesbian and Gay History* (Chicago: University of Chicago Press, 2007), 138–144; and Steve Pinkerton, "'New Negro' v. 'Niggeratti': Defining and Defiling the Black Messiah," *Modernism/modernity* 20, no. 3 (2013), 539–555.

14 Parker Tyler, letter to Ezra Pound, September 18, 1933, box 53, folder 2400, Ezra Pound Papers, Beinecke Rare Book and Manuscript Library, Yale University, New Haven, CT. Cited in Sam See, "Making Modernism New: Queer Mythology in *The Young and Evil*," *English Literary History* 76, no. 4 (2009): 1085.

15 Djuna Barnes, letter to Michael Perkins, July 19, 1971, series II, box 13, folder 32, Djuna Barnes Papers.

16 "Watchman, What of the Night?," *Gay*, June 7, 1971, 13–14; brackets in original. *Gay* was a New York City newspaper edited by Jack Nichols and Lige Clarke, published from 1969 to 1974.

17 Emily Coleman, letter to Djuna Barnes, October 27, 1935, series II, box 3, folder 7, Djuna Barnes Papers.

18 Wallace Thurman, *Infants of the Spring* (1932; Boston: Northeastern University Press, 1992), 194; hereafter cited in text.

19 Ezra Pound, *Hugh Selwyn Mauberley (Contacts and Life)*, in *Selected Poems 1908–1969* (London: Faber and Faber, 2004).

20 Colm Tóibín, introduction to *Another Country*, by James Baldwin (1963; Harmondsworth: Penguin, 2001), xii.

21 Djuna Barnes, *Nightwood* (1936; London: Faber and Faber, 2007), 189; hereafter cited in text.

22 See Herring, *Queering the Underworld*, 134, 228.

23 Charles Henri Ford and Parker Tyler, *The Young and Evil* (1933; Paris: Olympia, 2004), 63; hereafter cited in text.

24 Robert E. Hemenway, *Zora Neale Hurston: A Literary Biography* (Urbana: University of Illinois Press, 1997), 49.

25 Alain Locke, "Negro Youth Speaks," in *The New Negro: An Interpretation*, ed. Alain Locke (New York: Albert and Charles Boni, 1925), 49.

26 Henry Louis Gates, Jr., "The Trope of the New Negro and the Reconstruction of the Image of the Black," *Representations* 24, no. 1 (1988): 130; Anna Pochmara, *The Making of the New Negro: Black Authorship, Masculinity and Sexuality in the Harlem Renaissance* (Amsterdam: Amsterdam University Press, 2011), 57.

27 See Cary D. Wintz, *The Politics and Aesthetics of "New Negro" Literature* (New York: Garland, 1996); and Monica L. Miller, "The Black Dandy as Bad Modernist," in *Bad Modernisms*, ed. Douglas Mao and Rebecca L. Walkowitz (Durham: Duke University Press, 2006), 179–205.

28 Richard Bruce Nugent, *Gentleman Jigger* (New York: Da Capo Press, 2006), 168.

29 Pinkerton, "'New Negro' v. 'Niggeratti,'" 545.

30 *The Crisis* was founded in 1910 and edited by W. E. B. Du Bois. Still in print today, it was backed from its inception by the NAACP. Suzanne W. Churchill,

"Youth Culture in *The Crisis* and *Fire!!*," *The Journal of Modern Periodical Studies*, 1, no. 1 (2010): 64–99, 65, and note 3, 98.

31 Lee Edelman, *No Future: Queer Theory and the Death Drive* (Durham: Duke University Press, 2004), 11.

32 Richard Bruce Nugent, "Smoke, Lilies and Jade," in *Gay Rebel of the Harlem Renaissance*, ed. Thomas H. Wirth (Durham: Duke University Press, 2002), 80; hereafter cited in text.

33 Boone, *Libidinal Currents*, 226.

34 See Herring, *Queering the Underworld*, 136, 142.

35 John Emsley, *The Shocking History of Phosphorus: A Biography of the Devil's Element* (London: Pan Books, 2001).

36 Djuna Barnes, *Ryder* (1928; Normal, IL: Dalkey Archive Press, 1995), 139.

37 See, "Making Modernism," 1083.

38 Parker Tyler, *Magic and Myth of the Movies* (New York: Henry Holt and Co., 1947), xi.

39 See, "Making Modernism," 1075.

40 See Sean Latham, *The Art of Scandal: Modernism, Libel Law, and the Roman á Clef* (Oxford: Oxford University Press, 2009).

41 Tyler, *Magic and Myth*, 60–62.

42 Tyler, *Magic and Myth*, 59, xv.

43 Tyler, *Magic and Myth*, xix.

44 Herring, *Queering the Underworld*, 123.

45 Tyler, *Magic and Myth*, 188–189.

46 Kathryn Bond Stockton, *The Queer Child, or Growing Sideways in the Twentieth Century* (Durham: Duke University Press, 2009), 5.

47 See also Karín Lesnik-Oberstein and Stephen Thomson, "What Is Queer Theory Doing with the Child?," *Parallax* 8, no. 1 (2002): 35–46.

48 Tyler, *Magic and Myth*, 59.

49 Djuna Barnes, *Ladies Almanack* (1928; Manchester: Carcanet, 2006), 35.

50 Ibid., 35, 34.

51 Peter Burra, "Fiction," *The Spectator*, November 27, 1936; Clifton Fadiman, "Djuna Barnes," *The New Yorker*, March 3, 1937; Mark Van Doren, "Mouse Meat," *The Nation*, April 3, 1937; quotations located in series IV, box 1, folder 18, Djuna Barnes Papers.

52 Djuna Barnes, note on translator query, series II, box I, folder 5, Djuna Barnes Papers.

53 Ibid.

54 Djuna Barnes, letter to Emily Coleman, undated, series II, box 3, folder 24, Djuna Barnes Papers.

8

MICHAEL P. BIBLER

The Cold War Closet

For many in the twenty-first century, the image of the closet has become almost trite. Think of the hit cable television series *True Blood* (2008–2014), in which vampires have finally "come out of the coffin." The trope's pervasiveness stems in part from the heightened visibility of lesbian, gay, bisexual, transgender, and queer (LGBTQ) politics since the early 1970s, when the Gay Liberation Front implored sexual minorities to "come out," and the 1980s, when AIDS activists reinvigorated that call under the banner of "Silence = Death." Eve Kosofsky Sedgwick famously wrote that "[t]he closet is the defining structure for gay oppression in [the twentieth] century," and the trope's ubiquity in the twenty-first century is a testament to the success of "coming out" as one strategy for fighting that oppression.[1]

However, by framing LGBTQ politics as the progress from "in" to "out," from oppression to liberation, the closet also produces a certain myopia about earlier historical periods before the heady days of the 1970s. When viewed in terms of the closet, earlier periods can appear hopelessly and tragically "in" – dominated by secrecy and shame. And this view especially shapes common notions about the decades immediately preceding gay liberation: the Cold War era of the 1950s and 1960s. Indeed, it is impossible to talk about the early Cold War period without referring to the closet, not least because of the widespread social and political persecution of gays and lesbians during that time. And yet, a closer look at the gay and lesbian literature of that period also reveals a somewhat different use of the closet than readers in the twenty-first century might expect.

Secrecy and shame were, without question, part of the literary and cultural discourses surrounding homosexuality during the early Cold War, but writers invoked and explored the image of the closet in ways that might surprise us. In this period, literary representations of gays and lesbians ballooned exponentially, and shame, self-loathing, and suicide figured prominently in much of this literature. However, as writers sought a more public venue for writing about – and thus finding greater social acceptance for – homosexuality, they paradoxically held on to a particular model of the closet that was useful to them. This chapter argues that many writers pushed back against the public crackdowns and campaigns against lesbian and gay people not by embracing or lamenting the secrecy of the closet but by asking for the right to the *privacy* of the closet. Even as political activists were beginning to push for sexual civil rights during this period, writers were making a slightly different kind of plea. Attempting to reconfigure the public discourse of homosexuality in terms of privacy instead of only secrecy or shame, their writing makes the case that the social and political "problem" of being gay or lesbian was precisely that sexuality should not be a matter of public concern in the first place.

Theory and Historicism

Sedgwick's *Epistemology of the Closet*, one of the foundational texts of sexuality studies, shows how the closet works to structure a wide range of the binary relations that define "Western culture":

> I think that a whole cluster of the most crucial sites for the contestation of meaning in twentieth-century Western culture are consequentially and quite indelibly marked with the historical specificity of homosocial/homosexual definition. ... Among those sites are ... the pairings secrecy/disclosure and private/public. Along with and sometimes through these epistemologically charged pairings, condensed in the figures of "the closet" and "coming out," this very specific crisis of definition has then ineffaceably marked other pairings as basic to modern cultural organization as masculine/feminine, majority/minority, innocence/initiation, natural/artificial, new/old, growth/decadence, urbane/provincial, health/illness, same/different, cognition/paranoia, art/kitsch, sincerity/sentimentality, and voluntarity/addiction.

(72)

In obvious ways, Sedgwick's deconstructive reading of the closet has been especially generative for others seeking to understand and critique the wider ideological ties between sexuality and culture. However, although her work is grounded in the "historical specificity" of the nineteenth and twentieth centuries, other scholars have identified historical limitations built into her theoretical model.

Marlon B. Ross shows how Sedgwick constructs the closet as a "race-less paradigm" that ignores the racial and evolutionary theories of primitivism and civilization underlying the notion of "progress."[2] He agrees with Sedgwick that "[t]he 'coming out' or closet paradigm has been such a compelling way of fixing homosexual identification exactly because it enables this powerful narrative of progress ... in terms of the psychosexual development of an individual and the sociopolitical birth and growth of a legitimate sexual minority group" (163). But he also shows the dangerous limitations of conflating the closet with the concept of modernity, because that conflation implicitly defines the closet in invisibly racial terms that exclude non-white peoples and cultures. He writes: "[H]omosexual modernity is constructed not only in relation to a premodern European past before sexual parity gave rise to the uncloseting of a common identity. It is also constructed over and against the premodern present of traditional (that is, *primitive*) sexual practices being engaged in by those not privy to Europe's progress toward homosexual identity" (175).

Taking a different approach, the social historian George Chauncey has cautioned that the closet does not accurately describe the experiences and feelings of all historical subjects whom we might identify as gay or lesbian – including not only non-Western people and people of color, as Ross argues, but also those whom we might squarely associate with the modernity Sedgwick describes. In a famous rebuttal to Sedgwick, Chauncey writes:

> Nowhere does [the closet] appear before the 1960s in the records of the gay movement or in the novels, diaries, or letters of gay men and lesbians. The fact that gay people in the past did not speak of or conceive of themselves as living in a closet does not preclude us from using the term retrospectively as an analytic category, but it does suggest that we need to use it more cautiously and precisely, and to pay attention to the very different terms people used to describe themselves and their social worlds.[3]

Both Ross and Chauncey remind us that for all its usefulness in some respects, the closet can be a blunt tool for examining the wider cultural landscape of sexual diversity. But Chauncey's words also reveal the particular difficulty of reading the Cold War period of the 1950s and 1960s, when the image of the closet – or something like it – was only just beginning to make its appearance in gay and lesbian communities and literature.

Dating the emergence of the closet trope in its twenty-first-century meaning is difficult. The literary critic Henry Abelove argues that the first such usage can be traced to Frank O'Hara's 1958 poem "Ode: Salute to the French Negro Poets," in which "O'Hara points to the costs of the closet and of reticence more generally."[4] But the cultural geographer Michael P. Brown and historian Michael S. Sherry give the trope a later date of origin in the late 1960s, around the beginning of the gay liberation movement. Indeed, Sherry shows that earlier uses of the term did not carry the same meaning that it has in the twenty-first century. For example, he notes that a 1962 issue of the gay magazine *One* asked, "'Out from where? Out into what?' [and] mentioned no 'closet,' instead identifying 'coming out' as 'our slang phrase for coming from a majority and going to a minority.'" Sherry continues,

"*One* knew the need for 'wearing the mask' in a 'hostile world' that taught 'the evilness of homosexuality.' But 'the absolute necessity for secrecy from the majority' was something 'you learned quickly' *after* coming out – a protective device, not a place of hiding."[5]

This distinction between the closet as a place of hiding and a place of protection is crucial to understanding the early Cold War literary period, because it pushes us to rethink current discussions about the importance of shame in queer identity and queer history. Many scholars have asked how embracing, rather than avoiding, queer feelings of shame can help us reimagine theoretical and political discourses about sexuality. Activists have organized Gay Shame rallies to protest the neoliberal corporatization of Gay Pride events and the middle-class homonormativity of mainstream gay and lesbian identities.[6] And scholars such as Heather Love have built on the later work of Sedgwick, as well as that of Michael Warner, Douglas Crimp, and others, to argue that a critical embrace of the histories of queer violence, shame, and isolation "can help us see structures of inequality in the present." Love takes it as given that queer identity "is produced out of shame and stigma," and she argues that embracing those roots of queer identity reminds us to "refus[e] to write off the most vulnerable, the least presentable, and all the dead."[7]

However, although this turn toward the legacies of earlier forms of "shame and stigma" is important, overstating those legacies blinds us again to the contours of the historical landscape. For example, Chauncey argues that in the 1950s, shame was not the defining characteristic of gay life, even though Love takes for granted that it was: "[T]he correspondence and diaries produced by gay men in the mid-twentieth century, supposedly the heyday of homosexual abjection, often contain astonishingly detailed, exuberant, uninhibited, and unashamed accounts of their sexual experiences of a kind that it is hard to imagine many of their heterosexual contemporaries committing to paper."[8] Indeed, Chauncey argues that many queer people refused to succumb to the feelings of shame that were demanded by the heterosexual mainstream: "[T]he truly remarkable thing about 1950s queers was their refusal to play the role assigned them by the hostility of their own time and the condescension of history" (278). Instead of totally embracing or succumbing to shame, many Cold War queers turned away from the mainstream discourses of sexual deviance to write different stories. And it is in this turn that we can see the uniquely Cold War approach to the patterns of silence and disclosure that we associate with the closet. Although privacy is of course not far off from secrecy, and the closet is obviously a negotiation of both, Cold War writers might be better understood as challenging the stigma attached to secrecy by reclaiming notions of privacy for their own ends. Michael Warner writes that homosexuals "have neither privacy *nor* publicness. ... In the United States, the judiciary, along with the military and its supporters in Congress and the White House, has gone to great lengths to make sure that they will have neither. It is this deformation of public and private that identity politics – and the performative ritual of coming out – tries to transform."[9] However, during the Cold War period, before identity politics, many gay and lesbian writers sought this "deformation" not through public acts of coming out but through the reconfiguration of privacy into something that could provide both a respite from persecution and, importantly, a means to resist it.

The Cold War Context

As the historian Allan Bérubé and others have shown, the massive mobilizations of World War II helped foster a burgeoning gay subculture.[10] Young men and women mobilized away from the family found new companions and acquaintances who shared a same-gender attraction; and as they moved through metropolitan centers, many found bars and other public venues where they could gather and meet more people like themselves. After the war, many settled in these cities, and gay and lesbian subcultures became more and more visible. At the same time, two major studies of sexuality brought further public attention to the existence of gay people and gay communities: Alfred Kinsey and his cohort's *Sexual Behavior in the Human Male* (1948) and their subsequent *Sexual Behavior in the Human Female* (1953).

Partly as a result of this wider visibility, state agencies began to crack down on what increasingly became viewed – despite Kinsey's attempts to explain it otherwise – as "abnormal" and "immoral" behavior. The historian John D'Emilio writes that from 1950 onward, "the danger posed by 'sexual perverts' became a staple of partisan rhetoric," creating fears of a "homosexual menace" that prompted widespread dismissals of queers (and people who were thought to be queer) from civil service jobs, the military, the post office, schools, and so on.[11] In 1952, the American Psychiatric Association listed homosexuality as a pathology in the first edition of its *Diagnostic and Statistical Manual of Mental Disorders*. And as the historian David K. Johnson explains, the "Lavender Scare" about the homosexual threat to national security and the national body far outstripped the so-called "Communist Witch Hunts" associated with McCarthyism, with the federal government firing far more people for being gay than for being communist.[12]

Mirroring this crackdown, a good deal of writing from the 1950s and the 1960s offered unflattering, pernicious, and often tragic representations of lesbian and gay characters, partly as a way to push readers to strive for sexual and gender "normality." As Anna G. Creadick explains in rich detail, the pursuit of normality – social, cultural, and sexual – was nearly a national obsession that was integrally bound to the wish to define and defend U.S. culture against the supposed anti-individualism of communism. And in mainstream literature, gay characters were often tragic foils meant to highlight the need for achieving the straight (and white) normality of the heterosexual family. Usually these queer characters were punished with violence, depression, exile, and death – often suicide – because of their nonnormative desires. In particular, Creadick discusses James Jones's *From Here to Eternity* (1951), which was both a popular and critical success, as an emblematic post–World War text that "evokes, but then excises, homosexual or 'queer' desire and erects a public, predatory, violent male heterosexuality in its place." Creadick adds: "In synch with a postwar science of sexual 'facts,' Jones's 'realistic' fiction ... reflected and helped to constitute a cultural shift from 'queer' to 'normality' in postwar understandings of sexuality." [13]

Not surprisingly, as gays and lesbians became demonized in mainstream literature and the public sphere, this crackdown also produced a significant rise in queer political activism and even militancy. Johnson writes that the Lavender Scare's "success in eliminating thousands of suspected homosexuals from the government would also lead to its undoing, as gay men and lesbians began to organize politically to challenge what they came to see as an unjust government policy" (10). D'Emilio charts the evolution of this "homosexual emancipation movement" during the postwar decades, focusing particularly on the "homophile" groups the Mattachine Society and the Daughters of Bilitis. [14] Although these groups started with "radical beginnings" (57) through activists' ties to the radical left, they gradually adopted a platform that sought "credibility" (83) through educational and social programs meant to demonstrate the "respectability" (75) of "normal" homosexuals (83). Yet the seeds of radicalism did not die, and East Coast groups began to take more direct action by protesting and lobbying for equal rights and justice, thus laying the foundations for more radical programs of gay liberation following the Stonewall riots (150). Although the push toward "respectability" can be read as a retreat to the closet's invisibility, the wish to resist the regimes of queer oppression never died.

This homophobic atmosphere of the Cold War inevitably shaped the literature of gay and lesbian writers. Often writers had to bury their treatments of gay identity and gay life in stories of tragedy or deeply gothic, cryptic narratives. To some extent, much like the lives of gay and lesbian individuals, queer writers could not be as open and direct as they would have liked to be and still get their works published. And yet, despite these pressures, gay and lesbian writing does not wholly acquiesce to the homophobic status quo. As Sherry, Jaime Harker, Robert J. Corber, and many others have demonstrated, the explosion of gay and lesbian writing beginning in the late 1940s attempted to shift public perceptions of homosexuality. Sherry demonstrates at length how queer artists, particularly gay men, had a profound and widespread influence on postwar culture and the arts on all levels. Susan Stryker shows how cheap paperbacks and "queer pulp" became the "venue of choice" for bringing depictions and discussions of nonnormative sexualities to a mass audience, sometimes with notable monetary success.[15] And Harker shows how these queer influences and queer representations, especially in the pulp market, "contributed to a larger breakdown of cultural hierarchy" between popular, highbrow, and middlebrow art and literature.[16]

The increased visibility of homosexuality in art and literature of course helped fuel cultural suspicions and anxieties about gays and lesbians. Harker notes that many American novels with gay or lesbian protagonists succumbed to presenting "gay life" as "lurid" by regularly indulging in stereotypes and clichés: male "effeminacy," "narcissism," "predatory gay sexuality," "gay murder," "suicide … and the threat of suicide," "[a]bsent fathers and smothering mothers," and so on (15). And some negative themes and stereotypes continued to appear in even the most sympathetic gay literature up through the late 1960s, including Mart Crowley's important, although now somewhat maligned, Broadway hit *The Boys in the Band* (1968), the first commercially successful play to deal extensively and explicitly with gay themes and characters. But many gay novelists also used their writing to challenge prevailing assumptions. These works "encouraged readerly sympathy through the suffering of the main characters. … Postwar gay novels insisted that 'we' are just like 'you'" (14). Calling this group of texts the "gay protest novel" (12), Harker shows how some queer writers thus sought to "domesticate homosexuality, claiming it as a legitimately American phenomenon" (14).

This peculiar combination of stereotype and resistance in the gay protest novel and other types of writing reveals the difficulty of evaluating Cold War literature (and the arts in general) in terms of the closet. As writers sought to generate "readerly sympathy" for their gay and lesbian subjects, they seemed to back away from the narratives of radical resistance and pride that became the mainstay of post-Stonewall writing. And yet the increasing openness of gay and lesbian writing during these decades also suggests a refusal to accept the secrecy mandated by society through the image of the closet. Although this openness might be aided by the general expectation that writers (and other artists) are allowed to be bohemian, it is also partly a result of a growing public curiosity about gays and lesbians and their refusal to remain completely in the shadows or assimilate wholly into mainstream American society. Indeed, as Corber notes, many gay male writers of the time made it clear in their works that "the primary source of gay male oppression was not the inaccessibility of the American dream, but the regulatory fictions that governed the production of gender and sexual identity" – not the tragedy of the closet but the imposition of the closet's oppression from the outside.[17] Although they might not seem to take an open stance of pride and liberation, these works still resist the narrow confines of shame and quietism that we in the twenty-first century have come to associate with being in the closet.

Cold War Writing

How Cold War writers responded to gay oppression and navigated the structures of silence and disclosure varied wildly, of course. A detailed survey of these writers might not accomplish any more than simply showing how the image of the closet does not easily map on to this diverse literary landscape. Nevertheless, it is still worth touching on some of the most prominent writers and works of this period to recall the breadth of gay and lesbian writing in these decades. My aim in providing this cursory list is to show how we might form a better, more accurate picture of Cold War America by seeing how gay and lesbian writers imagined strategies of privacy to cope with and resist the landscape of police crackdowns, governmental oppression, and public discourses focused on deviance and shame. I then conclude with a closer look at two key texts that also imagine turning privacy into a force of resistance and retaliation, a move that can help us see more clearly the historically specific structures of the closet prior to gay liberation.

It is commonly understood that a new era of queer writing in American literature began with the publication of two novels in 1948: Truman Capote's *Other Voices, Other Rooms* and Gore Vidal's *The City and the Pillar*. Vidal's novel follows the ex-soldier Jim Willard as he drifts through several gay American subcultures. Although it offers a positive and frank portrayal of gay identity and life, the novel does end on a negative note, with Jim raping (or in the original ending, murdering) his boyhood friend for refusing to have sex with him. Capote's novel tells the story of young Joel Knox, who slowly comes to terms with his own gender deviance – and, by implication, homosexuality – by consciously aligning himself with his queer, cross-dressing cousin Randolph. This novel, which preceded Vidal's by a few months, is often heralded as the first gay novel with a positive ending to reach a mainstream audience, although it is obviously indebted to the southern gothic deconstruction of sexual and gender categories in the works of his slightly older contemporary, Carson McCullers. Yet Capote was also criticized throughout his career for not writing more explicitly gay stories afterward. Indeed, although no one could ever accuse Capote himself of being closeted, even this first novel's emphasis on multiple "rooms" would seem to invoke the image of the closet. But we should note that at the end of the novel, Joel accepts his sexuality by returning inside the house from the garden; his "coming out" is thus a kind of "going in" that does not map on to the domestic geography of the closet. Similarly, as I have argued elsewhere, his later short story "The Thanksgiving Visitor" (1967) returns to the complex architecture of the southern gothic to imagine a sexuality that is openly admitted yet still never described, again breaking down the binary structures of "in" and "out" associated with the closet.[18]

Tennessee Williams's work similarly weaves complex narratives and dramatic performances of silence and disclosure in ways that do not readily fit the more recent model of the closet. In *Cat on a Hot Tin Roof* (1955), for example, Brick's alcoholism is clearly rooted in his rejection of his friend Skipper after Skipper confesses his homosexual desires to Brick, as well as Brick's own panic about whether he might also be gay. *Suddenly, Last Summer* (1958) pushes these questions of confession and revelation further, with the whole play slowly winding toward Catherine's almost forced admission that her cousin Sebastian had been procuring sex with boys. But as many critics have noted, Williams's use of these tropes and structures of the closet are not so straightforward. As David Savran writes, "[t]hroughout Williams's work, the closet ... is the subject of innumerable metaphoric and metonymic transformations, a constantly shifting site of concealment and disclosure, speech and silence," a site that ultimately performs a dual function as "both a means of concealment and privileged perspective on both the dominant culture and what it seeks to police and contain."[19]

Corber offers another good example of how the closet functions in Williams's work. Although some have criticized Williams for not being more direct about the protagonist Mr. Krupper's homosexuality in the short story "Hard Candy" (1954), Corber shows how the story's "evasiveness" and "equivocations" prevent readers from showing Mr. Krupper the same dislike as the other characters who "deny his humanity" do (112). Thus, by "reproducing the structures of the closet" and making his homosexuality the story's "open secret," Williams "prevents our curiosity about Mr. Krupper from reducing him to an 'insensibly malign object.' Mr. Krupper's homosexuality becomes a sign not of his corruption but of his subjecthood, thereby discouraging us from positioning him as sexually other" (112). Obviously Williams did not adopt exactly the same relation to the closet in all his writing, and there is no question that he occasionally used the trope to link homosexuality to secrecy and shame. But Corber's analysis shows that Williams typically used the closet to open up the complexity of his characters and to allow us to develop an interest in them that goes beyond squeezing them into rigid sexual categories – in Corber's words, an interest that is more than "pornographic" (112). Here the secrecy of the closet becomes an open secret that not only grants a perspective on the regimes of hatred and oppression but also guarantees a privacy that makes the subject more complex because he is more unknowable.

Corber's reading of Williams offers a useful way to think about privacy in the works of two major Cold War poets: Elizabeth Bishop and Frank O'Hara. As with many works we would associate with the closet, Bishop's and O'Hara's poems often present queer themes with a subtlety that non-queer readers might miss entirely. But although their references to their queer relationships and their queer sexual politics might be viewed as oblique, neither Bishop nor O'Hara could ever be described as secretive to the point of hiding their sexuality. Building on the work of Joanne Felt Diehl and others, Steven Gould Axelrod argues that Bishop's poems, especially her 1955 collection *A Cold Spring*, "explore a range of ideas and feelings particular to … lesbian culture," even as their observational style, when viewed "from the standpoint of classical [i.e., nonsexual] politics[,] … may appear relatively innocuous."[20] This oblique engagement with lesbianism may seem to us like an act of closeting, but it is less an act of denial or suppression than it is what Kamran Javadizadeh calls a "performance of modesty" – an attempt to keep the private aspects of Bishop's personal life private.[21] Thus, although many of Bishop's poems "have controlled surfaces that deflect an easy gaze to the emotions beneath," as Gary Fountain writes, their "reticence and anonymity" are in fact part of a complex pose that is tied both to her artistic belief that it was not "proper for a poet to be so overtly 'confessional'" and to a more urgent "strategy for survival" that helped divert attention not only from her relationships with women but also, and more seriously, from "what she felt to be her [personal] failure in these relationships."[22]

According to Scott Herring, O'Hara, by contrast, was "quintessentially open – immediate, chatty, visible, and candid about his sexual preferences."[23] And yet, not unlike Bishop, his poetry also dwells on the minutiae of objects and seemingly mundane observations without commenting didactically on their larger political and sexual significance. The queer dimensions of poems such as "Poem (Lana Turner Has Collapsed!)" (1962) and "Having a Coke with You" (1960) are immediately recognizable and even gesture toward a utopian model of queer futurity, as José Esteban Muñoz has argued.[24] But O'Hara's unique form of descriptive poetics (what he called "Personism") also challenges the homosexual prohibitions of the Cold War era by refusing to reveal anything particularly meaningful about the identity of the speaking subject or about O'Hara himself. As Herring shows, O'Hara's attention to the impersonal details of everyday life render the poet's identity invisible through the public medium of the poem itself. Mediating the relationship between speaker and reader, O'Hara's poems "fashion a novel community of impersonal individuals who may never meet ... [but] instead gather over the object that is the personal poem" (425–426). In this way, much as Bishop cultivates privacy through modesty, O'Hara cultivates privacy through a "depersonalization" that simultaneously "reveals all, only to reveal nothing about himself" (425).

Some writers were, of course, less interested in deploying structures of secrecy or privacy in their writing, including John Rechy, Allen Ginsberg, and William S. Burroughs.[25] Yet even some writers of queer pulp explored the possibilities of privacy in ways that are only now beginning to be recognized and understood. Ann Bannon, the foremost writer of lesbian pulp, is well known for her series of books depicting, among other things, the butch-femme lesbian subculture of mid-century Greenwich Village. Although the five books collectively known for the central butch character as the *Beebo Brinker Chronicles* have garnered countless fans and admirers, Julian Carter argues that the sixth book, *The Marriage* (1960), has been largely neglected because its depiction of a marriage between a gay man and a lesbian does not appeal to newer generations of queer readers. As Carter explains, however, this "gay marriage" is not an attempt to keep the characters' queer desires in the closet; instead, it protects the couple from scrutiny and gives them access to the power and protections of middle-class life while still allowing them to pursue their queer desires. It "signals an emotionally satisfying resolution to the common gay dilemma of how to be socially conventional while erotically and emotionally deviant."[26] In addition to all of the other ways in which Bannon's novels exploit and challenge their readers' own feelings of shame, this novel also explores the power and advantages of privacy that the closet can afford.

Taking a slightly different approach, Patricia Highsmith's 1952 quasi-pulp novel *The Price of Salt* (which she originally published under the pseudonym Claire Morgan) offers an unprecedented happy ending for its lesbian protagonists – one that would seem to reject the image of the closet completely. And yet, the central characters Therese and Carol repeatedly respond to one of the central conflicts by asking for privacy. Throughout the novel, Carol's ex-husband continues to threaten to deny her all visiting rights with her daughter because of her lesbian affairs in the past, and once he gains evidence of her affair with Therese, he follows through on his threat. The heart of the threat would seem to be that Carol must cease all contact with Therese, retreat into the closet, and remain celibate. But Carol and Therese never seek to hide or deny their relationship – only to flee from her ex-husband's spying eyes in a cross-country car chase. What these women want is not to be invisible but to be left alone.

This reading of *The Price of Salt* can also help us think about how privacy plays out in another important gay text from the 1950s: James Baldwin's *Giovanni's Room* (1956). Similar to Capote's *Other Voices, Other Rooms*, Baldwin's novel seems to prefigure the trope of the closet by linking the narrator David's feelings of pleasure and shame with the room in which he enjoys his love affair with Giovanni. When they are alone in the room, David is happiest; but when the couple moves outside the room, such as to the gay bar, David becomes angry and troubled. It is easy to read this reaction as David's anxiety about his homosexuality and his refusal to "come out" both to himself and others. But we could also read David's reaction as his anxiety about being reduced to a one-dimensional figure by others who would "deny his humanity," as Corber writes about Mr. Krupper in Williams's "Hard Candy." This reading of privacy also helps explain why one of the most famous African American writers of this time would choose to write his most openly gay novel using white protagonists. Because African Americans had never really been granted the right to privacy in U.S. culture, and because the civil rights movement was demanding just and equal treatment in the *public* sphere, privacy simply could not form a very useful basis for creating models of complex, queer, black subjectivity in the 1950s (a possibility that may open new ways of thinking about the work of Baldwin's friend Lorraine Hansberry, who wrote letters to the gay periodicals *The Ladder* and *One* about politics, feminism, and gay rights). This reading of *Giovanni's Room* does not deny the other machinations of shame, secrecy, and self-loathing that we more often associate with the closet, but it also opens up the possibility for a more positive reading that asks us to think about the power of privacy.

Finally, I turn to two other Cold War novels to show how these writers transform the notion of privacy into a means of resistance and retaliation against homophobic American society. The first is Christopher Isherwood's *A Single Man* (1964), in which the protagonist George indulges in a revenge fantasy against a local newspaper editor who had "started a campaign against sex deviates":[27]

> Then, that newspaper editor, George thinks, how funny to kidnap him and the staff-writers responsible for the sex-deviate articles – and maybe also the police chief, and the head of the vice squad, and those ministers who endorsed the campaign from their pulpits – and take them all to a secret underground

movie studio where, after a little persuasion – no doubt just showing the red-hot pokers and pincers would be quite sufficient – they would perform every possible sexual act, in pairs and in groups, with a display of the utmost enjoyment. The film would then be developed and prints of it would be rushed to all the movie theaters. George's assistants would chloroform the ushers so the lights couldn't be turned up, lock the exits, overpower the projectionists, and proceed to run the film under the heading of Coming Attractions.

(38)

It is important that George's fantasy of revenge is not a turnabout where the secrets of the editors and the vice squad are discovered and revealed. Rather, George fantasizes about forcing these people to commit sexual acts for which, we assume, they have no desire – to act and become something they are not. George's fantasy is a fantasy of the closet insofar as he wants these people (presumably men) to adopt or perform publicly a sexuality that is different from their "true" identity. Yet it is not a fantasy of the closet that seeks to discover and reveal these men's inner secrets. Oddly, despite the remarkable detail of his fantasy, he still respects his victims' privacy.

Indeed, privacy is crucial to George. He refuses to tell any of his casual acquaintances that his partner Jim has died in a car crash, not because he wants to hide his sexuality but because he does not want them to know his business. Similarly, George and Jim's house occupies a secluded corner of their neighborhood: "[Y]ou could only get to it by the bridge across the creek; the surrounding trees and the steep bushy cliff behind shut it in like a house in a forest clearing" (20). Yet their secluded "island," as Jim calls it, again does not hide the fact of their relationship (20). George's straight, married neighbors all know them as a couple and even invite them over for meals. What the men enjoy is not secrecy but privacy. And this sense of privacy is what George feels has been violated by the newspaper editor. It is not that he fears being discovered and shamed for his homosexuality but that the sanctified spaces of his pleasure – his house and the various sites of gay cruising targeted by the editor, police chief, and vice squad – have been invaded by people who refuse to let him live as a gay man. Although Isherwood's novel still ends controversially with a gay death – George's – this pervasive emphasis on privacy makes it hard to read this novel strictly in terms that conflate the closet with secrecy and shame.

A similar fantasy of queer retaliation plays out in John Kennedy Toole's comic New Orleans novel *A Confederacy of Dunces*, which was not published until 1980 but was written at the height of the Cold War in 1963. Late in the novel, the protagonist, Ignatius Reilly, sees a young gay man dressed as a sailor and voices the same paranoid suspicion that was expressed over and over during the Lavender Scare: "This is extremely serious. ... Every

soldier and sailor that we see could simply be some mad decadent in disguise. My God! ... The United States is probably totally defenseless!"[28] But
Ignatius also quickly realizes that infiltrating the governments of the United
States and other global powers with queers in disguise could be a strategy
for world peace:

> How many of the military leaders of the world may simply be deranged old
> sodomites acting out some fake fantasy role? Actually, this might be quite ben-
> eficial to the world. It could mean an end to war forever. ... The power-crazed
> leaders of the world would certainly be surprised to find that their military
> leaders and troops were only masquerading sodomites who were only too
> eager to meet the masquerading sodomite armies of other nations in order to
> have dances and balls and learn some foreign dance steps. ... Perhaps you [gay
> people] are the hope for the future.
>
> (263)

Turning the homophobic fears of the state back onto itself, Ignatius plots
the formation of a global political movement that will secretly put gays and
lesbians in the highest seats of power and replace war with nondestructive,
hedonistic orgies.

Not surprisingly, Ignatius's ambition does not go to plan. At the launch
party for his campaign at the French Quarter apartment of the flamboyant
gay man Dorian Greene, Ignatius's prospective recruits ironically thwart
his scheme by doing exactly what he wants: partying. Ignatius fails precisely because these gay people are *too* gay. And if we read this spectacular failure in terms of the closet, we discover interesting and unorthodox
ways to think about the relationships between secrecy and power, privacy
and politics, and pleasure and identity. Essentially, Ignatius is asking these
queers to go back into the closet by making themselves undercover agents
so that they can change the political system and thus create a new world
in which queers could then be "out." Yet the novel's campily stereotypical
queers are already "out" and having fun, and they refuse to go back "in,"
even if it might make things better for them in the long run by stopping
the homophobic crackdowns of the Cold War era. However, even though
they are "out" personally, Toole's characters also remain "in" the political closet, because they refuse to challenge the political structures that
oppress them. As Dorian points out to Ignatius, the gays and lesbians of
the French Quarter all know the undercover cop Mancuso who regularly
dresses up to entrap gay men for solicitation. Yet instead of denounc-
ing this surveillance and demanding equal treatment, they either ignore
Mancuso or comically turn the state's power back on itself by report-
ing *him* for solicitation. They do not want to be involved with the politics of the state on any level and instead simply want the state to leave

them alone so that they can indulge in the pleasures of their daily lives. Although they mock the state in the figure of Mancuso, Toole's queer characters do not seek to transform the public sphere, because to them all the fun happens in private parties. And when Ignatius tries to force them "out" by pushing them into politics, the queer community pushes *him* out of the house. Thus, however much Toole's portrayal of the queer community appears to amount to a satirical critique, he ultimately contorts the boundaries between in and out in ways that reject secrecy in favor of a strangely liberated privacy.

This convoluted relationship between privacy, resistance, and a kind of sexual freedom characterizes much of the literature of the Cold War era. And although the freedom found within privacy is different from the sexual liberation of the 1970s, there were continuities between the two periods. Henry Abelove shows how the anticolonialist politics of Bishop, Baldwin, Ginsberg, O'Hara, and others influenced the similarly anticolonialist politics of the Gay Liberation Front (GLF). And this attention to historical continuities further challenges the common misconception that the Cold War was a period of languishing "in" the closet prior to the great "coming out" after Stonewall. However, Abelove also notes that most Cold War writers were (if they were still alive) ambivalent at best about the liberation politics of the 1970s (86). As this chapter has revealed, one way of accounting for this ambivalence is to pay closer attention to the changing shape of the image of the closet during that time. When "GLFers," as Abelove calls them, wrote that "we shall welcome your contribution to COME OUT," they invoked an image of the closet where being "in" meant secrecy and denial as well as shame and humiliation (86). Yet during the Cold War, with all the terror and violence hurled at the "homosexual menace," many writers sought to explore the positive aspects of the closet, where secrecy coincided with the potentially more empowering notion of privacy. For them, the closet could also be a source of power and safety, a window onto the structures of persecution and oppression and a force for imagining and representing the complexity of the human subject through art and literature. And although none of these writers took a naïvely utopian view of the closet's protective space, some of them did imagine ways of turning their request for privacy into fantasies of queer retaliation and unambiguous rejections of official sexual paradigms. This fantasy of using violence, espionage, and trickery in order to be left alone is hardly the image of liberation for which the GLF and others fought in the post-Stonewall era. But understanding the fantasies and meanings of privacy for queers during the Cold War might still offer unique opportunities for rethinking sexual politics today.

NOTES

1 Eve Kosofsky Sedgwick, *Epistemology of the Closet* (Berkeley: University of California Press, 1990), 71; hereafter cited in text.

2 Marlon B. Ross, "Beyond the Closet as Raceless Paradigm," in *Black Queer Studies: A Critical Anthology*, ed. E. Patrick Johnson and Mae G. Henderson (Durham: Duke University Press, 2005), 161, 163; hereafter cited in text.

3 George Chauncey, *Gay New York: Gender, Urban Culture, and the Making of the Gay Male World, 1890–1940* (New York: Basic Books, 1994), 6.

4 Henry Abelove, *Deep Gossip* (Minneapolis: University of Minnesota Press, 2003), 85; hereafter cited in text.

5 Michael S. Sherry, *Gay Artists in Modern American Culture: An Imagined Conspiracy* (Chapel Hill: University of North Carolina Press, 2007), 96. See also Michael P. Brown, *Closet Space: Geographies of Metaphor from the Body to the Globe* (New York: Routledge, 2000), 1–6.

6 See David M. Halperin and Valerie Traub, "Beyond Gay Pride," in *Gay Shame*, ed. David M. Halperin and Valerie Traub (Chicago: University of Chicago Press, 2009), 8–15.

7 Heather Love, *Feeling Backward: Loss and the Politics of Queer History* (Cambridge, MA: Harvard University Press, 2007), 30.

8 George Chauncey, "The Trouble with Shame," in *Gay Shame*, ed. David M. Halperin and Valerie Traub (Chicago: University of Chicago Press, 2009), 281; hereafter cited in text.

9 Michael Warner, *Publics and Counterpublics* (New York: Zone Books, 2005), 53.

10 See Allan Bérubé, *Coming Out under Fire: The History of Gay Men and Women in World War II* (New York: The Free Press, 1990), 98–127.

11 John D'Emilio, *Making Trouble: Essays on Gay History, Politics, and the University* (New York: Routledge, 1992), 59.

12 David K. Johnson, *The Lavender Scare: The Cold War Persecution of Gays and Lesbians in the Federal Government* (Chicago: University of Chicago Press, 2004), 2; hereafter cited in text.

13 Anna G. Creadick, *Perfectly Average: The Pursuit of Normality in Postwar America* (Amherst: University of Massachusetts Press, 2010), 97, 117.

14 John D'Emilio, *Sexual Politics, Sexual Communities: The Making of a Homosexual Minority in the United States, 1940–1970*, 2nd ed. (Chicago: University of Chicago Press, 1983), 4; hereafter cited in text.

15 Susan Stryker, *Queer Pulp: Perverted Passions from the Golden Age of the Paperback* (San Francisco: Chronicle Books, 2001), 8.

16 Jaime Harker, *Middlebrow Queer: Christopher Isherwood in America* (Minneapolis: University of Minnesota Press, 2013), 47; hereafter cited in text.

17 Robert J. Corber, *Homosexuality in Cold War America: Resistance and the Crisis of Masculinity* (Durham: Duke University Press, 1997), 5; hereafter cited in text.

18 See Michael P. Bibler, "How to Love Your Local Homophobe: Southern Hospitality and the Unremarkable Queerness of Truman Capote's 'The Thanksgiving Visitor,'" *MFS Modern Fiction Studies* 58, no. 2 (2012): 284–307.

19 David Savran, *Communists, Cowboys, and Queers: The Politics of Masculinity in the Work of Arthur Miller and Tennessee Williams* (Minneapolis: University of Minnesota Press, 1992), 104–105, 109.

20 Steven Gould Axelrod, "Elizabeth Bishop and Containment Policy," *American Literature* 75, no. 4 (2003): 858. See also Joanne Felt Diehl, "Bishop's Sexual Politics," in *Elizabeth Bishop: The Geography of Gender*, ed. Marilyn May Lombardi (Charlottesville: University Press of Virginia, 1993), 17–45, and the other essays in that volume.

21 Kamran Javadizadeh, "Elizabeth Bishop's Closet Drama," *Arizona Quarterly* 67, no. 3 (2011): 121.

22 Gary Fountain, "'Closets, Closets, and More Closets!' Elizabeth Bishop's Lesbianism," in *Queer Representations: Reading Lives, Reading Cultures*, ed. Martin Duberman (New York: New York University Press, 1997), 256, 256, 256, 256, 253.

23 Terrell Scott Herring, "Frank O'Hara's Open Closet," *PMLA* 117, no. 3 (2002): 416; hereafter cited in text.

24 José Esteban Muñoz, *Cruising Utopia: The Then and There of Queer Futurity* (New York: New York University Press, 2009), 5–9.

25 Rechy's novel *City of Night* (1963), a story about a male hustler, became a best-seller. Ginsberg's *Howl* (1955) resulted in an obscenity trial because of its frank depiction of gay sex, but Ginsberg also used the queer dimensions of his other writing to explore larger social, spiritual, and philosophical themes and to reach many readers beyond his bohemian and queer devotees. Burroughs's inclusion of queer sexuality in his work also caused scandal, but in keeping with the public dismissal of the most overt sexual writing, his 1952 manuscript *Queer* was not published until 1985.

26 Julian Carter, "Gay Marriage and Pulp Fiction: Homonormativity, Disidentification and Affect in Ann Bannon's Lesbian Novels," *GLQ: A Journal of Lesbian and Gay Studies* 15, no. 4 (2009): 585.

27 Christopher Isherwood, *A Single Man* (New York: Simon and Schuster, 1964), 36; hereafter cited in text.

28 John Kennedy Toole, *A Confederacy of Dunces* (New York: Grove Weidenfeld, 1980), 262; hereafter cited in text.

9

The Time of AIDS and the Rise of "Post-Gay"

While the 1970s saw the birth of avowedly gay and lesbian literature, the 1980s and 1990s saw an exponential increase in its production. As Robert McRuer notes, during this period, "literally thousands of novelists, poets, and playwrights published or performed works about gay people."[1] Writers' groups, literary magazines, and book reviews were "devoted entirely to gay and lesbian writing," and the annual Lambda Literary Awards (founded in 1989) "even provided institutional recognition of outstanding achievement in lesbian and gay literature."[2] In the 1980s, gay male fiction crossed over, although this much-remarked-upon phenomenon describes the adoption of gay titles by major publishers more than it does widespread consumption by straight audiences. Christopher Bram observes that during the 1980s and early 1990s, "thanks to the existence of the gay press and gay bookstores, gay-themed titles virtually sold themselves. ... It was the age of the gay midlist novel. Publishers could count on a small but solid profit while hoping an occasional novel would cross over into bigger sales."[3] Although lesbian literature was less likely to appear in the midlists of large- or medium-sized houses, a number of vigorous independent feminist publishers also catered to a healthy lesbian readership.

The outpouring of gay and lesbian literature since 1980 has responded to and helped shape key developments in gay and lesbian culture. It is around two of the most momentous of these developments – the AIDS epidemic and the phenomenon of "post-gay" – that this chapter is organized. Each of these developments has its own lineaments and each has had quite specific manifestations and ramifications; yet they are not unrelated. The AIDS crisis and the idea of post-gay both make central in public and literary discourse the issue of sexual identity, on the one hand, and the issue of sexual identity's undoing, on the other. The late twentieth century and the early twenty-first century have been characterized as much by challenges to the notions of gay and lesbian identity that were established during the 1970s as they have by continuations of those notions. It is the varied literary negotiations of these shifting perspectives on sexual identity that focuses this chapter.

The AIDS epidemic entailed an assertion of gay and lesbian politics that was arguably unmatched in vigor since the first flush of liberation in the early 1970s. But activist responses to AIDS also displaced the "ethnic" model of same-sexuality that had developed during the 1970s by shifting the emphasis of AIDS discourse from groups to (risky and safe) behaviors – a shift that was not only medically sensible but also politically crucial, as it undermined the stereotyping of AIDS as a "gay disease." This oscillation between the assertion and interrogation of identity is also evident in the idea of post-gay, a term I apply to a broad set of disparate, and even contradictory, trends that nevertheless share a rhetorical abandonment of defining features of 1970s gay and lesbian identity, culture, and politics.

In its most prominent manifestation, post-gay refers to an assimilationist discourse that declares that gays are no different from straights, apart from "who they love" and a few missing "rights." In this usage, post-gay indexes a historical moment in which, it is frequently claimed, gays and lesbians are accorded historically unprecedented levels of acceptance and representation and in which the need for distinctively LGBTQ ways of socializing, organizing sexuality, and viewing the world has fallen away.[4] But although post-gay rhetoric often appears to wish away gay culture, it continues to rely on the idea of discrete sexual identities. The popular assumption of a biological basis of sexuality is exemplary of the post-gay attitude in that it asserts but also downplays sexual identity, positing it as a benign genetic variation without necessary cultural significance.

Perhaps counterintuitively, this chapter also deploys post-gay to refer to the anti-assimilationist term "queer" that has named both a theoretical development and a way of living sexually nonnormatively since the early 1990s. I find it useful to group queer under post-gay because, like today's assimilationism, albeit on very different grounds, queer culture also rejects certain orthodoxies of the 1970s – including, most centrally, the idea of stable identities that are organized around same-sex desire. But (as many have noted) there is a tension between queer's foundational refusal of sexual identity and the proliferation of gendered and sexual identifications that, in practice, both queer theory and queer culture promote.

Identity can only be asserted, or indeed undone, in relation to the defining context of the group, and this chapter traces the representation of gay and lesbian identity in literature since 1980 in relation to two keywords for homosexual collectivity: "community" and "family." The idea of a gay and lesbian community only makes sense in the postliberation context, and assumptions about this idea's usefulness or validity shaped the representation and experience of same-sex identity throughout the 1980s and 1990s. "Family," the related but alternative term for gay and lesbian collectivities, came into popular use in the 1980s. For many gays and lesbians, who are often excluded or alienated from their families of birth, the idea of alternative kinship groups composed of friends, lovers, and ex-lovers provided a compensatory source of emotional sustenance. But, as Kath Weston notes in *Families We Choose*, an anthropological study of 1980s gay and lesbian San Francisco, "gay families [cannot] be understood apart from the families in which lesbians and gay men [have] grown up."[5] This tension and overlap between biological families and "families we choose" has proven to be galvanizing for gay and lesbian literature since 1980.

In what follows, I begin with an exploration of literary responses to AIDS, responses in which the interplay of individual and communal experience is central. The second section takes up the challenge that the politics of difference of the 1980s posed to the white supremacist assumptions of gay literature, exploring key black writers' representations of intersecting racial and sexual identities. The third section focuses on the transgressive queer fiction of the 1990s, with its in-your-face challenges to the so-called mainstreaming of gay identity. The final section turns to the phenomenon of contemporary post-gay writing, exploring related issues, such as to what extent U.S. literary culture has assimilated queerness and to what extent gay and lesbian literature has (as is often asserted to be the case) ceased to be a vital cultural force.

AIDS, Community, and Literary Form

Setting the scene for a tale of a casual sexual encounter in the early 1970s, the narrator of Jane DeLynn's *Don Juan in the Village* (1990) says, "I was poor then, and lived in a walk-up on the Bowery. And yet I was not unhappy, for I lived entirely for love. Much of the city did then, though it never will again."[6] DeLynn's novel of lesbian cruising shares with a number of gay male novels from the 1990s an elegiac perspective on the social and sexual experimentation of the 1970s – a perspective that is carried in titles such as Jack Fritscher's *Some Dance to Remember* (1990), Christopher Coe's *Such Times* (1994), Brad Gooch's *The Golden Age of Promiscuity* (1996), and Edmund White's *The Farewell Symphony* (1997). By bestowing the honorific of "love" on the promiscuity that energized gay New York in the postliberation, pre-AIDS period, DeLynn affectingly epitomizes the celebratory tone of these elegy-novels, a tone that contrasts markedly with the condemnation and disgust with which 1970s gay sexual culture was often painted in AIDS discourse, including that which emanated from some gay AIDS activists.

First described in 1981 (although not named as such until the following year), AIDS had a swift, devastating impact on the gay male population that abated only with the introduction of antiretroviral therapies around 1997. If the 1990s saw the publication of successful novelistic responses to AIDS, developing a literary response to the syndrome at first proved difficult. As Richard Canning notes, AIDS writing during the early years of the epidemic "was an especially tardy and uneven affair. ... Very few AIDS literary works appeared in the midst of the unfolding disaster, as those people closest to it struggled to comprehend, to care, to bury their dead and to look after their own health."[7] As works began to emerge from 1982 onward, some forms proved more fitting than others. In the view of many critics and writers, the novel, with its imperative of closure and its emphasis on individual experience, generally proved inadequate to the devastations of the syndrome. Shorter forms, such as lyric poetry and the short story, were often felt to deal more successfully with the epidemic.

It is not surprising that some of the most effective responses to AIDS were poetry, the literary medium that is typically associated with the elegiac impulse that seeks to make otherwise overwhelming grief tractable through the discipline of form. Collections such as Mark Doty's *My Alexandria* (1993) and *Atlantis* (1995) and Thom Gunn's *The Man with Night Sweats* (1992) deployed consummate poetic craft to respond to the epidemic. In his indicatively titled memoir *The Poetry of Healing* (1997), the poet-physician Rafael Campo eloquently describes the usefulness of "archaic" verse forms as a means of dealing with AIDS and contrasts them to other representations and experiences of the epidemic: "the regularity of resting brain wave activity in contrast to the disorganized spiking of a seizure ... the single-voiced, ringing chant of a slogan at an ACT UP rally in contrast to the indecipherable rumblings of an AIDS-funding debate on the Senate floor."[8]

The formal qualities of the short story – notably its contrary tendencies of narrative suspension and epiphany – also made it well suited to tackling the syndrome. In an interview, Edmund White said of *The Darker Proof* (1987), a collection of short stories about men living with AIDS that he coauthored with English writer Adam Mars-Jones, that the short story form afforded "a more angular and less predictable" approach to the "inevitable trajectory" of health, decline, and death that the novel virtually dictated.[9] Two of the most affecting AIDS texts are, indeed, collections of short stories: Allan Barnett's *The Body and Its Dangers* (1990) and Rebecca Brown's *The Gifts of the Body* (1994). The latter was written from the perspective of an AIDS caretaker, a role many lesbians adopted.[10]

The Darker Proof initiated a significant strategy in AIDS fiction by deliberately not naming the syndrome. In eliding the medical term, such fiction, as White puts it, sought to "show the human side" of the experiences of those intimate with AIDS.[11] Mobilizing a longstanding impulse of literary discourse, the AIDS fiction and poetry of the 1980s and 1990s sought to access experiential truths that were inaccessible to the discourses constructing AIDS as a biomedical problem. Thus Campo writes that AIDS poetry enabled a "richness of response" that counteracted the ineffectiveness of bland public health pronouncements in the face of continued risky sex. In place of those pronouncements, Campo continues, "I have found myself wishing that more poems would be written, in red graffiti spray-painted across vacant billboard – that more rules be broken, that the truth be told."[12] It is also perhaps the case that the reluctance to name the syndrome and – pace White – to represent death in many AIDS texts suggests, as Dale Peck writes, that it was felt that "literature might succeed in capturing the experience only by avoiding it, or at least not tackling it head on."[13] Peck's statement gestures toward the traumatic enormity of AIDS, which meant, for many writers, that its representation was paradoxically best managed through various modes of indirection. The novels mentioned at the start of this section often exhibit this tactic. Gooch's *The Golden Age of Promiscuity*, for instance, signals the end of the golden age of the 1970s only with a cameo in its closing pages by Gaëtan Dugas, the French-Canadian air steward identified as Patient Zero in Randy Shilts's *And the Band Played On* (1987), a much-criticized history of the emergence of AIDS. And White's autobiographic *The Farewell Symphony*, an epic chronicle of 1970s New York City, hurries through the deaths of the narrator's friends in its final few pages and breaks down completely when the narrator comes to the death of his lover.

Traumatic though it proved to be, AIDS is also characterized in gay literature as an experience that gives shape to the historical trajectory of a community. This historicization can often look like teleology, even eschatology. For instance, the protagonist of Robert Ferro's novel *Second Son* (1988) reflects that the "sterile, hopeless bathroom for the sick" is "the end of a line that had led from the center of countless dance floors, under dazzling lights, energy, protection, the insulation of endless youth."[14] But the celebratory note tends to override the ominous one, as in Ferro's subsequent description of gay men's experience of promiscuity as a "sudden bursting of beauty and exuberance into [their] lives ... the result of natural forces magnified by great numbers, into a phenomenon."[15] Here the figuration of promiscuity in terms of "natural forces" and "great numbers" provides a parallel to the epidemic spread of AIDS among gay men that picks up on the earlier image of the historical "line." The invocation of "beauty and exuberance," however, militates against the idea that AIDS is promiscuity's dark mirror image.

Either explicitly or implicitly, then, AIDS texts connect individual experiences of the syndrome with the collective, epidemiological experience of the gay community.[16] But many of these texts have been criticized for what they leave out about the AIDS experience – their unrepresentativeness on the basis of race, class, gender, and region. Although they are two of the more well-regarded AIDS novels, Coe's *Such Times* and Christopher Davis's *Valley of the Shadow* (1988) typify the focus on successful, white, metropolitan gay men for which such novels have been often criticized. These criticisms bespeak not only the urgencies of AIDS among various non-white and non-gay communities but also the impact of the politics of difference or of multiculturalism. Indeed, in the LGBTQ context, the politics of difference was given impetus by the AIDS crisis, as evidenced by debates over the representativeness of activist groups such as ACT UP.[17] It is to the assertion of a distinctively black LGBTQ literature during the 1980s and 1990s – a literature that fashioned its own distinctive responses to AIDS – that the next section turns.

The Difference That Race Makes

"*All the protagonists are blond; all the Blacks are criminal and negligible.*"[18] With this opening sentence, Joseph Beam's introduction to *In the Life* (1986) – the first anthology of writings by black gay men – registers its debt to a landmark collection of black feminist writings, *All the Women Are White, All the Blacks Are Men, But Some of Us Are Brave* (1982). Difference politics had an impact on feminist discourse and therefore on lesbian literary culture before it did on avowedly gay male writing, with writers such as Michelle Cliff, June Jordan, and Audre Lorde producing a substantial body of black lesbian literature by the early 1980s. In contrast, Beam's introduction points to the elision of the black gay presence both in white gay imagery and in the African American community's self-representation. Deploying the multiculturalist trope of visibility, Beam stresses the importance of a distinctively gay black male literature through a chiastic formulation: "[V]isibility is survival. ... Survival is visibility."[19]

Beam died of HIV/AIDS–related causes before completing the sequel to *In the Life, Brother to Brother.* Published in 1991 under the stewardship of the poet Essex Hemphill, *Brother to Brother*, like *In the Life*, is a miscellany of short fiction, autobiographical pieces, interviews, and poetry. It also tracks the intersection of blackness and gayness, but this imperative is given new urgency by AIDS. In his introduction, Hemphill writes that, rather than rendering the gay community more "responsible," the epidemic has made clear "how significant are the cultural and economic differences" between black and white gay men, as evidenced by the disproportionate number of black deaths.[20] *Brother to Brother* devotes a section to autobiographical and poetic representations of AIDS, with writers such as Walter Rico Burrell, David Frechette, and Assoto Saint providing potent doses of testimony and lament.

If the book in many ways stresses the embattled status of black gay men, Hemphill's introduction anticipates the flourishing of black gay literature. Hemphill draws more overtly than Beam did on the "heritage of Negritude" to posit black gay self-representation as distinct from both its white gay and black straight counterparts: "We must begin to identify what a black gay sensibility is; identify its esthetic qualities and components ... and then determine how this sensibility and esthetic relates to and differs from African American literature as a whole."[21] But although gayness makes an indelible difference to black identity for Hemphill, like Beam before him, he stresses the connection of black gay men to a community that disavows them: these "invisible brothers ... have *always* participated in the positive nurturing roles in the structures of family within the African American community."[22]

One popular version of the full representation of the intersection of race and gay sexuality for which Hemphill called was provided in the 1990s and early 2000s by the novels of E. Lynn Harris (who died in 2009). Harris's trilogy *Invisible Life* (1991), *Abide with Me* (1994), and *Just As I Am* (1999) narrates the search for romantic happiness and career success by Raymond Winston Tyler, Jr., a gay black attorney, and a range of similarly upwardly mobile, African American characters. As was the case for Beam and Hemphill, for Harris the difficulty of living in and contributing to the black community is definitive of gay African American existence, and that difficulty is again conveyed through the trope of invisibility. Raymond wishes to be "an asset to the black community," and narrative tension is generated in the third novel when he is nominated for a federal judgeship but is not endorsed by the NAACP or church groups.[23]

Harris tropes on racial and sexual passing with Raymond, who moves uncertainly between men and women in the first two books, describing his story as "the saga of the tragic sexual mulatto."[24] The sexual passing of Raymond and other gay and bisexual characters has damaging and sometimes tragic results. Harris anticipates the media panic of the 2000s about black men on the Down Low with an episode from the first book in which a young black woman, Candance, dies of AIDS-related complications from HIV passed on to her by her fiancé, who is Raymond's closeted ex-lover.[25] Indeed, the trilogy, which evolves in tandem with the television talk show genre, engages with a range of representations of sexuality from the 1990s mediascape, including trans identities and transphobia, child sexual abuse, Queer Nation and outing, and Jennie Livingston's 1990 documentary about urban black and Latino ballroom culture, *Paris Is Burning*. AIDS and the tense relations between gay men and the African American community are the trilogy's thematic mainstays, however. One of the central events of the second novel is the death from AIDS-related causes of Kyle, Raymond's gay best friend; and whereas Kyle is accepted and loved by his mother, Raymond's struggles with his father demonstrate one black gay man's relationship to the heteronormative majority. Race both sustains and divides the identities of the gay characters, who are subject to "fear of rejection, if not from their immediate family, then certainly from the African-American family as a whole."[26]

Whereas Harris's work derives much of its thematic energy from the discrepancy between black gay men and the African American "family," Jewelle Gomez's fantasy novel *The Gilda Stories* (1991) turns to the notion of "families we choose." Transforming the trope of vampirism, Gomez develops a surprising range of representations of sexuality, community, and race. Gilda, a slave girl, is initiated into a vampiric "family of friends" through an "exchange of blood" with a mother/lover figure in 1850, and the novel follows her immortal life through chapters that focus on different points in time, progressing into the future of the twenty-first century.[27] Literalizing "blood ties," the novel constitutes the exchange between vampires and human initiates as a means to "continually reshape" the "meaning" of "family."[28] HIV/AIDS informs *The Gilda Stories* in a still more indirect – indeed, transfigured – fashion than it does the novels mentioned in the previous section, with the potentially dangerous mingling of blood recuperated as a metaphor for vital interpersonal connection. The book thus imagines a world beyond or without AIDS through its inversion of the fatal riskiness of one of the syndrome's modes of transmission.

As a model of improved or idealized social relations, the vampire family is not reducible to a metaphor for homosexual community. But in describing this family, Gomez provocatively reinscribes the phobic notion of homosexual recruitment in positive terms: to initiate a human is to bring him or her into what the book calls "the life," echoing the African American vernacular term for same-sexuality.[29] At the same time, the trope of vampirism suggests the distance of the lesbian individual from the traditional African American community. Gilda involves herself in the African American community at various key moments (such as the aftermath of slavery and the Black Power period), but she is unable to become too attached, given that her (immortal) "life separate[s] her from them."[30]

The Queer Moment

Whereas gay and lesbian African American texts of the 1980s and 1990s characteristically represent same-sexuality as paradoxically both marginal and central to the African American world, the queer texts of the early 1990s and thereafter parade their marginality, emphasizing their divergences from straight culture and "mainstream" gay culture alike. This is not to say that ideas of community organized around same-sexuality disappear altogether – though they do in some works, such as Dennis Cooper's "George Miles" novels, which obsessively elaborate claustral scenarios of sexualized murder.[31] Rather, images of community in queer literature tend to be fragmentary or threatened. Queer culture (which includes queercore punk music and the New Queer Cinema) emerged out of discontent with a gay and lesbian world that was seen as bland and commercialized, as overwhelmingly white and polite (although most queer culture has been white-authored).[32] This discontent with the supposed complacencies of the gay and lesbian world was also apparent in the 1990s in the academy with the emergence of queer theory and in the critique of so-called mainstreaming that was voiced by some LGBTQ activists.[33] A brief glance at some landmark anthologies of the time illustrates the kinds of differences that queer made, or attempted to make, to the gay and lesbian literary scene.

Published in 1992 and edited by Cooper, the indicatively titled *Discontents: New Queer Writers* is presented as a "wakeup call to future gay literary anthologies" from "the vast, diverse, and growing anti-assimilationist queer movement": "writers and comix artists" (such as Dorothy Allison, Alison Bechdel, Robert Glück, Gary Indiana, Dale Peck, and Sarah Schulman) who "refuse the compromises necessary for mainstream success."[34] Like *Discontents*, Marci Blackman and Trebor Healy's *Beyond Definition: New Writing from Gay and Lesbian San Francisco* (1994) positions itself as a founding text, with a preface by Susie Bright that looks forward to "imitators" – somewhat paradoxically for a text that announces in its title its endorsement of queer individualism, or, as Bright puts it, the refusal of "irritating labels."[35] Due to its limited geographical reach, this anthology's roll call of writers is less familiar than that of *Discontents*, although it is notable for the inclusion of an early piece by Michelle Tea, who later documented San Francisco's queer dyke scene in the autobiographical novel *Valencia* (2000).

The introduction to Amy Scholder and Ira Silverberg's *High Risk* (1991), a self-styled "anthology of forbidden writings," explicitly addresses the intertwined crises of AIDS and the culture wars of the late 1980s and early 1990s that were associated with government arts funding (several of the artists targeted by conservative commentators and legislators were queer and/or produced art concerned with AIDS).[36] *High Risk* strikes a more embattled and indeed apocalyptic tone than *Discontents* or *Beyond Definition*, with Silverberg stating that in "a time of increasing oppression and censorship," in which "the dominant culture forces disenfranchisement on more people, and encourages homogeneity, the number of groups labeled 'transgressive' grows exponentially."[37] Although it is not explicitly or exclusively queer, *High Risk* nevertheless features many of the writers now associated with queer literature, such as Cooper, Glück, Indiana, DeLynn, and David Wojnarowicz. Celebrating various forms of outlawry, *High Risk* set the coordinates for the mini-boom in transgressive queer literature of the 1990s. Drug taking, sadomasochism, sex work, and tenuous existences in the blasted bohemia of 1980s downtown New York are prominent in the collected pieces, and various combinations of these elements define novels such as Bruce Benderson's *User* (1994), Linda Yablonsky's *The Story of Junk* (1997), and Wojnarowicz's memoir *Close to the Knives* (1991). *High Risk*'s introduction somewhat awkwardly juxtaposes the shock of the book's contents with the equal-opportunity bromide that promises "a balanced anthology of lesbian, gay and heterosexual writers from various ethnic backgrounds."[38] By embracing the politics of diversity, however, *High Risk* also gestures toward the deliquescence of the firmly ethnic gay identity that queer endorsed. Even as queerness features *as* an identity, its apposition in the anthology with other marginalized ethnic and sexual identities indicates the queer impulse to jettison established gay and lesbian culture.

Although the moment of queer is defined by an upswell of new political and artistic energies, most of the queer writers mentioned did not emerge at this time, but had already been publishing for one or even two decades. Their formal experimentalism and/or the confronting nature of their sexual representation, however, often set them at odds with both heteronormative literary culture and its gay counterpart. The discrepancy that these writers tended to experience between their interests and "mainstream" gayness was remedied for some of them in forms of cross-generational identification. Thus, Dennis Cooper, who refers regularly in interviews to "the deep alienation I feel and have always felt from gay-centric culture," identifies with the nihilistic energies of 1980s punk, despite having come of age in the early 1970s.[39] And Eileen Myles, a writer of revelatory anecdotal poems and memoir-novels, describes finding an artistic home among the "weird and adorable young dykes" of the 1990s, contrasting contemporary queer dykedom with "the taboo-laden feminism" of her youth in the 1970s.[40]

Robert Glück, another writer from this group, is less alienated from conventional gay culture. Glück is a founder of the loose-knit, largely

Bay Area–based New Narrative movement that during the 1980s developed a hybrid aesthetic combining autobiographical material with
critical-theoretical awareness in order to explore a gay identity figured as
both fragile and imperative, both individual and collective (Steve Abbott,
Bruce Boone, and Kevin Killian are other writers associated with the movement). For New Narrative writers, Glück writes, "the theme of obsessive
romance did double duty, de-stabling the self and asserting gay experience."[41] Glück's novels *Jack the Modernist* (1986) and *Margery Kempe*
(1994) are exemplary, juxtaposing the self-shattering of sexuality with a
lovingly rendered account of a community of friends and lovers in gay San
Francisco. Far less sympathetic to metropolitan gay culture, Gary Indiana's
splenetic novels of downtown New York, *Horse Crazy* (1989), *Rent Boy*
(1993), and *Do Everything in the Dark* (2003), implicate contemporary gay
identity within what Sarah Schulman calls "the gentrification of the mind,"
which, for veterans of Lower East Side bohemia, is the cultural counterpart
of the 1990s gentrification of the district's bricks and mortar.[42]

With regard to the representation of LGBTQ community, Schulman's
novels occupy a halfway point between Glück's gentleness and Indiana's
excoriations. Schulman's *People in Trouble* (1990) is a fictionalization of
ACT UP New York's formation, which figures AIDS, homelessness, and
gentrification as linked signs of "the beginning of the end of the world."[43]
But although *People in Trouble* ends despairingly with the assertion that
in the face of these developments, "there was nothing more to say," communal energy and anger animates the book: the protagonist Molly experiences self-recognition at AIDS activist meetings "with her people," which
contrasts with the destructive intimacy she experiences in a romance with a
married woman who continues to wield her heterosexual privilege.[44] In *Rat
Bohemia* (1995), Schulman returns to the concerns of *People in Trouble* –
AIDS and the destruction of the once-vibrant downtown scene – but the
despair is overwhelming, and the plot stutters to a halt. ACT UP is "like a
family" for the lesbian protagonist, but it is a highly dysfunctional one that
is prone to infighting and accusations.[45]

The Post-Gay Moment?

Whereas Schulman continues to hold tenuously to the hope represented by
the idea of community, post-gay writers, by contrast, might be thought of
as retreating from gay collectivity to within the confines of the family. The
two best-known post-gay writers, David Leavitt and Michael Cunningham,
who both began publishing in the 1980s, exemplify this dynamic. Leavitt
and Cunningham have garnered the credentials of establishment literary

recognition: both were from the beginnings of their careers widely reviewed in major journals, magazines, and newspapers; and both published stories early on in their careers in *The New Yorker*. Many regarded the arrival of Leavitt and then Cunningham on the scene as signaling, at last, genuine "cross-over" fiction: novels and stories featuring gay material that had appeal for straight audiences. Although Edmund White, the most famous gay literary writer to emerge in the 1970s, proudly claims the title of "gay author," both Leavitt and Cunningham reject it, seeing themselves as exploring "larger" concerns. However, for unsympathetic gay critics, the palatability and putative universalism of both authors' work has entailed the sanitization and marginalization of gay life.

In Leavitt's short story collection *Family Dancing* (1984) and his novel *Equal Affections* (1989), gay material is uneasily integrated into middle-class family dramas. In the story "Territory," for example, a gay man's relationship with his lover is framed entirely by his relationship with his mother, whom the two men are visiting. It is the mother's gaze that triggers a brief outburst of "fierce pride" in his sexuality as well as the more persistent experiences of "embarrassment" and "shame."[46]

Cunningham's breakthrough novel *A Home at the End of the World* (1990) explores elective as well as conventional family structures, but his attitude toward queer kinship is far more ambivalent than that of Gomez. The novel configures its three main characters – a gay man, a straight woman, and a straight man – in a nontraditional reproductive unit, but its most compelling episodes concern the two male characters' childhoods in conventional bourgeois homes. The novel both insists on and undermines the idea of elective kinship, with its main characters alternately describing themselves as a family and rejecting the idea: "We are nothing like a family"; "You know, you're going to drive me crazy with this family shit."[47] Tentative from the start, this family ultimately comes apart, with the female member becoming unable to tolerate the "zaniness" of being "in love with two men at once" and leaving with the infant.[48] Although the novel is lukewarm about the viability of a queer version of the family, it does, however, make it thematically central. Gay life, on the other hand, is marginalized (despite much of the novel taking place in 1980s downtown Manhattan). The gay protagonist's "half-lover," with whom he sustains a years-long sexual relationship somewhat implausibly free of emotional entanglement, is admitted into the family only when he is dying of AIDS.[49] Indicative of Cunningham's understated rendition of the major concerns of other gay fiction of the 1980s and 1990s, the syndrome is relegated to a subplot.

Similarly, in Cunningham's *The Hours* (1998), the impact of AIDS is, as Richard Canning puts it, "contained, even diminished" by the novel's "complex narrative structure."[50] An homage to Virginia Woolf's novel *Mrs. Dalloway* (1925), *The Hours* alternates between days in the lives of three different women at different points in the twentieth century: Virginia Woolf, planning *Mrs. Dalloway* but subject to suicidal despair in 1923; Laura Brown, a Californian housewife similarly beset by depression who reads Woolf's novel in 1951; and Clarissa Vaughn, living in 1990s New York and, like Woolf's Clarissa Dalloway, planning a party, in this case for a brilliant gay writer dying of complications from AIDS. The novel imitates Woolf's fluidly free indirect narration, recalls her epiphanic tonalities, and elaborately reworks incidents from *Mrs. Dalloway*, so that Clarissa's kiss with Sally Seton is echoed in an incipiently homoerotic kiss between Laura and a female friend, and the shell-shocked Septimus's death is replayed in the fatal fall of the gay writer, who is suffering from AIDS-related dementia.

Although this death points to the tragic significance of AIDS, the novel barely touches on the messy realities of embodied gay lives and the complex interrelations between gay individuals and gay communities. Cunningham's Clarissa is a lesbian whose comfortable, coupled life is denigrated by the reimagined Miss Kilman, a caricatured queer theorist besotted with Clarissa's straight daughter. If the novel ignores the idea of LGBTQ community, it incorporates the queer moment of the 1990s only to dismiss it.

But although Leavitt and Cunningham received plaudits in part by downplaying gay content, rumors in the twenty-first century of the death of gay literature have been exaggerated. Less fiction is marketed as "gay" by major houses these days, but gay and (to a lesser extent) lesbian authors continue to be published by them. Additionally, small presses and university presses, as well as online publication forums, have increasingly acted as vehicles for queer literary expression, which continues to be vigorous and diverse. A recent example of that vigor and diversity, which brings together the concerns of AIDS, identity, and community that have run through this chapter, is Samuel Delany's novel *Through the Valley of the Nest of Spiders* (2012). This mammoth (800-page) work, which combines pornography, utopia, realism, and science fiction, hardly fits the profile of the gay midlist novel of earlier decades (it was published by the small LGBTQ press Magnus). Tracing a decades-long love affair between two working-class southerners living in an idyllic rural gay colony called the Dump, *Through the Valley* is virtually plot-free, yet it cumulatively achieves an affecting sense of the rewards of gay intimacy and gay community. The novel's many pornographic scenes develop the idea of promiscuous sex as a community-building practice that characterizes Delany's earlier "pornotopian" novel *The Mad Man* (1994) and his nonfiction work *Times Square Red, Times Square Blue* (1999).[51] Yet although *Through the Valley*'s conclusion envisions a future in which

HIV/AIDS has apparently been eradicated, the sex scenes are insistently safe, and HIV testing is mandatory in the Dump. Early twentieth-century hetero-normative American culture, and arguably gay culture as well, have in many ways forgotten AIDS, but Delany's novel attests to the ethical necessity of remembering it. And although Delany's future is more sexually tolerant than our present, this tolerance does not entail the disappearance of gay identity or culture – which post-gay rhetoric often seems to suggest is the logical or desirable outcome of the increasing acceptance of homosexuality. In its imaginatively rich rendition of an exclusively gay community, *Through the Valley* points to, and embodies, the enduring relevance of gay culture and literature in the twenty-first century.

NOTES

1 Robert McRuer, *The Queer Renaissance: Contemporary American Literature and the Reinvention of Lesbian and Gay Identities* (New York: New York University Press, 1997), 1.
2 Ibid., 1–2.
3 Christopher Bram, *Eminent Outlaws: The Gay Writers Who Changed America* (New York: Twelve, 2012), 238.
4 In a representative statement of this position, the journalist Dan Martin states: "As we march towards true equality, the whole idea of a 'gay culture' becomes more and more meaningless as the world accepts the truth that gay people aren't all the same." Dan Martin, "The Lady Gaga Backlash Begins," *The Guardian*, April 20, 2011; quoted in Dennis Altman, *The End of the Homosexual?* (St. Lucia: University of Queensland Press, 2013), 205.
5 Kath Weston, *Families We Choose: Lesbians, Gays, Kinship* (New York: Columbia University Press, 1991), 3.
6 Jane DeLynn, *Don Juan in the Village* (New York: Pantheon, 1990), 223.
7 Richard Canning, "The Literature of AIDS," in *The Cambridge Companion to Gay and Lesbian Writing*, ed. Hugh Stevens (Cambridge: Cambridge University Press, 2011), 136.
8 Rafael Campo, *The Poetry of Healing: A Doctor's Education in Empathy, Identity, and Desire* (New York: Norton, 1997), 166.
9 Kay Bonetti, "An Interview with Edmund White," *Missouri Review* 13, no. 2 (1990): 97.
10 See, for instance, Nancy Stoller, "Lesbian Involvement in the AIDS Epidemic: Changing Roles and Generational Differences," in *Women Resisting AIDS: Feminist Strategies of Empowerment*, ed. Beth E. Schneider and Nancy E. Stoller (Philadelphia: Temple University Press, 1995), 270–285.
11 Bonetti, "Interview with Edmund White," 97.
12 Campo, *Poetry of Healing*, 188, 189.
13 Dale Peck, "Foreword: Preaching to the Converted," in *Vital Signs: Essential AIDS Fiction*, ed. Richard Canning (New York: Carroll and Graf, 2007), viii.
14 Robert Ferro, *Second Son* (New York: Crown, 1988), 57.
15 Ibid., 90.

16 On the interplay between "personal" and "population" narratives in AIDS literature, see Richard Canning, introduction to *Vital Signs: Essential AIDS Fiction*,
   ed. Richard Canning (New York: Carroll and Graf, 2007), xxxvi–xxxviii; and
   Steven Kruger, *AIDS Narratives: Gender and Sexuality, Fiction and Science*
   (New York: Routledge 1996), 75–83.

17 See, for instance, Jennifer Brier, *Infectious Ideas: AIDS and US Politics,
   1980–2006* (Chapel Hill: University of North Carolina Press, 2009).

18 Joseph Beam, "Introduction: Leaving the Shadows Behind," in *In the
   Life: A Black Gay Anthology*, ed. Joseph Beam (Boston: Alyson, 1986), 13;
   emphasis in original.

19 Ibid., 14, 15. Beam quotes from a 1984 article he wrote for Philadelphia's
   Gay News.

20 Essex Hemphill, introduction to *Brother to Brother: New Writings by Black
   Gay Men*, ed. Essex Hemphill (Boston: Alyson, 1991), xix.

21 Ibid., xxi, xxvii.

22 Ibid., xxviii, xxvii.

23 E. Lynn Harris, *Invisible Life* (New York: Anchor, 1994), 262.

24 E. Lynn Harris, *Just As I Am* (New York: Anchor, 1995), 148.

25 For a critique of the Down Low explanation of high HIV rates among black
   women, including its racist assumptions, see Russell Robinson, "Racing the
   Closet," *Stanford Law Review* 61, no. 2 (2009): 1463–1534. Although "Down
   Low" did not take on its present-day connotation until the 2000s, media alarm
   about secretly bisexual black men passing on HIV to their female partners is
   evident from the late 1980s onward. See Cathy J. Cohen, *The Boundaries of
   Blackness: AIDS and the Breakdown of Black Politics* (Chicago: University of
   Chicago Press, 1999), 229.

26 Harris, *Just As I Am*, 221.

27 Jewelle Gomez, *The Gilda Stories* (Ithaca: Firebrand, 1991), 31, 120.

28 Ibid., 69.

29 Ibid., 38.

30 Ibid., 112.

31 See Dennis Cooper, *Closer* (New York: Grove Weidenfeld, 1989); Dennis
   Cooper, *Frisk* (New York: Grove Weidenfeld, 1991); Dennis Cooper, *Try*
   (New York: Grove, 1994); Dennis Cooper, *Guide* (New York: Grove, 1997);
   and Dennis Cooper, *Period* (New York: Grove, 2000).

32 On queercore, see Michael Du Plessis and Kathleen Chapman, "Queercore: The
   Distinct Identities of Subculture," *College Literature* 24, no. 2 (1995): 45–58. On
   the New Queer Cinema, see Michele Aaron, ed., *New Queer Cinema: A Critical
   Reader* (New Brunswick: Rutgers University Press, 2004).

33 On queer theory, see, for instance, Annamarie Jagose, *Queer Theory*
   (Melbourne: Melbourne University Press, 1996). On mainstreaming, see Urvashi
   Vaid, *Virtual Equality: The Mainstreaming of Gay and Lesbian Liberation*
   (New York: Anchor, 1995).

34 Dennis Cooper, introduction to *Discontents: New Queer Writers*, ed. Dennis
   Cooper (New York: Amethyst, 1992), xi.

35 Susie Bright, introduction to *Beyond Definition: New Writing from Gay
   and Lesbian San Francisco*, ed. Marci Blackman and Trebor Healey (San
   Francisco: Manic D, 1994), 12.

36 See Robert Bolton, ed., *Culture Wars: Documents from the Recent Controversies in the Arts* (New York: New Press, 1992).

37 Ira Silverberg, introduction to *High Risk: An Anthology of Forbidden Writings*, ed. Ira Silverberg and Amy Scholder (New York: Plume, 1991), xvi.

38 Ibid.

39 Quoted in Daniel Reitz, "Dennis Cooper," *Salon*, May 5, 2000, http://www.salon.com/2000/05/04/cooper/.

40 Eileen Myles, "My Intergeneration," *Village Voice*, June 20, 2000, http://www.villagevoice.com/2000-06-20/news/my-intergeneration/. For Myles's work, see, for instance, her poetry *Not Me* (New York: Semiotext(e), 1991); her novel *Chelsea Girls* (Santa Rosa, CA: Black Sparrow, 1994); and her non-fiction collection *The Importance of Being Iceland: Travel Essays in Art* (Los Angeles: Semiotext(e), 2009).

41 Robert Glück, "Long Note on New Narrative," *Narrativity* 1 (2000), http://www.sfsu.edu/~newlit/narrativity/issue_one/gluck.html.

42 See Sarah Schulman, *The Gentrification of the Mind: Witness to a Lost Imagination* (Berkeley: University of California Press, 2012).

43 Sarah Schulman, *People in Trouble* (London: Sheba, 1990), 1.

44 Ibid., 228, 208.

45 Sarah Schulman, *Rat Bohemia* (New York: Plume, 1995), 84.

46 David Leavitt, *Family Dancing* (New York: Knopf, 1984), 20, 6.

47 Michael Cunningham, *A Home at the End of the World* (New York: Farrar, Straus and Giroux, 1990), 253, 313.

48 Ibid., 255.

49 Ibid., 114.

50 Canning, "Literature of AIDS," 136.

51 For Delany's definition of "pornotopian fiction," see Samuel R. Delany, *Shorter Views: Queer Thoughts and the Politics of the Paraliterary* (Hanover: Wesleyan University Press/University Press of New England, 1999), 133.

PART III

Critical Approaches

IO

L. H. STALLINGS

Gender and Sexuality

> Mapmakers, and others, who draw important things for a living, do not want us to know this.
>
> – Nikky Finney, "The Clitoris"

Starting in the later twentieth century, American literary studies was transformed by intersectional analyses of gender and sexuality. Critics' awards mark this shift in a variety of ways, with more than 100 book awards designated for excellence in American literature and literary studies. Some of these are mainstream, like the National Book Award; others are prominently shaped by the politics of gender and sexuality, such as the Lambda Literary Award. Although these awards continue to recognize excellence and achievement, the production of more awards and the categories within the awards demonstrate an awareness of absences and presences still being contained, controlled, and mapped by certain empires and their designations of what is universally proper culture and knowledge – rationality, empiricism, science, and technology. Despite the fact that American literature has always maintained a commitment to freedom and democracy, it has not always been successful at distinguishing itself from these empires of knowledge that make freedom and democracy impossible. From the 1970s onward, however, gender and sexuality became subjects of inquiry in American literary studies, which allowed for a more complex reflection on such themes. From post-structuralist concerns about subjectivity to queer theory's challenging of identity politics, the intersectional analytic of gender and sexuality in literary studies emerged from under the hooded regimes of power, knowledge, and culture, just as quotidian discourse about the unmapped and feminine flesh that Nikky Finney writes about in her National Book Award–winning collection of poetry *Head Off and Split* did despite medical omissions of its existence and important function in women's lives.

Finney's win and acceptance speech underscore why the intersection of gender and sexuality alters American literary studies.[1] The awards and their histories seldom linger on how intersections make possible such creative excellence and undo empire. Such was the case for *Head Off and Split*, a collection of poems metaphorically shaped by a fishmonger's question to a young African American girl: "Head off and split? Translation: Do away with the watery gray eyes, the impolite razor sharp fins, the succulent heart, tender roe, delicate sweet bones."[2] Finney's conclusion about the girl answering yes or no to the question suggests that what sustains, feeds, enlivens, and liberates cannot be left in the hands of another, even if the labor is messy, tedious, and difficult. Making new knowledge is trying work, but it is necessary. Taking a cue from this award-winning book of poetry, this chapter discusses how prioritizing the intersection of gender and sexuality in American literary studies has allowed marginalized groups and writers to shift a field that had been implicitly beholden to empires of knowledge and rule, white heteropatriarchy, and liberal settler colonialism into one that has intuited the changing same of empire's rule. There are two themes that demonstrate how gender and sexuality studies and theories have intervened in empire's order of knowledge and rule in American literary studies from the late twentieth century to the early twenty-first century: (1) archaeology and resurrection and (2) literature's engagement with culture.

Temples of Conflicts and Gender: Literary Archaeology vs. Literary Resurrection

Jean I. Marsden's 2002 essay "Beyond Recovery: Feminism and the Future of Eighteenth Century Studies" understands that the legacy of recovering women's texts has been a celebratory movement of women's culture that risks foregoing the necessary critical rigor demanded by other professional fields of study. Marsden explains her concern by focusing on issues such as the "seeming obscurity of the object of research," its worth, and, "most crucially, the ways in which we project ourselves onto the writers we recover and the consequences of such projection for our scholarship."[3] Although Marsden was right to be concerned about the pattern of discovering women writers and claiming them, sometimes falsely so, as foremothers of twentieth-century feminism, moving beyond recovery is not an option. Moreover, because we know about the proliferative use of writing pseudonyms and the everyday ordinary experience of racial and sexual passing in some marginalized people's lives and writing, moving beyond recovery should not always be the most utilized option. Rather, we should look toward the motivations for and conflicts of recovery efforts on behalf of feminist and queer scholars across race, ethnicity, and class. Archaeology, with its goal of preserving and making history, provides evidence of preliterate, and more ancient literate, civilizations, but it has also been a tool of empire in which academics believe that empirical evidence is more important than sacred texts and spaces are. Feminist literary studies and scholarship has been both archaeology and resurrection. Myths about resurrection inform us that it is never a solitary and individual act. There is the resurrector and the resurrected. The act is done in accord with persons intent on improving on or saving someone or something. However, this particular means of doing criticism transitioned into an archaeology of knowledge in the late 1960s. After the methods of recovery were carried out by critics aligned with the 1960s women's liberation movement and sexual revolution in the United States, the remaining work of infusing more critical rigor resurfaced two decades later in feminist literary criticism and theory, because identity politics came to be an issue of contention that recovery methods alone could not address. Even though these movements provided the political capital to justify unearthing and making known women's accomplishments in literature, the models for recovery signaled an activist strain. This recovery of women's texts, although initially a matter of canons and historicizing traditions, had implications beyond the classroom. As canonicity continued to be challenged by marginalized groups, new theoretical interventions emerged. Because, as Audre Lorde once explained, the transformation of silence into language and an appreciation of difference are necessary for making gender and sexuality valued categories of analysis in American literary studies, the initial means for doing so were and should remain collective and collaborative.[4]

Notable texts that did so included Susan Gubar and Sandra Gilbert's *The Madwoman in the Attic* (1979) and their coedited *Norton Anthology of Literature by Women* (1985). When classifying the nature of their collaboration, Gilbert described it as "the hither-to unmapped continent of a women's literary tradition, whose countries we had never been taught."[5] Their work on authors such as Jane Austen, the Brontë sisters, George Eliot, Emily Dickinson, and Elizabeth Barrett Browning led to the recovery of other women writers who may have been ignored because their works deviated from male paradigms and aesthetics. Elaine Showalter, Catharine R. Stimpson, Wendy Martin, and Carolyn Heilbrun went on to recover and analyze women authors outside of the Victorian era, such as Aphra Behn, Virginia Woolf, and Simone de Beauvoir. Showalter's *The Female Malady* (1985) and *Sexual Anarchy* (1990) established "gynocriticism" as a model meant to "construct a female framework for the analysis of women's literature, to develop new models based on the study of female experience, rather than to adapt male models and theories."[6] These latter two works became part of an ongoing discussion about and criticism of essentialism in feminist theories that were later placed on other women's work as well.

Gynocriticism, in fact, depended on an essential female body and a universal experience of womanhood that analyses of race and sexuality as categories and the recovery of non-white texts were undoing. Whereas white women located their foremothers in Victorian, Renaissance, and Greek traditions, women of color turned elsewhere. Paula Gunn Allen's *Sacred Hoop: Recovering the Feminine in American Indian Traditions* (1986) looks toward Native American folklore figures and tales of the corn maiden and spider woman to establish an intersectional approach of gynocriticism and indigenous populations. Alice Walker's *In Search of Our Mother's Gardens* (1983) includes a resurrection narrative in which she tells the story of visiting Zora Neale Hurston's grave – a narrative that inspired subsequent generations of scholars. Critics such as Hazel Carby, Barbara Christian, Frances Smith Foster, Deborah McDowell, Nellie McKay, Valerie Smith, Cheryl Wall, and Susan Willis likewise reconstructed black womanhood by exploring writers such as Anna Julia Cooper, Alice Dunbar Nelson, Jessie Fauset, Harriet Jacobs, Rebecca Jackson, Frances Ellen Harper, Pauline Hopkins, Nella Larsen, Ann Petry, and others. As Carby suggested in *Reconstructing Womanhood* (1987), such archival work and texts indicated that the basis of black feminist literary theory relied on questioning womanhood: in order for black women to become orators or published writers, they had to "confront the dominant domestic ideologies and literary conventions of womanhood which excluded black women from the definition of 'woman.'"[7] Simultaneously, texts such as Trinh T. Minh-ha's *Woman, Native, Other: Writing Postcoloniality and Feminism* suggested that "she who 'happens to be'" a (non-white) Third World member, a woman, and a writer is bound to go through the ordeal of exposing her work to abuse, praises, and criticisms that either ignore, dispense with, or overemphasize her racial and sexual attributes.[8] Similarly, Lisa Lowe's "Heterogeneity, Hybridity, Multiplicity: Asian American Differences" (1991) and her later *Immigrant Acts: On Asian American Cultural Politics* (1996) examined the importance of the hyphenated immigrant identity for writers such as Maxine Hong Kingston, Lydia Lowe, and Amy Tan. The growth of scholarly journals and edited collections likewise enabled these developments with the rise of prominent women's studies journals such as *Boundaries, Camera Obscura, Conditions, differences, Feminist Studies, Hypatia, NWSA Journal* (now *Feminist Formations*), *Signs, Sojourner*, and *Women's Studies*.

Numerous anthologies, such as *Feminisms: An Anthology of Literary Theory and Criticism* (1991), *But Some of Us Are Brave: All the Women Are White, All the Blacks Are Men: Black Women's Studies* (1982), and

Dragon Ladies: Asian American Feminists Breathe Fire (1997), did the same in the last two decades of the twentieth century. They served as collaborative and communal texts for women across the broad spectrum of racial and sexual identities. In their introduction to *Feminisms*, for instance, Robyn R. Warhol and Diane Price Herndl discuss how difficult it was in the late 1980s to teach a course on feminist theory and fiction because of practical concerns about textbook issues, the limited access to scholarly feminist journals, and the intensive labor of locating and reproducing articles for the class. They assert that the goal of their compilation was to solve the following dilemma:

> Most collections of feminist criticism contain twelve to fifteen essays which represent either a particular methodology or are focused on a specific subject. When such anthologies do attempt to represent a variety of methodological approaches, their limited space prevents any attempt at real comprehensiveness. Generally, if an anthology focuses on French feminist theories, it excludes Anglo-American approaches; if it brings together work on minority literature, it leaves out "mainstream" subjects.[9]

Although Warhol and Herndl's words are true, the one commonality shared by all of these anthologies was an understanding of the importance of literature, fiction, criticism, and theory as a site for analyzing gender and sexuality.[10] Barbara Smith's *Homegirls: A Black Feminist Anthology* could have just as easily been called a Black feminist literary anthology, given that many of its contributors were poets and fiction authors. Gloria Anzaldúa's and Cherríe Moraga's *This Bridge Called My Back: Writings by Women of Color* (1981) and Anzaldúa's *Making Face, Making Soul: Haciendo Caras* (1990) and *Borderlands/La Frontera: The New Mestiza* (1987) focus on language, voice, and indigenous cultures of Chicana women. Each of these anthologies demonstrated that the line between feminist activism, criticism, and literary creativity was not as segregated as it could have been in the twenty-first century. As feminists moved in and throughout the academy in the late twentieth century, some came to regard their work in disciplinary and professional terms by incorporating specific jargon and theory that staunchly situated them on one side, whereas others invested in activist and creative approaches that could garner a mass audience and political support for feminist movements within and outside university halls. After the 1980s, debates about essential gender identity and the feminist production of knowledge about gender and sexuality were positioned as being either in the rational/logical realm or in the affective/creative realm and once again brought into question the pros and cons of simply recovering texts and applying current models of reading gender and sexuality to them.

This initial focus on the recovery of women's texts and the close reading of gender was eventually followed by a growing separation of sexuality from gender in lesbian and gay literary studies. During this development, the recovery of LGBTQ writers shared a similar impetus as the one that led to the recovery and critical evaluation of texts by women writers. From European literature of the Renaissance and Victorian eras to American literature of various periods and movements, gender variation, same-sex desire, homoeroticism, and interracial sex became as worthy of investigation as heterosexual women were in feminist literary studies. Writers such as Sappho, Oscar Wilde, Allen Ginsberg, and James Baldwin offered scholars an entry point for recovery and valuable evidence for highlighting the significance of sexual fluidity in literary representations. Ann Allen Shockley's "The Black Lesbian in American Literature: An Overview" (1979) was one of the first essays to signal the need for the recovery of racialized lesbian texts and to express how such discoveries might lead to conflicts for marginal populations seeking acceptance by a wider literary community. It was the poet-activist Adrienne Rich's essay "Compulsory Heterosexuality and Lesbian Existence" (1980) – especially its promotion of terms such as "lesbian existence" and "lesbian continuum" to connote the presence of lesbians throughout history and its array of woman-identified experiences – that then corroborated Shockley's quest and emphasized why literature would be an interventional site for shifting sexuality studies that had centered on white heteronormative communities, and vice versa. Carla Trujillo's *Chicana Lesbians: The Girls Our Mothers Warned Us About* (1991) then dissected compulsive heterosexuality and its parameters of Anglo domination and forced assimilation for Chicana/o sexualities.

Despite the emergence of independent presses such as Alyson Press, Naiad Press, Aunt Lute Press, South End Press, and Kitchen Table Press, gender segregation continued to coincide with racial segregation, and gay and lesbian literature for many mainstream publishers came to focus on white communities. Catherine E. McKinley's *Afrekete: An Anthology of Black Lesbian Writing* (1995), Joseph Beam's *In the Life: A Black Gay Anthology* (1986), and Essex Hemphill's *Brother to Brother: New Writings by Black Gay Men* (1991) were politically successful projects, but they were commercially limited. Explicit representations of gay and lesbian sexuality occurred when the erotica genre and anthology flourished in the 1990s. *Erotique Noire: Black Erotica* (1992), *Best Lesbian Erotica* (1996), and *Best Gay Erotica* (1996) were profitable erotica anthologies whose demand resulted in second printings and long-standing series collection.

In the scholarly arena, examinations of literary sexual icons and lesser-known figures were also greatly enhanced by the critical work of the French philosopher Michel Foucault. The publication and translation of Foucault's three-volume study *The History of Sexuality* (1976–1984; English translations, 1978–1986) deeply influenced dissertations and monographs about sexuality, power, and identity.[11] As critics used the ideologies from Foucault's work in addition to feminist theory, psychoanalysis, and post-structuralism, queer theory emerged as a dominant paradigm of analysis for gender and sexuality. The proliferation of queer theory in literary studies was also driven by a need to analyze texts that had been previously understudied or deemed inappropriate during past eras as a result of unique aesthetics and themes. Additionally, as the HIV/AIDS epidemic impacted the society, culture, and health of various communities, literature became a tool that interrupted the political silence and stigmatization of bodies that had been medically and scientifically marked as sexually deviant. As with Eros and Thanatos, desire and death were representationally linked in biopolitical warfare and sealed together by what was then thought to be first documented case of HIV/AIDS in 1981. Having been influenced by AIDS activism, for instance, Eve Kosofsky Sedgwick's *Epistemology of the Closet* (1990) deployed queer theory to analyze the words of Herman Melville, Marcel Proust, and Wilde to dismantle the binaries between homosexuality and heterosexuality and to demonstrate that literature offers readers counternarratives to the medical and scientific discourses that have been dominant since the nineteenth century. Feminist theory and women's studies contributed to the formation of lesbian and gay studies, and from there, queer theory, queer of color critique, disability studies and crip theory, and trans theory and transgender studies emerged as critical interventions to tackle the sexual problematics of white empire.

Sexual Problematics: Text/Body/Desire/Embodiment

Once the work of John D'Emilio, Annamarie Jagose, Michael Warner, and others had expanded the boundaries of queer theory, it became clear that the disciplinary boundaries between history, literature, sociology, and anthropology were dissolving as they further articulated the intersectional knowledge inherent in analyses of gender and sexuality. Lee Edelman's *Homographesis* (1994), for one, tackled sexual identity politics, the HIV/AIDS crisis, homophobia, and racism. Moreover, questions of form in literature and the usefulness of theory were taken up in ways that had everything to do with sexuality as an object of analysis and cultural aesthetics that was employed by creative writers to affectively capture the feeling of sex. Such endeavors were not easy to do in a time period mired in conservatism, erotophobia, and anti-intellectualism. In her discussion of the academic and intellectual isolation of scholars engaged with the history of sexuality and university failures to hire such individuals, Lisa Duggan suggests three reasons for the dismal options for scholars of sexuality: "the trivialization of sexuality, the making of sexuality as solely psychological and biological subject matter, and the failure to understand the importance of the production and organization of sexualities."[12] Duggan argued that "the history of sexuality should not have to hide itself under the supposedly 'broader' rubric of cultural history, any more than women's history should have to hide itself within family history."[13] Yet American literature reveals that histories of sexuality were being marked somewhere other than in the discursive and linear narratives of history. The fiction of Dorothy Allison, Rita Mae Brown, William S. Burroughs, and Emma Perez, as well as the poetry of Cheryl Clarke, Marilyn Hacker, Essex Hemphill, Audre Lorde, and Amy Lowell point to the relevance of cultural memory in changing how gender and sexuality are imagined and regulated in the Americas. Additionally, the themes and forms employed in novels such as Arturo Islas's *The Rain God* (1984), Gayl Jones's *Corregidora* (1975), Samuel R. Delany's *Hogg* (1995), and Leslie Feinberg's *Stone Butch Blues* (1993) demanded that critics locate interdisciplinary strategies to adequately address the ways in which these novels' depictions of sexuality and gender threatened to undo empirical and imperialist hierarchies of knowledge about gender and sexuality. Each novel privileged nonliterary forms, subcultures, and controversial subjects, and their very forms came to embody queerness on the page. Because so much of queer theory's foundations are situated in literary studies' explorations of gender and sexuality, one might argue that the coupling of literary studies and feminist studies gave rise to queer theory as a field that was more than a discipline invested in general histories of sexuality. The incorporation of different aesthetics from various artistic mediums also helped better capture how these new concerns with gender and sexuality required more than historical, sociological, and anthropological narratives.

The use of nonliterary culture within creative and critical writing also propelled new forms that captured the rapidly changing intersection of gender with sexuality in American literature and literary studies. American literature and literary studies from the 1980s onward was a large part of the culture wars in which gender and sexuality issues had become defining markers of difference between conservative and liberal values. With Boy George, Michael Jackson, Prince, David Bowie, Sylvester, Annie Lennox, Madonna, Grace Jones, and Cyndi Lauper visibly and sonically defining the intersection of gender and sexuality, literature and literary criticism and theory of the late twentieth century delved into the highs and lows of culture. Film and cinema studies, which consistently borrowed

from narratological and psychoanalytic theory, were transformed by
lucrative porn industries and empires in New York and California's San
Fernando Valley. The celebration and visibility of porn stars such as Jerry
Butler, Vanessa Del Rio, Heather Hunter, Angel Kelly, Hypatia Lee, John
Leslie, Tracy Lord, and Randy West demonstrated a proliferation of sexual representation and imagery with which not everyone was comfortable. Because it was no longer underground, pornography forced some
feminists to engage (hetero)sexuality as they never had earlier. Debates
about art, porn, and censorship ushered in porn studies, which incorporated critical legal theory, critical race theory, feminist theory, and film
and literary studies. Anti-porn sentiments were expressed in fiction and
essays written by Susan Brownmiller, Andrea Dworkin, Audre Lorde,
Catherine McKinnon, and Alice Walker. Eventually, Linda Williams's
Hard Core: Power, Pleasure and the "Frenzy of the Visible" (1989) coun-
tered the feminist panic about porn, and although it is not a literary trea-
tise, its reliance on a standard literary studies approach to narrative is
patent. Williams insists that hardcore pornography is a "genre among
genres" that "consists of sexual action in, and as, narrative."[14] These conversations about what is obscene and what is art, in addition to if and
how sexuality can be represented outside of patriarchal modes, illuminated disagreements about inclusion and exclusions in the canon making
of American literary studies that had existed for some time.

When one represents race, class, nation, ability, and sexuality in certain
forms or genres, those representations, texts, or studies are composed out
of cultural elements that are never simply apolitical signs and signifiers.
Throughout these shifts, scholars continued to ask: When critics and students go in search of lost texts, what are their reasons and for what will
their efforts be used? What factors shape the various forms, genres, and
categories of these textual strategies? The answers to such questions reveal
that as more narratives and novels are unearthed from various archives,
more diverse theories will be needed to assess them. One major problem
with early recovery and resurrection in American literary studies was that it
centered on a proper and moral subject or text. Moreover, this proliferation
of recovery of women's and LGBT texts did little to help us understand the
differences between sexuality and gender that seem obvious now. Feminist
studies, gender theory, and queer theory helped, but it was especially cultural studies that enabled the delinking of literary studies from its basic
foundations of morality and truth, as Hayden White's and Foucault's works
about author, text, and narrative have shown.[15] Their claims forcibly mat-
tered to the intersection of gender and sexuality as well as its prior suppression, because almost every identity, form of knowledge, and research

method – even the illegible and silenced ones – has had to negotiate both gender and sexuality in monolithic and linear ways.

Indeed, as excessive as the production of feminist anthologies had become by the end of the 1990s, the importance of such anthologies to concepts of interdisciplinarity, collaboration, and intersectionality cannot be overemphasized, given that all three indicate that no singular truth or approach is ever sufficient. There was also a rise in scholarly journals focused on sexuality and culture. Literature and literary studies changes how the study of sexuality can be discussed, and marginalized sexualities motivate us to try to find alternative discursive mechanisms to discuss them, but sometimes language is not enough. As Judith Butler once explained, "language is always less than 'clarifying' when it comes to desire. Desire will be that which guarantees a certain opacity in language, an opacity that language can enact and display, but without which it cannot operate."[16]

Some literary scholars found encouragement in writers who valued other cultural artifacts in their literary representations of sexuality and gender. In order to challenge conventions of how to present gender and sexuality, as well as literary forms associated with the colonization of knowledge and people, writers and scholars turned to oral traditions, autobiography, music, comics, visuality, southern gothic traditions, and speculative and science fiction genres. They used these genres to represent the possible intersections of gender and sexuality with race, class, and disability and to showcase the various histories of sexualities that had taken place in spite of efforts to erase or not acknowledge them. Kathy Acker, Alison Bechdel, Octavia Butler, Jewelle Gomez, Randall Kenan, Ursula K. Le Guin, and Audre Lorde made it necessary to find less traditional means of analyzing gender and sexuality in literature. As Greg Thomas asks:

> When questions of gender and sexuality are on the table for discussion, even if sex and eroticism or embodiment in general are not, who asks how they get there? What form should they take or not take? Why do they communicate explicit and/or implicit scenarios of race, class, empire? Which specific order of knowledge dictates the limited shape and purpose of such inquiries, artificially separating race, gender, class, and sexuality, without recognizing this is a very specific intellectual operation rooted in a very specific intellectual culture and history? … It remains necessary to determine what is just, progressive, or radical about any instant of this criticism itself, particularly if it cannot analyze its complicity with the sexual politics of white Western imperialism – past, present, and, unfortunately, future.[17]

The future of American literature and its representations of gender and sexuality have been explored in anti-imperialist ways across genres that have been deemed low culture or popular fiction, but it took Donna Haraway's

"A Cyborg Manifesto: Science, Technology, and Socialist-Feminism in the Late Twentieth Century" (1985) and *Primate Visions: Gender, Race, and Nature in the World of Modern Science* (1989) to further change such opinions. Haraway initiated new developments with regards to the critique of biology, technology, and the social construction of gender. As one of the most relevant feminist essays of the late twentieth century, "A Cyborg Manifesto" could not have been written were it not for the influence of a genre that has been historically dismissed as not being serious literature: science fiction. As the Black Studies scholar Sylvia Wynter had also insisted in her pivotal essays, "The Ceremony Must Be Found: After Humanism" (1984) and "Beyond Miranda's Meanings: Un/Silencing the 'Demonic Ground' of Caliban's Women" (1990), questions about embodiment, what it means to be human, and the order of truth, power, and knowledge shape our very conceptions of gender and sexuality as well as our disciplining of each, and thus the creative frames of narrative can be as useful as a critique of the biological. Whether it is Jewelle Gomez's *The Gilda Stories* (1991), Katherine Forrest's *Daughters of a Coral Dawn* (1984), Terry de la Peña's *Margins* (1992), or Audre Lorde's *The Cancer Journals* (1980), the numerous ways in which readers learn to comprehend what it means to be human and post-human compel us to locate a more radical theory of sexuality.

Gayle Rubin was one of the premier advocates for more radical theories of sexuality. In her canonical essay "Thinking Sex: Notes for a Radical Theory of the Politics of Sexuality" (1984), Rubin stands up for sexual nonconformists as she tracks the moral melodramatic narratives of sexuality. By dissecting legal cases about prostitution and homosexuality, as well as cultures of obscenity, pornography, and sex education, Rubin argues that "a radical theory of sex must identify, describe, explain, and denounce erotic injustice and sexual oppression," and she suggests that sexual essentialism was currently impeding the development of such theory.[18] Her argument about sex-negativity in Western sexualities became the basis for theories of sex-positivity. Rubin's "The Traffic in Women: Notes on the Political Economy of Sex" (1975) provides a Marxist reading of women's oppression in a capitalist society by considering the ways in which concepts such as family work to organize a sex/gender system. Rubin was not alone in her approach of focusing on marginalized groups and social economies. Before there was a formalized queer of color critique, as seen in Jennifer DeVere Brody and Dwight A. McBride's *Callaloo* special issue, "Plum Nelly: New Essays in Black Queer Studies" (2000), and E. Patrick Johnson and Mae Henderson's *Black Queer Studies: A Critical Anthology* (2005), Hortense J. Spillers took up the sexual economy of slavery and provided dense and theoretically sophisticated appraisals of gender, sexuality, and race. Writing during a time when black feminists were engaged in a disagreement over theory and practice, Spillers blended her interests in African American Studies, feminist theory, psychoanalysis, and black cultural studies to challenge Western histories of sexuality and gender, which ignored captive bodies. In her most cited essay, "Mama's Baby, Papa's Maybe: An American Grammar Book" (1987), Spillers turns to the slave narrative to demonstrate how gender regimes are dismantled or made invalid when applied to captive bodies and how racialized bodies become labeled as abnormally gendered when they are defined in terms of the white subjectivity of the humanity denied to them. Spillers's argument that African American men must "say yes to the female within" became kindling for other ways of thinking about black masculinity and race.[19]

Noting the significance of language, land, culture, and spirituality as elements that contribute to constructs of sexuality and gender, Gloria Anzaldúa and Cherríe Moraga's edited collection, like their single-author creative critical writings, demonstrates that the women's movement and feminism were not ever simply white, middle-class, heterosexual political organizations. Anzaldúa's examination of how religion, border laws and politics, and colonization impact Chicana women was informed by her belief that "the work of the mestizo consciousness is to break down the subject-object duality."[20] Anzaldúa's "mestiz[a] consciousness" offered a theory about binaristic models of gender and sexuality that could address the wounded psyche of Chicana women. Taking up the multiple identities and experiences of Chicana women, Anzaldúa's "mestiz[a] consciousness" foreshadowed the idea of becoming in queer theory, and Anzaldúa insists that the mestiza "has discovered that she can't hold concepts or ideas in rigid boundaries. … She operates in a pluralistic mode – nothing is thrust out, the good the bad and the ugly."[21] Like Anzaldúa, Andrea Smith's call for sexual decolonization and queering of hierarchies in *Conquest: Sexual Violence and American Indian Genocide* (2005) offers an analysis of how colonization often depended on the control of Amerindian women's bodies through sexual violence and terrorism.

Taking her lead from the previously mentioned feminist approaches, Robyn Wiegman created feminist scholarship that interrogated whiteness as a category of race, while also thinking through questions of gender and sexuality. In *American Anatomies: Theorizing Race and Gender* (1995), Wiegman offers antiracist and antisexist critiques. By documenting the body as readable text and visuality as its primary economy, Wiegman explores how race figures into how gendered subjectivity can be liberating or limited depending on other factors of the body and subject experience. Through comparative readings of American literature and culture, Wiegman theorizes the possibility of different genealogies of feminist traditions, which also results in a divergence from second-wave feminism and its conception of the masculine and patriarchy. Other American literary scholars performed similar feats to change the direction of black feminist thought. In the 1980s, Deborah McDowell boldly took up the debate about theory versus praxis that had been epitomized in Barbara Smith's "Toward a Black Feminist Criticism" (1977) and later in Barbara Christian's "The Race for Theory" (1988). McDowell did not just take a side and leave it at that. Her "New Directions for Black Feminist Criticism" (1980) provided a solid example of what literary theory could offer in order to more comprehensively explicate various black women's lives, literature, and culture. In that essay, she called for "firmer definitions of lesbians and lesbian literature" in black feminist criticism.[22] Despite her critique of Smith's lesbian readings of *Sula* (1973), McDowell later provided her own queer reading of a black woman's novel. *"The Changing Same": Black Women's Literature, Criticism, and Theory* (1995) challenged definitions of literary theory that encapsulated it as "a very particular practice," and one of the field-changing essays in that collection remains an essay on Nella Larsen that documents homoeroticism and its racialization.[23]

The 1990s was a decade of more gender and sexuality scholars following up on Haraway's and Wynter's projects to undo gender and move the oppressive bonds of patriarchy. One of most heralded U.S. critics of gender, sexuality, and the body to do so was Judith Butler. *Gender Trouble: Feminism and the Subversion of Identity* (1990) and *Bodies That Matter: On the Discursive Limits of "Sex"* (1993) are two theoretical works that have influenced fields beyond feminist studies, including disability studies and trans studies. Beginning in both texts with observations on language and subjectivity, Butler builds on the works of Jacques Derrida, Foucault, Luce Irigaray, Julia Kristeva, Jacques Lacan, and Monique Witting. *Gender Trouble* was an amalgamation of post-structuralist, psychoanalytical, and feminist methods that theorized gender, sex, and sexuality as performative. After deconstructing both sex and gender as socially constructed, Butler then goes on to delink desire from gender. In *Bodies That Matter*, she extends her analysis of performativity, engages critiques of the concept, and asks demanding questions such as, "[H]ow can one read a text for what does not appear within its own terms, but which nevertheless constitute the illegible conditions of its own legibility"?[24]

Likewise, Judith (Jack) Halberstam charges feminist theory to consider how science and technology studies change "the social relationship between gender and science, sexuality and biology, feminism and the politics of artificiality," so that we can see how "gendered representations are technological productions."[25] Later, in an analysis of Bram Stroker's *Dracula*, Halberstam theorizes the technologies of monstrosity, that is, "the production of monstrosity ... monstrous of race, monstrous class, or monstrous sex."[26] These early essays clearly serve as the foundation for the trajectory of her most noted works: *Skin Shows: Gothic Horror and the Technology of Monsters* (1995), *Female Masculinity* (1998), and *In a Queer Time and Place: Transgender Bodies, Subcultural Lives* (2005). In these last two books, Halberstam privileges cultural texts and performance. *Female Masculinity* uncouples masculinity from the biological male body and confronts lesbian-feminist phobias over the butch lesbian. With analyses covering eighteenth-century tribades and twentieth-century drag kings, Halberstam argues that minority and female masculinities serve as crucial sites for revealing how masculinity is performative and provide a "focus on certain categories of butchness without presuming that they represent early stages of transsexual identity and without losing their specificity as masculine identifications within a female body."[27]

During this same era, Roderick A. Ferguson's *Aberrations in Black: Toward a Queer of Color Critique* (2003), David L. Eng's *Racial Castration: Managing Masculinity* (2001), Siobhan B. Somerville's *Queering the Color Line: Race and the Invention of Homosexuality in American Culture* (2000), and Gayatri Gopinath's *Impossible Desires: Queer Diasporas and South Asian Public Cultures* (2005) likewise exemplified why literary and cultural studies continues to be important to disciplinary interventions into the study of gender and sexuality, especially in regards to people of color.[28] These studies of sexuality and difference interrogate American literary studies' ideas of chronology, geography, race, and gender in literary history and its emphasis on structures and movements that have been shaped by unacknowledged imperialist endeavors.

Over the years, feminist criticism and theory has thus made literary studies more interdisciplinary as a result of its interrogation of authorship, authority, and subjectivity. As a result, literary studies wrestled with its elitist class origins, which privileged the masculine, rationality, and written literacies. Yet this field certainly made feminist studies, as well as other disciplines, more queer and trans with its arguments about what constitutes a text. It is the intersection of gender and sexuality in American literature that makes evident Finney's claim at the beginning of this chapter that the things that are unmapped, inconsistently measured, and misdiagnosed about the body allow the possibility of one day making a poem that challenges empires of knowledge with affective exchanges of knowledge.[29]

NOTES

1 See Nikky Finney, "Acceptance Speech for the National Book Award for Poetry," http://nikkyfinney.net/acceptance.html.
2 Nikky Finney, "Resurrection of the Errand Girl: An Introduction," in *Head Off and Split* (Evanston, IL: Northwestern University Press, 2011), 3.
3 See Jean I. Marsden, "Beyond Recovery: Feminism and the Future of Eighteenth Century Studies," *Feminist Studies* 28, no. 3 (2002): 658.
4 Audre Lorde, "The Transformation of Silence into Language," in *Sister Outsider: Essays and Speeches* (Freedom, CA: Crossing, 1984), 40–44.
5 See National Book Critics Circle, "Video: Sandra Gilbert and Susan Gubar Accept Sandrof for Lifetime Achievement," March 1, 2013, http://bookcritics.org/blog/archive/video-sandra-gilbet-and-susan-gubar-accept-sandrof-for-lifetime-achievement.
6 Elaine Showalter, "Toward a Feminist Poetics," in *The New Feminist Criticism: Essays on Women, Literature and Theory*, ed. Elaine Showalter (London: Virago, 1986), 131.
7 Hazel Carby, *Reconstructing Womanhood: The Emergence of the Afro-American Woman Novelist* (New York: Oxford University Press, 1987), 6.
8 Trinh T. Minh-ha, *Woman, Native, Other: Writing Postcoloniality and Feminism* (Bloomington: Indiana University Press, 2009).
9 Robyn R. Warhol and Diane Price Herndl, introduction to *Feminisms: An Anthology of Literary Theory and Criticism*, ed. Robyn R. Warhol and Diane Price Herndl (New Brunswick: Rutgers University Press, 1991), x.
10 French feminist theory engaged Freud, Lacan, and Derrida to rethink questions of language and subjectivity as they related to women's bodies. Although French feminist writings by Hélène Cixous, Luce Irigaray, Julia Kristeva, and Monique Witting can be traced to the mid-1970s, translations of their work, and therefore its use by U.S. non-Francophone critics, occur with greater frequency in the 1980s.
11 Michel Foucault, *The History of Sexuality*, vol. 1, *An Introduction*, trans. Robert Hurley (New York: Vintage, 1978); Michel Foucault, *The History of Sexuality*, vol. 2, *The Use of Pleasure* (New York: Vintage, 1990); Michel Foucault, *The History of Sexuality*, vol. 3, *The Care of the Self* (New York: Vintage, 1988).
12 Lisa Duggan, "The Discipline Problem: Queer Theory Meets Lesbian and Gay History," in *Sex Wars: Sexual Dissent and Political Culture*, ed. Lisa Duggan and Nan D. Hunter (London: Routledge, 1995), 195.
13 Ibid., 196.
14 Linda Williams, *Hard Core: Power, Pleasure and the "Frenzy of the Visible"* (Berkeley: University of California Press, 1989), 121.
15 Hayden White, "The Value of Narrativity in the Representation of Reality," *Critical Inquiry* 7, no. 1 (1980): 5–27; and Michel Foucault, "What Is an Author?," in *Language, Counter-Memory, Practice*, ed. Donald F. Bouchard, trans. Donald F. Bouchard and Sherry Simon (Ithaca: Cornell University Press, 1977), 124–127.
16 Judith Butler, "Desire," in *Critical Terms for Literary Study*, ed. Frank Lentricchia and Thomas McLaughlin (Chicago: University of Chicago Press, 1990), 369.

17 Greg Thomas, *The Sexual Demon of Colonial Power: Pan-African Embodiment and Erotic Schemes of Empire* (Bloomington: Indiana University Press, 2007), 155.

18 Gayle Rubin, "Thinking Sex: Notes for a Radical Theory of the Politics of Sexuality," in *Pleasure and Danger: Exploring Female Sexuality*, ed. Carole Vance (Boston: Routledge, 1992), 267–319.

19 Hortense J. Spillers, "Mama's Baby, Papa's Maybe: An American Grammar Book," *diacritics* 17, no. 2 (1987): 79.

20 Gloria E. Anzaldúa, *Borderlands/La Frontera: The New Mestiza* (San Francisco: Aunt Lute, 1987), 80.

21 Ibid., 79.

22 See Deborah E. McDowell, "New Directions for Black Feminist Criticism," *Black American Literature Forum* 14, no. 4 (1980): 154.

23 Ibid., 153.

24 Judith Butler, *Bodies That Matter: On the Discursive Limits of "Sex"* (New York: Routledge, 1993), 37.

25 Judith Halberstam, "Automating Gender: Postmodern Feminism in the Age of the Intelligent Machine," *Feminist Studies* 17, no. 3 (1991): 439–440.

26 Judith Halberstam, "Technologies of Monstrosity: Bram Stoker's *Dracula*," *Victorian Studies* 36, no. 3 (1993): 334.

27 Judith Halberstam, *Female Masculinity* (Durham: Duke University Press, 1998), 152.

28 Ferguson uses African American literature to read against the grain of canonical sociology and its concepts of racial difference. Eng juxtaposes the psychoanalytic work of Freud, Lacan, and Fanon against the literature of Asian American and Asian diasporic writers. Somerville exposes how the constructions of race and sexuality in the United States are intertwined legally, socially, and biologically in early twentieth-century cinema and African American literature. Gopinath challenges conventional and nationalistic concepts of the diaspora that privilege bloodlines, descent, and authenticity by examining queerness as it is presented in South Asian literature and culture.

29 In addition to the queer theorists Sedgwick, Butler, and Halberstam, affect theory and studies about gender, sexuality, and time have been produced and forged by theorists such as Sara Ahmed, Lauren Berlant, Elizabeth Freeman, Brian Massumi, Sianne Ngai, and Ann Stoker. Most notable is Halberstam, who, in relying on theories of temporality, picks up her earlier discussion of the transsexual figure to discuss how queer communities live in an alternate time paradigm. By arguing for prolonged adolescence, Halberstam challenges "reproductive time" and offers a revision of subcultural theory. For Halberstam's discussion of reproductive time, see *In a Queer Time and Place: Transgender Bodies, Subcultural Lives* (New York: New York University Press, 2005), 10.

I I

KYLA WAZANA TOMPKINS

Intersections of Race, Gender, and Sexuality: Queer of Color Critique

José Esteban Muñoz, Presente

Given how varied queer people of color are in our histories, cultures, and strategies for expression and survival in the Americas, it is impossible to fully take account of us in one chapter. This essay is an abbreviated account of the field that has come to be known as "queer of color critique" over the past thirty years, focusing on a few keywords and themes. In what follows, I narrate some of the overlapping histories of queer communities of color as they resonate and reverberate across the shared trajectories and cultural productions that emerged from modernity, modern and neoliberal capitalism, the evolution of race and racism, and the colonial and neocolonial encounters and diasporas of the past 500-odd years.

Although the phrase "queer of color critique" only came into usage recently, we can trace the origins of the collusion between constructions of race and sexuality in the Americas to the particular expression of sexual violence, Christian and colonial militarism, and homophobic racism that came into existence during and that has survived since the colonial encounters between Europeans, Africans, and indigenous peoples.[1] As scholars of settler colonialist discourse have shown, violence toward and a fear of non-heteronormative sexualities (as defined by Euro-American Christianity) were firmly in place during the first centuries of the colonial encounter – particularly in the violence toward indigenous peoples who showed what was, for Europeans, nonnormative gender and sexual expression, including what we might now recognize as same-sex oriented, inter- or transgendered ways of living.[2]

This violence took place across the Americas, as Spanish, English, and French colonial forces sought to destroy the nations and cultures that were already in place by using geopolitical disruption (forced migration and the displacement of native peoples from their sovereign lands), the breaking up of family networks (native boarding schools and the sexualized and cultural violence that took place there), disciplinary regimes (the Inquisition and other colonial bodies that criminalized gender nonnormativity, sodomy, and forms of same-sex desire), and bald, naked violence (for instance, Balboa's setting of dogs upon indigenous peoples in what is now Peru for their "sins" of sexual transgression and for dressing as women). All of these actions laid the groundwork for a logic that framed indigenous peoples as feminized or animalistic, thereby installing European colonialism as patriarchal and heteronormative and, above all, claiming the modern category of "human" for European whites only.

Thus, as the foundational racial violences that underlie the modern nation-states that now comprise these continents were being laid down and concretized, categories of normative and nonnormative sexuality were constructed alongside and over them. Obviously these were not limited to indigenous peoples, given that similar forms of racialized aggression took place as part of the logic of chattel slavery and also recurred as sex panics attached to later waves of immigration.[3] Chattel slavery, for instance, sanctioned and even built into its own economic project sexual violences against African men, women, and children, who were at times categorized as breedable stock and therefore as nonhuman inventory holding a great deal of economic investment. Having been denied citizenship and therefore legibility as subjects who deserved protection under the law, slaves were seen as lacking the right to consent and control over their persons: to be a slave – male or female, adult or child – was to be available to white rape, and yet also to have that selfsame act denied *as* rape. To be black then was to be always already sexualized as against white citizens and therefore to be always and already deviant.[4] Throughout U.S. history, we can see similar legal, juridical, and disciplinary violence deployed against other racialized groups: in the immigration laws that restricted Asian women's immigration to the United States and created bachelor societies of Asian American men as a cheap labor force, while also publicly deriding Asian men as both feminized and sexually dangerous, for instance.[5]

Queer of color critique articulates queer theory from the heart of these and other histories, although at times it also intervenes in and complicates mainstream and Euro-American queer theory. For instance, by claiming the oceanic traumas and sensations of the middle passage – the time and space of the slave ship's voyage from Africa to the Americas – as a site from which to theorize black queerness, Omise'eke Natasha Tinsley notes that "fluidity" has been a central symbol of queer theory for the past fifteen years: "[Q]ueer theory has harnessed the repetitive, unpredictable energy of currents, waves, and foam to smash and wash into bits many I's from the gendered self to the sexed body, from heterocentric feminist speech to homonormative gay discourse."[6] Tinsley's rethinking of fluidity as a trope of queer theory demands that it be reworked from the point of view of its unexamined debt to the black Atlantic: "To become an expansively decolonizing practice, queer theory must adjust its vision to see what has been submerged in the process of unmarking whiteness and global northernness. ... In the black queer time and place of the door of no return, fluid desire is neither purely metaphor nor purely luxury."[7]

Tinsley's important intervention places hemispheric African diasporic history at the productive heart of a decolonizing queer theory/practice. Grounding her argument in readings of the Caribbean writers Eliot Bliss, Dionne Brand, Mayotte Capecia, Michelle Cliff, and Ida Faubert, she argues that alongside these terrible – terror-filled and terrorizing – experiences of violence, forms of cultural, familial, and emotional expression emerged and survived, which testifies not only to the determined refusal of these many peoples to disappear but also to their ongoing political objections to the systems under which they labored. (And here we might also think of the more experimental work of Claude McKay, especially the 1929 novel *Banjo*, in which he celebrates and examines the migratory lives of African, Afro-Caribbean, and African American workers, folding diasporic homosociality into a radical critique of capital).[8] Recent work on *mati* women in Suriname, for instance – working-class women whose sexual and emotional practices refuse easy distinctions between heterosexual and lesbian life but many of whose primary relationships are formed with women – hypothesizes that although the term "*mati*" means "same-sex lover," it likely emerged etymologically from the term "shipmate," as in "s/he who survived the middle passage with me."[9] The discursive and material violence attached to the production of erotic categories of normative and nonnormative being is real, of course, but what is also clear is that the queerness, as it were, of peoples of color emerges from the fire of modernity's historical forges and has an energy to survive and create that is fiercely its own. One might also consider the separation of theory from literature to be another form of discursive violence, one that is linked to hierarchies of normativity. As feminist literary critics have shown, and as the important literary contributions of women of color feminism have demonstrated, one is hard pressed to separate queer of color theory from queer of color cultural production in terms of fiction, poetry, dance, film and other forms of creativity.[10]

Indeed, as the warrior-like term "fierce" testifies, the aesthetics of queer of color life are tied to the daily work of creating and thriving in a phobic world, to the beauty, courage, and humor that emerge out of and as psychic and physical survival at the individual, familial, and community levels.[11] Struggle and liberation are key terms here, and thus the history and cultural production attached to global liberation struggles must be understood as historical antecedents to the contemporary lives and cultural production of queers of color in the Americas. These include but are not limited to: indigenous resistance movements; Third World nationalist and postcolonial struggles; trade unionist and socialist movements and the Marxist intellectual traditions attached to them; first-, second-, and third-wave feminism, in particular the enormous and important body of writing that emerged from the cultural and political arms of women of color feminism; the Chicana/ Chicano movements, or *El Movimiento*; transnational and pan-African black radicalism; transgender rights movements; disability rights movements; the civil rights and Black Power movements; and, finally, the modern gay and lesbian rights movement.

All of these histories undergird and feed the logic, literature, and body of thought that has come to be known as queer of color critique, and they are expressed in theater, poetry, political manifestos, novels, anthologies, dance, performance, and also at the everyday level of the gesture – the snap, the twist, the turn, the strut, the jack, the twerk, the twirl of the fancy dance, the lift of a skirt, the one-two step of the *merengue*, the switch of a hip and the cock of an eyebrow, the twitch of the lip, and the languid wave – that forms the world-making strategies of people of color in the Americas. To engage with queer of color life in the Americas is to be humbled and dazzled by its richness and its courage; to be fully present to it is to be moved affectively and politically by what might be yet unleashed if we move closer to its utopic possibilities.

In ranging from political thought to art to daily life, queer of color writing and cultural expression can hardly be captured in this one essay. The next three sections each attempt to take account of a few overlapping terms by way of an initial gesture. The first section takes account of the complicated role that the nation state has played in queer of color life; the second looks at the interlinked notions of exile, diaspora, and movement as they have been claimed by queer of color writing; and the third takes up performance, aesthetics, and erotics.

State, Nation, and Violence

In her 1987 *Borderlands/La Frontera*, Gloria Anzaldúa theorizes her identity as a queer Chicana beyond the geographical boundaries of the nation-state: "As a *mestiza* I have no country, my homeland cast me out; yet all countries are mine because I am every woman's sister or potential lover."[12] Using the cultures that exist along and upon the U.S.-Mexican border (cultures that predate the establishment of that border in 1848 with the signing of the Treaty of Guadalupe Hidalgo) as a model from which to theorize mixed-race consciousness, or *mestizaje*, alongside her queerness, Anzaldúa sees lesbian identity as a universal quality that exceeds the limits of the nation-state.[13] In this view, queerness and her mestiza consciousness refute any sense of belonging to one bordered nation. Instead, she occupies a space outside the nation-state, making mestiza consciousness an identity that takes up the exclusion of queers and border citizens from the state as a place from which to theorize non-binaristic and alternative forms of belonging.

And yet, despite Anzaldúa's utopic vision – in the sense that José Esteban Muñoz defined utopia, via Ernst Bloch, as "relational to historically situated struggles … the hopes of a collective" but also as a kind of queer futurity, as the not-yet arrived – for most people, the state proves to be something far more intractable at the present time.[14] Extending the work of feminist critics of liberalism and neoliberalism in particular, Roderick A. Ferguson has argued that the state, the nation, and citizenship itself are always articulated as universals that are normatively heterosexual and white, both producing and obscuring populations of color as always and already non-heteronormative and sexually deviant. As Ferguson argues, the nation-state has historically solicited (and forced) the labor of non-white populations by offering the promise of limited forms of citizenship – which is understood here as both legal and social membership in the nation-state – while simultaneously policing those same populations along the lines of sexual propriety and social hygiene. Drawing from the archive of black feminist and lesbian literary criticism and African American literature, for instance, Toni Morrison's *Sula* (1973), James Baldwin's *Go Tell It on the Mountain* (1953), and Richard Wright's *Native Son* (1940), Ferguson argues that it is precisely from the point of view of these "surplus populations" that we might begin to produce a critique of capitalism, and therefore of the nation-state: "[W]e must see the gendered and eroticized elements of racial formations as offering ruptural – i.e., critical – possibilities."[15] Culture, he argues, is one place where those critical possibilities are deployed: "U.S. women of color feminism helped to designate the imagination as a social practice under contemporary globalization."[16]

Given the foundational violence against queer people of color as both sexual and racialized subjects that underlies the formation of state citizenship as always and already white and heterosexual, it is no surprise that the nation-state emerges as more of a problem than as a site for solutions in queer of color critique, and indeed, recent queer of color and feminist critique has begun to critique a "rights-based" – that is, "state-based" – approach to social change. This coming-together of women of color feminism, queer theory, and critical race theory has also drawn energy from and contributed to disability and transgender thought, in particular the work of Dean Spade, whose writing on the law in relation to transgender activism has fundamentally reshaped strategies for queer of color activism by questioning recognition, inclusion, and incorporation projects and instead focusing on the strategic alliances that have been formed in relation to the administrative violence of judicial-industrial complexes.[17]

In examining the relationships between queers of color and the nation-state, queer of color theorists have described the strategies queers employ to survive within, dismantle, and/or (dis)identify with the nation-state, developing trenchant critiques of the strategies the state uses to mobilize gay and lesbian rights for nationalist ends as well as, in turn, critiquing the strategies that mainstream gay and lesbian organizations have deployed to engage the state as a site from which to leverage limited and problematic forms of political power, including, for instance, marriage rights and the right to serve in the military. These relationships reveal dialectical tensions between national belonging and exclusion, and between complicity in and subjection to state violence and neglect.

In the years since 9/11 and the restructuring of the modern U.S. war machine during George W. Bush's presidency, the paradoxical relationship between queer belonging and queer abjection has been respatialized along transnational lines. Taking into account the wars in Afghanistan and Iraq as well as the deployment of anti-Muslim sentiment along the ideological tracks laid down by orientalism, queer of color theorists have turned their attention to the relationship between the rights-oriented discourse of equality and protection within the modern nation-state, on the one hand, and the logics with which the state justifies its exercise of violence against foreign countries and their peoples, on the other hand. In the period following 9/11, as Jasbir Puar and Amit Rai have written, "the construct of the terrorist relies on a knowledge of sexual perversity (failed heterosexuality, Western notions of the psyche, and a certain queer monstrosity)."[18] That is to say, the perverse and socially dangerous qualities that defined queerness in the period leading up to 9/11 were, after that national trauma, displaced onto the Arab (and, as Puar shows, the South Asian) subject. As Puar argues, this displacement has occasioned the eruption of a new mainstream gay and lesbian politics that she terms "homonationalism," in which gay and lesbian organizations increasingly advocate for the right to gain normative forms of citizenship and national belonging, including the right to marry and the right to serve in the military.[19]

Within this logic, gay and lesbian rights become part and parcel of the new militarized normal, which is then deployed against people of color and racialized others overseas (and, of course, domestically, where poor people of color continue to disproportionately join the military). It is exactly at this political intersection that we must ask: What is the price of normative belonging to the nation-state? This deep investment in conservative forms of citizenship has produced a reformist logic – one that Chandan Reddy finds articulated in Nella Larsen's novel *Quicksand* (1928) – in which "the liberal state embodies and figures the ethical fulcrum without which the movements and claims for equality would be both ineffective and dead."[20]

As the debates around and responses to California's Proposition 8 – a 2008 ballot initiative banning gay and lesbian marriage that was passed by voters – demonstrated, these new political formations have resulted in the further exclusion of people of color from gay and lesbian politics. In one stunning example of the tone-deafness around race in the main-stream gay and lesbian rights movement, in the days leading up to the vote, anti–Proposition 8 interest groups ran an advertisement urging voters to consider gay and lesbian marriage as analogous to interracial marriage, arguing that the 1967 *Loving v. Virginia* case, in which an interracial het-erosexual couple appealed to the Supreme Court for the right to marry, and which ultimately struck down all laws banning interracial marriage, was but a precedent to the current marriage rights debate. This strategy, how-ever, did not only ignore the historic hostility toward interracial marriage in black communities, thus striking a discordant and condescending note at a pressing political moment. It also presaged the later backlash against com-munities of color on the part of gay and lesbian organizations who blamed the passage of Proposition 8 on those communities, publicly deploying the unfair and historically ungrounded idea that communities of color are more homophobic than white communities are.

Exacerbating this grievous political algebra, *The Advocate* then ran a cover story on December 16, 2008, with the title "Gay Is the New Black," a statement that both occluded the ongoing struggle for political and eco-nomic equity for African American communities and emptied out the history of that struggle in order to make blackness a signifier of revolutionary and thereby commodifiable chic. Of course, as it turned out, it was in fact the Church of Jesus Christ of Latter-Day Saints (itself an organization that has been historically targeted for its nonnormative and yet hyper-heterosexual family organization) that was later revealed to be financially instrumental in pushing Proposition 8 and in targeting communities and voters of color, in a logic that echoed the later complaints of pro-gay marriage groups.

The state, as juridical structure, and the nation, as an ideological concept and discursive force that structures ideas of who belongs and who does not belong within its borders, thus continue to impact and shape the everyday lives of the nation-state's queer citizens as well as the lives of the queer non-citizens – migrant workers and undocumented peoples, for instance – who reside there. When "multiplied," as Ferguson terms it, as and with race, we also begin to see that queers – in particular, those queers of color living in poverty – are disproportionately targeted by state violence, as well: as, for instance, in the case of transgendered sex workers who experience either police aggression or police indifference to the many forms of violence visited upon them. This violence lies atop a particularly modern paradox of the U.S. nation-state, which rests its claims to liberal democracy upon a mythology of equal rights and protections under the law for all of its citizens and inhabitants and yet, as critics of liberalism have shown, in fact produces everyday ideologies by which many of those citizens and inhabitants, by dint of racial and sexual difference or economic inequality, are excluded.

Returning to Anzaldúa's vision of the stateless queer, we might also think about the occlusion of indigenous peoples from her analysis, which posits a borderland, or transnational identity, but in doing so, and particularly in doing so via a mixed-race model of *mestizaje*, in essence renders invisible the existence of sovereign nations internal to the nation-state itself. The realities of reservation as well as urban Native American life – even the fundamental fact that from within an indigenous epistemology, the U.S. nation-state (the source to which we turn for rights-based claims) lies atop many sovereign indigenous nations that continue to resist settler colonialism – attest to the fact that we cannot take on an unnuanced relationship to the nation and state, as either the source, or even a resource, for larger dreams of social and political change.[21]

Home, Belonging, and Movement

In a seminal sequence in the now classic 1991 film *Paris Is Burning*, Dorian Corey explains what a "house" is:

A house – they're families for a lot of children who don't have families. But this is a new meaning of family. The hippies had families. And no one thought nothing about it. It wasn't a question of a man and a woman and children which we grew up knowing as family – it's a question of a group of human beings in a mutual bond.[22]

The question of belonging and the normative function of the home – particularly as families of origin – as well as the rethinking of the very nature of house and home are at the heart of queer critique, if only because so many queers experience the family as a site of violence and rejection – one is reminded here of Audre Lorde's vexed relationship with her mother in *Zami: A New Spelling of My Name: A Biomythography* (1982), or the protagonist's struggles with his preacher father in *Go Tell It on the Mountain*.[23] This should come as no surprise given the central place of the family as a cornerstone of heterosexual and patriarchal structures; and yet even in a period in which gays and lesbians have begun to win limited (and, as discussed in the previous section, contested) civil rights victories in the courts and in Congress, in fiction, film, and queer of color politics, the trope of the queer as exile or refugee from the family continues, whether in the mythology of gay migration from small town or rural areas to urban areas or in the hard material realities of transgendered and queer kids who escape from their homes into the precarity of street life, as do the "children" of the voguing houses. And yet, as the exiled protagonist of Monique Truong's *The Book of Salt* (2004) reminds us, the primal wound of familial and parental rejection remains behind as a longing for home.[24]

In short, mobility, movement, and the vexed issues of having a home or belonging continue to linger in queer of color writing, performance, and theory, just as indeed they do in queer life and cultural production more broadly. These themes take many forms. For instance, the turn to the study of transnational queer literary cultures, as discussed at length by Martin Joseph Ponce in Chapter 14, has opened up the idea that movement, migration, and immigration across national and hemispheric lines are central and important experiences that are occluded when we imagine "gay community" to be largely static or nationally bounded. As artists and scholars have shown, queer transnational migration takes a variety of forms, as do the various queer diasporas that have shaped queer of color critique. Whether by forced migration, displacement, refugee movement, choice, or removal, non-white peoples have come to the Americas and have moved within the Americas in a variety of different trajectories, some of which are linear – for instance, immigration to and settlement within the United States – and some of which are not – for example, moving to the United States and returning regularly to, or splitting time between, the United States and a country of origin.

Displacing the nation-state as a central and normalizing analytic lens through which we view queer life throws the close ties between nationalism and heteropatriarchy into stark relief. David L. Eng's work on the intersections between queerness and diasporic life, for instance, argues that the similar tropes of migration from home – of movement away from origins – and static or traditional notions of home and family as they unfold in diasporic movement and in the anti-normative possibilities of queerness might make happy bedfellows of the two. Taking up R. Zamora Linmark's 1995 *Rolling the R's*, a novella that tells the story of a group of queer and straight pan-Asian and Pacific immigrant teenagers in Honolulu, he writes that "rather than demanding the abnegation of homeland ... into standard narratives of immigration, assimilation and settlement, the queer diaspora ... emphatically substitutes a queer affiliation that preserves individual histories of development ... [predicated] on the engagement of racial, gender, class and national differentials for its social efficacy and engagement. ... This is what a diaspora organized around queerness potentially offers."[25] Similarly, in her work on cultural production in the South Asian diaspora, Gayatri Gopinath argues that "a queer diasporic framework productively exploits the analogous relation between nation and diaspora on the one hand, and between heterosexuality and queerness on the other. ... Queerness is to heterosexuality as the diaspora is to the nation."[26]

A queer diasporic imaginary then offers a site from which to rethink the romance of filial belonging that has undergirded certain conservative forms of liberal citizenship, but it has also produced imaginative forms of transnational belonging that weave together multiple cultural trajectories and produce new forms of affiliation and creativity. Lawrence La Fountain-Stokes's work on Puerto Rican artists in the Bronx borough of New York City, for instance, documents how the performance work of Arthur Avila and Elizabeth Marrero makes "Nuyorico" a site of queer utopian possibility in which "neighborhood-based transgressive performance and local interventions offer new social visions and spaces for Puerto Ricans and other queer people of color ... a concept that riffs off the tradition of Nuyorican cultural resistance that has been a hallmark of diasporic Puerto Rican life."[27]

This sense of being "between and afar" also finds expression in Rinaldo Walcott's theorizing of a "homopoetics" of queer Caribbean life in diaspora that occupies a place of privilege – of being a queer migrant whose very queerness is both grounded in its roots and enabled by its absence from a "home" that criminalizes queer life and sex. Placing himself in conversation with Edouard Glissant, Hilton Als, Audre Lorde, and M. Jacqui Alexander, Walcott argues that "the work of diaspora and or Caribbean extensions outside the archipelago and the ethics of speaking from 'away' can draw on the poetics of the region to speak back in ways that ethically inform a politics of the possible there and here."[28]

This sense that movement, migration, and displacement offer valuable metaphors and material histories through which to rethink queerness has found expression in a queer of color theory that also seeks to upend and reconsider how subjectivity itself is formed. Sara Ahmed's work on affect and orientation finds its roots in the school of Western philosophy called phenomenology, but it is also grounded in her experiences of migration. Her reading of the terms "queer" and "orientation" as well as "Orientalism" point to how the notion of being a sexualized subject is a matter of being in motion, of "turning" toward one thing or the other; she points out that the Indo-European roots of the word "queer" point to a notion of "twist-ing": "Queer is, after all, a spatial term which then gets translated into a sexual term, a term for a twisted sexuality that does not follow a straight line." Belonging somewhere and finding a home, she argues, is a matter of "extending one's body into space"; it is a matter of finding one's direc-tion, one's orientation toward others; it is a matter of settling into the "new contours of what we could call livable or inhabitable space."[29] Similarly, writing about *queer latinidad*, that is, the broad contours of the queer cul-ture that emerge from Spanish-speaking postcolonial nations, Juana María Rodríguez speaks of queer identity as "situatedness in motion: embodiment and spatiality."[30] Divas, for instance, "are a breathing, swishing, eruption of the divine, a way of being in the world, of claiming power as movement, glances, voice, body and style."[31]

Queers of color, and in particular those queers of color defined in and through various diasporic movements, have taken up the conditions and strategies of their own displacement as political epistemology and aesthetic project. This dislocatedness and critical "orientation" toward home and homeland are not without pain: exile and the melancholy of not belonging, of being "away," mark queer of color life and cultural production with a sense of loss that is irrefutable. And yet, these migrations have also rewritten queerness as a category by reclaiming mobility as a productive site experi-ence from which to rethink the political work of sexual and racial non-normativity: What would it mean to rethink "the movement" from within movement itself?

This project would entail, as Muñoz argues in his readings of queer artists and authors such as Frank O'Hara, LeRoi Jones, and Elizabeth Bishop, let-ting go of totalizing political goals, that is, letting go of the "ends" of polit-ical work and instead focusing on the "here and now" as a time and space whose deficiencies spur us on to imagine queerness as a utopian futurity that never arrives: "[U]topia is a stage, not merely a temporal stage, like a phase, but also a spatial one."[32] Here, Muñoz shifts from the motif of movement to that of gesture: "Queer utopia is a modality of critique that speaks to quo-tidian gestures as laden with potentiality. The queerness of queer futurity, like the blackness of a black radical tradition, is a relational and collective modality of endurance and support. ... It is a being in, toward, and for futurity."[33] Queer of color critique arrives at this project by embracing movement as an experience of never-quite-arriving and therefore allowing for the possibility of what-yet-may-be.

Performance, Erotics, and Aesthetics

On a street in downtown Cuba, a *transformista* named Lili saunters out of her apartment to the sound of catcalls and insults from her neighbors; a transvestite strolls along an urban lake to the sounds of Billie Holliday; a group of young gay men sashay through Washington Square Park as though it were a fashion runway; a butch Latina lesbian in baggy clothes, gold chains, and a do-rag moves slowly downstage, marking each step with a satisfied "uh"; a white man falls in love with a female Chinese opera singer who is biologically male; another falls in love with a transvestite mixed-race woman who only later reveals her penis.[34] Each of these scenes from the canon of critical performances, ethnographic restagings, and cultural productions by queers of color points us to the centrality of performance to queer of color life; each of these subjects walks his or her own fine line between spectacular artifice, a brave truthfulness about who he or she is, and a kind of quotidian danger that freights each bodily gesture with a will-to-be-visible and, even more, a will-to-survive.

In recent years, performance studies has grown in importance as a critical space from within which to examine and render visible modes of living that have been historically obscured. "Performance" can mean many things, and indeed, as Sean Metzger argues in Chapter 2, like "queer," it is a contested term, one whose very contestation is at the heart of its critical power. Performance may mean an aesthetic or theatrical event; it may also point to the fulfilling of social norms – ways of walking, talking, and "doing" selfhood – that make one's self legible and acceptable to the social world. As the performances cited at the beginning of this section also suggest, the everyday and aesthetic performances of queers of color speak to ways of being – of moving, of speaking, of dancing, and of living – that collapse those distinctions. To be different – to be brown, to be queer, or to be trans, for instance – in a deeply normative world is by definition to be theatrical, in part because to be unapologetically visible in a world that would much rather you were invisible, or even dead, is by definition to be an event. These performances then are forms of *doing* selfhood and of claiming theatricality in such a way as to defy a world that is determined to erase the very subject who makes the performance possible. As Muñoz, building on other theorists, showed in his important work

Disidentifications, to enact those performances is also to engage in "world-making" that "delineates the ways in which performances – both theatrical and everyday rituals – have the ability to establish alternate views of the world. ... They are oppositional ideologies that function as critiques of oppressive regimes of 'truth' that subjugate minoritarian people."[35]

Muñoz's idea of "disidentification" has been central to reshaping the field of queer of color theory, as well as performance studies. For Muñoz, disidentification is a technology by which subaltern peoples, especially queers of color, identify with parts of dominant culture, borrowing and reshaping those parts in order to build lives and worlds within which they can survive. We might understand performance, then, as both ephemeral but also vital to, and defining of, queer of color life. Given its dependence on visuality, citation, and spectacle, performance is an exercise in aesthetics; that is, performance interacts and plays with viewers' sensory experiences of and responses to an object or person.

These performances are, of course, culturally and historically specific, and yet there are resonances across many of these differences. Consider, for instance, concepts like beauty, drama, and realness. In his seminal discussion of diasporic Filipino men's "self-making" practices, Martin F. Manalansan IV unpacks the terms "biyuti" and "drama," which are popularly used in *swardspeak*, an everyday language spoken by Filipino gay men that borrows from English and Tagalog.[36] Referencing the English word "beauty" but deploying it to different ends than the source to which it refers, "biyuti," as Manalansan describes it, variously describes selfhood, physical feminine beauty, countenance, or emotional disposition. Similarly, "drama," a term that most clearly refers to the everyday work of performing the self, draws on theatrical conventions and idioms. Both of these terms, as Manalansan shows, are framed in the particular and shifting terms of diasporic *bakla* (loosely queer in terms of gender or sexual nonnormativity) culture, and they borrow at times from Tagalog television and cinema melodramas.

The centrality of aesthetics and cultural borrowing to queer of color life is also present in a term like "realness," which refers, specifically in drag ball culture, to the precision with which a performance mimics the original. And yet, these are not simply aspirational imitations, as categories such as "Butch Queen First Time at a Drag Ball" from the film *Paris Is Burning* suggests; rather, these are knowing performances of performances that send up the original, to a certain extent the performer, and the culture that pits them against each other.

Aesthetics form, then, a political language within which a community both speaks to itself and with which members may recognize each other. Here one might also think of the "dandy" tradition, taken up by lesbians

of color throughout the twentieth and twenty-first centuries (by performers and blues women such as Moms Mabley and Bessie Smith), in which
women borrowed from and dressed in the sharpest of men's fashions. This
particular expression of female masculinity references but is also distinct
from butchness and has historically (although not exclusively, as current
expressions of "boi" fashion and desire attest) found its erotic counterpart
in queer femme style. Aesthetic performance and playfulness, that is, become
part of infusing the everyday with eroticism, which is understood loosely, as
Lorde defined it in her foundational essay "The Uses of the Erotic," as

> the open and fearless underlining of my capacity for joy ... so every level upon
> which I sense also opens to the erotically satisfying experience, whether it is
> dancing, building a bookcase, writing a poem, examining an idea. ... And that
> deep and irreplaceable knowledge of my capacity for joy comes to demand
> from all of my life that it be lived within the knowledge that such satisfaction
> is possible.[37]

Eroticism, as Lorde understood it in her revolutionary essay, is sexual; but
more than that, erotics refers to the infusing of the everyday with a feeling of
belonging to and expansively enacting a sense of alignment between self and
world. Queer of color critique's interest in performance brings this spectacu-
larity, this commitment to wielding visibility against a phobic public sphere,
into sharp relief and finds political value in the courage that queers of color
contribute to everyday aesthetic practices, ranging from literature, drama,
poetry, essays, autobiography, and dance to the movement of bodies in the
space and time of everyday life.

NOTES

Although this essay bears my name as author, it was structured and initially
researched in collaboration and with the generous participation of Emily A. Owens,
who is presently completing her dissertation entitled "Fantasies of Consent: Black
Women's Sexual Labor in 19th Century New Orleans" at Harvard University. The
essay bears the imprint of her fierce intelligence and energy, and my only regret is
that we were not able to write it together. The readings and research were also completed with the contributions and participation of my Queer of Color Critique class
at Pomona College in the fall of 2014. It has been my goal to write this piece as col-
laboratively as possible, borrowing from the model of collective writing spearheaded
by women of color feminism, in particular the collectives that produced the critical
anthologies *This Bridge Called My Back*, *Home Girls: A Black Feminist Anthology*,
and many others. The writing here echoes my colleagues' and students' ideas, and
any lapses or gaps are my fault alone.

1 The term itself, however, is generally credited to Roderick A. Ferguson,
   Aberrations in Black: Toward a Queer of Color Critique (Minneapolis: University
   of Minnesota Press, 2003).

2 See Scott Lauria Morgensen, "Settler Homonationalism: Theorizing Settler Colonialism within Queer Modernities," *GLQ: A Journal of Lesbian and Gay Studies* 16, no. 1–2 (2010): 105–131; Mark Rifkin, *When Did Indians Become Straight? Kinship, the History of Sexuality, and Native Sovereignty* (New York: Oxford University Press, 2011); Andrea Smith, "Queer Theory and Native Studies: The Heteronormativity of Settler Colonialism," *GLQ: A Journal of Lesbian and Gay Studies* 16, no. 1–2 (2010): 41–68; and Zeb Tortorici, "Against Nature: Sodomy and Homosexuality in Colonial Latin America," *History Compass* 10, no. 2: (2012): 161–178.

3 See Bruce Burgett, "Sex, Panic, Nation," *American Literary History* 21, no. 1 (2009): 67–84.

4 See, for instance, Darieck Scott, *Extravagant Abjection: Blackness, Power, and Sexuality in the African American Literary Imagination* (New York: New York University Press, 2010).

5 Peter Boag, *Same-Sex Affairs: Constructing and Controlling Homosexuality in the Pacific Northwest* (Berkeley: University of California Press, 2003); Jennifer Ting, "Bachelor Society: Deviant Heterosexuality and Asian American Historiography," in *Privileging Positions: The Sites of Asian American Studies*, ed. Gary Y. Okihiro, Marilyn Alquizola, Dorothy Fujita Rony, and K. Scott Wong (Pullman: Washington State University Press, 1995); Madeline Y. Hsu, "Unwrapping Orientalist Constraints: Restoring Homosocial Normativity to Chinese American History," *Amerasia Journal* 29, no. 2 (2003): 230–253; and Nayan Shah, *Contagious Divides: Epidemics and Race in San Francisco's Chinatown* (Berkeley: University of California Press, 2001).

6 Omise'eke Natasha Tinsley, "Black Atlantic, Queer Atlantic: Queer Imaginings of the Middle Passage," *GLQ: A Journal of Lesbian and Gay Studies* 14, no. 2–3 (2008): 203.

7 See Tinsley, "Black Atlantic," 206. See also Omise'eke Natasha Tinsley, *Thiefing Sugar: Eroticism between Women in Caribbean Literature* (Durham: Duke University Press, 2010).

8 I thank my student William Mullaney for his thesis and insights into McKay's *Banjo*.

9 Tinsley, "Black Atlantic," 208; Gloria Wekker, *The Politics of Passion: Women's Sexual Culture in the Afro-Surinamese Diaspora* (New York: Columbia University Press, 2006).

10 As Barbara Christian, wrote in "The Race for Theory," *Cultural Critique* 6 (1987): 51–63: "I am inclined to say that our theorizing (and I intentionally use the verb rather than the noun) is often in narrative forms, in the stories we create, in riddles and proverbs, in the play with language, since dynamic rather than fixed ideas seem more to our liking. How else have we managed to survive with such spiritedness the assaults on our bodies, social institutions, countries, our very humanities" (52). The foundational writing of women of color feminism in the 1980s and 1990s laid potent claim to literature, in particular to poetry, as a writing practice from which experience could be theorized. Examples include Cherríe Moraga and Gloria Anzaldúa, *This Bridge Called My Back: Writings by Radical Women of Color* (New York: Kitchen Table Women of Color Press, 1981); and Barbara Smith, *Home Girls: A Black Feminist Anthology* (New York: Kitchen Table/Women of Color Press, 1983).

11 The term "warrior" was claimed by Audre Lorde in her self-titling as "black, lesbian, mother, warrior, poet." See Joan Wylie Hall, *Conversations with Audre Lorde* (Jackson: University Press of Mississippi, 1990), vii.

12 Gloria Anzaldúa, *Borderlands/La Frontera: The New Mestiza* (San Francisco: Aunt Lute Books, 2012), 102.

13 Ibid., 106.

14 José Esteban Muñoz, *Cruising Utopia: The Then and There of Queer Futurity* (New York: New York University Press, 2009), 3.

15 Ferguson, *Aberrations in Black*, 17. See also Grace Hong, *The Ruptures of American Capital: Women of Color Feminism and the Culture of Immigrant Labor* (Minneapolis: University of Minnesota Press, 2006).

16 Ibid., 117.

17 See Dean Spade, *Normal Life: Administrative Violence, Critical Trans Politics and the Limits of the Law* (Brooklyn: South End Press, 2011).

18 Jasbir Puar and Amit Rai, "Monster, Terrorist, Fag: The War on Terrorism and the Production of Docile Patriots," *Social Text* 20, no. 3 (2002): 117–148.

19 See Jasbir Puar, *Terrorist Assemblages: Homonationalism in Queer Times* (Durham: Duke University Press, 2007).

20 Chandan Reddy, *Freedom with Violence: Race, Sexuality, and the US State* (Durham: Duke University Press, 2011), 9.

21 Here one might consider Mark Rifkin's insights in *When Did Indians Become Straight?* about how queer and other liberation movements have either co-opted ideas of Native American kinship or occluded Native sovereignty claims in order to articulate their own political agendas. For counterexamples to these strategies drawn from the canon of Native American LGBTQ literature, see Rifkin's discussions of Beth Brant's 1992 story collection *Mohawk Trail* as well as Craig Womack's 2001 *Drowning in Fire*.

22 Quoted in *Paris Is Burning*, directed by Jennie Livingston (Miramax, 1991).

23 James Baldwin, *Go Tell It on the Mountain* (New York: Vintage Books, 2013); Audre Lorde, *Zami: A New Spelling of My Name: A Biomythography* (Berkeley: Crossing Press, 1982).

24 Monique Truong, *The Book of Salt* (New York: Mariner Books, 2004).

25 David L. Eng, *Racial Castration: Managing Masculinity in Asian America* (Durham: Duke University Press, 2001), 226.

26 Gayatri Gopinath, *Impossible Desires: Queer Diasporas and South Asian Public Cultures* (Durham: Duke University Press, 2005), 11.

27 Lawrence La Fountain-Stokes, *Queer Ricans: Cultures and Sexualities in the Diaspora* (Minneapolis: University of Minnesota Press, 2009), 132.

28 Rinaldo Walcott, "Queer Returns: Human Rights, the Anglo-Caribbean, and Diaspora Politics," *Caribbean Review of Gender Studies* 3 (2009): 7.

29 Sara Ahmed, *Queer Phenomenology: Orientations, Objects, Others* (Durham: Duke University Press, 2006), 67, 66, 11.

30 Juana María Rodríguez, *Queer Latinidad: Identity Practices, Discursive Spaces* (New York: New York University Press, 2003), 5.

31 Rodríguez, *Queer Latinidad*, 24.

32 Muñoz, *Cruising Utopia*, 99.

33 Ibid., 91.

34 See, respectively, Jafari S. Allen, *¡Venceremos?: The Erotics of Black Self-Making in Cuba* (Durham: Duke University Press, 2011); *Tongues Untied*, directed by Marlon T. Riggs (Frameline, 1989); *Paris Is Burning*, directed by Jennie Livingston; Elizabeth Marrero, *El Barrio Con Macha*, YouTube video, 8:48, 2008, posted by "FX GAY TV," https://www.youtube.com/watch?v=WZFzNV7fICI; David Henry Hwang, *M. Butterfly* (New York: Plume Publishing, 1993); and *The Crying Game*, directed by Neil Jordan (Miramax, 1992).

35 José Esteban Muñoz, *Disidentifications: Queers of Color and the Performance of Politics* (Minneapolis: University of Minnesota Press, 1999), 195.

36 Martin F. Manalansan IV, *Global Divas: Filipino Gay Men in the Diaspora* (Durham: Duke University Press, 2003), ix.

37 Audre Lorde, "The Uses of the Erotic: The Erotic as Power," in *Sister Outsider: Essays and Speeches by Audre Lorde* (Berkeley: Crossing Press, 2007), 56–57.

12

JUDITH ROOF

Psychoanalytic Literary Criticism of Gay and Lesbian American Literature

In September 1909, Sigmund Freud and Carl Jung lectured at Clark University in Worcester, Massachusetts. Under the heading "The Origin and Development of Psychoanalysis," Freud delivered five lectures introducing his version of European psychoanalysis to an American audience. Jung, too, gave lectures at the Clark event and also at Fordham University in New York University three years later. At the time, Freud was not well known for his theoretical work on sexuality; although *Three Essays on the Theory of Sexuality* appeared in German in 1905, it was not translated into English until 1910. Freud's studies of hysterical patients, *Studies in Hysteria* (with Josef Breuer) (1895) and *Fragment of an Analysis of a Case of Hysteria* ("The Dora Case") (1905), located his patients' hysteria in their repressed sexual desires, including – in Dora's case – homosexual desires.[1] Differing from the theories of the earlier sexologists Richard von Krafft-Ebing and Havelock Ellis, Freud's *Three Essays* understood human sexuality as having the possibility of different sexual "aims" and "objects."[2] Individuals, Freud believed, might wish for sexual union or merely to look at, be seen by, punish, or be punished by – all "aims" – a variety of sexual objects: people of the same sex, the other sex, fetish objects, animals, and so on. In contrast to sexologists who hypothesized that homosexualities were the result of gender inversion, where the mind of one gender was present in the body of the other sex, Freud's theories were more dynamic and varied, relying more on ideas of an individual's unconscious wishes and desires as the keys to sexual behavior.

During the 1930s and 1940s, other schools of psychoanalytic thought developed, including Carl Jung's theory of archetypes and the collective unconscious, which de-emphasized sexuality and focused instead on the individual's integration into a larger social consciousness.[3] Melanie Klein, who worked primarily with children, along with Otto Rank and later D. W. Winnicott, began a psychoanalytic school premised on an individual's relationships with internal objects, such as a psychically incorporated ideal of his or her mother or father.[4] Known as object relations theory, this approach also de-emphasized sexuality in favor of an individual's development as it was influenced by encounters with others. Although Jung's ideas founded a literary criticism based on myths and archetypes that was prominent in the 1960s and 1970s, neither Jung nor object relations theorists offered much to the psychoanalytic criticism of literature and sexuality.

In contrast, almost at the moment of its inscription, Freudian psychoanalysis became a mode of literary criticism. Freud himself undertook analyses of Sophocles' *Oedipus Rex* and Shakespeare's *Hamlet* in *The Interpretation of Dreams* (1900) and of E. T. A. Hoffman's *The Sandman* in *The Uncanny* (1917–1919).[5] He considered the motivations for creative writing in his 1908 "Creative Writers and Day-Dreaming."[6] Ernest Jones, a psychoanalyst and Freud's biographer, offered another psychoanalytic reading of *Hamlet*.[7] Edgar Allen Poe's "The Purloined Letter" took center stage in a protracted exchange of psychoanalytic criticism when one of Freud's disciples, Marie Bonaparte, presented an extended analysis of the text.[8] Another Freudian analyst, Jacques Lacan, also interpreted the Poe text.[9] Lacan took up and continued to develop Freud's understandings of sexuality as basic to human desire and subjectivity, although Lacan declared in *Seminar XX* that there "is no sexual relation" and that individuals unconsciously take up positions as "lover/beloved" and believe that one can "have it all, or not have it all" regardless of biological sex.[10] The theories of both Freud and Lacan have become the primary bases for an American practice of psychoanalytic literary criticism and analyses of representations of homosexuality and lesbian sexuality.

What Is Psychoanalytic Criticism?

In "To Open the Question," Shoshana Felman explores the ambiguous relationship between psychoanalytic theories and literary criticism.[11] Rejecting the idea that either term – psychoanalysis or literature – is subordinate to the other, Felman suggests that the ideal of a psychoanalytic criticism is "a real exchange ... between two different bodies of language and between two different modes of knowledge."[12] Psychoanalysis and literature treat the same material: human experience, perceptions, and language. The "two domains, indeed," Felman suggests, "implicate each other, each one finding itself enlightened, informed, but also affected, displaced, by the other."[13]

Throughout much of the history of psychoanalytic literary criticism, however, critics have deployed psychoanalysis to focus on "the author, the reader, or the fictive persons of the text," as Peter Brooks observes.[14] These three themes elicit a psychoanalytic treatment as if they were analysands – those undergoing psychoanalysis. Using clues from literary texts, this mode of psychoanalytic criticism deploys the basic themes and processes of analysis, assuming for each object: that there is a latent (i.e., unexpressed) meaning; that this meaning can be inferred by analyzing the clues in the details and omissions of a manifest or expressed text; and that a critic will thus find a hidden secret or theme that accounts for the author's/reader's/character's motivations, pleasures, and/or processes. Brooks warns against using analytic tools "in a wholly thematic way," partly because doing so occurs in a context that is very different from an actual psychoanalytic context (which involves a complex transferential relationship between analyst and analysand). The assumptions of this mode of analysis derive from inapposite analogies between literature and psychical processes. A text is not a psyche, for example; nor is it something akin to a dreamwork through which one might analyze an author.

By noting that "we sense that there ought to be, that there must be, some correspondence between literary and psychic process, that aesthetic structure and form, including literary tropes, must somehow coincide with the psychic structures and operations they both evoke and appeal to," Brooks ultimately appeals to Freud's more dynamic theories as a way to understand narrative.[15] Brooks shows how our conceptions of narrative play out the same dynamic between wanting to end (death drive) and wanting to continue (Eros) that Freud maps in *Beyond the Pleasure Principle,* and he proffers a theory of narrative that deploys psychoanalysis as a dynamic model for both a literary form and a mode of criticism. In "Freud's Masterplot," Brooks demonstrates parallels between Freud's estimations of the dynamic psychical forces of life and the dynamic forces that are at work in narrative both as an effect of its structure and in the way narrative structure operates in specific narrative.[16] Because he can locate a middling delay and dalliance, Brooks regards such material as involving too much sameness, including, possibly, the hint of homosexual interludes or other sexual dalliances that prevent narrative closure in heterosexual reproductive felicity. Brooks's parallels suggest another intersection between literature and psychoanalysis in that both address the same question of desire – the desire produced by the text and the desire of readers.

The question of desire inaugurates questions about sexuality that haunt Brooks's analysis of narrative, especially insofar as the dominant shape of narrative veers toward a closure that can be understood as the joinder of opposites, whereas the middle hosts the indeterminacy of dalliances and desire. Although earlier modes of psychoanalytic literary criticism, such as Charles Mauron's *psychocritique,* had attempted to discern authors' psychical themes via repeated motifs in their oeuvres, other critics employed psychoanalytic tactics as a way to read texts to discern the sexual "identities" of their authors.[17] These identities are, of course, usually gay male or lesbian identities, and they are understood as needing a cover during historical periods when gay and lesbian desires were not readily accepted. Although they are not overtly psychoanalytical, "encodement" theories employ reading strategies that are similar to the psychoanalytic practice of reading between the lines: manifest expressions both hide and reveal a hidden latent meaning available to those, like psychoanalysts, who know how to read the code. Hence some 1980s criticism of lesbian texts, such as Catharine Stimpson's readings of Gertrude Stein's self-representations in "The Somagrams of Gertrude Stein," see Stein's texts as a disguised rendition of identity and experience that lesbian readers will be able to decode and understand.[18] Eve Kosofsky Sedgwick's *Epistemology of the Closet* also engages with "'reader relations,' as sites of definitional creation, violence, and rupture in relation to particular readers, particular institutional circumstances."[19] Although Sedgwick's reading focuses on the "performative aspects of texts," especially in relation to the categorical binaries that constitute the divisions between heterosexual and homosexual, it also relies in part on economies of readerly identification, a psychoanalytic concept that grounds most notions of readers' relations to texts.[20]

Roland Barthes, however, offers another approach to readers' textual desire. Derived from the same psycho-dynamics as those in Brooks's dynamic model of narrative, Barthes's *The Pleasure of the Text* discusses the pleasures of following readers' desire despite the structure and impetus of the text.[21] He suggests that textual erotics do not come from a reader succumbing to the oedipalized character of narrative, which produces both answers and closure, but instead they exist in a text's "gaps" – its discontinuities, loose ends, and "abrasions."[22] As Barthes explains: "Is not the most erotic portion of a body *where the garment gapes?* In perversion (which is the realm of textual pleasure) there are no 'erogenous zones' (a foolish expression besides); it is intermittence, as psychoanalysis has so rightly stated, which is erotic."[23]

These psychodynamic modes of literary criticism, which were premised primarily on narrative theory's readings of Freud's *Beyond the Pleasure Principle*, his concepts of identification, and his analytic practices of interpreting narrative and textual cues, contrast with the more structured concepts offered by object relations theorists. Sedgwick continues her interest in an object relations approach to issues of sexuality in her study of Marcel Proust, *The Weather in Proust*, where she considers the links between Proust's various difficulties (sleeping in strange places, asthma, and so on) as well as the novel's structure to be manifestations of a fear that may be just as much an anxiety about success as one about failure.[24] Sedgwick eschews the oedipal character of the Freudian dynamic in favor of considering Proust's aesthetic responses in relation to the introjected parental objects favored by Melanie Klein.

Psychoanalysis and Post-Stonewall Criticism

Issues of sexuality became more prominent in American literary criticism in the late 1960s and 1970s when both feminist and gay rights movements began to emerge as platforms for literary critique. In 1970, Brian Reade published *Sexual Heretics: Male Homosexuality in English Literature from 1850 to 1900.*[25] Jane Rule published *Lesbian Images* in 1975, and critics began considering the role of lesbian and gay male characters in writing by Virginia Woolf, D. H. Lawrence, E. M. Forster, William Shakespeare, James Baldwin, Walt Whitman, Willa Cather, Herman Melville, Ernest Hemingway, Henry James, Christopher Isherwood, Carson McCullers, Amy Lowell, Marcel Proust, Joseph Conrad, Andre Gide, Jean Genet, Sappho, Jean Cocteau, Arthur Rimbaud, and Paul Verlaine.[26] But during the period from the 1960s to 1980, most critical discussions of gay males and lesbians in literature were concerned with gay and lesbian themes, aesthetics, and general representations. Only with the feminist move toward psychoanalysis in the 1980s did studies of lesbian and gay male literature begin to utilize the tools and concepts of psychoanalysis.

With the rise of Lacanian psychoanalysis in France in the 1960s and 1970s, critics paid new attention to issues of sexual difference and sexuality. Such French feminist theorists as Luce Irigaray and Julia Kristeva worked with and responded to Lacan's psychoanalytic concepts, seeing those concepts both as a repetition of patriarchal notions of sex and gender roles and as a way to reveal and critique those roles. Even more clearly than Freud, Lacan did not think that gender roles aligned with biological sexes. Lacan mapped a logic of *sexuation*, in which a subject's desire is complexly positioned according to the question of whether one is lover or beloved and whether one does or does not believe that someone can have it all. Lacan locates these possibilities not in relation to specific sexes or genders but instead in relation to psychical structures (such as neuroses or perversion) themselves.

Lacan's work was first published in translation in the United States in 1977 in a collection of written essays, *Ecrits.*[27] (Most of Lacan's work took the form of oral seminars.) In 1985, the feminist psychoanalyst Juliet Mitchell and the critic Jacqueline Rose translated and published some of Lacan's seminar work on feminine sexuality, including material on female homosexuality, in *Feminine Sexuality: Jacques Lacan and the école freudienne.*[28]

Other feminist work that explored the intersections of sexuality, gender, and feminism emerged in the 1980s, including extended critiques of Freud's missed analysis of Dora's homosexual desires in his *Fragment of an Analysis of a Case of Hysteria*. Jane Gallop explored the complexities of sex, gender, desire, and psychoanalysis in her 1984 study *The Daughter's Seduction*.[29] Teresa de Lauretis, too, began to combine semiotics with psychoanalysis in her work on gender and film in *Alice Doesn't: Feminism, Semiotics, Cinema* (1984).[30]

Most of this feminist psychoanalytic criticism was concerned with issues of sexual difference. Very little attention was paid to questions of lesbian sexuality, because most commentary about lesbians in literature involved issues of visibility – how lesbians were represented in literary texts, the ways lesbian desire might be encoded, and how lesbian communities fostered literary traditions. Feminist psychoanalytic criticism tended to ignore issues of lesbian sexuality: many of the collections of feminist criticism published in the 1970s and 1980s contained at most one or two essays focused on lesbian literature or lesbians in literature, and none of these took a psychoanalytic approach, especially because many lesbian feminist critics saw psychoanalysis as patriarchal. Only when a writer was herself lesbian would there be any consideration of the representations of lesbian sexuality, and those studies were mostly thematic. Such authors as Colette, Virginia Woolf, Djuna Barnes, Carson McCullers, and Willa Cather attracted a literary critical approach to lesbian sexuality in their works, but most of the critical attention focused on questions of reading, as in Jean Kennard's essay "Ourself behind Ourself: A Theory for Lesbian Readers."[31]

Whereas feminism worked through psychoanalysis's understandings of sexual difference, very little overtly psychoanalytic work appeared on male homosexual issues in literature. Several essays appeared in the 1970s treating male homosexuality as either a theme or an underlying authorial identity. The pioneering work of Leo Bersani, however, commences a discussion about sexual life, the subject, sexual identities, and aesthetics. In his 1987 essay "Is the Rectum a Grave?," Bersani explores the masochism of sexuality as an experience that shatters the subject, an analysis that was particularly resonant to gay men during a period of increasing panic about AIDS.[32] Because it was entwined with psychoanalytic concepts of subjectivity, sexuality, and experience, Bersani's earlier work on the novels of Honoré de Balzac, Samuel Beckett, and Marcel Proust raises questions about critical approaches that focus on aesthetic production as both hiding and revealing writers' subjective structures and fantasies. In addition to countering psychoanalytic approaches that focus on the author as the locus of textual meaning, in "Psychoanalysis and the Aesthetic Subject" Bersani suggests that

aesthetic production parallels the anxieties adherent to a subject's encounters with the world as both anxieties and aesthetics engage "the horror of
undifferentiated being."[33] Whereas sexual encounters offer one experience
of this shattering, aesthetic objects inscribe another, and Bersani sees each
of these as bridged by "fantasy" as possibly "a major site of our connected-
ness to the world ... It represents the terms in which the world inheres in the
fantasizing subject."[34]

In his work specifically addressing homosexuality, Bersani identifies what
David Kurnick describes as "the unresolved, perhaps unresolvable, tension
between identity's contents and its formal patterning."[35] He resolves this
problem of impossibly unresolvable questions of gay identity in his 1995
book *Homos* by considering homosexuality "an anti-identitarian identity."[36]
This identity, which is not one, may operate as "a seductive sameness," but
it also undergirds the ways specific texts resolve the problem of desire.[37]
In his commentary on the work on Proust's writing in his *The Culture of
Redemption*, for example, Bersani traces a trajectory in which the question of desire moves to a fascination with style for its own sake: the truth
of desire becomes an aesthetic issue with an aesthetic answer.[38] Bersani's
interest in issues of identity, fantasy, and aesthetics also informs his work
on psychoanalysis itself, especially the writings of Sigmund Freud. His 1986
study *The Freudian Body* again undertakes the question of "how might the
esthetic be conceived as a perpetuation and replicative elaboration of mas-
ochistic sexual tensions?"[39]

Psychoanalytic Criticism after 1990

Integrating psychoanalysis, sexuality, subjectivity, and aesthetics, Bersani's
work ushered in a different practice of psychoanalytic literary criticism after
1990. Along with the encounters of feminism and psychoanalysis, psychoanalytic criticism began to focus more on larger questions of subjectivity,
theories of narrative, and cultural analysis. The advent of queer theory also
shifted the question of identity, challenging identitarian assumptions while
also reasserting them, in a way that is resonant with Bersani's conclusions,
at a locus of non-identitarian identity. Pushing against notions of subjective identity premised on sexual desire, however, stultified psychoanalytic
approaches to individual texts, displacing psychoanalytic inquiry to the
realm of theory. Initially, psychoanalysis's relocation as a meta-theoretical
discourse had to do with the ways in which it appeared to endorse rigidly
gendered and sexed positions, as many feminist critics had argued. Judith
Butler's deployment of concepts from psychoanalysis, such as melancholia
and identification, were conflated with analogies to J. L. Austin's concept

of a "performative" in which language accomplishes what it says in being said (i.e., the marital "I do"), and this conflation resituated Freudian psychoanalysis as part of the combination of discourses through which individuals became gendered subjects.[40] Although Butler's account of gender in *Gender Trouble* has little direct connection to identities comprised in relation to sexual orientation, its reformulation of genders as contingent effects of repetition seemed to open up possibilities for less rigid understandings of sexualities, especially insofar as conceptions of sexual orientation seemed to depend on binary understandings of gender and sexual difference.

Butler extended her theory of gendering to literary texts in her 1993 *Bodies That Matter*, in which she deploys her theory in relation to the works of such authors as Willa Cather and Nella Larsen.[41] My own *A Lure of Knowledge: Lesbian Sexuality and Theory* examined the ways in which psychoanalysis echoed cultural narratives of lesbian desire as a point of failure and return.[42] Teresa de Lauretis's *The Practice of Love* continued the development of a theory of gender and discourse, focusing on a specifically psychoanalytic theory of lesbian desire.[43] Annamarie Jagose offered a rigorous analysis of the complex theory and practice of lesbian textual practice in her 1994 study *Lesbian Utopics*, and Elizabeth Grosz took the conversation one step further, proposing a shift from the etiologies of lesbian desire to a consideration of future possibility in "Refiguring Lesbian Desire," which was published in the 1994 anthology *The Lesbian Postmodern*.[44] These latter two texts take Freudian psychoanalytic understandings of lesbian sexuality into account as part of their considerations of lesbian desire and potential.

Several critics also furthered narrative theory's understandings of the interrelations between narrative, sexualities, and psychoanalysis in the 1990s. Following Peter Brooks's "Freud's Masterplot," Barthes's *The Pleasure of the Text*, and de Lauretis's reading of narrative's gendered positions in "Desire in Narrative," narrative theory in the 1990s began to consider the ways in which narrative might be read oppositionally (Ross Chambers in *Room for Maneuver*), as a dynamic sexual schematic (my *Come as You Are: Sexuality in Narrative*), and in relation to a desire for the body (Peter Brooks's *Body Work: Objects of Desire in Modern Narrative*).[45]

Theorists of lesbian desire clearly had a head start in the development of psychoanalytical theories of sexuality, most likely because of a feminist interest in psychoanalysis in the 1980s. Apart from the work of Bersani, most critics of gay male literature did not become engaged in psychoanalytic work until the mid-1990s. Thomas Yingling's socio-materialist study *Hart Crane and the Homosexual Text* commenced the decade with a consideration of how homosexuality relates to the "material" practices of language by pushing style and tradition while still retaining a tension between public performance and private knowledge.[46] Tim Dean also took up the tensions of a "poetics of privacy" in the work of Hart Crane in an early essay in his critical oeuvre that focuses on the intercalations of psychoanalysis, gay male sexuality, and cultural politics.[47] Bersani, Dean, and Christopher Lane form the nucleus of a psychoanalytic gay male criticism from the 1990s to the present. In parallel to the lesbian feminist psychoanalytic theory that grew out of feminism and psychoanalysis, gay male psychoanalytic theory shifted its focus from individual authors to meta-theoretical questions of gay subjectivity, sexuality, and public cultures – a theorizing that shifted more to a Lacanian than a Freudian lexicon. Although Lacan considered himself a Freudian analyst, Lacan's conceptual vocabulary also deploys the insights of twentieth-century philosophy, linguistics, mathematics, and topological theory; Lacanian psychoanalysis offers a more nimble and complex conception of subjectivity and sexuality that is less cemented to both patriarchy and heteronormativity.

Lane and Dean charted the direction of psychoanalytic gay male criticism, with Lane investigating Victorian masculinity from a psychoanalytic perspective and writing about Foucault's relations to homosexuality. Lane's seminal edited collection, *The Psychoanalysis of Race*, brings another crucial set of discourses into psychoanalytic consideration.[48] Dean's psychoanalytic criticism considers a range of topics, from the work of Butler and Lee Edelman to James Joyce, Joseph Conrad, Foucault, Bersani, AIDS, performance theory, and psychoanalytic theory itself, which culminated in his *Beyond Sexuality* (2000), as well as essays on Lacan and the work of Slavoj Žižek.[49] Both critics engage with questions of public/private, the possibilities of politics, questions of the future of gay subjects, and issues of intimacy, and they also elaborate an increasingly Lacanian sexual discourse.

The role that psychoanalytic criticism played in gay and lesbian criticism grows in the 1990s, in part because this decade also marked the emergence of anthologies of gay and lesbian literary criticism and theory. Although these collections combined literary criticism with more meta-critical and theoretical topics, it is clear that psychoanalysis had become a part of the critical discourse in gay and lesbian literary criticism. *Lesbian and Gay Studies: An Introduction* (1997) includes a section on "Psychoanalysis and Sexual Identity" contributed by Lane;[50] *The Gay '90s: Disciplinary and Interdisciplinary Formations in Queer Studies* also appeared in 1997, and it included an essay by Thomas Yingling titled "Homosexuality and the Uncanny: What's Fishy in Lacan," which examined Lacan's essay "La signification du phallus" in relation to male homosexuality and Manuel Puig's *El beso de la mujer araña*.[51] Martin Duberman's capacious *A Queer*

World: The Center for Lesbian and Gay Studies Reader (1997) includes not only an entire section on psychology but also a number of essays that rely on psychoanalytic concepts in their analyses of such problems as identity, civil rights, and questions of community.[52]

Psychoanalytic Criticism in the Twenty-First Century

The apotheosis of studies in sexuality and psychoanalysis was Tim Dean and Christopher Lane's 2001 anthology *Homosexuality and Psychoanalysis*,[53] although other contributors also rethought the American literary tradition in terms of homosexuality and psychoanalysis, including, most notably, William Jeffs, who presented a thorough portrait of the state of the field in *Feminism, Manhood, and Homosexuality: Intersections in Psychoanalysis and American Poetry*.[54] A collection of twenty-two essays from key thinkers in psychoanalytic theory, lesbian and gay studies, and sexual cultures, Dean and Lane's book marked the end of long but subtle hostilities between the mental health establishment and lesbian and gay scholars. That "the mental health establishment routinely used to consider same-sex desire as a form of illness," Dean and Lane suggest, produced a longstanding "adversarial" relationship between psychoanalysis and gay and lesbian cultures.[55] But they also quickly note that Freud himself understood "homosexuality as part of everybody's sexual constitution and thus not in itself a problem."[56] The problem becomes, as the editors point out, "social attitudes" toward same-sex desires.[57]

However, to launch a new wave of psychoanalytically informed interrogations of the social, the psychical, and the cultural requires, as Dean and Lane observe, a recognition that neither psychoanalysis nor homosexuality are terms that signify any singular phenomenon; rather, both represent a range of approaches, possibilities, positions, and practices. The productive intersection of psychoanalysis with gay and lesbian studies also represents a process that involves the interrogation of both terms. The easy identification of psychoanalysis with repressive pathology had become a very complex and nuanced idea that was centered on the formation of subjectivity and the operations of desire, thanks in part to the increased availability of the work of Lacan. As designations of same-sex desire, *lesbian* and *gay* were overwritten by the more inclusive and less specific designation *queer* as both a gesture against repressive normativity and also as a category that conflated questions of gender, sex, transgender, transsex, intersex, bisexuality, and most issues relating to both gender and sexual display and identity. As a discipline that concerns itself with the formation of the subject, psychoanalysis addresses the multiple issues of sexual difference, gender, and desire as intrinsic parts of subject formation, offering one way of thinking about the complex interrelations between these phenomena.

Psychoanalysis as a critical method became less prominent with the rise of queer theory, because beliefs in psychoanalysis's dependence on normativity and binary sex/gender roles seemed to make it less useful in a terrain that willfully eschews these concepts. Insofar as psychoanalytic processes, such as reading a "latent" meaning through a "manifest" text, or deploying common concepts, such as "identity" and "desire," became part of critical discourse, psychoanalytic discourse continues to be a part of the critical environment. Freudian psychoanalysis, however, continued by the work of Lacan, maps a wide range of desiring and identificatory possibilities that emerge in unpredictable combinations in the production of individual subjects, as Ellie Ragland outlines in *The Logic of Sexuation: From Aristotle to Lacan* (2004).[58] One effect of psychoanalysis's perverse sexual logics, paradoxically, is the work of Gilles Deleuze and Félix Guattari, who, in pushing back against what they envision as psychoanalysis's reign of constricted, oedipalized desire, theorize a generalized pervasive and unconstricted desire on the part of subjects who exist in intertwined, dynamic, networked systems of relations. Rosi Braidotti employs Deleuze and Guattari's theories in her examination of feminist possibility in *Metamorphosis: Towards a Materialist Theory of Becoming* (2002).[59]

Another effect of the move to queer theory was a shift from questions of desire in sexuality to issues of the drive. In *No Future: Queer Theory and the Death Drive* (2004), Lee Edelman links Freud's notion of the drive – the continuous unconscious urge without goal or object – to cultural positionings of homosexualities.[60] In *Freud's Drive: Psychoanalysis, Literature, Film* (2010), Teresa de Lauretis also theorizes the centrality of the drive as the nonspecific impetus that produces an excess of affect without ever finding closure.[61] Deploying the concept of the drive enables literary critics and gay, lesbian, and queer theorists finally to avoid the duplicities of psychoanalysis's presumptions of heteronormativity in order to engage a more dynamic concept of subjectivity.

Case Study: The Work of Djuna Barnes

One of the texts de Lauretis considers in *Freud's Drive* is Djuna Barnes's 1936 modernist classic *Nightwood*. "It is queer," she asserts,

> not simply because of all of the far-from-normative sexual interactions between and within human bodies alluded to in the doctor's monologues, or because the novel's main characters are homosexuals, transvestites, possibly transexual, circus freaks, and even non-human animals. The heart of sex in

> *Nightwood* is sexuality without solution and trauma without resolution –
> sexuality as an unmanageable excess of affect that can find textual expression
> only in a figural, oracular language, in hybrid images and elaborate conceits,
> or in the stream of allusions, parables, and prophesies with which the doctor
> attempts to fill the chasm between language and the real.[62]

De Lauretis's reading of *Nightwood* as an "unmanageable excess of affect"
offers a solomonic solution to the contradictory readings of both Barnes's
Ladies Almanack and *Nightwood* in the preceding decade.[63]

The history of criticism of Djuna Barnes's work is not only intertwined
with psychoanalysis; its interpretations also trace the increasingly sophisticated possibilities of psychoanalytic readings as they matured. In "'A
Nose-Length into the Matter': Sexology and Lesbian Desire in Djuna
Barnes's *Ladies Almanack*," Christine Berni traces the ways in which the
Ladies Almanack challenges sexology in its rendition of sexual desire as
being "thoroughly multiple, shifting, and contradictory."[64] Berni interprets
Barnes's text as resisting sexology's normative binaries and also complicat-
ing contemporaneous conceptions "of lesbianism as inversion" that were
typical of such sexologists as Havelock Ellis and permeated the work of
Sigmund Freud.[65]

Berni's reading takes a tack that is different from earlier debates over the
strategic significance of Barnes's work, which are represented on the one
hand by Karla Jay's biographical reading of *Ladies Almanack* as Barnes's
resentment toward the wealthy Natalie Barney and her circle, whose members the book satirizes, and on the other hand by Susan Sniader Lanser's
reading of the text as a "'refusal of phallocentrism' and a reclamation of 'the
positivity of the female body and the lesbian experience.'"[66] These different
readings, which appeared from the late 1970s to the 1990s, themselves track
the evolution and increasing sophistication of feminist psychoanalytic literary criticism from author- (and identity-)centered interpretations to understandings of texts as themselves enacting parts of larger conversations about
sexual difference, gender, and sexualities.

Nightwood has also inspired contradictory readings centered on similar understandings of psychoanalysis and sexuality. Susana S. Martins's
"Gender Trouble and Lesbian Desire in Djuna Barnes's *Nightwood*" maps
the text's previous contradictory readings as both "a celebration of homosexuality and as a homophobic portrayal of a failed relationship."[67] Like
Berni, Martins finds a third ground by pulling back a step – by seeing
Nightwood not as a polemic but as a way of contesting gender categories
themselves. Noting that Barnes was interested in psychoanalysis, Martins
suggests that *Nightwood* is a challenge to Freudian ideas: "[Barnes] works
through and against patriarchal structures, sometimes seeming complicit

with patriarchal discourse, in an attempt to articulate the woman-to-woman desire that could hardly exist in the theories being published by Freud at the time of the novel's conception and writing."[68] Martins goes further to assert that "the text also works at the more radical task of deconstructing seemingly fundamental binaries: male/female, mind/body, and culture/nature."[69]

As understandings of subjectivity and sexuality continue to become increasingly sophisticated, so too will psychoanalytic criticism of gay and lesbian American literature continue to mark a terrain for the increased understanding of desire, the drive, the relationships between subjects and the socius, and the ways in which literature inscribes it all. With the increasing visibility of modes of thinking that derive from systems theory, the work of Deleuze and Guattari, and attempts by such theorists as Michel Serres (in both *Parasite* and *Genesis*) to recast the problems of dialectical and oppositional thinking that derive from structuralism, the ways in which critics and theorists understand issues of sexuality will be further enriched.[70] Critics continue to consider the problems of the "subject," "identity," "the sexual," and the sociopolitical.

NOTES

1 Sigmund Freud and Josef Breuer, "Studies on Hysteria (1893–1895)," in *The Standard Edition of the Complete Psychological Works of Sigmund Freud*, trans. James Strachey, 24 vols. (London: Hogarth, 1955), 2; Sigmund Freud, "Fragment of an Analysis of a Case of Hysteria (1901–1905)," in *The Standard Edition of the Complete Psychological Works of Sigmund Freud*, trans. James Strachey, 24 vols. (London: Hogarth, 1955), 7:1–122.

2 Sigmund Freud, "Three Essays on the Theory of Sexuality (1901–1905)," in *The Standard Edition of the Complete Psychological Works of Sigmund Freud*, trans. James Strachey, 24 vols. (London: Hogarth, 1955), 7:125–172.

3 Carl Jung, *Man and His Symbols* (New York: Dell, 1968).

4 Melanie Klein, *Selected Melanie Klein*, ed. Juliet Mitchell (New York: Free Press, 1987); D. W. Winnicott, *Winnicott on the Child* (New York: Da Capo, 2002).

5 Sigmund Freud, "The Uncanny (1917–1919)," in *The Standard Edition of the Complete Psychological Works of Sigmund Freud*, trans. James Strachey, 24 vols. (London: Hogarth, 1955), 17:217–256.

6 Sigmund Freud, "The Interpretation of Dreams (First Part) (1900)," in *The Standard Edition of the Complete Psychological Works of Sigmund Freud*, trans. James Strachey, 24 vols. (London: Hogarth, 1955), 4; and Sigmund Freud, "Creative Writers and Day-Dreaming (1906–1908)," in *The Standard Edition of the Complete Psychological Works of Sigmund Freud*, trans. James Strachey, 24 vols. (London: Hogarth, 1955), 9:141–154.

7 Ernest Jones, *A Psycho-Analytic Study of "Hamlet"* (Ann Arbor: University of Michigan Library, 1922).

8   Edgar Allen Poe, "The Purloined Letter," in *Collected Works of Edgar Allen Poe: Tales and Sketches 1843–1849*, ed. Thomas Ollive Mabbot (Cambridge, MA: Belknap Press of Harvard University Press, 1978); Marie Bonaparte, *The Life and Works of Edgar Allan Poe: A Psychoanalytic Interpretation*, trans. John Rodker (New York: Humanities Press, 1971).

9   Jacques Lacan, "Seminar on the 'Purloined Letter,' " trans. Jeffrey Mehlman, *Yale French Studies* 48, no. 48 (1972): 39–72.

10 Jacques Lacan, *On Feminine Sexuality, The Limits of Love and Knowledge 1972–1973: Encore, The Seminar of Jacques Lacan*, Book XX, ed. Jacques-Alain Miller, trans. Bruce Fink (New York: Norton, 1988).

11 Shoshana Felman, "To Open the Question," in *Literature and Psychoanalysis*, ed. Shoshana Felman (Baltimore: Johns Hopkins University Press, 1982), 5–10.

12 Ibid., 6.

13 Ibid.

14 Peter Brooks, "The Idea of a Psychoanalytic Literary Criticism," *Critical Inquiry* 13, no. 2 (1987): 334–348.

15 Ibid., 334.

16 Peter Brooks, "Freud's Masterplot: Questions of Narrative," in *Literature and Psychoanalysis*, ed. Shoshana Felman (Baltimore: Johns Hopkins University Press, 1982), 280–300.

17 Charles Mauron, *Des métaphores obsédantes au mythe personnel: Introduction à la psychocritique* (Paris: Corti, 1964).

18 Catharine Stimpson, "The Somagrams of Gertrude Stein," *Poetics Today* 6, no. 1–2 (1985): 67–80.

19 Eve Kosofsky Sedgwick, *Epistemology of the Closet* (Berkeley: University of California Press, 1990), 3.

20 Ibid.

21 Roland Barthes, *The Pleasure of the Text*, trans. Richard Miller (New York: Hill and Wang, 1975).

22 Ibid., 11.

23 Ibid., 9–11.

24 Eve Kosofsky Sedgwick, *The Weather in Proust*, ed. Jonathan Goldberg (Durham: Duke University Press, 2012).

25 Brian Reade, *Sexual Heretics: Male Homosexuality in English Literature from 1850 to 1900* (London: Routledge and Kegan Paul, 1970).

26 Jane Rule, *Lesbian Images* (New York: Doubleday, 1975).

27 Jacques Lacan, *Ecrits*, trans. Alan Sheridan (New York: Norton, 1977).

28 Juliet Mitchell and Jacqueline Rose, eds., *Feminine Sexuality: Jacques Lacan and the école freudienne*, trans. Jacqueline Rose (New York: Norton, 1985).

29 Jane Gallop, *The Daughter's Seduction: Feminism and Psychoanalysis* (Ithaca: Cornell University Press, 1982).

30 Teresa de Lauretis, *Alice Doesn't: Feminism, Semiotics, Cinema* (Bloomington: Indiana University Press, 1984).

31 Jean Kennard, "Ourself behind Ourself: A Theory for Lesbian Readers," *Signs* 9, no. 4 (1984): 647–662.

32 Leo Bersani, *Is the Rectum a Grave? And Other Essays* (Chicago: University of Chicago Press, 2010).

33 Leo Bersani, "Psychoanalysis and the Aesthetic Subject," *Critical Inquiry* 32, no. 2 (2006): 166.

34 Ibid., 171.

35 David Kurnick, "Embarrassment and the Forms of Redemption," *PMLA* 125, no. 2 (2010): 400.

36 Leo Bersani, *Homos* (Cambridge, MA: Harvard University Press, 1995), 101.

37 Ibid., 150.

38 Leo Bersani, *The Culture of Redemption* (Cambridge, MA: Harvard University Press, 1990).

39 Leo Bersani, *The Freudian Body: Psychoanalysis and Art* (New York: Columbia University Press, 1986), 43.

40 Judith Butler, *Gender Trouble: Feminism and the Subversion of Identity* (New York: Routledge, 1990).

41 Judith Butler, *Bodies That Matter: On the Discursive Limits of "Sex"* (New York: Routledge, 1993).

42 Judith Roof, *A Lure of Knowledge: Lesbian Sexuality and Theory* (New York: Columbia University Press, 1991).

43 Teresa de Lauretis, *The Practice of Love: Lesbian Sexuality and Perverse Desire* (Bloomington: Indiana University Press, 1994).

44 Annamarie Jagose, *Lesbian Utopics* (New York: Routledge, 1994); Elizabeth Grosz, "Refiguring Lesbian Desire," in *The Lesbian Postmodern*, ed. Laura Doan (New York: Columbia University Press, 1994), 67–84.

45 Ross Chambers, *Room for Maneuver: Reading Oppositional Narrative* (Chicago: University of Chicago Press, 1991); Judith Roof, *Come as You Are: Sexuality and Narrative* (New York: Columbia University Press, 1996); Peter Brooks, *Body Work: Objects of Desire in Modern Narrative* (Cambridge, MA: Harvard University Press, 1993).

46 Thomas Yingling, *Hart Crane and the Homosexual Text* (Chicago: University of Chicago Press, 1990).

47 Tim Dean, "Hart Crane's Poetics of Privacy," *American Literary History* 8, no. 1 (1996): 83–109.

48 Christopher Lane, ed., *The Psychoanalysis of Race* (New York: Columbia University Press, 1998).

49 Tim Dean, *Beyond Sexuality* (Chicago: University of Chicago Press, 2000).

50 Christopher Lane, "Psychoanalysis and Sexual Identity," in *Lesbian and Gay Studies: A Critical Introduction*, ed. Andy Medhurst and Sally Munt (London: Cassell, 1997), 160–175.

51 Thomas Yingling, "Homosexuality and the Uncanny: What's Fishy in Lacan," in *The Gay '90s: Disciplinary and Interdisciplinary Formations in Queer Studies*, ed. Thomas A. Foster (New York: New York University Press, 1997), 191–198.

52 Martin Duberman, ed., *A Queer World: The Center for Lesbian and Gay Studies Reader* (New York: New York University Press, 1997).

53 Tim Dean and Christopher Lane, eds., *Homosexuality and Psychoanalysis* (Chicago: University of Chicago Press, 2001).

54 William Jeffs, *Feminism, Manhood, and Homosexuality: Intersections in Psychoanalysis and American Poetry* (New York: Peter Lang, 2003).

55 Dean and Lane, *Homosexuality and Psychoanalysis*, 3.
56 Ibid.
57 Ibid., 4.
58 Ellie Ragland, *The Logic of Sexuation: From Aristotle to Freud* (Albany: State University of New York Press, 2004).
59 Rosi Braidotti, *Metamorphosis: Towards a Materialist Theory of Becoming* (Cambridge: Polity, 2002).
60 Lee Edelman, *No Future: Queer Theory and the Death Drive* (Durham: Duke University Press, 2004).
61 Teresa de Lauretis, *Freud's Drive: Psychoanalysis, Literature, Film* (London: Palgrave, 2010).
62 Ibid., 244–245.
63 Ibid., 128.
64 Christine Berni, "'A Nose-Length into the Matter': Sexology and Lesbian Desire in Djuna Barnes's *Ladies Almanack*," *Frontiers: A Journal of Women's Studies* 20, no. 3 (1999): 83.
65 Ibid., 84.
66 Susan Sniader Lanser, "Speaking in Tongues: *Ladies Almanack* and the Discourse of Desire," in *Silence and Power: A Reevaluation of Djuna Barnes*, ed. Mary Lynn Broe (Carbondale: Southern Illinois University Press, 1991), 156–168, quoted in Berni, "A Nose-Length into the Matter," 45.
67 Susana S. Martins, "Gender Trouble and Lesbian Desire in Djuna Barnes's *Nightwood*," *Frontiers: A Journal of Women's Studies* 20, no. 3 (1999): 109.
68 Ibid., 110.
69 Ibid.
70 Michel Serres, *The Parasite*, trans. Lawrence R. Schehr (Minneapolis: University of Minneapolis Press, 2007); and Michel Serres, *Genesis*, trans. Genevieve James and James Nielson (Ann Arbor: University of Michigan Press, 1997).

13

MELISSA JANE HARDIE

Post-Structuralism: Originators and Heirs

Contact

Samuel R. Delany has long been an elder statesman of gay and lesbian writing and his work spans improbable boundaries: Delany is a distinguished academic without formal academic qualifications and a literary pioneer whose most prominent work has been in a formerly marginal genre, science fiction. His 1999 *Times Square Red, Times Square Blue* offers an exemplary queer object for beginning to orient an account of the relationship between post-structuralism, its originators and heirs, and gay and lesbian American literature. The book is composed of two essays. The first, "Times Square Blue," recounts social and sexual encounters in the movie theaters clustered around Times Square before its family-friendly renovation in the 1990s. The second, "… Three, Two, One, Contact: Times Square Red," offers a series of arguments that are propelled by the first part of the book and elaborate its implications. This second part is distinguished in important ways from the first: it examines three theses; it breaks in several places into parallel text, where anecdote and digression accompany but remain separate from the elaboration of those theses; and it presents in primarily scholarly prose (although not in "academic" style) its argument about important zones of "interclass contact and communication conducted in a mode of good will," where the "class war" that rages "constantly and often silently in the comparatively stabilized societies of the developed world … perpetually works for the erosion of the social practices through which interclass communications takes place and of the institutions holding those practices stable."[1]

In Delany's hands, good will becomes a heuristic for thinking concertedly about how unplanned forms of "contact and communication" are fostered through liaisons that are either explicitly sexual or conducted under the auspices of the consumption of sexual content. Delany details an array of encounters in the movie houses he visited, encounters that might once have been seen as metonyms for unequal social status and covert sexual identity – as indices, in other words, of marginalization and oppression. Instead, Delany identifies the structural circumstances in which such encounters took place (profit-taking that targeted those who lacked better options), their historical particularities, and their transience, and he locates a powerful possibility in their midst. These encounters demonstrate that rigid categories of sexual identification are untenable in light of the fluid and transient forms of identification and contact that are made in the cinemas. They likewise show that the relationship between theory and practice is complicated and mutually informing. Finally, they offer a finely tuned account of how sexuality is performed and staged in context-specific ways, where crude models of sexual identification, such as identifying through object choice, collapse alongside the sheer diversity of sexual appetites, practices, and interests. In all of these demonstrations, Delany's nuanced writing resembles the work of post-structuralist theory in gay and lesbian studies, and not coincidentally, this work is staged in the context of the consumption of texts – in his case, cinema, but for queer theory, more commonly literature. The literary in some senses almost always locates the argumentative detail, as well as sometimes the argument, of post-structural theory concerned with sexuality. Such a heuristic serves equally well, then, when thinking about how post-structuralism as a theory has mingled with gay and lesbian literary writing, given that contact and communication between theory and praxis are conducted within and in spite of institutions that serve to either bring them together or keep them apart. Those institutions may be more or less formal – university departments, reading groups, intimate conversational habits, and so on – but they share with the theaters that Delany describes an opportunity to see what happens when those who are not conventionally aligned are brought together.

Delany, in fact, reports that an editor who read "an early draft" of "Times Square Blue" asked him: "But what ... went on in those movie theaters, before they were closed? Let me see some of that."[2] Delany added at first "a single paragraph," and "[a]ll the extensions of the piece since that version ... around which the earlier material now forms a sort of locative parergon – have grown from that one paragraph."[3] The phrase "locative parergon" suggests a very particular mode of disclosure incited by the editor's question. The initial draft becomes a supplement (parergon), securing to a time and place (locative) the writing that extends it. In so doing, Delany's use of the word parergon alerts us to a key moment in the history of post-structuralism. In *The Truth in Painting*, Jacques Derrida locates the problem of defining works of art through their intrinsic character, a quality defined by a boundary or border, or "parergon." He argues that the supplemental boundary itself is necessarily in some way continuous with the work of art.[4] Delany's "locative parergon" exemplifies this logic, insofar as what was written to amplify the essay replaced its locating but bounding content. This kind of reversal, familiar in the logic of post-structural writing, is not merely a way to gloss or understand the architectonic efficiencies of Delany's unusual method; rather, it helps amplify the possibilities revealed elsewhere in the essay with similar thematic elucidations of the liberating effects of interclass contact. The elegance of Delany's mode of writing comes not just from its capacity to show what happens in the theater but equally from its ability to act out the transport between what is inside and what is outside. Such transport characterizes the complex relationship between literary theory, post-structuralism, and literature. The material produced to frame or gloss the body of the text does not become merely its supplement but instead is integral to the whole. In turn, the integrity of the whole is always suspect, because it relies on what was "after" it – beyond it temporally or spatially – to confirm that it *is* whole.

The distinct emphasis on the literary throughout this body of work is perhaps boded in the etymological freight that "queer" was given by Eve Kosofsky Sedgwick in *Tendencies*, where she notes that "[q]ueer is a continuing moment, movement, motive – recurrent, eddying, *troublant*. The world 'queer' itself means *across* – it comes from the Indo-European root –*twerkw*, which also yields the German *quer* (transverse), Latin *torquere* (to twist), English *athwart* … The immemorial current that *queer* represents is antiseparatist as it is antiassimilationist. Keenly, it is relational, and strange."[5] By troubling distinctions and meaning alike, queer comes to represent what cuts across or athwart conventional distinctions, and literary language becomes an ideal location for such troubling possibilities.

Of course, establishing an origin for post-structuralism requires comparable flexibility. Michel Foucault's status as an originator, for instance, carries with it also his development of "genealogical critique," wherein historical relations are distanced from a model of historical progression and instead linked to one of epistemic process in which the contours of power relations in each episteme are visible in their archaeological effects. Rather than seeing a particular contemporary moment in terms of its current power struggles, a genealogical critique traces the relationship between different past practices by investigating the range of institutions that, when combined, constitute the particular dynamic of a moment. So instead of considering how, for instance, an oppressive heterosexuality instituted discriminatory practices toward non-heterosexual subjects, genealogical analyses explored the ways in which heterosexuality itself was created as a back-formation through the desire or drive to identify varieties of sexuality that failed to conform to a model of proper functioning, a model they themselves conspired to create.

In the same way, determining what constitutes "gay" or "lesbian" identity becomes complicated when addressed through the lens of post-structural thought, where skepticism reigns with regard to either or both constructivist and essentialist arguments about identity. Judith Butler's powerful critique of essentialist ideas of gender, allied with the concept of "trouble," radically recast feminist identity politics in light of the implications of Foucault's decentering of essentializing categories of identity. Butler's work turned instead to thinking about how identity is performed, arising not as the result of an essential core of gendered subjectivity but rather as an internalization and repetition of gender norms. For Butler, the thematic of passing in American literature offered an ideal representation of the incompleteness and performative nature of identities taken to be core. For Sedgwick, the nature of epistemology itself was at stake in the ways literary texts organized themselves around questions of secrecy and sexuality. Her work, which powerfully determined the ambit of queer theory's repurposing of insights derived from post-structuralism, turned on a number of axioms, after Foucault, to establish what she called an "epistemology of the closet."[6] Through this epistemology, she investigated contrasting accounts of the minoritizing and universalizing of gay and lesbian subjects to suggest that arguments about causation – for instance, the now popular account of sexuality as biologically determined – are indebted to and reliant on fractured certainties about what it means to know *anything*, and they are oriented around the matter of sexual disclosure. In place of confident or sturdy schemes to describe these thorny issues, Sedgwick demotes robust certainty around categories and identity and promotes an ethical "not knowing." With her own training in literary analysis and previous work on the gothic and on homosociality, it is not surprising that literary models of knowing were fundamental to Sedgwick's analysis, and the nuanced ways of saying and not saying that characterizes literariness are exemplified by her use of a writer like Henry James to tease out the implications of a closet epistemology.

The Speaker's Benefit: Michel Foucault in America

The most compelling originary moment for the purposes of this chapter was the 1978 publication of Robert Hurley's English translation of Foucault's *The History of Sexuality, Volume 1: An Introduction*. Its reception inaugurated a critical encounter between gay and lesbian studies as they were then conceived and the pressure of post-structural theories of subjectivity and identity that will come to prominence in the United States after the English translation of Derrida's *Of Grammatology* in 1976.[7] Foucault visited the United States during the mid-seventies, initially at the invitation of Leo Bersani, to lecture across the country, although he was located for the most part at the University of California, Berkeley. At a time when gay and lesbian communities were engaged with the vexed question of the relationship between liberation, feminism, and identity politics, and before the effects of HIV/AIDS refocused political energy during the 1980s, Foucault's trenchant delineation of the "birth of the homosexual" aligned this identity with the very powers that were arrayed against it. Foucault mocks the egregious representation of the Victorian period as one that instituted repressive decorum by opening *History* with a parody of "the imperial prude ... emblazoned on our restrained, mute, and hypocritical sexuality" in order to question "the story" that between the "frankness" of the early seventeenth century and the "monotonous nights of the Victorian bourgeoisie," sexuality was brought indoors and "carefully confined."[8] In Foucault's hands, a contemporary advocacy of speech against repression facilitates a critical misrepresentation: "This discourse on modern sexual repression holds up well, owing no doubt to how easy it is to uphold. A solemn historical and political guarantee protects it" (5). He offers instead a more compromising set of promises and benefits that arise from representing of sexuality in terms of its repression:

> [T]here may be another reason that makes it so gratifying for us to define the relationship between sex and power in terms of repression: something that one might call the speaker's benefit. If sex is repressed, that is, condemned to prohibition, nonexistence, and silence, then the mere fact that one is speaking about it has the appearance of a deliberate transgression. A person who holds forth in such language places himself to a certain extent outside the reach of power; he upsets established law; he somehow anticipates the coming freedom.
>
> (6)

Foucault makes of the association of sexuality, its representation, and its liberation something more complex than a politics of freedom. He argues against a version of the history of sexuality that offers a "chronicle of an increasing repression" and suggests as its antidote "nothing less than a transgression of laws. A lifting of prohibitions, an irruption of speech, a reinstating of pleasure" (5).

Instead of asking why we are repressed or how might we overcome repression, Foucault asks why we say we are repressed, and he offers the *repressive hypothesis* to explain our insistence. For Foucault, the power and promise that are associated with speaking of sex are tied to the power of preaching: "[A] great sexual sermon ... has swept through our societies over the last decades" (7). Sexual discourse has not been repressed but rather "subjected to a mechanism of increasing incitement" (12), and that incitement to discourse is evidenced by both a proliferation of talk about sex and the "implantation" (36) of perversity, because "[o]ur epoch has initiated sexual heterogeneities" (37). Foucault identifies here the creation of a "*scientia sexualis*," where scientific parsing of sexual taxonomies was aided by a marriage of the routine of the laboratory with the impulse to confess (51).

Foucault dates the birth of the homosexual to 1870, a birth generated by a nineteenth-century shift in classification that meant juridical identification of forbidden acts could give way to taxonomies that created a new "specification of individuals" (42–43). The homosexual was born precisely when it was no longer understood by its sexual acts but rather by its characterization through "a certain quality of sexual sensibility": "The sodomite had been a temporary aberration; the homosexual was now a species" (43). Rather than offering a rallying point for liberatory politics or a coherent psychological "truth," the homosexual became one element of the "entomological" categorization of perverts, from a field of multifarious activity to a schema of classification identities that were to be codified and minutely distinguished – an incitement, in other words, to discourse. The administration of sexuality became the means by which power and knowledge came together equally in the adoption of this *scientia sexualis* and in its contestation: Foucault notes that the creation of categories of perversion enabled not only their description but also a "reverse" discourse, where

> homosexuality began to speak in its own behalf … often in the same vocabulary, using the same categories by which it was medically disqualified. There is not, on the one side, a discourse of power, and opposite it, another discourse that runs counter to it. Discourses are tactical elements or blocks operating in the field of force relations.
>
> (101–102)

The "irruption of speech" associated with the repressive hypothesis in turn becomes implicated in a more complex terrain than one characterized only by oppression and liberation, a territory where the question of normativity reigns. Arguments that depend on establishing homosexuality as a normal, biological condition are therefore enmeshed in precisely the same *scientia sexualis* that gives context and meaning to arguments concerning homosexuality's deviance. Whereas the parergon signified the lack of integrity of an object to Derrida, attempting to "fix" the unitary subject *homosexual* similarly undoes the category. Post-structuralism's prizing open of categories such as *homosexual* establishes that such labors of classification undo and redo their own work in their attempts to establish meaning. As Derrida so controversially put it, there is "nothing outside the text": rather than finding a truth in putting words to things, such attempts at a *scientia sexualis* rely instead on all that lies outside such denotations – the "locative parergon" that Delany describes.[9]

Butler's Passing

"How can something operate as an origin if there are no secondary consequences which retrospectively confirm the originality of that origin?"[10] In her extension and elaboration of Foucault's work, Butler offered a way to think through questions of sexual subjectivity that implicate gender, race, and other forms of formerly essentialized identity. Rather than constituting the grounds upon which gendered identity builds itself, gender and sexual identity arises as a parody of itself:

> The parodic or imitative effect of gay identities works neither to copy nor to emulate heterosexuality, but rather, to expose heterosexuality as an incessant and panicked imitation of its own naturalized idealization. That heterosexuality is always in the act of elaborating itself is evidence that it is perpetually at risk, that is, that it 'knows' its own possibility of becoming undone: hence, its compulsion to repeat which is at once a foreclosure of that which threatens its coherence.[11]

By recasting heterosexuality not as the biological "truth" of sexual difference and desire but rather as a parody of itself always at risk, and so always in action, Butler moved the terrain of post-structural anti-normativity through a critically inverse logic. In this inverted scheme, gender and sexual identity reveals itself only in its performance of itself: when it is stripped of its foundational status, these repetitions render gender and sexuality more problematic with each iteration. It is in this elaboration that the risk is exposed, and in the "compulsion to repeat" what is revealed is not a natural relationship between essence or identity and action or practice but precisely a constitutive incoherence, a failure to match one with the other. Heterosexuality becomes not essential but performative: a constant procession of acts of representation of itself that point to no inner truth.

Although Butler's work makes frequent recourse to the world of textual elaboration to show how these mechanisms frame the representation of gender and sexuality, she also ambitiously casts the question in terms of other forms of classification and sequestration. Just as Delany uses the instance of inter-class contact to frame a reading of sexually charged encounters, Butler pushes arguments about sexual identity by considering a constellation of essentialized identities in terms of their compulsive repetitions and incessant ideations. In particular, Butler shifts her arguments about performativity into thinking through other relationships, for instance, "the relationship between feminism, psychoanalysis, and race studies."[12] In her reading of Nella Larsen's 1929 novel *Passing*, Butler opens the question of "the assumption of sexual positions" to scrutiny in terms of not only a "heterosexualizing symbolic" but also "a complex set of racial injunctions" (167). In her reading of the story, which dramatizes the passing as white of Clare Kendry, Clare's rekindled friendship with Irene Redfield precipitates conflict over the question of racial identity and the facts of segregation: although Irene has chosen to identify as African American and live in Harlem, Clare's husband is a racist and unaware of his wife's connection to the African American community. Between the two women there exists a push-pull that generates the narrative action of the story, and Larsen's registration of ambivalence is routed explicitly through questions of racial identity and more covertly through an account of a sexualized dynamic between the women that is never staged as such but is characterized through heightened affect and tragic incident in the story. Rather than read the story as revelatory of a sexual identity allegorized by other forms of covert secrecy, Butler suggests that the convergence of homosexuality and the implicit fear of miscegenation generated by passing reminds us that "the reproduction of the species will be articulated as the reproduction *of* relations of reproduction, that is, as the cathected site of a racialized version of the species in pursuit of hegemony through perpetuity, that requires and produces a normative heterosexuality in its service" (167).

Against the "privileging of sexual difference" as "*the* question for our time" (and evident in the work of philosophers such as Luce Irigaray), Butler offers a much more nuanced account of the machinery that produces "relations of reproduction" (167). For her, these relations are what are reproduced, just as the parodic reiterations of heterosexual or gendered performance are the work of gendering and sexual normativity. As Butler notes, the "question of what can and cannot be spoken, what can and cannot be publicly exposed" is raised in relation to both the issue of passing and the issue of sexual desire between the women, and this structure makes the two intrinsically paired in the work of representing how relations of normative heterosexuality are implicated in the two forms of secret otherness (169). Even though Irene criticizes Clare's passing, Butler notes that Irene herself is engaged in "many of the same social conventions of passing as Clare" and is implicated in the same hegemonic regime that pulls each into performing something she might not be (169). This is possible precisely, in Butler's terms, because each act of passing, or not passing, conforms to a performative logic that both hides and reveals what is dissociated from it and by it – secure sexual and racial identification. As Butler notes, Clare's repugnant husband calls her "Nig" despite his ignorance of her ostensible identity. He sees her as "a kind of love toy," which indicates that within his dangerous ignorance lies a form of paradoxical knowingness: it "suggests that he knows or that there is a kind of knowingness in the language he speaks"; at the same time, it secures his non-knowing, because "if he can call her that and remain her husband, he cannot know" (171). Butler aligns this structural oscillation with the structure of the fetish, where desire is generated by an impossible object that one loves despite being cognizant of its impossibility. For Butler, it is the "knowing" capacity of language itself that focuses the production of normative heterosexuality in the inextricable bonds of knowing and not knowing that are distributed among characters in the story, whether that be the opaque articulation of desire between Irene and Clare or the more densely paradoxical relation signaled by the "love toy" nickname.

Sedgwick's Closet of Unknowing

The role of "not knowing" becomes even more critical in the work of Eve Kosofsky Sedgwick, most strikingly in a book that opens with a series of decisive and assured axioms. Sedgwick commences her epochal *Epistemology of the Closet* with the extravagant claim that "many of the major nodes of thought and knowledge in twentieth-century Western culture as a whole are structured – indeed fractured – by a chronic, now endemic crisis of homo/heterosexual definition, indicatively male, dating from the end of the nineteenth century."[13] Although Sedgwick's focus is on homosexuality, and (white) male homosexuality in particular, it is unmistakable that her general hypotheses about the closet and its sometimes inhabitants are almost misleadingly congruent with her series of "axiomatic" open secrets around the question of what people have done both with each other and by themselves sexually. Although Sedgwick fears that her book locates ideal subjects of its analysis at the expense of other sexual subjects, she institutes two reciprocal moves. One is that the analysis can be elastic in its range, and the other is that the matter of homosexuality is always embedded in these discourses, even if the material that clusters around it misleadingly suggests otherwise in its content. One of Sedgwick's initial queries is related to the very primacy of the homo/heterosexual definition itself, as opposed to, say, the masturbator as a singular sexual subject. Why, she asks, does the gender of the sexual object necessarily predominate as the axis of sexual classification? Referring to the "entomologized" parsing of sexual object choice that Foucault uses to characterize the nineteenth-century sexology that finally shrank the number of sexual categories to fundamentally two, she locates a variety of alternate sexual subjectivities (9).

It is a historical rather than predicative fact, Sedgwick argues, that the homo/heterosexual definition has gained the particular role it now plays in the exercise of sexual knowledge and ignorance. For Sedgwick, this fact provides the grounds upon which to analyze sexual identification and utterance (the preformatted nature of sexual nomination) through rhetorical analyses of texts as diverse as simple speech acts and convoluted narrative fictions. Sedgwick's work adopts many of the practices of philosophical speculation, but at its heart lies an argument against logic as the best or most voluble means to argue disclosure that aligns logic with common sense and against rhetoric while also noting that "the particular kinds of skills that might be required to produce the most telling interpretations have hardly been a valued part of the 'common sense' of this epistemologically cloven culture" (12).

Literary truths are truths in the world, or truths that are an effect of textual sense in all its contradictory logic. For Sedgwick, the audacity of her claim lies in rendering the "cloven" nature of epistemological culture per se via the homo/heterosexual divide, but it is equally audacious for placing center stage a long meditation on the role of literary language and its interpretation as generative of the most telling disclosures of sexual identity. Sedgwick analyzes the closet as both a mobile literary metaphor and a way to think about the incarcerations of linguistic effects: about how words constrain, inhibit, and exemplify the things we mean them to mean. Sedgwick notes that the closet is an ideal figure through which to deconstruct not only knowledge but equally importantly ignorance, which, like knowledge, should be understood as both plural (as varieties of ignorances) and in all its specificity (subject to detailed examination) (8). Sedgwick notes that in these deconstructive moves she wants to "make use in sexual-political thinking of the deconstructive understanding that particular insights generate, are lined with, and at the same time are themselves structured by particular opacities" (8). In other words, ignorance is no longer simply the opposite of knowledge but instead its deconstructive other, much as the parergon is both separate from and intrinsic to the art object. This exploration of the closet asks us to consider how we use words to tell things about others and ourselves through obliquity, incomplete utterances, and other forms of indirect description.

Sedgwick labels the introduction of *Epistemology of the Closet* "Introduction: Axiomatic," and she notes that "the book not only has but constitutes an extended introduction" (12). The bulk of her book consists of a series of lengthy readings of literary texts, confining the structure of axiomatic assertion to her perambulatory introduction and the first chapter, which explore the crises of definition constellated around the closet. Along the same lines, her comment identifies the content that follows the introductory – analysis of the literary – as introductory as well. The introduction figures the axiom as the basis not only of her particular argument but also of her epistemological argumentation in general. Sedgwick outlines Foucault's axiomatic assertions about sexual knowledge before adopting the axiomatic as the properly grounding rhetorical structure for the prefatory material to a text that will remain, at best, introductory. She writes that she understands Foucault's "demonstration … that modern Western culture has placed what it calls sexuality in a more and more distinctively privileged relation to our most prized constructs of individual identity, truth, and knowledge" to have had "results" that become "axiomatic" in her own work (3). Such an argumentative dependence on Foucault inserts Sedgwick's innovative analysis into a daisy chain of theoretical cogitation in such a way as to forecast the proliferate effects of her own analysis. It institutes a pattern of demonstration, result, and axiom that is as prosperous for her own work as his.

Describing her work as introductory establishes Sedgwick's aspiration that the text's value will ultimately be heuristic. For Sedgwick, "knowingness" is associated with "the deadening pretended knowingness by which the chisel of modern homo/heterosexual crisis tends, in public discourse, to be hammered most fatally home" (12). Axiomatic reasoning resembles "knowingness" but is crucially different. "Taken as read" is subtly distinct from "already known"; it replaces the regime of assumption with the practice of literalism (taking as read) as a metaphoric enunciation of what may (indeed, must) be assumed. Axioms are assumptions that must be taken at face value: they must be conceded without interrogation. They point, here, to their history but not to their etiology. This distinction is crucial. Citing Foucault as the originator of the axiom that serves as the operative premise for her own work, Sedgwick historicizes without turning back to investigate either the demonstration or its result. Sedgwick, in effect, liberates her argument from the prefatory imperative to prove its premises, arguing instead, and later, through the apparent proof of literary interpretation, which is situated both literally and figuratively as posterior to the elaboration of axioms.

In so doing, Sedgwick's argumentative innovation involves two key and related strategies. The first is her deployment of terms such as hypothesis, demonstration, result, axiom, and algorithm. The second strategic innovation is her elaboration of the generative distinction between argued modalities of homosexuality, which locate homosexuality either through universalizing or minoritizing discourses. Sedgwick raises this issue through two different concerns, which are related in complex ways throughout the course of her introduction. First, she notes the location of the homo/het-erosexual definition both as an issue of primary importance "for a small, distinct, relatively fixed homosexual minority" and as "an issue of contin-uing, determinative importance in the lives of people across the spectrum of sexualities" (1). Secondly, she notes "the contradiction between seeing same-sex object choice on the one hand as a matter of liminality or tran-sitivity between genders, and seeing it on the other hand as reflecting an impulse of separatism – though by no means necessarily political separat-ism – between genders" (1–2).

Universalizing discourses, which see homosexuality as one point on an arc of sexual preference, compete with minoritizing discourses that locate homosexuality as a minority specialization and see homosexuals as contra-dictorily placed in terms of their gender cohort. Gender-separatist under-standings of homosexuals as epitomizing gender types likewise compete with gender-transitive understandings, which characterize gender instead as mutable and impossible to locate and identify these as paradoxically deter-mining characteristics exemplified by the homosexual. One might draw from those two types of identification an argument about both the nature of sexual discourses and the nature of critical theory. Sedgwick's analysis, which is peculiarly apropos in thinking about matters of sexuality, is not inappropriately cognate with her own positioning as a literary theorist who is attempting to address sweeping cultural, political, and social questions within the sometimes glacially paced and opaquely contextual practice of literary reading. A constitutive element of queer theory has always been that its disciplinary affiliations are diffuse. Although it would be fair to say that Sedgwick's work is aligned with the perverse orientation of literary analysis, it would be equally fair to say that the work's impact has been substantial in myriad disciplines, and its propulsive energies have been impossible to contain. Sedgwick's own trajectory was unpredictable; her influence was profound.

Affect

In 1995, an essay cowritten by Sedgwick and Adam Frank, "Shame in the Cybernetic Fold," served as an early indicator that the so-called "affective turn" would become a dominant preoccupation for literary studies in the wake of the significant directions that both Butler and Sedgwick augured in their work at the beginning of the decade. Sedgwick and Frank's essay reproduces the kind of revisionist manifesto that constituted *Epistemology of the Closet*, and it too begins with a series of assertions of certainty whose performative value is familiarly queer. It begins: "Here are a few things theory knows today. / Or, to phrase it more fairly, here are a few broad assumptions that shape the heuristic habits and positing procedures of theory today."[14] The essay subsequently introduces their edited collection of Tompkins' writing, *Shame and Its Sisters*. Tomkins, a relatively neglected psychologist whose work received renewed attention after the publication of their collection, linked in indissoluble ways the physical and psychological experience of affect, and the troubling of easy assignations of either biological or psychological origins for feelings became as much a central drive in Sedgwick's work via Tomkins as did restituting value in feeling as a source of action that is always implicated in thinking (thus the title of her 2003 monograph *Touching Feeling*).

Especially in the formidable body of work of Lauren Berlant, and pervasively within the work in queer theory that followed Butler and Sedgwick, thinking about affect became an ingrained concern in writing about gay and lesbian literature and a collection point for diverse inter- and multi-disciplinary thinkers. Ann Cvetkovich's writing, to cite another example, exemplifies the way queer work turned to questions of public culture and negative affect in thinking through the next iteration of gay and lesbian studies (in particular, the study of trauma).[15] For Berlant, the notion of an "intimate public sphere" reanimated questions of private and public identity through the delineation of an affective dimension, particularly in the mass products of "women's culture." Throughout her theorization, the critical question is one of affective relation – thinking about how attachments are formed, through which fantasies they are formed, and what relations are entailed in their formation.

In *Cruel Optimism*, for example, Berlant explores the ways in which aspirational attachments are formed to precisely those forms and fantasies that inhibit prosperity. In her introduction, Berlant writes that she is "extremely interested in generalization: how the singular becomes delaminated from its location in someone's story or some locale's irreducibly local history and circulated as evidence of something shared."[16] That interest is continuous with the kind of problematic that Sedgwick posed in *Epistemology*, and it is structurally cognate with the work of literary exemplification and "delamination" that has always accompanied post-structural approaches to gay and lesbian literature in writings such as Sedgwick's and Butler's. It is not merely (or even) that generalization is possible but rather how it proceeds. Berlant thus thinks through generalization and the "teachable" with the help of Mary Gaitskill's novel *Two Girls, Fat and Thin* (1991) in a chapter whose relation to Sedgwick's work is explicit from its first citation (of Sedgwick's 1995 poetry collection *Fat Art, Thin Art*), from the content of that citation (the electric

conjugation "thinkiest"), and from its original composition as a contribution to a *festschrift* dedicated to Sedgwick (285). Berlant "delaminates"
the story of Gaitskill's novel to think through what she describes as dialectical impulses between distinct modes of embodiment articulated in her
work and Sedgwick's. Literary exemplification here performs equally well
the service of addressing an intimate and critical project. In fact, its service
is to render these two dialectically entwined. Between the "two girls" of
the novel lies Anna Granite, an Ayn Rand stand-in who orients the women
to one another despite their quite different relationships to her. Although
the two girls are themselves historically incapable of the mode of intimate
disclosure their interaction prompts, Berlant writes that "they both register ambivalence and embarrassment toward the need they feel to tell each
other something, which is not at all their usual practice" (44). This ambivalence and embarrassment registers on the affective scale that characterizes
shame as psychological and social affect and locates the ambivalence and
embarrassment attendant on bodily over-presence (the ambivalent registration of a body's "thereness"). In their interaction, Justine and Dorothy
attempt to feel what Berlant describes as "negative density," or "dense
moments of sensuality" whose inhabitation "stops time, makes time, and
saturates the lived, imagined, and not-yet-imagined world" (137).

Gaitskill's pair in this respect occupy a similar temporality to the one
occupied by Clare and Irene in *Passing*, where only the maintenance
of strict attention to temporality (identity before and after passing, or
before and after marriage, for instance) permits everyday life, and yet
another form of irresistible negative attachment draws an alternative
scheme for the women. Berlant's exemplar links the chapter's entangling
of Sedgwick's work and person with her own to the literary problem
of exemplarity, where "smarts" and "thinkiness" are tied to the words'
"root[s] in physical pain ... [i]t is as though to be smart is to pose a threat
of impending acuteness" and "[i]n this sense smartness is the opposite of
eating, which foregrounds the pleasure of self-absorption, not its sting"
(139). In her transformative reading of the novel, Berlant engages the
way in which it calls on an assessment of "what affective events are,"
by "tracking repetition, form, and norm" wherein "the motive and aim
of the aesthetic education are to train the viscera," and yet "an aesthetic
that values the beauty of fantasy or of form can believe too much that the
viscera are saying something undistorted when we encounter the scene
of its investments" (138–139). This paradox provides an aesthetic frame
for the "cruel optimism" around which the book centers its analysis of
affective attachments, itself framed by her intimate public attachment to
Sedgwick's writing.

Inheritance

Given the grounds upon which post-structural thought decentered questions of identity and affiliation, it makes sense that its heirs interrogated queerness through a diverse set of fresh possibilities. That such an ambivalence around questions of classification and identity might bear unexpected fruit was already evident in Teresa de Lauretis's adoption of the phrase "queer theory" in a special issue of *differences* in 1991, but what that phrase means is, like most things, liable to change. In 1996, for example, Annamarie Jagose noted that after its minting, de Lauretis "abandoned" the term "barely three years later, on the grounds that it had been taken over by those mainstream forces and institutions it was coined to resist."[17] In the coauthored introduction to *The Routledge Queer Studies Reader* that was published sixteen years later, Jagose and Donald E. Hall write: "In broad stroke, queer studies is the institutionalization of a new – or at least newly visible – paradigm for thinking about sexuality that emerged simultaneously across academic and activist contexts in the early 1990s, constituting a broad and unmethodical critique of normative models of sex, gender and sexuality."[18] These two distinct ways of framing queer studies' relations to institutional knowledge demonstrate the pliability of the term during the past two decades, not least because it has migrated away from the primarily literary focus of writers such as Sedgwick. The term "queer" has been adapted for experimental and political reuse and given fresh treatment since the 1990s work of Butler and Sedgwick. More recently, the "broad strokes" of queer studies has embraced variations on the theme of sexuality studies in the work of critics such as Berlant, Kathryn Bond Stockton on the "queer child," and José Esteban Muñoz on "disidentification." In each case, a paradoxical relationship between pleasure (the erotic) and discipline – from opprobrium to censure to prohibition and erasure, from cruelty to optimism – becomes a central problematic whose parsing was aided by post-structural theory.

Heather Love's influential *Feeling Backward: Loss and the Politics of Queer History* opens with her observation that a "central paradox of any transformative criticism is that its dreams for the future are founded on a history of suffering, stigma, and violence."[19] This paradox inhabited or even animated the work of post-structuralist thought in gay and lesbian studies in the 1980s and 1990s when it broke from the politics of liberation and equality. Rather than resolving the paradox, though, post-structuralism sought ways to rethink the terms themselves, not because liberation and equality were ever abandoned as goals but because history itself made their status complicated. Love writes that "[o]ppositional criticism opposes not only existing structures of power but also the very history that gives it meaning."[20] To come to grips with the work of representation, one must do more than merely oppose its hurtful content: revisionist readings of representations of gay and lesbian lives, for example, could only do so much while remaining content with identifying and refuting stereotypes and other forms of oppression. As Love suggests, focusing on the elimination of forms of oppression and their representation has the consequence of removing from view the very conditions under which identities were formed and the context against and within which they thrived. How to account for a more ambivalent or double-faced relationship to the facts of "suffering, stigma, and violence" became a focal question for post-structuralist queer theory.

David Halperin puts this matter slightly differently in *How to Be Gay*:

> And when gay liberation has done its work, what then? Will gay male culture, of the subcultural variety I have described here, wither away? Will it lose its appeal? Will gay men of the future be unable to understand, except in a kind of pitying or embarrassed way, why their forebears who lived in the twentieth and twenty-first centuries found so much meaning, so much delight in heterosexual cultural norms that excluded them, at least insofar as such forms contained no explicit representations of gay men or gay male life?[21]

Halperin identifies specific reading strategies that create senses of identity or identification within the very texts that seem to bar those identities from representation. This is one common way in which the history of queer identity might be recovered: through the assumption that readers forge deconstructive relationships with the representations that ostensibly obliterate them. Halperin asks a question that sits alongside the paradox that Love identifies and narrows its focus to the way in which texts are read, and therefore appreciated, against the grain of representation itself. It offers two propositions: that we read in more complex ways than simply accepting particular historical representations at face value, and that we acknowledge these practices as historically specific and vulnerable to the vicissitudes of time. Halperin also identifies another anxiety concerning the loss of time- and place-specific reading strategies to later generations of readers, a concern that points to the vexed question of the relationship between generations of queer readers, writers, and the textual forms that are important to them.

That these insights are indebted to the work of post-structuralism is clear when we consider how Halperin identifies Foucault in changing the way in which such readings are made. In his influential book *Saint Foucault*, he writes that the "queer politics" of Foucault are not an identity politics as such but a "horizon of possibility whose precise extent and heterogeneous scope cannot in principle be delimited in advance."[22] The only way to define "queer" in this sense is as "oppositional ... *whatever* is at odds with the normal, the legitimate, the dominant."²³ This terminology is grounded in Halperin's understanding of the critical insights offered by Foucault's theorization of sexuality, and it establishes Foucault as an originator in the field of post-structuralism through his historical argument against normative categories and essentialized sexual identity.

A final word of caution: articulating a relationship between originators and heirs is also compromised or normalizing unless the movement from past to present is allowed a certain flexibility. Although post-structuralism has developed its own historical paths and desire lines, making oneself available to the rich contextualizing moments out of which critical debates emerged is as fundamental to the work of the heir as furthering the line is. Foucault's prominence as a theorist of queer subjectivity coincided with the rise in activism and excited critical thinking that accompanied the HIV/AIDS crisis. It leaves as its legacy both the work that pushes strongly toward a future-oriented idea of queer theory as enabling a better, more secure, and more visible franchise within the body politic and the work of critics for whom such goals remained critically suspect.²⁴ These theories also ask more of texts than that they facilitate or clarify how literary representation figures or enhances understandings of gay and lesbian identifications, except where these various nonnormative and disorienting understandings of the problem of identity make plain. This project itself becomes one of a new inclusiveness and one that offers unexpected readings of texts. The unexpected could even be considered their hallmark.

NOTES

1 Samuel R. Delany, *Times Square Red, Times Square Blue* (New York: New York University Press, 1999), 111.
2 Ibid., xv.
3 Ibid., xv–xvi.
4 Jacques Derrida, *The Truth In Painting*, trans. Geoff Bennington and Ian McLeod (Chicago: University of Chicago Press, 1987), 15–147.
5 Eve Kosofsky Sedgwick, *Tendencies* (Durham: Duke University Press, 1993), xii.
6 Eve Kosofsky Sedgwick, *Epistemology of the Closet* (Berkeley: University of California Press, 1990).
7 Jacques Derrida, *Of Grammatology*, trans. Gayatri Chakravorty Spivak (Baltimore: Johns Hopkins University Press, 1976).
8 Michel Foucault, *The History of Sexuality*, vol. 1, *An Introduction*, trans. Michael Hurley (New York: Vintage, 1980), 3; hereafter cited in text.
9 Derrida, *Of Grammatology*, 163.

10 Judith Butler, "Imitation and Gender Insubordination," in *Inside/Out: Lesbian Theories, Gay Theories*, ed. Diana Fuss (New York: Routledge, 1990), 22.

11 Butler, "Imitation and Gender Insubordination," 22–23.

12 Judith Butler, "Passing, Queering: Nella Larsen's Psychoanalytic Challenge," in *Bodies That Matter: On the Discursive Limits of "Sex"* (New York: Routledge, 1993), 167; hereafter cited in text.

13 Sedgwick, *Epistemology of the Closet*, 1; hereafter cited in text.

14 Eve Kosofsky Sedgwick and Adam Frank, "Shame in the Cybernetic Fold: Reading Silvan Tomkins," *Critical Inquiry* 21, no. 2 (1995): 496.

15 See Ann Cvetkovich, *An Archive of Feelings: Trauma, Sexuality, and Lesbian Public Cultures* (Durham: Duke University Press, 2003); and Ann Cvetkovich, *Depression: A Public Feeling* (Durham: Duke University Press, 2012). An edited collection such as David M. Halperin and Valerie Traub's *Gay Shame* (Chicago: University of Chicago Press, 2010) demonstrates not least in its provocative titling and identification of shame in particular as an affect with deep resonant compatibility with "gay" that one of the unexpected but most richly diverse areas in which work after post-structuralism would thrive would be in thinking through affects and their textual representation.

16 Lauren Berlant, *Cruel Optimism* (Durham: Duke University Press, 2011), 12; hereafter cited in text.

17 Annamarie Jagose, *Queer Theory* (Melbourne: Melbourne University Press, 1996), 127.

18 Donald E. Hall and Annamarie Jagose, with Andrea Bebell and Susan Potter, *The Routledge Queer Studies Reader* (London and New York: Routledge, 2013), xvi.

19 Heather Love, *Feeling Backward: Loss and the Politics of Queer History* (Cambridge, MA: Harvard University Press, 2009), 1.

20 Love, *Feeling Backward*, 1.

21 David M. Halperin, *How to Be Gay* (Cambridge, MA: Harvard University Press, 2012), 432.

22 David M. Halperin, *Saint Foucault: Towards a Gay Hagiography* (Oxford: Oxford University Press, 1997), 62.

23 Halperin, *Saint Foucault*, 62.

24 For example, Lee Edelman (whose *Homographesis* forged the most strongly post-structural or deconstructive methodology in queer theory) maintains such skepticism throughout his later work. In *No Future: Queer Theory and the Death Drive* (Durham: Duke University Press, 2004), he identifies in queer a force against the "reproductive futurity" that centers political imagination. Ways of thinking from present to future, given the premises that animate post-structuralism, are complicated. Kathryn Bond Stockton's reframing of the queer child as "growing sideways" in *The Queer Child, or Growing Sideways in the Twentieth Century* (Durham: Duke University Press, 2009) exemplifies the kind of strategies that post-structuralism both required and enabled in the wake of its own reorganization of categories of identification and liberation.

14

MARTIN JOSEPH PONCE

Transnational Queer Imaginaries, Intimacies, Insurgencies

To bring to bear a transnational analytic to the study of queer U.S. literature is to interrogate the national frame of "America" as the organizing principle of literary and sexual history and to open up the field to hemispheric, oceanic, postcolonial, and diasporic approaches. Queer scholarship in this outernational vein includes materialist analyses of globalization's heterogeneous impacts on local sexual economies as well as ethnographic explorations of diverse gender and sexual categories, terminologies, and practices in non-Western cultures;[1] studies of queer migrations in terms of sexual and economic opportunities, cultural differences, immigration law, and political asylum;[2] and examinations of transnational activist formations in the areas of global health, international human rights, and visual culture and new media.[3] Despite the varied methodologies employed, transnational approaches to sexuality have enabled scholars, as the anthropologist Elizabeth Povinelli and historian George Chauncey write, to "map the movements of people, capital, and images across national boundaries; follow the desires, aspirations, and desperations that prompted these movements; and chronicle the effects of these movements on sexual subjectivities, identifications, and intimate practices."[4]

One significant convergence between transnational U.S. literary and queer studies lies in their shared critiques of American political and sexual exceptionalism and the developmental narratives of capitalist and queer progress that underlie those fantasies. Donald Pease writes that the former developed in the 1930s and the Cold War period as a discourse "characterized by its account of the United States's unique place in world history – the 'redeemer nation,' 'conqueror of the world's markets,' and, more recently, the 'global security state.'"[5] Jasbir Puar has extended this definition into the domain of sexuality by examining recent "homonationalist" formations and processes that seek to "[rehabilitate] some – clearly not all or most – lesbians, gays, and queers to US national citizenship" for the sake of presenting "the United States as a properly multicultural heteronormative but nevertheless gay-friendly, tolerant, and sexually-liberated society," while simultaneously excluding other racialized and "terrorist" bodies from that space of belonging.[6] Far from undermining the power of "heterosexuality as the norm," homonationalism, Puar elaborates, "fosters nationalist homosexual positionalities which then police nonnationalist non-normative sexualities" and "enables a transnational discourse of US queer exceptionalism vis-à-vis perversely racialized bodies of pathologized nationalities" (51).

In light of the cautionary critiques of U.S. exceptionalism and homonationalism, the globalization of "gay" identity, and what Inderpal Grewal and Caren Kaplan describe as "the tradition-modernity split [...] in which the United States and Europe are figured as modern and thus as the sites of progressive social movements, while other parts of the world are presumed to be traditional, especially in regard to sexuality,"[7] the following readings are organized into rubrics which recognize and challenge those presumptions: immigration to America, imaginative reclamations of queered homelands and borderlands, ambivalent returns to overseas homelands and the politics of international sex tourism, queer critiques of the postcolonial nation-state, and Two-Spirit/queer Native critiques of U.S. settler colonialism. Neither discrete nor comprehensive, these rubrics are meant to serve as heuristic devices for exploring the manifold lines of flight, desire, and inquiry called forth – and called for – by this diverse body of literature.

Queering Immigration

Gender and sexually nonconforming people on the move in search of more hospitable locales to enact and express their dissident desires, embodiments, and subjectivities is a common theme in queer literature and life. But recent scholarship has interrogated the archetypal "sexual geography," as Kath Weston describes it, "in which the city represents a beacon of tolerance and gay community, the country a locus of persecution and gay absence,"[8] as well as the sexual exceptionalist claims of America outlined above. Such skepticism is worth bearing in mind when dealing with José Garcia Villa's autobiographical stories in the collection *Footnote to Youth: Tales of the Philippines and Others* (1933), one modernist example of the braiding together of immigration and queer eroticism.[9] These texts narrate his journey from the Philippines (which was then under U.S. colonial rule) to New Mexico (where he briefly attended college) to New York (where he ultimately settled) through a series of episodic, impressionistic, "spiritually" oriented stories stitched together by numbered paragraphs.

Each of the stories in "Wings and Blue Flame: A Trilogy" begins with a scene of loss and traces the unnamed narrator's efforts at substitutions.

After being sent by his father to study in the United States in "Untitled Story," the narrator seeks to recuperate the loss of his homeland and his girlfriend, Vi, by forming attachments with both male and female students at the University of New Mexico (including David, Georgia, and Aurora). The second installment, "White Interlude," disrupts the first story's heterosexual resolution between the narrator and Aurora by opening with the loss of David, whose poverty prevents him from continuing to enroll at the university. In the trilogy's final story, "Walk at Midnight: A Farewell," the narrator becomes intensely attached to Jack, essentially David's substitute, who fails to reciprocate the narrator's love and causes the latter emotional distress. Playing on the Catholic notion of the Virgin Birth ("Then after I had breathed of the beating of His heart God passed me into my mother and in a night in August I was born" [117]), this story implies that the primordial separation from God, coupled with the narrator's growing recognition that Jack will never "love me even as I love him" (122), indicates that the narrator can only be made "whole" by reunion with the divine in death, a desire that erupts in the penultimate paragraph: " – I am hungry for You, O God!" (130). However, in this climactic moment of torment and temptation, the narrator turns away from the seductions of God's love ("stronger God ran His fingers through my hair") and purges the human love object from within himself as he is lying on the New Mexico mesa: "I was taking Jack out of me and giving him to the earth and to the sky, and the white flowers in my hands were my gifts of forgiveness" (130).

In the oblique story "Young Writer in a New Country," Villa eschews erotic reciprocation as the precondition for belonging, instead claiming autobiographical writing as the means of his own rebirth: "I, father of tales. Fathering tales I became rooted to the new land. I became lover to the desert. Three tales had healed me" (301–302). Although the narrator's "cool white birth in a new land" (301) may seem to signal an identification with white Americanness, and although his arrival in New York City would seem to reinscribe a narrative of queer metronormativity,[10] the conclusion of "Young Writer" ends on a much more ambivalent note:

> Will the native land forgive? Between your peace and the peace of a strange
> faraway desert – Between your two peaces –
> O tell softly, softly. Forgive softly.

(303–304)

Neither wholly triumphant nor utterly disillusioned, the ending evokes a narrator suspended between his "native land" and the Southwest desert, idealized spaces of "peace" for which his New York existence seems to yearn.[11]

Imagining Queer Homelands and Borderlands

Whereas Villa's modernist autobiographical stories remain relatively silent about the impact of racial and sexual difference on social acceptance in the United States during the Depression years, Audre Lorde's "biomythography" *Zami: A New Spelling of My Name* (1982) makes explicit some of the oppressive social forces that hinder possibilities of belonging for African American lesbians from the interwar through the Cold War periods. *Zami* traces the autobiographical narrator Audre's life in Harlem as the daughter of Caribbean immigrants and her coming into being as a self-identified black lesbian, in part through the intimate relationships she forges with several black and white women, including Gennie, Ginger, Bea, Eudora, Muriel, and Afrekete.

Although it is mostly set in the United States, the text's transnational dimensions are crucial to its intersectional approach to race and sexuality. In Mexico City, Audre experiences for the first time a sense of racial "affirmation" when "seeing my own color reflected upon the streets in such great numbers."[12] This sense of racial comfort in Mexico abruptly ends after Audre leaves Eudora in Cuernavaca and returns to New York. In the 1950s, there were "few other Black women who were visibly gay" (177), and the downtown lesbian scene "reflected the ripples and eddies of the larger society that had spawned it": "But when I, a Black woman, saw no reflection in any of the faces there week after week, I knew perfectly well that being an outsider in the Bagatelle had everything to do with being Black" (220). Whereas her white partner Muriel insists on the parallel forces of sexual and racial subordination – "that she and all gay-girls were just as oppressed as any Black person, certainly as any Black woman" – Audre realizes that this misrecognition contributes to the rift between them (204). Near the end of the narrative, Audre fulfills her unarticulated "long[ing] for other Black women" (224) with Afrekete, a black singer with whom she spends the summer of 1959 and to whom she dedicates several italicized, eroticized paeans (249–252).

In a sense, both the racism of New York and the mutually pleasurable relationship with Afrekete provoke Audre to look outside U.S. borders for a sense of belonging, for that "amorphous and mystically perfect place called 'home'" (71) that her mother's nostalgic stories of Grenada had evoked – "a place I had never been to but knew well out of my mother's mouth" (13). In the epilogue, the adult Audre draws on her mother's idealized memories of Carriacou, a place that Audre could not find on a map for years but that became a "magic place" in her child's mind (14), and projects a utopian space beyond the racial-gender-sexual hierarchies that stratify U.S. society. This space enables the conferral of "a new spelling of my name," replacing "the term 'Lesbian' of Greek origin," as Carol Boyce Davies points out, "with the term 'Zami' of Caribbean/creole origin [as] an important attempt at redefinition":[13] "*Zami. A Carriacou name for women who work together as friends and lovers*" (255). The biomythography closes with Lorde rediscovering and bringing near a diasporic home in Carriacou ("Once *home* was a long way off") that localizes and legitimizes female relationality and same-sex desire through a reclamation of the maternal line: "There it is said that the desire to lie with other women is a drive from the mother's blood" (256).

Gloria Anzaldúa's *Borderlands/La Frontera: The New Mestiza* (1987) similarly posits and draws on transnational feminine figures to construct the queer "new mestiza." By complicating absolute distinctions between state-imposed boundaries, Anzaldúa theorizes the borderlands in political ("the Texas-U.S. Southwest/Mexican border") as well as "psychological," "sexual," and "spiritual" terms.[14] Such zones of encounter and proximity, in which "two or more cultures edge each other" (19), however, are prone to conflict and violence, wounding and transfusing, smearing and queering:

> The U.S.-Mexican border *es una herida abierta* where the Third World grates against the first and bleeds. And before a scab forms it hemorrhages again, the lifeblood of two worlds merging to form a third country – a border culture.
> [...] *Los atravesados* live here: the squint-eyed, the perverse, the queer, the troublesome, the mongrel, the mulato, the half-breed, the half dead; in short, those who cross over, pass over, or go through the confines of the "normal."
>
> (25)

To account for these contentious conditions of prohibition and possibility, Anzaldúa tracks a colonial history from the Spanish conquistadors of the sixteenth century to the U.S.-Mexican War and the 1848 Treaty of Guadalupe Hidalgo to the contemporary era of northward migration ("the return odyssey to the historical/mythological Aztlán" that is now known as the U.S. Southwest [33]), aggressive border control, and exploited gendered labor in the region.

Through its challenging of U.S. colonialism and racism as well as Chicano sexism and homophobia, *Borderlands* engages a multivalent critique made possible through movement – "I had to leave home so I could find myself" (38) – and through the "rebellion" of acting "against two moral prohibitions: sexuality and homosexuality" (41). However, for Anzaldúa, departure is neither a "betrayal" of home nor a flight into mainstream U.S. queer culture (43). Rather, Anzaldúa reimagines home by reinterpreting colonial, masculinist, and sexist Mexican/Chicano understandings of female figures like La Virgen de Guadalupe, Malinche, and La Llorona,[15] and also by reclaiming ancient female deities such as *Coatlicue* ("Goddess of birth and death" [68]; "symbol of the fusion of opposites" [69]) through a process that Debra A. Castillo terms a "poetic genealogy with pre-Columbian Aztecs."[16] Anzaldúa summarizes the tactics practiced by the new mestiza, who develops a "new consciousness – a *mestiza* consciousness" (102): "She reinterprets history and, using new symbols, she shapes new myths. She adopts new perspectives toward the darkskinned, women and queers. She strengthens her tolerance (and intolerance) for ambiguity" (104). Such queer feminist reckonings with colonial and nationalist histories and ancient indigenous mythologies are, of course, inescapably political and have themselves been subject to critique and revision.[17]

Queer Returns

To be sure, not all reachings across geocultural borders are imaginatively or historically oriented. Han Ong's satirical novel *The Disinherited* (2004) narrates the forty-four-year-old Roger Caracera's return to the Philippines from the United States for the reading of his father's will and his attempts to divest himself of his $500,000 inheritance as rapidly and anonymously as possible. His most concerted efforts at disbursing the unwanted money focus on Pitik Sindit. Years earlier, Roger had received from his Uncle Eustacio $60,000, which he learns was originally intended for Pitik but was redirected to himself to ensure the family's good name. Roger's indignation at his relatives' homophobia gets complicated, however, when he discovers that Pitik Sindit "turned out to be not a man, not even a young man, but a boy."[18] By the time Roger tracks down the boy in Madame Sonia's "House of Beauty and Pain," Pitik is a fifteen-year-old erotic dancer known as Blueboy who performs for older foreign men.

By alluding to international gay sex tourism and cross-age, cross-race liaisons, *The Disinherited* juxtaposes two crisscrossing modes of desire: a young, neocolonial Filipino subject's desire for an idealized America(n) and a white American man's desire for Southeast Asian youths. Pitik understands the allure of his dancing not as dehumanizing objectification but as a magnetic "pull" so powerful that it beckons admirers from across the seas and holds them "in this country" (255). Unlike Roger, who treats Pitik like a son, Feingold, the American to whom Pitik had been promised by Madame Sonia, is shamelessly enthralled by Pitik. A self-identified "lover of boys," Feingold reverses the tropes of American freedom and Third World repression, contending that "America is not the First World [...] It has its backward aspects too" (282). He avers that "Thailand and the Philippines" represent "more tolerant locales" (321) when it comes to his predilections.

MARTIN JOSEPH PONCE

In contrast to Roger's view of man-boy relationships as connoting "master and slave" and "hunter and prey" (287), Feingold insists that commerce and romance are not incompatible: "[In] this part of the world what Blueboy and I represent is entirely natural" (282).

Whereas Feingold and the patrons at Madame Sonia's seek pleasures abroad that are forbidden at home, Pitik himself adopts the very opposite position. In his "fairy tale," Pitik would meet a white, wealthy American man who is "so besotted with the boy that he had to have Pitik by his side" and who would fly him away from his sordid world of poverty and queer-phobia (199). In the end, however, Pitik winds up with neither Roger nor Feingold; his fantasies are terminated by the reputation-conscious Caracera family, and his romantic desires are transmuted into spectral "implacable" revenge as he haunts Roger's New York screening of the World War II film *Fiesta of the Damned* in the final scene (368).

Lawrence Chua's novel *Gold by the Inch* (1998) similarly explores themes of return and gay sex tourism but with a twist. In this formally fragmented text, it is not the (stereo)typical older white man who cruises for young brown flesh but instead an unnamed, working-class, twenty-three-year-old ethnic Chinese immigrant who visits Southeast Asia after ten years of liv-ing in New York and engages in a tumultuous affair with a handsome Thai hustler named Thong. Because the narrator returns to Bangkok, Thailand, and his birthplace of Penang, Malaysia, after breaking up with his white boyfriend Jim, a cocaine addict who treated him like a "decorative com-panion,"[19] some critics have suggested that his relationship with Thong "reverses" the racial and class objectifications to which he was subjected by his white partners.[20] It is important to note, though, that interlaced in this drama of intraracial same-sex eroticism is a less sensational, but no less sig-nificant, narrative of family reintegration whereby the protagonist attempts to reconcile with his distant, abusive father (whom he visits in Honolulu en route to Bangkok) and to piece together the details of his grandmother who died during World War II: "Did she even exist? Or is she just another one of the fragments of stories that my family passes around between silences? Stories prompted by my thirst for origins" (70). His effort at reconnecting to his homeland only grows more desperate after his search for his grand-mother's story (however ironically mocked it is) comes up short: "There is no prepackage of identity or ethnic heritage left to possess. No folk tales passed on from Grandmother's knee" (135).

Scarred by his relationships with Jim and his father in the United States, alienated upon his return to Southeast Asia, and left unsatisfied at his grand-mother's grave, the narrator negotiates and localizes his desire for belonging in Thailand through his desire for Thong. He initially claims sameness with

230

Thong based on their shared occupations as hustlers (13) and fantasizes that they are "[p]erfect lovers" (29), but he eventually comes to recognize that "you [Thong], whom I'd thought my twin, were nothing like me. [...] You would never love anyone, anything, as much as I loved you now" (37). This fear of the unequal intensities of attraction is further complicated by the semi-commercial nature of their relationship, which makes it impossible for the narrator to discern whether Thong stays with him out of mutual affection or for the money. Even as economic mediation adulterates the erotic, it also provides the narrator with some semblance of distanced composure, a shield against emotional vulnerability in the face of Thong's assaulting beauty and his impervious, unreadable demeanor. Their turbulent relationship finally dissolves when Thong "[v]iciously" accuses him of simply being another tourist – "This is just a vacation for you, isn't it?" (201) – and the narrator internally acquiesces to the charge: "In the end, you are just an American darker than the rest, doing things in Thailand you can never do at home" (201).

The text's ambiguous conclusion implicates the reader, as well. Reverting back to his edgy cynicism, the narrator resumes the role of hustler but aims his address at the reader. Likening book to body and reading to a kind of voracious voyeurism, the narrator refuses to indulge the reader's wish "for some kind of closure" and instead proffers his cocaine-laden body "naked on the bed" (207): "Your face travels the cold expanse of my body. Inhaling. Devouring" (208). In the end, then, *Gold by the Inch* issues "a cautionary critique" not only of the exploitative transnational Asian subject but also of the privileged consumer of postcolonial gay fiction.[21]

Queer Postcoloniality

Other literary engagements with overseas homelands have combined the critiques of sexual-economic commodification and exploitation found in *The Disinherited* and *Gold by the Inch* with critiques of repressive, heteronormative postcolonial nation-states.[22] Set during the martial law regime of Ferdinand Marcos (a regime supported by U.S. military and economic aid), Jessica Hagedorn's novel *Dogeaters* (1990), for example, features Joey Sands, a queer, half-Filipino, half-black DJ at a gay club in Manila who sustains his heroin addiction through prostitution. Although his ambitions to hook up with a rich foreigner (man or woman) echo Pitik Sindit's, his week-long affair with a German film director, Rainer, ends with Joey inadvertently witnessing the opposition senator's assassination. His story shifts dramatically from participating in Manila's seedy underworld of underage sex shows, shower dancers, drugs, and hustling to being led into the mountains by a group of underground guerrilla rebels. There he meets up with the former beauty queen and daughter of the opposition senator, Daisy Avila, who had "denounce[d] the beauty pageant as a farce, a giant step backward for all women";[23] joined her rebel lover Santos Tirador; been captured, interrogated, and gang-raped in one of the government security force's detention camps; been released on condition of exile; and subsequently snuck back into the country under a new name.

Although the entry of a former gay hustler and beauty queen into a guerrilla formation comprised of indigenous, provincial, and urban figures may not constitute a utopian alternative to the highly stratified, highly surveyed milieu of Manila, it nevertheless provides a potential space of resistance to state authoritarianism for queer and feminist figures. Some critics have argued that Joey Sands's queerness goes underground along with his former identities, lifeways, and sense of individual control, but the novel does not portray this alleged sexual submergence as a necessary precondition of his acceptance into the rebel camp.[24] Also noteworthy is the fact that although queer, or *bakla*, figures like the First Lady's tailor, Chiquiting Moreno, and her loyal "homosexual constituents" (217) seem to collude with the dictatorship,[25] it is the shower dancer Boy-Boy who serves as the conduit between the urban and provincial sites of resistance. A seemingly apolitical emblem of sexual commodification by global gay tourism, Boy-Boy turns out to be part of the underground and helps Joey escape Manila by bringing him into the care of the guerrilla forces.

Moving from the Pacific to the Caribbean, Michelle Cliff's novel *No Telephone to Heaven* (1987) parallels *Dogeaters* in their shared concerns with neocolonial class and color hierarchies, state and resistant forms of violence, the transformation of an upper-class female protagonist who renounces her privilege and aligns herself with the less fortunate, and the connection forged between the female protagonist and her queer ally as they join a group of resistance fighters. *No Telephone to Heaven* also draws on the trajectory of the return narrative: the light-skinned, well-off Clare Savage moves from Jamaica to New York with her parents and younger sister and spends her high school and college years there during the Civil Rights era; she attends graduate school in London, the capital of the imperial "mother-country,"[26] where she studies European literature and art and witnesses a racist, anti-immigrant rally; she has an affair in Europe with an African American veteran of the Vietnam War who suffers from PTSD and an incurable wound; and finally she returns to her homeland – literally, to her grandmother's home – to serve as a schoolteacher of history and, in the end, as part of a socially diverse "band" of guerrilla soldiers who "were making something new" (5).

Clare's narrative of coming into political consciousness is aided by Harry/Harriet, a transgender nurse and healer whose mother was a maid and whose father was Clare's employer. When Clare visits Kingston during a break from graduate school, the two of them bond by sharing intimate life histories. Harry/Harriet reveals that s/he was raped by a white officer at age ten but insists that the violation "did not make me the way I am" (128); s/he emphasizes that "what he did to me is" not "a symbol for what they did to all of us" (129). As they grow closer, Clare says to her companion, "Harry, you make me want to love you" (130), and she admits to herself that she does not find Harry/Harriet "strange" but rather feels "[a]t home with" hir (131).[27] Most significant, it is Harry/Harriet who tells Clare, "Come home. I'll be here. Come back to us, once your studies are finished" (127). In Harry/Harriet's mind, commitment is incumbent on all of them: "[T]he time will come for both of us to choose. For we will have to make the choice. Cast our lot. Cyaan live split. Not in this world" (131). Eventually, Clare chooses to return to Jamaica and assist the guerrillas by allowing them to recultivate the "ruination" (8) surrounding her grandmother's house, and Harry/Harriet vows to let "Harriet live and Harry be no more" (168).

Although both characters die when an unknown element betrays the guerrillas' raid on an Anglo-American movie set (where a sanitized version of the Maroon leaders Nanny and Cudjoe is perversely being filmed) and the soldiers are gunned down by aerial fire, it is nonetheless clear that the novel not only sympathizes with Clare's and Harriet's political choices but also makes room for those – a "light-skinned woman, daughter of landowners" (5) and a "strange [...] boy-girl" (21) – who might otherwise be excluded from grassroots activist groups because of their skin color, class, sexuality, or gender expression. The critique of queer/transphobia that Harriet encounters is especially salient given Jamaica's notoriety for being deeply homophobic – a condition whose history is traceable to British colonialism and African slavery and a bias that Jamaican American writers like Cliff, Thomas Glave, and Patricia Powell have strongly contested.[28]

Two-Spirit/Queer Native Decolonizations

The multivalent critiques of both Western imperialisms and postcolonial nationalisms found in Hagedorn's and Cliff's novels are also central to Two-Spirit/queer Native literature. As Andrea Smith has argued, queer of color and queer diasporic analyses have tended to overlook the ways in which their privileging of mobility, diaspora, and hybridity "depend ideologically on the disappearance of Native peoples," the bracketing of settler colonialism, and the failure to account for "alternative forms of nationalism that are not structured by nation-states."[29] Thus, although Two-Spirit/queer Native scholarship and art engage in some of the tactics outlined earlier in the chapter – historically tracking and reclaiming culturally specific traditions and practices of gender and sexual diversity; producing queer critiques of heteronormative colonial and national formations – the particular interventions of the field lie in the primacy of dismantling settler colonialism and asserting Native sovereignty.

Although the publication of Two-Spirit/queer Native literature in English, as Lisa Tatonetti notes, extends back to the work of Maurice Kenny (Mohawk) in the 1970s,[30] I close here with a brief consideration of Deborah Miranda's (Ohlone/Costanoan-Esselen) *Bad Indians: A Tribal Memoir* (2013). This multigenre, multimedia text traces the enduring legacies of eighteenth- and nineteenth-century Spanish colonial missionary discourses and practices on California Indians, Miranda's historical ancestors, her immediate family members, and herself. The violence perpetrated by the Spanish priests and soldiers on California mission Indians through strict temporal, carceral, and corporeal disciplinary measures served to instill the values and rituals of Catholicism and uproot Native knowledges and worldviews. Such violence and cultural replacement extended to the arena of sexuality through rape and other forms of sexual abuse as well as through the demonizing of what the Spanish authorities called *joyas*.[31]

Miranda fittingly evokes what she elsewhere calls the "gendercide" of the *joyas* and those figures' survival into the present through a trickster tale.[32] Arriving toward the end of the book, the comic story "Coyote Takes a Trip" erupts into what is otherwise nonfiction colonial, family, and personal history. Focalized through Coyote's perspective, the tale narrates Coyote's dissatisfaction with Venice Beach ("He's lost his mojo" [179]), his decision to visit his brother in New Mexico, and his eventual recognition that one of the three "old *viejas*" on the bus – "one black, one *India*, one Korean" (180) – is actually not a typical lady. Although he had been checking her out on the bus, it is not until Coyote gets up at his stop and his baggy pants fall down, "his butt hanging out" and "his pride and joy" aimed "right at eye level with the old *Indita*," that Coyote realizes "that was no little old lady. The qualities that had so intrigued Coyote, that mix of strength and serene femininity … that old lady was a glammed-up – *and impressed* – old man" (183). As Coyote sees her "giving him the *eye*," perhaps out of admiration, he feels his mojo return. But he is also provoked into recalling "that old word" used to describe his admirer, who is "[n]ot exactly a man" (183). Reversing the historical narrative of Spanish colonialism leading to shame and fear ("They called us monsters" [31]), Coyote's recollection moves backward in time from the derogatory contemporary word *joto* ("No, older than that, and sweeter") to the Spanish-era term *joya* ("Nope, still Spanish, and just thinking it conjured up vile images of humiliation") to the Chumash *'aqi*, "a word that meant honor, medicine, truth" and that he had tellingly learned "long ago on a warm beach" from "a Ventureño with sparkling eyes and a ticklish belly" (184). As though he is enacting spatially the temporal recovery of the "sweeter" word for the Two-Spirit figure, Coyote reverses tracks and decides to seek out Juanita around Venice Beach: "Now he knew where his mojo had gone, and he was gonna be there waiting when it came back this afternoon" (185). Although Miranda notes that the historic *joyas'* "male-female liminality" enabled them to serve as "undertakers" who "possessed the necessary training to touch the dead or handle burials without endangering themselves,"[33] here she playfully accords the contemporary *'aqi* Juanita – una *vieja* at that! – the role of reinvigorating Coyote's mojo and pulling him out of his sodden funk. Indeed, Juanita's revitalizing, erotic capacity directly counters the quotations that Miranda inserts into the tale of colonial Spanish soldiers and Franciscan friars denigrating the *joyas* as "abominable" and "execrable" (178) creatures whose gender transitive roles result in "unspeakably sinful act[s]" (184).

In this respect, "Coyote Takes a Trip" both references and undermines the notion that queerness requires travel, that transnational movement represents the transgression of restrictive national boundaries. Coyote does not have to reach Albuquerque to retrieve his mojo; nor does Juanita need to move out of her Chumash ancestral homeland along the California coast to remain an *'aqi* or to entice a partner. Indeed, the story makes clear that the reciprocal relationship between the two figures occurs not through dramatic border-crossing transformations but precisely in the mundane, if serendipitous, transactions of everyday life: "Hell," Coyote thinks to himself at the end, "he might even help carry the groceries" (185). By imagining himself joining Juanita's domestic space in southern California, Coyote implies an understanding of "indigenous nationhood [and home] as already queered."[34]

Two-Spirit/queer Native literature and scholarship call critical attention not only to the history of heteronormative settler colonialism, the decimation or distortion of indigenous gender and sexual diversities, and mainstream appropriations of non-heterosexual Native embodiments but also to the very notion of U.S. sexual and political exceptionalism mentioned at the start of this chapter. Immigrating to America in hopes of experiencing sexual freedom, petitioning for gender-sexual asylum, and seeking rights, recognition, and protection through legal reform – these practices are underwritten by an implicit faith in the integrity and authority of the U.S. nation-state, an often blind faith that Native perspectives, recalling the realities of colonial conquest and genocide, enable us to perceive.

In this context, we might hear José Garcia Villa's quiet closing question, which ostensibly refers to his Philippine homeland, resonate anew: "Will the native land forgive?"

NOTES

1 See, for example, Dennis Altman, "Rupture or Continuity? The Internationalization of Gay Identities," *Social Text* 48, no. 3 (1996): 77–94; Tom Boellstorff, *A Coincidence of Desires: Anthropology, Queer Studies, Indonesia* (Durham: Duke University Press, 2007); Arnaldo Cruz-Malavé and Martin F. Manalansan, eds., *Queer Globalizations: Citizenship and the Afterlife of Colonialism* (New York: New York University Press, 2002); Neville Hoad, *African Intimacies: Race, Homosexuality, and Globalization* (Minneapolis: University of Minnesota Press, 2007); Gayatri Gopinath, *Impossible Desires: Queer Diasporas and South Asian Public Cultures* (Durham: Duke University Press, 2005); Peter A. Jackson, "Capitalism and Global Queering: National Markets, Parallels among Sexual Cultures, and Multiple Queer Modernities," *GLQ: A Journal of Lesbian and Gay Studies* 15, no. 3 (2009): 357–395; Martin F. Manalansan, *Global Divas: Filipino Gay Men in the Diaspora* (Durham: Duke University Press, 2003); and Lisa Rofel, *Desiring China: Experiments in Neoliberalism, Sexuality, and Public Culture* (Durham: Duke University Press, 2007).

2 See, among others, Lionel Cantú, *The Sexuality of Migration: Border Crossings and Mexican Immigrant Men*, ed. Nancy A. Naples and Salvador Vidal-Ortiz (New York: New York University Press, 2009); Brad Epps, Keja Valens, and Bill Johnson González, eds., *Passing Lines: Sexuality and Immigration* (Cambridge, MA: Harvard University, David Rockefeller Center for Latin American Studies, 2005); and Eithne Luibhéid and Lionel Cantú, Jr., eds., *Queer Migrations: Sexuality, U.S. Citizenship, and Border Crossings* (Minneapolis: University of Minnesota Press, 2005).

3 See, for instance, Chris Berry, Fran Martin, and Audrey Yue, eds., *Mobile Cultures: New Media in Queer Asia* (Durham: Duke University Press, 2003); Marc Epprecht, *Sexuality and Social Justice in Africa: Rethinking Homophobia and Forging Resistance* (London: Zed Books, 2013); Joseph Massad, "Re-Orienting Desire: The Gay International and the Arab World," *Public Culture* 12, no. 2 (2002): 361–385; Nadine Naber, *Arab America: Gender, Cultural Politics, and Activism* (New York: New York University Press, 2012); and Simon Watney, "AIDS and the Politics of Queer Diaspora," in *Negotiating Lesbian and Gay Subjects*, ed. Monica Dorenkamp and Richard Henke (New York: Routledge, 1995), 53–70.

4 Elizabeth A. Povinelli and George Chauncey, "Thinking Sex Transnationally: An Introduction," *GLQ: A Journal of Lesbian and Gay Studies* 5, no. 4 (1999): 446.

5 Donald Pease, "Exceptionalism," in *Keywords for American Cultural Studies*, ed. Bruce Burgett and Glenn Hendler (New York: New York University Press, 2007), 109.

6 Jasbir K. Puar, *Terrorist Assemblages: Homonationalism in Queer Times* (Durham: Duke University Press, 2007), 38, 39; hereafter cited in text.

7 Inderpal Grewal and Caren Kaplan, "Global Identities: Theorizing Transnational Studies of Sexuality," *GLQ: A Journal of Lesbian and Gay Studies* 7, no. 4 (2001): 669.

8 Kath Weston, "Get Thee to a Big City: Sexual Imaginary and the Great Gay Migration," *GLQ: A Journal of Lesbian and Gay Studies* 2, no. 3 (1995): 262.

9 José Garcia Villa, *Footnote to Youth: Tales of the Philippines and Others* (New York: Scribner's, 1933); hereafter cited in text.

10 For an illuminating critique of queer metronormativity, see Scott Herring, *Another Country: Queer Anti-Urbanism* (New York: New York University Press, 2010).

11 For a more detailed version of this argument, see Martin Joseph Ponce, "José Garcia Villa's Modernism and the Politics of Queer Diasporic Reading," *GLQ: A Journal of Lesbian and Gay Studies* 17, no. 4 (2011): 575–602.

12 Audre Lorde, *Zami: A New Spelling of My Name: A Biomythography* (New York: Crossing, 1982), 156; hereafter cited in text.

13 Carol Boyce Davies, *Black Women, Writing and Identity: Migrations of the Subject* (London: Routledge, 1994), 90. For a recent queer diasporic reading of *Zami*, see Stella Bolaki, "'New Living the Old in a New Way': Home and Queer Migrations in Audre Lorde's *Zami*," *Textual Practice* 25, no. 4 (2011): 779–798.

14 Gloria Anzaldúa, *Borderlands/La Frontera: The New Mestiza* (1987; San Francisco: Aunt Lute Books, 1999), 19; hereafter cited in text.

15 For a broader discussion of these figures and of Chicana lesbian literature more generally, see Catrióna Rueda Esquibel, *With Her Machete in Her Hand: Reading Chicana Lesbians* (Austin: University of Texas Press, 2006).

16 Debra A. Castillo, "Anzaldúa and Transnational American Studies," *PMLA* 121, no. 1 (2006): 263.

17 See, for example, Castillo, "Anzaldúa and Transnational American Studies"; Sheila Marie Contreras, "Literary Primitivism and 'the New Mestiza,'" *Interdisciplinary Literary Studies* 8, no. 1 (2006): 49–71; and María Josefina Saldaña-Portillo, *The Revolutionary Imagination in the Americas and the Age of Development* (Durham: Duke University Press, 2003), 278–282.

18 Han Ong, *The Disinherited* (New York: Farrar, Straus and Giroux, 2004), 141; hereafter cited in text.

19 Lawrence Chua, *Gold by the Inch* (New York: Grove Press, 1998), 55; hereafter cited in text. The novel implies that the narrator had served as a kind of "kept boy" for other johns as well – e.g., "Your rich boyfriends indulged you in all the polished crevices of Europe and North America, but the vines always drag you back here" (19).

20 See Stephen Hong Sohn, "'Valuing' Transnational Queerness: Politicized Bodies and Commodified Desires in Asian American Literature," in *Transnational Asian American Literature: Sites and Transits*, ed. Shirley Geok-lin Lim, John Blair Gamber, Stephen Hong Sohn, and Gina Valentino (Philadelphia: Temple University Press, 2006), 100; and Youngsuk Chae, "Neocolonial Global Capitalism and Imperial Desire in Lawrence Chua's *Gold by the Inch*," *MFS Modern Fiction Studies* 57, no. 4 (2012): 157.

21 Sohn, "'Valuing' Transnational Queerness," 107. Sohn reads the narrator as addressing his former boyfriend, Jim, and not the reader.

22 The postcolonial state's homophobic heterosexualization – condemning homosexuality as a "white man's disease" or as a sign of Western colonial incursion and decadence – constitutes the inverse of Western sexual exceptionalism. See, for example, M. Jacqui Alexander, *Pedagogies of Crossing: Meditations on Feminism, Sexual Politics, Memory, and the Sacred* (Durham: Duke University Press, 2005), 21–65, 181–254.

23 Jessica Hagedorn, *Dogeaters* (New York: Penguin, 1990), 108; hereafter cited in text.

24 See Rachel C. Lee, *The Americas of Asian American Literature: Gendered Fictions of Nation and Transnation* (Princeton: Princeton University Press, 1999), 101; and Stephen Hong Sohn, "From Discos to Jungles: Circuitous Queer Patronage and Sex Tourism in Jessica Hagedorn's *Dogeaters*," *MFS Modern Fiction Studies* 56, no. 2 (2010): 317–348.

25 See Sohn, "From Discos to Jungles," 336–338.

26 Michelle Cliff, *No Telephone to Heaven* (New York: Plume, 1996), 109; hereafter cited in text.

27 For an excellent reading of the eroticism between Harry/Harriet and Clare, see Omise'eke Natasha Tinsley, *Thiefing Sugar: Eroticism between Women in Caribbean Literature* (Durham: Duke University Press, 2010), 169–200.

28 See Cliff's essay collection *If I Could Write This in Fire* (Minneapolis: University of Minnesota Press, 2008); Thomas Glave's short story collections *Whose Song? and Other Stories* (San Francisco: City Lights, 2000) and *The Torturer's Wife* (San Francisco: City Lights, 2008), and his essay collections *Words to Our Now: Imagination and Dissent* (Minneapolis: University of Minnesota Press, 2005) and *Among the Bloodpeople: Politics and Flesh* (New York: Akashic Books, 2013); and Patricia Powell's novels *A Small Gathering of Bones* (Boston: Beacon Press, 1994) and *The Pagoda* (New York: Knopf, 1998). On homophobia in Jamaica, see Suzanne LaFont, "Very Straight Sex: The Development of Sexual Morés in Jamaica," *Journal of Colonialism and Colonial History* 2, no. 3 (2001): n.p.; Rebecca Schleifer, *Hated to Death: Homophobia, Violence, and Jamaica's HIV/AIDS Epidemic* (New York: Human Rights Watch, 2004).

29 See Andrea Smith, "Queer Theory and Native Studies: The Heteronormativity of Settler Colonialism," *GLQ: A Journal of Lesbian and Gay Studies* 16, no. 1–2 (2010): 54, 59.

30 Lisa Tatonetti, "Indigenous Fantasies and Sovereign Erotics: Outland Cherokees Write Two-Spirit Nations," in *Queer Indigenous Studies: Critical Interventions in Theory, Politics, and Literature*, ed. Qwo-li Driskill, Chris Finley, Brian Joseph Gilley, and Scott Lauria Morgensen (Tucson: University of Arizona Press, 2011), 155–156. My sincere thanks to Lisa Tatonetti for generously sharing with me her ongoing research on queer Native literatures.

31 Deborah A. Miranda, *Bad Indians: A Tribal History* (Berkeley: Heyday Books, 2013); hereafter cited in text.

32 Deborah A. Miranda, "Extermination of the *Joyas*: Gendercide in Spanish California," *GLQ: A Journal of Lesbian and Gay Studies* 16, no. 1–2 (2010): 253–284.

33 Miranda, "Extermination of the *Joyas*," 266.

34 Smith, "Queer Theory and Native Studies," 54.

SELECTED GUIDE TO FURTHER READING

Bibliographies, Anthologies, and Readers

Abelove, Henry, Michèle Aina Barale, and David M. Halperin, eds. *The Lesbian and Gay Studies Reader*. New York: Routledge, 1993.

Beam, Joseph, ed. *In the Life: A Black Gay Anthology*. Boston: Alyson, 1986.

Canning, Richard, ed. *Vital Signs: Essential AIDS Fiction*. New York: Carroll and Graf, 2007.

Elledge, Jim, ed. *Masquerade: Queer Poetry in America to the End of World War II*. Bloomington: Indiana University Press, 2004.

Foster, Jeannette Howard. *Sex Variant Women in Literature: A Historical and Quantitative Survey*. 1956. London: Frederick Muller, 1958.

Hemphill, Essex, ed. *Brother to Brother: New Writings by Black Gay Men*. Boston: Alyson, 1991.

Jay, Karla, and Allen Young, eds. *Out of the Closets: Voices of Gay Liberation*. New York: Douglas, 1972.

Lavender Culture. New York: Jove, 1978.

McKinley, Catherine E., and L. Joyce DeLaney, eds. *Afrekete: An Anthology of Black Lesbian Writing*. New York: Anchor Books, 1995.

Moraga, Cherríe, and Gloria Anzaldúa, eds. *This Bridge Called My Back: Writings by Radical Women of Color*. Watertown, MA: Persephone, 1981.

Morse, Carol, and Joan Larkin, eds. *Gay and Lesbian Poetry in Our Time: An Anthology*. New York: St. Martin's, 1988.

Nestle, Joan, ed. *The Persistent Desire: A Femme-Butch Reader*. Boston: Alyson, 1992.

Roberts, J. R. *Black Lesbians: An Annotated Bibliography*. Tallahassee: Naiad, 1981.

Scholder, Amy, and Ira Silverberg, eds. *High Risk: An Anthology of Forbidden Writings*. New York: Plume, 1991.

Queer Literary and Cultural Theories

Anzaldúa, Gloria. *Borderlands/La Frontera: The New Mestiza*. 1987. San Francisco: Aunt Lute Books, 2012.

Berlant, Lauren. *Cruel Optimism*. Durham, NC: Duke University Press, 2011.

Berlant, Lauren, and Michael Warner. "Guest Column: What Does Queer Theory Teach Us about X?" *PMLA* 110, no. 3 (1995): 343–349.

Bersani, Leo. *Is the Rectum a Grave? And Other Essays*. Chicago: University of Chicago Press, 2009.

Butler, Judith. *Gender Trouble: Feminism and the Subversion of Identity.* New York: Routledge, 1990.
  Bodies That Matter: On the Discursive Limits of "Sex." New York: Routledge, 1993.
Cvetkovich, Ann. *An Archive of Feelings: Trauma, Sexuality, and Lesbian Public Cultures.* Durham, NC: Duke University Press, 2003.
Dean, Tim. *Beyond Sexuality.* Chicago: University of Chicago Press, 2000.
Delany, Samuel R. *Times Square Red, Times Square Blue.* New York: New York University Press, 2001.
Edelman, Lee. *No Future: Queer Theory and the Death Drive.* Durham, NC: Duke University Press, 2005.
Ferguson, Roderick A. *Aberrations in Black: Toward a Queer of Color Critique.* Minneapolis: University of Minnesota Press, 2003.
Foucault, Michel. *The History of Sexuality.* Vol. 1: *An Introduction.* Translated by Robert Hurley. New York: Vintage, 1990.
Freeman, Elizabeth. *Time Binds: Queer Temporalities, Queer Histories.* Durham, NC: Duke University Press, 2010.
Halberstam, Judith. *In a Queer Time and Place: Transgender Bodies, Subcultural Lives.* New York: New York University Press, 2005.
  The Queer Art of Failure. Durham, NC: Duke University Press, 2011.
Herring, Scott. *Another Country: Queer Anti-Urbanism.* New York: New York University Press, 2010.
Jagose, Annamarie. *Inconsequence: Lesbian Representation and the Logic of Sexual Sequence.* Ithaca: Cornell University Press, 2002.
Johnson, E. Patrick. "'Quare' Studies, or (Almost) Everything I Know about Queer Studies I Learned from My Grandmother." *Text and Performance Quarterly* 21, no. 1 (2001): 1–25.
Lorde, Audre. *Sister Outsider: Essays and Speeches.* Freedom, CA: Crossing, 1984.
Muñoz, José Esteban. *Cruising Utopia: The Then and There of Queer Futurity.* New York: New York University Press, 2009.
Sedgwick, Eve Kosofsky. *Epistemology of the Closet.* Berkeley: University of California Press, 1990.
  Tendencies. Durham, NC: Duke University Press, 1993.
  "Paranoid Reading and Reparative Reading, or, You're So Paranoid You Probably Think This Introduction Is about You." In *Novel Gazing: Queer Readings in Fiction,* edited by Eve Kosofsky Sedgwick, 1–37. Durham, NC: Duke University Press, 1997.
Smith, Barbara. "Toward a Black Feminist Criticism." *Conditions: Two* 1, no. 2 (1977): 25–44.
Stockton, Kathryn Bond. *The Queer Child, or Growing Sideways in the Twentieth Century.* Durham, NC: Duke University Press, 2009.
Warner, Michael. *The Trouble with Normal: Sex, Politics, and the Ethics of Queer Life.* New York: Free Press, 1999.

Nineteenth-Century Queer Literatures

Abelove, Henry. *Deep Gossip.* Minneapolis: University of Minnesota Press, 2003.
Bauer, Dale M. *Sex Expression and American Women Writers, 1860–1940.* Chapel Hill: University of North Carolina Press, 2009.

Bennett, Paula. "The Pea That Duty Locks: Lesbian and Feminist-Heterosexual Readings of Emily Dickinson's Poetry." In *Lesbian Texts and Contexts: Radical Revisions*, edited by Karla Jay and Joanne Glasgow, 104–125. New York: New York University Press, 1990.

Coviello, Peter. *Tomorrow's Parties: Sex and the Untimely in Nineteenth-Century America*. New York: New York University Press, 2013.

Erkkila, Betsy. "Whitman and the Homosexual Republic." In *Walt Whitman: The Centennial Essays*, edited by Ed Folsom, 153–171. Iowa City: University of Iowa Press, 1994.

Fetterley, Judith, and Marjorie Pryse. *Writing out of Place: Regionalism, Women, and American Literary Culture*. Urbana: University of Illinois Press, 2003.

Kent, Kathryn R. *Making Girls into Women: American Women's Writing and the Rise of Lesbian Identity*. Durham, NC: Duke University Press, 2003.

Looby, Christopher. "The Literariness of Sexuality: Or, How to Do the (Literary) History of (American) Sexuality." *American Literary History* 25, no. 4 (2013): 841–854.

Moon, Michael. "'The Gentle Boy from the Dangerous Classes': Pederasty, Domesticity, and Capitalism in Horatio Alger." *Representations* 19 (1987): 87–110.

Disseminating Whitman: Revision and Corporeality in Leaves of Grass. Cambridge, MA: Harvard University Press, 1993.

Ohi, Kevin. *Henry James and the Queerness of Style*. Minneapolis: University of Minnesota Press, 2011.

Rifkin, Mark. *When Did Indians Become Straight? Kinship, the History of Sexuality, and Native Sovereignty*. Oxford: Oxford University Press, 2011.

Warner, Michael. "Thoreau's Bottom." *Raritan* 11, no. 3 (1992): 53–79.

Modern and Modernist Queer Literatures, 1900–1945

Boone, Joseph Allen. *Libidinal Currents: Sexuality and the Shaping of Modernism*. Chicago: University of Chicago Press, 1998.

Chauncey, George. *Gay New York: Gender, Urban Culture, and the Making of the Gay Male World, 1890–1940*. New York: Basic Books, 1994.

Cobb, Michael L. "Insolent Racing, Rough Narrative: The Harlem Renaissance's Impolite Queers." *Callaloo* 23, no. 1 (2000): 328–351.

Dickie, Margaret. *Stein, Bishop, and Rich: Lyrics of Love, War, and Place*. Chapel Hill: University of North Carolina Press, 1997.

Duggan, Lisa. *Sapphic Slashers: Sex, Violence, and American Modernity*. Durham, NC: Duke University Press, 2000.

Galvin, Mary E. *Queer Poetics: Five Modernist Women Writers*. Westport, CT: Greenwood Press, 1999.

Goldberg, Jonathan. *Willa Cather and Others*. Durham, NC: Duke University Press, 2001.

Herring, Scott. *Queering the Underworld: Slumming, Literature, and the Undoing of Lesbian and Gay History*. Chicago: University of Chicago Press, 2007.

Holcomb, Gary Edward. *Claude McKay, Code Name Sasha: Queer Black Marxism and the Harlem Renaissance*. Gainesville: University Press of Florida, 2007.

Jarraway, David R. *Going the Distance: Dissident Subjectivity in Modernist American Literature*. Baton Rouge: Louisiana State University Press, 2003.

Lindemann, Marilee. *Willa Cather: Queering America*. New York: Columbia University Press, 1999.

Love, Heather. *Feeling Backward: Loss and the Politics of Queer History*. Cambridge, MA: Harvard University Press, 2007.

Marra, Kim, and Robert A. Schanke, eds. *Staging Desire: Queer Readings of American Theater History*. Ann Arbor: University of Michigan Press, 2002.

Nealon, Christopher. *Foundlings: Lesbian and Gay Historical Emotion before Stonewall*. Durham, NC: Duke University Press, 2001.

Salvato, Nick. *Uncloseting Drama: American Modernism and Queer Performance*. New Haven: Yale University Press, 2010.

See, Sam. "Making Modernism New: Queer Mythology in *The Young and Evil*." *English Literary History* 76, no. 4 (2009): 1073–1105.

Somerville, Siobhan B. *Queering the Color Line: Race and the Invention of Homosexuality in American Culture*. Durham, NC: Duke University Press, 2000.

Stimpson, Catharine R. "The Somagrams of Gertrude Stein." *Poetics Today* 6, nos. 1–2 (1985): 67–80.

Vogel, Shane. *The Scene of Harlem Cabaret: Race, Sexuality, Performance*. Chicago: University of Chicago Press, 2009.

Wirth, Thomas H. "Introduction." In *Gay Rebel of the Harlem Renaissance: Selections from the Work of Richard Bruce Nugent*, 1–61. Durham, NC: Duke University Press, 2002.

Yingling, Thomas E. *Hart Crane and the Homosexual Text: New Thresholds, New Anatomies*. Chicago: University of Chicago Press, 1990.

Cold War and Liberation Literatures

Bergman, David. *The Violet Hour: The Violet Quill and the Making of Gay Culture*. New York: Columbia University Press, 2004.

Bibler, Michael P. *Cotton's Queer Relations: Same-Sex Intimacy and the Literature of the Southern Plantation, 1936–1968*. Charlottesville: University of Virginia Press, 2009.

Bronski, Michael. "Introduction." In *Pulp Friction: Uncovering the Golden Age of Gay Male Pulps*, edited by Michael Bronski, 1–21. New York: St. Martin's Griffin, 2003.

Corber, Robert J. *Homosexuality in Cold War America: Resistance and the Crisis of Masculinity*. Durham, NC: Duke University Press, 1997.

Garber, Linda. *Identity Poetics: Race, Class, and the Lesbian-Feminist Roots of Queer Theory*. New York: Columbia University Press, 2001.

Harker, Jaime. *Middlebrow Queer: Christopher Isherwood in America*. Minneapolis: University of Minnesota Press, 2013.

Hogeland, Lisa Maria. *Feminism and Its Fictions: The Consciousness-Raising Novel and the Women's Liberation Movement*. Philadelphia: University of Pennsylvania Press, 1998.

Keenaghan, Eric. *Queering Cold War Poetry: Ethics of Vulnerability in Cuba and the United States*. Columbus: Ohio State University Press, 2009.

McBride, Dwight A., ed. *James Baldwin Now*. New York: New York University Press, 1999.

Savran, David. *Communists, Cowboys, and Queers: The Politics of Masculinity in the Work of Arthur Miller and Tennessee Williams*. Minneapolis: University of Minnesota Press, 1992.

Sherry, Michael S. *Gay Artists in Modern American Culture: An Imagined Conspiracy*. Chapel Hill: University of North Carolina Press, 2007.

Stryker, Susan. *Queer Pulp: Perverted Passions from the Golden Age of the Paperback*. San Francisco: Chronicle, 2001.

Warner, Sara. *Acts of Gaiety: LGBT Performance and the Politics of Pleasure*. Ann Arbor: University of Michigan Press, 2012.

Wasley, Aidan. *The Age of Auden: Postwar Poetry and the American Scene*. Princeton: Princeton University Press, 2010.

Wolf, Stacy. *A Problem Like Maria: Gender and Sexuality in the American Musical*. Ann Arbor: University of Michigan, 1999.

Zimmerman, Bonnie. *The Safe Sea of Women: Lesbian Fiction, 1969–1989*. Boston: Beacon, 1990.

AIDS Literatures and Contemporary Queer Literatures

Clum, John M. *Something for the Boys: Musical Theater and Gay Culture*. New York: St. Martin's, 1999.

Cvetkovich, Ann. "Drawing the Archive in Alison Bechdel's *Fun Home*." *Women's Studies Quarterly* 36, nos. 1–2 (2008): 111–128.

Davidson, Guy. *Queer Commodities: Contemporary US Fiction, Consumer Capitalism, and Gay and Lesbian Subcultures*. New York: Palgrave Macmillan, 2012.

Dolan, Jill. *Utopia in Performance: Finding Hope at the Theater*. Ann Arbor: University of Michigan Press, 2005.

Holland, Sharon P. "To Touch the Mother's C(o)untry: Siting Audre Lorde's Erotics." In *Lesbian Erotics: Practices and Critiques*, edited by Karla Jay, 212–226. New York: New York University Press, 1995.

Martínez, Ernesto Javier. *On Making Sense: Queer Race Narratives of Intelligibility*. Stanford: Stanford University Press, 2012.

McRuer, Robert. *The Queer Renaissance: Contemporary American Literature and the Reinvention of Lesbian and Gay Identities*. New York: New York University Press, 1997.

Muñoz, José Esteban. *Disidentifications: Queers of Color and the Performance of Politics*. Minneapolis: University of Minnesota Press, 1999.

Murphy, Timothy F., and Suzanne Poirier, eds. *Writing AIDS: Gay Literature, Language, and Analysis*. New York: Columbia University Press, 1993.

Rifkin, Mark. *The Erotics of Sovereignty: Queer Native Writing in the Era of Self-Determination*. Minneapolis: University of Minnesota Press, 2012.

Rodríguez, Richard T. *Next of Kin: The Family in Chicano/a Cultural Politics*. Durham, NC: Duke University Press, 2009.

Román, David. *Acts of Intervention: Performance, Gay Culture, and AIDS*. Bloomington: Indiana University Press, 1998.

Ross, Marlon B. "'What's Love but a Second Hand Emotion?' Man-on-Man Passion in the Contemporary Black Gay Romance Novel." *Callaloo* 36, no. 3 (2013): 669–687.

Scott, Darieck. *Extravagant Abjection: Blackness, Power, and Sexuality in the African American Literary Imagination.* New York: New York University Press, 2010.

Viego, Antonio. "The Place of Gay Male Chicano Literature in Queer Chicana/o Cultural Work." In *Gay Latino Studies: A Critical Reader*, edited by Michael Hames-García and Ernesto Javier Martínez, 86–104. Durham, NC: Duke University Press, 2011.

Transnational Queer Literary and Cultural Studies

Bolaki, Stella. "'New Living the Old in a New Way': Home and Queer Migrations in Audre Lorde's *Zami*." *Textual Practice* 25, no. 4 (2011): 779–798.

Cohler, Deborah. "Teaching Transnationally: Queer Studies and Imperialist Legacies in Monique Truong's *The Book of Salt*." *Radical Teacher* 82 (2008): 25–31.

Doyle, Laura. "Transnational History at Our Backs: A Long View of Larsen, Woolf, and Queer Racial Subjectivity in Atlantic Modernism." *Modernism/Modernity* 13, no. 3 (2006): 531–559.

Eng, David L. *The Feeling of Kinship: Queer Liberalism and the Racialization of Intimacy.* Durham, NC: Duke University Press, 2010.

Gopinath, Gayatri. *Impossible Desires: Queer Diasporas and South Asian Public Cultures.* Durham, NC: Duke University Press, 2005.

Pecic, Zoran. *Queer Narratives of the Caribbean Diaspora: Exploring Tactics.* New York: Palgrave Macmillan, 2013.

Ponce, Martin Joseph. *Beyond the Nation: Diasporic Filipino Literature and Queer Reading.* New York: New York University Press, 2012.

Tinsley, Omise'eke Natasha. *Thiefing Sugar: Eroticism between Women in Caribbean Literature.* Durham, NC: Duke University Press, 2010.

Zaborowska, Magdalena J. *James Baldwin's Turkish Decade: Erotics of Exile.* Durham, NC: Duke University Press, 2009.

INDEX

Cambridge Companions to...

TOPICS

Printed in the United States
By Bookmasters